MUSIC FOR THE SOUL

MUSIC FOR THE SOUL

Daily Readings for a Year from the
Writings of Alexander Maclaren

Selected and arranged by the Rev. George Coates

AMG
PUBLISHERS
Chattanooga, TN 37422

Music for the Soul
© 1996 by AMG Publishers
All rights reserved.

Second Edition originally published by Hodder and Stoughton, 1905

ISBN: 0-89957-218-9

Library of Congress Catalog Card Number: 96-79878

Printed in the United States of America.
01 00 99 98 97 96 5 4 3 2 1

Foreword

This new edition of *Music for the Soul* comes from the second edition of Maclaren's work published in 1905. These daily devotional readings were selected from Maclaren's writings and arranged by the Rev. George Coates.

In this new edition we have sought to preserve the classical style of Maclaren, but in order to bring the power of these readings to modern readers, we felt that it was necessary to update the spelling and punctuation in accordance with how our language has changed over the years. Readers should also note that the points of current history mentioned by Maclaren are from the latter half of the nineteenth century. Scripture references have also been inserted in brackets, to make it more convenient for the reader to consult passages of the Bible that Maclaren quotes or mentions.

Music for the Soul contains 366 daily readings—one for each day of the year, including Februrary 29, for leap year. We have preserved Rev. Coates's helpful subject index, which the reader will find in the back pages of the book and we have added our own scripture index, which is an addition to the scripture index of the original work.

Introduction to the Original Edition

The cultivation of the spiritual side of the devotional life is the purpose for which this book has been compiled. No words can possibly describe the absolute necessity of cultivating a higher tone in the spiritual life of the Christians of this age; and it may be asserted, without fear of contradiction, that Dr. Alexander Maclaren's writings supply ample food for devotion and meditation. Every sentence he utters is full to overflowing of spiritual power and unction. He is the master of the art of how to touch the human soul by the simple, God-appointed method of preaching the Gospel in all the majesty and glory of an experimental force. He believes, therefore he speaks; and such speaking cannot fail to reach the heart. God has used this great preacher in the spiritual up-building of multitudes of Christians the world over, and in the salvation of many who, through the influence of his burning words, have been brought from "darkness to light, and from the power of Satan unto God."

Every Christian should have his Day-book of Devotional Reading, not to be used instead of the Word of God, but along with it. Contact with souls whose experience of God's grace and mercy has revealed ripened acquaintance with Him who is the Life and the Light of men is manifestly helpful to all believers in a common Savior. Since Thomas à Kempis, Bogatzky, Dr. J. R. Miller, and others have given to us their wonderful devotional meditations, the "Daily Devotional Book" has been a recognized companion of the devout life. Let the Bible, the living Word of the living Christ, be our first and chief book, but by its side, and as a helper to its proper devotional study, let the Christian gather some taper-lights from the men and women whose spiritual inspiration is assured, and whose hearts and lips have been touched with a live-coal from off God's altar. "Let the word of Christ dwell in you richly, in all wisdom."

The preparation of the volume has been a help and inspiration to the compiler. The subject headings and the Scripture passages have been selected with great care, and are suggestive, as far as it was possible, of the thoughts contained in the quotations from Dr. Maclaren. Full textual and subject indices will be found at the end.

I desire to acknowledge my obligation to Dr. Maclaren for his ready and gracious acquiescence in the preparation and publication of this work; also to Messrs. Macmillan and Co., the "Christian Commonwealth Publishing Co., Limited," and Messrs. Alexander and Shepheard for permission to make extracts from the published volumes of Dr. Maclaren's Sermons.

I send the book forth in the earnest hope and with the prayer that the "Daily Readings" may be a means of spiritual quickening and stimulus to all who are seeking for a fuller baptism of the Holy Spirit.

G. COATES

October, 1897

Daily Readings for a Year

IN REMEMBRANCE OF CHRIST

This do in remembrance of me—1 Cor. 11:24

"Do all in the name of the Lord Jesus" [Col. 3:17]. Do this in remembrance of Christ, or, as Paul expresses it, "discerning the Lord's body" [1 Cor. 11:29], not only *because you are in danger of forgetting*, but do this *because you remember*. Do this, not only in order that your reminiscences may be strengthened, but do it because they *are* strong. Seeing the Lord's body, discerning His presence, loving that which you discern—do this! And in like manner, "Whatsoever ye do, in word or deed, do all in the name of the Lord Jesus." Do all, that is to say, for the sake of the character, as revealed to you, of Him whom you love; do it all, giving thanks unto God and the Father by Him. And then, in the parallel passage, "Whatsoever ye do, do it heartily" [Col. 3:23]—that is one principle; and next, as the foundation of all real heartiness, do it "as to the Lord." This is the foundation, and the limitation as well; for it is only when we do it "heartily, as to the Lord," that earnestness is kept from degenerating into absorption, and that a man, while working with all his might, and "diligent in business" [Prov. 22:29], shall also be "fervent in spirit." The motive is the same: in the Communion it is the remembrance of the Lord; in the ordinary life it is "in the name of the Lord Jesus." Is that sacred motive one which is kept for select occasions, and for what we call special acts of worship? It is to be feared that the majority of Christian people do with that Divine reason for work, "the love of Christ constraineth us" [2 Cor. 5:14], as the old Franks (to use a strange illustration) used to do with their long-haired kings—they kept them in the palace at all ordinary times, gave them no power over the government of the kingdom, only now and then brought them out to grace a procession, and then would take them back again into their reverential powerlessness. That is very like what Christian people do, to a very large extent, with that which ought to be the rule of all their lives and the motive of all their work. We sit down to the communion, and we do *it* "in the name of the Lord Jesus"; we commemorate Him there. When we come to pray, we speak to Him and in His Name. Our high tides of devotion do not come so often as the ties of the sea; and then for the rest of our time there is the long stretch of foul, oozy, barren beach when the waters are out, and all is desolation and deadness. That is not what a Christian man ought to be. There is no action of life which is too great to bow to the influence of "This do in remembrance of Me"; and there is no action of life which is too small to be magnified, glorified, turned into a solemn sacrament, by the operation of the same motive.

THE PRESENT THE PROPHECY OF THE FUTURE

Stretching forward to the things which are before, I press on towards the goal—
Phil. 3:13, 14

Childhood is the prophecy of maturity. "The child is father of the man"; the bud foretells the flower. In the same way, the very imperfections of the Christian life, as it is seen here, argue the existence of another state where all that is here in the germ shall be fully matured, and all that is here incomplete shall attain the perfection which alone will correspond to the power that works in us. Think of the ordinary Christian character. The germ is there, and more than the germ. As one looks at the crudity, the inconsistencies, the failings, the feebleness of the Christian life of others, or of one's self, and then thinks that such a poor, imperfect exhibition is all that so Divine a principle has been able to achieve in this world, one feels that there must be a region and a time where we shall be all which the transforming power of God's Spirit can make us. True, the very inconsistencies of Christians are as strong a reason for believing in the perfect life of heaven as their purities and virtues. We have a right to say mighty principles are at work after Christian souls—the power of the Cross, the power of love essaying to obedience, the power of an indwelling Spirit; and is this all that these great forces are going to effect on human character? Surely a seed so precious and Divine is somewhere and some time to bring forth something better than these few poor half-developed flowers, something with more lustrous petals and richer fragrance. The plant is clearly an exotic here; does not its obviously struggling growth here tell of warmer suns and richer soil where it will be at home?

There is a great deal in every man, and most of all in Christian men and women, which does not fit this present. All other creatures correspond in their capacities to the place where they are set down; and the world in which the plant or the animal lives, the world of their surroundings, stimulates to activity all their powers. But that is not so with a man, "Foxes have holes, birds of the air have nests" [Matt. 8:20]. They fit exactly and correspond to their "environment." But a man!—there is an enormous amount of waste faculty about him if he is only going to live in this world. There is a great deal in every nature, and most of all in a Christian nature, which is like the packages that emigrants take with them, marked "not wanted on the voyage." These go down into the hold, and they are only of use after landing in the new world. If I am a son of God, I have got much in me that is "not wanted on the voyage"; and the more I grow into His likeness, the more I am thrown out of harmony with the things around me in proportion as I am brought into harmony with the things beyond.

"Neither death, nor life, nor things present, nor things to come, nor height, nor depth, nor any other creature" [Rom. 8:38, 39], shall be able to break that tie and banish the child from the conscious grasp of a Father's hand. Dear brother and sister, can you say, "Now am I a child of God"?

Then you may patiently and peacefully face that dim future.

January 3

TODAY

Today, if ye will hear his voice, harden not your hearts—Heb. 3:15

I say nothing about other reasons for prompt action, such as that every moment makes it harder for a man to turn to Jesus Christ as his Savior. The dreadful power of habit weaves chains about him, thin at first as a spider's web, solid at last as an iron fetter. Associations that entangle, connections that impede, grow with terrible rapidity. And if it is hard for you to turn to your Lord now, it will never be easier, and will certainly be harder.

And, dear friend, "today"—how long is it going to last? Of course, I know that all the deepest reasons for your being a Christian remain unaffected if you were going to live in the world forever. And, of course, I know that the gospel of Jesus Christ is as good to live by as it is to die by. But, notwithstanding, common sense says that if our time here is so uncertain as we know it to be, there is no time to put off. You and I have to die, whether we find a convenient season for it or not. And perhaps we have to die before we find Felix's "convenient season" [Acts 24:25] to send for Paul or Paul's Master. So, in the narrowest sense of the word, "Today . . . harden not your hearts."

But I dare say some of you, and especially some of you young people, may be kept from accepting Jesus Christ as your Savior, and serving Him, by a vague disinclination and dread to make so great a change. I urge you, do not give a feather's weight to such considerations. If a change is right, the sooner it is made the better. The shrinking all passes when it is made, just as a bather recovers himself when once his head has been plunged beneath the water.

And some of you may be kept back because you know that there are sins that you will have to unveil if you become Christians. Well, do not let that keep you back either. Confession is healing and good and sweet to the soul, if it is needful for repentance. Sins that men have a right to know hurt as long as they are hid, and cease to hurt when they are acknowledged, like the fox beneath the Spartan boy's robe, that gnawed when it was covered up, and stopped biting when it was revealed.

So, dear friend, you hear Christ speaking to you in His Word, in His servants, in the depths of your hearts. He speaks to you of a dying Savior, of His infinite love, of His perfect sacrifice, of a complete salvation, a cleansed heart, a blessed life, a calm death, an open heaven for each, if we will take them. "See that ye refuse not him that speaketh" [Heb. 12:25].

OUR RELATION TO OUR LORD

To us there is but one God, the Father, of whom are all things, and we in him—
1 Cor. 8:6

Every act of our life sets forth some aspect of our Lord and of our relation to Him, from the moment when we open our eyes in the morning—as those do who, having slept the sleep of sin, awake to righteousness, all through the busy day, when our work may speak to us of His that worketh continually, and our rest may prophesy to us of the "rest that remaineth for the people of God" [Ex. 16:23]; and our journeyings may tell of the journey of the soul of God, and our home may testify of the home which is above the skies—up to the hour when night falls, and sleep, the image of Death, speaks to us of the last solemn moment, when we shall close the eyes of our body on earth, to open those of our soul on the realities of eternity; when we shall no more "see through a glass, darkly; but then face to face" [1 Cor. 13:12]. All things, and all acts, and this whole wonderful universe, proclaim to us the Lord our Father, Christ our love, Christ our hope, our portion, and our joy! Oh, if you would know the meaning of the world, read Christ in it! If you would see the beauty of earth, take it for a prophet of something higher than itself! If you would pierce beneath the surface and know the sanctities that are all about us, remember that when He took bread and wine for a memorial of Him, He did not profane thereby, but consecrated thereby, all that He left out, and asserted the same power and the same prerogative, in lower degree, but as really and truly, for everything which the loving eye should look upon, for everything which the believing heart should apprehend! All is sacred. The world is the temple of God. Everywhere there are symbols and memorials of the living God.

Is it not something to have a principle which, while leaving events in all their power to tell upon us, yet prevents anything from pressing upon us with an overwhelming weight? Would it not be grand if we could so go through life as that all should be not one dead level, but one high plateau, as it were, on the mountaintop there, because all rested upon "Whatsoever ye do, in word or deed, do all in the name of the Lord Jesus" [Col. 3:17]? It is possible—not to our weak faith, perhaps; but the weakness of the faith is not inevitable. It is possible, though we *be* surrounded by many things that make it very hard. It is possible, and therefore it is *duty*. It is possible, and therefore the opposite is not merely a neglect, but is positive *sin*. Oh, to have my life equable like that; with one high, diffusive influence through it all; with one simple consecration placed upon it— that one motive: "The love of Christ constraineth us" [2 Cor. 5:14]! Why, it is like one of those applications of power you have often seen, when a huge hammer is lifted up, and comes down with a crash that breaks the granite in pieces, or may be allowed to fall so gently and so true that it touches, without cracking, a tiny nut beneath it. The *one* principle, mighty and crashing when it is wanted; and yet coming down with gentle, accurately-proportioned force on *all* life. Or, to take a higher illustration: it is like that mighty power that holds a planet in its orbit, in the wild weltering wastes of solitary space; and yet binds down the sand-grain and dust-mote to its place. Or, higher and truer still, the love of Christ that constraineth us makes us equable, calm, consistent, in shadowy but real copy of the everlasting tranquillity of our Father in heaven.

THE HEAVY COST OF THE WORLD

What shall it profit a man, if he shall gain the whole world, and lose his own
soul?—Mark 8:36

You get nothing for nothing in the world's market. It is a big price that you have to pay before these mercenaries will come to fight on your side. Here is a man that "succeeds in life," as we call it. What does it cost him? Well, it has cost him the suppression, the atrophy by disuse of many capacities in his soul which were far higher and nobler than those that have been exercised in his success; it has cost him all his days; it has possibly cost him the dying out of generous sympathies and the stimulating of unwholesome selfishness. He has bought his prosperity very dear. If people would estimate what they pay for gold (in an immense majority of cases) in treasure that cannot be weighed and stamped, they would find it to be about the dearest thing in God's universe; and that there are few men who make worse bargains than the men who give *themselves* for worldly success, even when they receive what they give themselves for.

Some of you know how much what you call enjoyment has cost you. Some have bought pleasure at the price of innocence, of moral dignity, of stained memories, of polluted imaginations, of an incapacity to rise above the flesh; and some have bought it as the price of health. The world has a way of getting more than it gives.

At best, if you are not Christian men and women, whether you are men of business, votaries of pleasure, seekers after culture and refinement, or anything else, you have given Heaven to get earth. Is that a good bargain? Is it much wiser than that of a horde of naked savages that sell a great tract of fair country, with gold-bearing reefs in it, for a bottle of rum and a yard or two of calico? What is the difference? You have been fooled out of the inheritance which God meant for you; and you have received for it transient satisfaction, and partial as it is transient. If you are not Christian people, you have to buy this world's wealth and goods at the price of God and of your own souls. And I ask you if that is an investment which recommends itself to your common sense. Oh, my brother, "what shall it profit a man, if he gain the whole world, and lose" himself? Answer the question.

Only he that is "a man in Christ" has come "to the measure of the stature of a perfect man" [Eph. 4:13]. There, and there alone, do we get the power which will make us full-grown. There alone does the soul get hold of that good soil in which, growing, it becomes as a rounded, perfect tree, with leaves and fruits in their season. All other men are half-men, quarter-men, fragments of men, parts of humanity exaggerated, and contorted, and distorted from the reconciling whole which the Christian ought to be, and in proportion to his Christianity is on the road to be, and one day will assuredly and actually be a "complete man, wanting nothing": nothing maimed, nothing broken, the realization of the ideal of humanity, the renewed copy "of the second Adam, the Lord from heaven."

A SHOWING FORTH OF CHRIST'S DEATH

Bearing about in the body the dying of the Lord Jesus, that the life also of Jesus might be made manifest in our body—2 Cor. 4:10

This showing forth of Christ's death is the truest explanation and definition that we can give of the process by which a Christian soul grows up into the likeness of its Lord. The death of the Lord Jesus, as a death *for us*, and the ground of our hope, is to be shown forth in our daily walk, as a death working *in us*, and the ground of our conduct. There is not only the atoning and sacrificial aspect in Christ's death on the Cross, but there is this likewise, that it stands as the example of the way by which we are, in our measure and place, to "mortify our members which are upon the earth" [Col. 3:5], because we are dead with Him, and our lives are "hid with Christ in God" [Col. 3:3]. *Here*, then, we say, "That death was *for me*, and I trust it"; in our common life we are to say, "That death is working *in me*, and I am becoming conformable unto the image of His death, that I may know Him, and the power of His resurrection, and so attain to the resurrection of the dead" [Phil. 3:10, 11]. And as sacred as is the one form of memorial, so sacred is the other; and closer than the outward sign which expresses the outward fact upon which we hope, is the inward reality by which alone the outward fact becomes the basis of our hope and the reason for our confidence. No man manifests the death of Christ by any outward act of communion or worship who is not feeling it daily in his own soul; and no man has any right to say, "I am trusting in that death as a sacrifice and salvation," who does not feel and show that he is built on Christ, and that Christ's death is in him a power to change him into His own likeness. It is in vain for us to say that we are relying on Christ, unless Christ be in us, slaying the old man and quickening the new. The one test of true faith is the inward possession of the Lord's Spirit; and between the sacrifice on the Cross and me the sinful man, there is no real union effected, nor any imputation and transference of merits, unless with it, proof of it, and consequence of it—and proof of it *because* consequence of it—there be likewise the *flowing-over* from the Cross to me of the life that was in Him, and of the death that He died. "Ye do show the Lord's death till He come" [1 Cor. 11:26] not only, nor chiefly, when you take the bread and the wine in remembrance of Him, but when, in daily contact with sin, in daily practice of that bitter and yet most sweet lesson of self-denial and sacrifice, you crucify the old man with his affections and lusts, [see Eph. 4:22] and rise again into "newness of life" [Rom. 6:4] The fact is better than the symbol—the inward communion more true than the outward participation. Just in proportion as His flesh and His blood are better and more vivifying than the bread and wine which feeds the body, in the same proportion is the manifestation of His death in life a nobler thing than the manifestation of His death at any table.

KNOWLEDGE AND LOVE

Though I have the gift of prophecy, and understand all mysteries and all knowledge, . . . but have not charity, I am nothing—1 Cor. 13:2

A man may know all about Christ and His love without one spark of love in his heart. There are thousands of people who, as far as their heads are concerned, know quite as much of Jesus Christ and His love as any of us do, and could talk about it and argue about it, and draw inferences from it, and have the whole system of evangelical Christianity at their fingertips. It is at their fingertips; it never gets any nearer to them than that.

There is a knowledge with which love has nothing to do, and it is a knowledge that with many people is all-sufficient. "Knowledge puffeth up," says the Apostle in First Corinthians 8:1, into an unwholesome bubble of self-complacency that will one day be pricked and disappear—nothing; but charity (love) buildeth up a steadfast, slowly-rising, solid fabric. There are two kinds of knowledge: the mere rattle of notions in a man's dry brain, like the seeds of a withered poppy-head—very many, very dry, very hard—that will make a noise when you shake it; and there is another kind of knowledge, which goes deep down into the heart, and is the only knowledge worth calling by the name, and that knowledge is the child of love. Love, says Paul, is the parent of all knowledge. We know, really know, any emotions of any sort whatever only by experience. You may talk forever about feelings, and you teach nothing about them to those who have not experienced them. The poets of the world have been singing about love ever since the world began. But no heart has learned what love is from even the sweetest and deepest songs. Who that is not a father can be taught paternal love by words, or can come to a perception of it by an effort of mind? And so with all other emotions. Only the lips that have drunk the cup of sweetness or of bitterness can tell how sweet or how bitter it is; and even when they, made wise by experience, speak out their deepest hearts, the listeners are but little the wiser unless they too have been initiated in the same school. Experience is our only teacher in matter of feeling and emotion, as in the lower regions of taste and appetite. A man must be hungry to know what hunger is; he must taste honey or wormwood in order to know the taste of honey or wormwood; and in like manner he cannot know sorrow but by feeling its ache, and must love if he would know love. Experience is our only teacher, and her school fees are heavy. Just as a blind man can never be made to understand the glories of sunrise or the light upon the far-off mountains; just as a deaf man may read books about acoustics, but they will not give him a notion of what it is to hear Beethoven—so we must have love *to* Christ before we know what love to Christ is, and we must consciously experience the love *of* Christ ere we know what the love of Christ is; and we must have love *to* Christ in order to have a deep and living possession of the love *of* Christ, though reciprocally it is also true that we must have the love of Christ known and felt by our answering hearts, if we are ever to love Him back again.

"He must be loved, ere that to you
He will seem worthy of your love."

THE SANCTITY OF LOVE

That ye . . . may be able to comprehend with all saints what is the breadth, and length, and depth, and height, and to know the love of Christ, which passeth knowledge—Eph. 3:17-19

Before we can love an unseen person and believe in his love, we must know about him by the ordinary means by which we learn about all persons outside the circle of our sight. So, before the love which is thus the parent of deep, true knowledge, there must be the knowledge by study and credence of the record concerning Christ, which supplies the facts on which alone love can be cherished. The understanding has its part to play in leading the heart to love, and then the heart becomes the true teacher. "He that loveth not, knoweth not God, for God is love" [1 John 4:8]. He that, because Christ dwells in his heart, is rooted and grounded in love, will be strengthened to know the love in which he is rooted. The Christ within us will know the love of Christ. We must first "taste," and then we shall "see" that the Lord is good, as the Psalmist puts it with deep truth [Ps. 34:8]. First the appropriation and feeding upon God, then the clear perception by the mind of the sweetness in the taste. First the enjoyment, then the reflection of the enjoyment. First the love, and then the self-consciousness of the love of Christ possesses and the love to Christ is experienced, which is knowledge. There is another condition laid down in these words, "That ye may be able to comprehend with all saints." That is to say, our knowledge of the love of Jesus Christ depends largely on our sanctity. If we are pure, we shall know. If we were wholly devoted to Him, we should wholly know His love to us; and in the measure in which we are pure and holy, we shall know it. That heart of ours is like some reflecting telescope; the least breath of earth upon the mirror will cause all the starry sublimities that it should shadow forth to fade and become dim. The slightest moisture in the atmosphere, though it be quite imperceptible where we stand, will yet be dense enough to shut our the fair, shining, snowy summits that girdle the horizon there, and to leave nothing visible but the lowliness and commonplaceness of the prosaic plain.

If you want to know the love of Christ, that love must purify your souls. But then you must keep your souls pure, assured of this, that only the single eye is full of light, and that they who are not "saints" grope in the dark even at mid-day, and while drenched by the sunshine of His love, are unconscious of it altogether. And so we get that miserable and mysterious tragedy that men and women walk through life, as many of you are doing, in the very blaze and focus of Christ's love, and never behold it, nor know anything about it.

THE INDWELLING CHRIST

That Christ may dwell in your hearts by faith—Eph. 3:17

There must be an indwelling Christ in order to have an experience, deep and stable, of His love. Then we shall know the love which we thus experience. But how comes that indwelling? That is the question for us. The knowledge of His love is blessedness, is peace, is love, is everything. That knowledge arises from our fellowship with, and our possession of, the love of God which is in Jesus Christ. How does that fellowship with, and possession of, the love of God in Jesus Christ come? That is the all-important question. What is the beginning of everything? "That Christ may dwell in your hearts by faith." There is the gate through which you and I may come, and by which we must come if we are to come at all into the possession and perception of Christ's great love. Here is the path of knowledge. First of all, there must be the knowledge which is the mere work of the understanding, bringing to us the facts of Christ's life and death for us. This we have to take with the hand of our simple understanding. And then you must turn these truths from mere notions into life. It is not enough to know the love that God has to us in that lower sense of the word "knowledge." Many of you know that, who never received blessing out of it all your days, and never will, unless you change. Besides the "knowing," there must be the "believing" of the love. You must translate the notion into a living fact in your experience. You must pass from the simple work of understanding the Gospel to the higher act of faith. You must not be contented with knowing, you must trust.

And if you have done that, all the rest will follow; and the little, narrow, low doorway of humble, self-distrusting faith, through which a man creeps on his knees, leaving outside all his sin and his burden, opens out into the temple palace—a large place in which Christ's love is imparted to us all.

When the sunbeams fall upon a mirror, it flashes in the light, because they do not enter its cold surface. It is a mirror, because it does not drink them up, but flings them back. The contrary is the case with the sentient mirrors of our spirits. In them the light must first sink in before it can ray out. They must be filled with the glory before the glory can stream forth. They are not so much like a reflecting surface as like a bar of iron which needs to be heated right down to its obstinate black core before its outer skin glow with the whiteness of a heat that is too hot to sparkle. The sunshine must fall on us, not as it does on some lonely hill-side, lighting up the gray stones with a passing gleam that changes nothing, and fades away, leaving the solitude to its sadness; but as it does on some cloud cradled near its setting, which it drenches and saturates with fire till its cold heart burns, and all its wreathes of vapor are brightness palpable, glorified by the light which lives amid its mists. So must we have the glory sink into us before it can be reflected from us.

WHO IS YOUR KING?

Choose you this day whom ye will serve—Josh. 24:15

You should deliberately decide whether or not Jesus Christ is to be your Savior and your King. Deliberately decide! God has given us that awful [full of awe] gift of choice, and thereby has laid upon us a tremendous weight of responsibility which separates us from all the less endowed, and sometimes (because less endowed) more happy creatures around us. And what do men do with it for the most part? I wonder how many of us have drifted into our "opinions," as we are pleased to call them, by quite another process than that of an intelligent weighing of the force of evidence. I wonder how many of us have, what we say, with unconscious self-condemnation, fallen into ways and habits of action which we never consciously resolved should be our masters. I believe, for my part, that the most of the life of the bulk of men is lived without any adequate exercise of their own deliberate volition and determination. Sadly, too, many of us seem to think that Nansen's way of getting to the North Pole is the best way of getting through the world—to put ourselves into a current and let it carry us. We drift. We do not decide, or, if we do, we let deliberate choice be coerced by inclination, and let wishes put their claws into the scale, and drag it down. Or we allow our environment to settle a large part of our beliefs and of our practices. It must settle a great deal of both for all of us; and none of us can get rid of the pressure of the surrounding atmosphere. But we are meant to be hammers, and not anvils; to mold circumstances, not to be battered and molded by them; to exercise a deliberate choice, and not to be like dead fish in the river, who are carried by the stream—or like derelicts in the Atlantic, that go floating about for years, and never reach any port at all, but are caught by the currents, and are slaves of every wind that blows.

Youth is the time for hope. The world lies all before us, fair and untried. The past is too brief to occupy us long, and its farthest point too near to be clothed in the airy purple which draws the eye and stirs the heart. We are conscious of increasing powers which crave for occupation. It seems impossible but that success and joy shall be ours. So we live for a little while in a golden haze; we look down from our peak upon the virgin forests of a new world that roll away to the shining waters in the west; and then we plunge into their mazes to hew out a path for ourselves, to slay the wild beasts, and to find and conquer rich lands. But soon we discover what hard work the march is, and what monsters lurk in the leafy coverts, and diseases hover among the marshes, and how short a distance ahead we can see, and how far off it is to the treasure-cities we dreamed of; and if at last we gain some cleared spot whence we can look forward, our weary eyes are searching mostly for a place of rest, and all our hopes have dwindled to hopes of safety and repose. If you have God for your "enduring substance," you can face all varieties of condition, and be calm, saying:

"Give what Thou canst, without Thee I am poor,
And with Thee rich; take what Thou wilt away."

The amulet that charms away disquiet lies here.

HIDDEN FROM THE WISE AND PRUDENT

I thank Thee, O Father, Lord of heaven and earth, because thou hid these things from the wise and prudent, and hast revealed them unto babes—Matt. 11:25, 26

There is no royal road into the sweetness and the depth of Christ's love for the wise or the prudent. The understanding is no more the organ for apprehending the love of Christ than is the ear the organ for perceiving light, or the heart the organ for learning mathematics. Blessed be God! The highest gifts are not bestowed upon the clever people, on the men of genius and the gifted ones, on the cultivated and the refined—but they are open for all men; and when we say that love is the parent of knowledge, and that the condition of knowing the depths of Christ's heart is simple love, which is the child of faith, we are only saying in other words what the Master embodied in His thanksgiving prayer, "I thank Thee, Father! Lord of heaven and earth, because Thou hast hid these things from the wise and prudent, and hast revealed them unto babes."

And that is so, not because Christianity, being a foolish system, can only address itself to fools; not because Christianity, contradicting wisdom, cannot expect to be received by the wise and the cultured—but because a man's brains have as little to do with his acceptance of the Gospel of Jesus Christ as a man's eyes have to do with his capacity of hearing a voice. Therefore, seeing that the wise and prudent, and the cultured, and the clever, and the men of genius are always the minority of the race, let us vulgar folk, that are neither wise, nor clever, nor cultured, nor geniuses, be thankful that that has nothing to do with our power of knowing and possessing the best wisdom and the highest treasures; but that upon this path the wayfaring man, though a fool, shall not err, and all narrow foreheads and limited understandings, and poor, simple, uneducated people, as well as philosophers and geniuses, have to learn of their hearts and not of their heads, and, by a sense of need and a humble trust and a daily experience, have to appropriate and suck out the blessings that lie in the love of Jesus Christ. Blessed be His name! The end of all aristocracies of culture and superciliousness of intellect lies in that great truth, that we possess the deepest knowledge and the highest wisdom when we love and by our love.

There is no true wisdom which does not rest calmly upon a basis of truthfulness of heart, and is not guarded and nurtured by righteousness and purity of life. Man is one—one and indissoluble. The intellect and the conscience are but two names for diverse parts of the one human being, or rather they are but two names for diverse workings of one immortal soul. And though it be possible that a man may be enriched with all earthly knowledge, while his heart is the dwelling-place of all corruption; and that, on the other hand, a man may be pure and upright in heart, while his head is very poorly furnished and his understanding very weak—yet these exceptional cases do not touch the great central truth, "The fear of the Lord is the beginning of wisdom, and the knowledge of the Holy is understanding" [Prov. 9:10].

THE MANIFESTED LOVE OF THE CHRIST

It is high as heaven; what canst thou do? deeper than hell; what canst thou know?
The measure thereof is longer than the earth, and broader than the sea—
Job 11:8, 9

We have no measure by which we can translate into the terms of our experience, and so bring within the grasp of our minds, what was the depth of the step which Christ took at the impulse of His love, from the Throne to the Cross. We know not what He forewent; we know not, nor ever shall know, what depths of darkness and soul-agony He passed through at the bidding of His all-enduring love to us. Nor do we know the consequences of that great work of emptying Himself of His glory. We have no means by which we can estimate the darkness and the depth of the misery from which we have been delivered, nor the height and the radiance of the glory to which we are to be lifted. And until we can tell and measure by our compasses both of these two extremes of possible human fate, till we have gone down into the deepest abyss of a bottomless pit of growing alienation and misery, and up above the highest reach of all unending progress into light and glory and God-likeness, we have not stretched our compasses wide enough to touch the two poles of this great sphere—the infinite love of Jesus Christ. So we bow before it: we know if we possess it with a knowledge more sure and certain, more deep and valid, than our knowledge of all but ourselves; but yet it is beyond our grasp, and towers above us inaccessible in the altitude of its glory, and keeps beneath us in the profundity of its condescension.

And, in like manner, this known love passes knowledge, inasmuch as with all our experience of it, our experience is but a little of it. We are like the settlers on some great island continent—as, for instance, on the Australian continent, for many years after its first discovery—a thin fringe of population around the seaboard, here and there, and all the great reach within, the bosom of the land, untraversed and unknown. So, after all experience the love of Jesus Christ, we have but skimmed the surface, but touched the edges, but received, filtered as it were, a drop of what, if it should come upon us in fullness of flood, like a Niagara of love, would overwhelm our spirits. So we have within our reach not only the sorrow of limited affections which bring gladness into life when they come, and darkness over it when they depart; we have not only human love which, if I may so say, is always lifting its finger to its lips in the act of bidding us adieu—but love which will abide with us forever. Men die; Christ lives. We can exhaust men; we cannot exhaust Christ. We can follow other objects of pursuit, all of which have limitation to their power of satisfying, and fall upon the jaded sense sooner or later, or sooner or later are wrenched away from the aching heart. But here is a love into which we can penetrate very deep and fear no exhaustion; a sea, if I may so say, into which we can cast ourselves, nor dread that like some rash diver flinging himself into shallow water where he thought there was depth, we may be bruised and wounded, but we may find in Christ the endless love that an immortal heart requires.

SECRET DISCIPLESHIP

And after this Joseph of Arimathea, being a disciple of Jesus, but secretly for fear
of the Jews, besought Pilate that he might take away the body of Jesus . . . And
there came also Nicodemus, which at the first came to Jesus by night—
John 19:38, 39

While Christ lived, Joseph of Arimathea and Nicodemus had been unfaithful to their convictions; but His death, which terrified and paralyzed and scattered His avowed disciples, seems to have shamed and stung them into courage. They came now, when they must have known that it was too late to lavish honor and tears on the corpse of the Master whom they had been too cowardly to acknowledge while acknowledgment might yet have availed. How keen an arrow of self-condemnation must have pierced their hearts as they moved in their offices of love, which they thought He could never know, around His dead corpse!

They were both members of the Sanhedrin: the same motives, no doubt, had withheld each of them from confessing Christ; the same impulses united them in this too late confession of discipleship. Nicodemus had had the conviction, at the beginning of Christ's ministry, that he was at least a miraculously attested and God-sent teacher. But the fear which made him steal to Jesus by night—the unenviable distinction which the Evangelist pitilessly reiterates at each mention of him—arrested his growth, and kept him dumb when silence was treason.

Joseph of Arimathea is described by two of the Evangelists as "a disciple"; by the other two as a devout Israelite, like Simeon and Anna, "waiting for the Kingdom of God." Luke informs us that he had not concurred in the condemnation of Jesus, but leads us to believe that his dissent had been merely silent. Perhaps he was more fully convinced than Nicodemus, and at the same time even more timid in avowing his convictions. These two contrite cowards, as they try to atone for their unfaithfulness to their living Master by their ministrations to Him dead, are true examples of secret disciples. They were restrained from the avowal of the Messiahship of Jesus by fear. There is nothing in the organization of society at this day to make any man afraid of avowing the ordinary kind of Christianity which satisfies the most of us; rather it is the proper thing with most of us middle-class people to say that in some sense or other we are Christians. But when it comes to a real avowal, a real carrying out of a true discipleship, there are as many and as formidable, though very different, impediments in the way today from those which blocked the path of these two cowards. In all regions of life it is hard to work out into practice any moral conviction whatever. How many of us are there who have beliefs about social and moral questions which we are ashamed to avow in certain companies for fear of the finger of ridicule being pointed at us? It is not only in the church, and in reference to purely religious belief, that we have the curse of secret discipleship, but it is everywhere. Wherever there are moral questions which are yet the subject of controversy, and have not been enthroned with the hallelujahs of all men, you get people that carry their convictions shut up in their own breasts, and lock their lips in silence, when there is most need of frank avowal. The political, social, and moral conflicts of this day have their "secret disciples," who will come only out of their holes when the battle is over, and will then shout with the loudest.

THE CAUSES OF SECRET DISCIPLESHIP

Can any hide himself in secret places, that I shall not see him? saith the Lord.
Do not I fill heaven and earth? saith the Lord—Jer. 23:24

In a society like ours, in which the influence of Christian morality affects a great many people who have no personal connection with Christ, it is not always enough that the life should preach, because over a very large field of ordinary daily life the underground influence, so to speak, of Christian ethics has infiltrated and penetrated, so that many a tree bears a greener leaf because of the water that has found its way to it from the river, though it be planted far from its banks. Even those who are not Christians live outward lives largely regulated by Christian principle. The whole level of morality has been heaved up, as the coast line has sometimes been by hidden fires slowly working, by the imperceptible gradual influence of the gospel.

So it is sometimes necessary that you should *say*, "I am a Christian," as well as that you should live like one. Ask yourselves, dear friends, whether you have buttoned your great coats over your uniforms, that nobody may know whose soldier you are. Ask yourselves whether you have sometimes held your tongues because you knew that if you spoke, people would find out where you came from and what country you belonged to. Ask yourselves have you ever accompanied the witness of your lives with the commentary of your confession? Did you ever, anywhere but in a church, stand up and say, "I believe in Jesus Christ, His only Son, *my* Lord?"

And then ask yourselves another question: Have you ever dared to be singular? We are all of us in this world often thrust into circumstances in which it is necessary that we should say, "So do not I because of the fear of the Lord." Boys go to school. They used to always kneel down at their bedsides and say their prayers when they were at home; they do not like to do it with all those critical and cruel eyes—fixed upon them; and so they give up prayer. A young man comes to Manchester, goes into a warehouse, pure of life, and with a tongue that has not blossomed into rank fruit of obscenity and blasphemy. And he hears at the next desk there, words that first of all bring a blush to his cheek, and he is tempted into conduct that he knows to be a denial of his Master. And he covers up his principles, and goes with the tempters into evil. I might sketch a dozen other cases, but I need not. In one form or other we all have to go through the same ordeal. We sometimes have to dare to be in a minority of one, if we will not be untrue to our Master and to ourselves.

REASONS FOR UNFAITHFULNESS

Moreover, it is required in stewards, that a man be found faithful—1 Cor. 4:2

The reasons for the unfaithfulness of Joseph of Arimathea and Nicodemus are put by John in a very blunt fashion: "for fear of the Jews." That is not what we say to ourselves; some of us say, "Oh! I have gone beyond outward organizations. I find it enough to be united to Christ. The Christian communities are very imperfect: there is not any of them that I quite see eye to eye with; so I stand apart, contemplating all, and happy in my unsectarianism." Yes! I quite admit the faults, and suppose that as long as men think at all, they will not find any church which is entirely to their mind; and I rejoice to think that some day we shall all outgrow visible organizations—when we get there where the seer "saw no temple therein." Admitting all that, I also know that isolation is always weakness, and that if a man stand apart from the wholesome friction of his brethren, he will get to be a great diseased mass of oddities, of very little use either to himself or to men or to God. It is not a good thing on the whole that people should fight for their own hands; and the wisest thing any of us can do is, preserving our freedom of opinion, to link ourselves with some body of Christian people and to find in them our shelter and our home. But these two were moved by "fear." They dreaded ridicule, the loss of position, the expulsion from Sanhedrin and synagogue, social ostracism, and all the armory of offensive weapons which would have been used against them by their colleagues.

So with us, the fear of loss of position comes into play. I have heard of people saying, "Oh! We cannot attach ourselves to such and such a community; there is no society for the children." Then, many of us are very much afraid of being laughed at. Ridicule, I think, to sensitive people, in a generation like ours, is pretty nearly as bad as the old rack and the physical torments of martyrdom. We have all become so nervous and high-strung nowadays, and depend so much upon other people's good opinion, that it is a dreadful thing to be ridiculed. Timid people do not come to the front and say what they believe and take up unpopular causes, because they cannot bear to be pointed at and pelted with the abundant epithets of disparagement which are always flung at earnest people who will not worship at the appointed shrines, and have sturdy convictions of their own.

Ridicule breaks no bones. It has no power, if you make up your mind that it shall not have. Face it, and it will only be unpleasant for a moment at first. When a child goes into the water to bathe, he is uncomfortable till his head has been fairly under water, and then, after that, he is all right. So it is with the ridicule which out-and-out Christian faithfulness may bring on us. It only hurts at the beginning, and people very soon get tired. Face your fears, and they will pass away. It is not perhaps a good advice to give unconditionally, but it is a very good one in regard of all moral questions. Always do what you are afraid to do. In nine cases out of ten it will be the right thing to do. If people would only discount "the fear of men which bringeth a snare" [Prov. 29:25] by making up their minds to it, there would be fewer dumb dogs and secret disciples haunting and weakening the church of Christ.

THE MISERIES OF SECRET DISCIPLESHIP

And the children of Israel did secretly those things that were not right against the Lord their God—2 Kgs. 17:9

How much Joseph of Arimathea and Nicodemus lost!—all those three years of communion with the Master; all His teaching, all the stimulus of His example, all the joy of fellowship with Him! They might have had a treasure in their memories that would have enriched them for all their days, and they had flung it all away because they were afraid of the curled lip of a long-bearded Pharisee or two.

And so it always is, the secret disciple diminishes his communion with his Master. It is the valleys which lay their bosoms open to the sun that rejoice in the light and warmth; the narrow clefts in the rocks that shut themselves grudgingly up against the light, are all dank and dark and dismal. And it is the men that come and avow their discipleship that will have the truest communion with their Lord. Any neglected duty puts a film between a man and his Savior; any conscious neglect of duty piles up a wall between you and Christ. Be sure of this, that if from cowardly or from selfish regard to position and advantages, or any other motive, we stand apart from Him, and have our lips sealed when we ought to speak, there will steal over our hearts a coldness: His face will be averted from us, and our eyes will not dare to seek, with the same confidence and joy, the light of His countenance.

What you lose by unfaithful wrapping of your convictions in a napkin, and burying them in the ground, is the joyful use of the convictions, the deeper hold of the truth by which you live and before which you bow, and the true fellowship with the Master whom you acknowledge and confess. And when these men came to Christ's corpse, and bore it away, what a sharp pang went through their hearts! They woke at last to know what cowardly traitors they had been. If you are a disciple at all, and a secret one, you will awake to know what you have been doing, and the pang will be a sharp one. If you do not awake in this life, then the distance between you and your Lord will become greater and greater; if you do, then it will be a sad reflection that there are years of treason lying behind you. Nicodemus and Joseph had the veil torn away by the contemplation of their dead Master. You may have the veil torn away from your eyes by the sight of the enthroned Lord; and when you pass into the heavens, may even there have some sharp pang of condemnation when you reflect how unfaithful you have been.

Blessed be His name! The assurance is firm that if a man be a disciple, he shall be saved; but the warning is sure that if he be an unfaithful and secret disciple, there will be a lifelong unfaithfulness to a beloved Master to be "purged away so as by fire" [1 Cor. 3:15].

THE CURE OF SECRET DISCIPLESHIP

Then shall the lame man leap as a hart, and the tongue of the dumb sing; for in the wilderness shall waters break out, and streams in the desert—Is. 35:6

Joseph of Arimathea and Nicodemus learned to be ashamed of their cowardice, and their dumb lips learned to speak, and their shy, hidden love forced for itself a channel by which it could flow out into the light; because of Christ's death. And in another fashion that same death and Cross is for us, too, the cure of all cowardice and selfish silence. The sight of Christ's Cross makes the coward brave. It was no small piece of courage for Joseph to go to Pilate and avow his sympathy with a condemned criminal. The love must have been very true which was forced to speak by disaster and death. And to us the strongest motive for stiffening our vacillating timidity into an iron fortitude, and fortifying us far above the fear of what man can do to us, is to be found in gazing upon His dying love who met and conquered all evils and terrors for our sakes.

That Cross will kindle a love which will not rest concealed, but will be like "the ointment of the right hand which bewrayeth itself" [Prov. 27:16]. I can fancy men to whom Christ is only what He was to Nicodemus at first, "a teacher sent from God," occupying Nicodemus's position of hidden belief in His teaching, without feeling any need to avow themselves His followers; but if once into our souls there has come the constraining and the melting influence of that great and wondrous love which died for us, then, dear brethren, it is unnatural that we should be silent. If those for whom Christ has died should hold their peace, the stones would immediately cry out. That death, wondrous, mysterious, terrible, but radiant and glorious with hope, with pardon, with holiness for us and for all the world—that death smites on the chords of our hearts, if I may so speak, and brings out music from them all.

The sight of the Cross not only leads to courage, and kindles a love which demands expression, but it impels to joyful surrender. Joseph gave a place in his own new tomb, where he hoped that one day his bones should be laid by the side of the master against whom he had sinned—for he had no thought of a resurrection. Nicodemus brought a lavish, almost an extravagant, amount of costly spices, as if by honor to the dead he could atone for treason to the living. And both the one and the other teach us that if once we gain the true vision of that great and wondrous love that died on the Cross for us, then the natural language of the loving heart is—

"Here, Lord! I give *myself* away;
'Tis all that I can do."

If following Him openly involves sacrifice, the sacrifice will be sweet, so long as our hearts look to His dying love. All love delights in expression, and most of all in expression by surrender of precious things, which are most precious because they give love materials which it may lay at the beloved's feet. What are positions, possessions, reputations, capacities, perils, losses, selves, but the sweet spices which we are blessed enough to be able to lay upon the altar which glorifies the giver and the gift? The contemplation of Christ's sacrifice—and that alone—will so overcome our natural selfishness as to make sacrifice for His dear sake most blessed.

THE MARK OF THE BEAST

Whatsoever a man soweth, that shall he also reap—Gal. 6:7

Wherever a human nature is self-centered, God-forgetting, and therefore God-opposing (for whoever forgets God defies Him), that nature has gone down below humanity, and has touched the lower level of the brutes.

Men are so made as that they must either rise to the level of God or certainly go down to the level of the brute. And wherever you get men living by their own fancies, for their own pleasure, in forgetfulness and neglect of the sweet and mystic bonds that should knit them to God, there you get "the image of the beast and the number of his name" [Rev. 15:2].

And besides that godless selfishness, we may point to simple animalism as literally the mark of the beast. He who lives not by conscience and by faith, but by fleshly inclination and sense, lowers himself to the level of the instinctive brute-life, and beneath it, because he refuses to obey faculties which they do not possess; and what is nature in them is degradation in us.

Look at the unblushing sensuality which marks many "respectable people" nowadays. Look at the foul fleshliness of much of popular art and poetry. Look at the way in which pure animal passion, the lust of the flesh, and the lust of the eye, and the love of good things to eat, and plenty to drink, is swaying and destroying men and women by the thousands among us. Look at the thin veneer of culture over the ugliest lust. Scratch the gentlemen, and you find the monster. Is it much of an exaggeration, in view of the facts of English life today, to say that all the world wanders after and worships this beast?

Sin is like a great forest-tree that we may sometimes see standing up in its leafy beauty, and spreading a broad shadow over half a field; but when we get around on the other side, there is a great, dark hollow in the very heart of it, and corruption is at work there. It is like the poison-tree in travelers' stories, tempting weary men to rest beneath its thick foliage, and insinuating death into the limbs that relax in the fatal coolness of its shade. It is like the apples of Sodom, fair to look upon, but turning to acrid ashes on the unwary lips. When we come to grasp the sweet thing that we have been tempted to seize, there is a serpent that stands up among all the flowers.

The message of love can never come into a human soul, and pass away from it unreceived, without leaving that spirit worse, with all its lowest characteristics strengthened, and all its best ones depressed, by the fact of rejection. If there were no judgment at all, the natural result of the simple rejection of the Gospel is that, bit by bit, all the lingering remains of nobleness that hover about the man, like scent about a broken vase, shall pass away; and that, step by step, through the simple process of saying, "I will not have Christ to rule over me," the whole being shall degenerate, until manhood becomes devilhood, and the soul is lost by its own lack of faith.

THE MERCY OF GOD

Thy mercy, O Lord, is in the heavens—Psalm 36:5

"Mercy" or "loving-kindness" in the Old Testament is very nearly equivalent to the New Testament "love"; or perhaps still more nearly equivalent to the New Testament "grace." Both the one and the other mean substantially this—active love communicating itself to the creatures that are inferior and that might have expected something else to befall them. Mercy is a modification of love, inasmuch as it is love to an inferior. The hand is laid gently upon the man, because if it was laid with all its weight it would crush him. It is the stooping goodness of a king to a beggar.

And mercy is likewise love, in its exercise to persons that might expect something else, being guilty. As a general coming to a body of mutineers with pardon and favor upon his lips, instead of with condemnation and death; so God comes to us, forgiving and blessing. All His goodness is forbearance, and His love is mercy, because of the weakness, the lowliness, and the ill desert of us on whom the love falls. All the attributes of the Divine nature, all the operations of the Divine hand, lie within the circle of His mercy—like a diamond set in a golden ring. Mercy, or love, flowing out in blessings to inferior and guilty creatures is the root and ground of all God's character; it is the foundation and impulse of all His acts. Modern science reduces all modes of physical energy to one, for which it has no name but—energy. We are taught by God's own revelation of Himself—and most especially by His final and perfect revelation of Himself in Jesus Christ—to trace all forms of Divine energy back to one which David calls mercy, which John calls love.

It is last as well as first, the final upshot of all revelation. The last voice that speaks from Scripture has for its special message "God is love." The last voice that sounds from the completed history of the world will have the same message, and the ultimate word of all revelation, the end of the whole majestic unfolding of God's purposes, will be the proclamation to the four corners of the universe, as from the trump of the Archangel, of the name of God as Love.

The northern and the southern pole of the great sphere are one and the same a straight axle through the very heart of it, from which the bounding lines swell out to the equator, and towards which they converge again on the opposite side of the world. So mercy is the strong axletree, the northern pole and the southern, on which the whole world of the Divine perfections revolves and moves.

"Thy mercy is in the heavens," towering up above the stars, and dwelling there, like some Divine ether, filling all space. The heavens are the home of light, the source of every blessing, arching over every head, rimming every horizon, holding all the stars, opening into abysses as we gaze, with us by night and by day, undimmed by the mist and smoke of earth, unchanged by the lapse of centuries, ever seen, never reached, bending over us always, always far above us.

And so the mercy of God towers above us, and stoops down towards us; rims us all about, and arches over us all; sheds down its dewy benedictions by night and by day; is filled with a mission stars, and light points of beauty and of splendor, is near us ever to bless and succor, to help, and holds us all in its blue round.

GOD'S FAITHFULNESS

Thy faithfulness reacheth unto the clouds—Psalm 36:5

God's faithfulness is in its narrowest sense His adherence to His promises. It implies, in that sense, a verbal revelation, and definite words from Him pledging Him to a certain line of action. "Hath he said, and shall He not do it?" [Num. 23:19]. He will not alter the thing that is gone out of His lips. It is only a God who has actually spoken to men who can be a "faithful God." He will not palter with a double sense, keeping His word of promise to the ear, and breaking it to the hope.

But not only His articulate promises, but also His own past actions, bind Him. He is always true to these, and not only continues to do as He has done, but discharges every obligation which His past imposes on Him. The ostrich was said to leave its eggs to be hatched in the sand; men bring men into positions of dependence, and then lightly shake the responsibility from careless shoulders. But God accepts the cares laid upon Him by His own acts, and discharges them to the last farthing. He is a "faithful Creator." Creation brings obligations with it; obligations on the creature; obligations on the Creator. If God makes a being, God is bound to take care of the being that He has made. If He makes a being in a given fashion, He is bound to provide for the necessities that He has reacted. According to the old proverb, "if He makes mouths, it is His business to feed them." And He recognizes the obligation. His past binds Him to certain conduct in His future. We can lay hold on the former manifestation, and we can plead it with Him. "Thou hast been and therefore Thou must be." "Thou has taught me to trust in Thee; vindicate and warrant my trust by Thy unchangeableness." So His word, His acts, and His own nature, bind God to bless and help. His faithfulness is the expression of His unchangeableness. "Because He could swear by no greater, He sware by Himself."

"Thy faithfulness reacheth to the clouds." Strange that the fixed faithfulness should be considered with reference to the very emblems of instability. The clouds are unstable; they whirl and melt and change. Strange to think of the unalterable faithfulness as reaching to them. May it not be that the very mutability of the mutable may be the means of manifesting the unalterable sameness of God's faithful purpose, of His unchangeable love, and of His ever consistent dealings? May not the apparent incongruity be a part of the felicity of the bold words? Is it not true that earthly things, as they change their forms and melt away, leaving no track behind, phantomlike as they are, do still obey the behests of that Divine faithfulness, and gather and dissolve, and break in the brief showers of blessing or short, sharp crashes of storm at the bidding of that steadfast purpose which works out one unalterable design by a thousand instruments, and changeth all things, being itself unchanged? The thing that is eternal, even the faithfulness of God, dwells amid it, and shows itself through the things that are temporal, the flying clouds of change.

MERCY AND FAITHFULNESS

To show forth thy lovingkindness in the morning, and thy faithfulness
every night—Psalm 92:2

Weave the lovingkindness, or mercy, and faithfulness of God together, and see what a strong cord they are on which a man may hang, and in all his weakness be sure that it will never give nor break. Mercy might be transient and arbitrary, but when you braid in "faithfulness" along with it, it becomes fixed as the pillars of Heaven, and immutable as the throne of God. Only when we are sure of God's faithfulness can we lift up thankful voices to Him, "because His mercy endureth forever." A despotic monarch may be all full of tenderness at this moment to some subject, and all full of wrath and sternness the next. He may have a whim of favor today and a whim of severity tomorrow, and no man can say, "What doest thou?" But God is not a despot. He has, so to speak, "decreed a constitution." He has limited Himself. He has marked out His path across the great wide region of possibilities of the Divine action—He has buoyed out His channel on that ocean; and has declared to us His purposes.

And so we can rely on God, as astronomers can foretell the motions of the stars. We can plead His faithfulness along with His love, and feel that the one makes sure that the other shall be from everlasting to everlasting. The next beam of the divine brightness is righteousness. "Thy righteousness is like the great mountains." Righteousness, not in its narrow sense of stern retribution, which gives to the evildoer the punishment that he deserves. There is no thought here, whatever there may be in other places in Scriptures, of any opposition between mercy and righteousness; but the notion of righteousness here is a broader and greater one. It is just this, to put it into other words, that God has a law for His being to which He conforms; and that whatsoever things are fair and lovely and good and pure down here, those things are fair and lovely and good and pure up there; that He is the archetype of all excellence, the ideal of all moral completeness; that we can know enough of Him to be sure of this—that what we call right He loves, and that what we call right He practices.

Unless we have that for the very foundation of our thoughts of God, we have no foundation to rest on. Unless we feel and know "the Judge of all the earth doeth right" [Gen. 18:25], and is right, and law and righteousness have their home and seat in His bosom, and are the expressions of His inmost being, then I know not where our confidences can be built. Unless Thy righteousness, like the great mountains, surrounds and guards the low plain of our lives, they will lie open to all foes.

THE SEA OF GLASS

And before the throne there was a sea of glass like unto crystal—Rev. 4:6

The sea of glass cannot be any part of the material creation, for the symbolism has provided for that otherwise. There seems to be but one explanation of it, and that is that it means the aggregate of the Divine dealings. "Thy judgments are a mighty deep." "Oh, the depth of the riches, both of the wisdom and of the knowledge of God! How unsearchable are His judgments and His ways past finding out!" That great ocean of the judgment of God is crystalline—clear, though it be deep. Does it seem so to us? We stand before the mystery of God's dealings, often bewildered, and not seldom reluctant to submit. The perplexity rising from their obscurity is often almost torture and sometimes leads us into Atheism, or something like it. And yet here is the assurance that this sea is crystal clear; and if we cannot look to its lowest depths, that is not because there is any mud or foulness there, but partly because our eyes are uneducated to search its depths. In itself it is transparent, and it rises and falls without "mire or dirt," like the blue Mediterranean on the marble cliffs of the Italian coast. If it be clear as far as the eye can see, let us trust that beyond the reach of the eye the clearness is the same.

And it is a crystal ocean as being calm. They who stand there have gotten the victory and bear the image of the Master. By reason of their conquest, and by reason of their sympathy with Him, they see that what to us, tossing upon its surface, appears such a troubled and tempestuous ocean, is calm and still. As from some height, looked down upon, the ocean seems a watery plain, and all the agitation of the billows has subsided into a gentle ripple on the surface; so to them looking down upon the sea that brought them thither, it is quiet—and their vision, not ours, is the true one.

Just as we fit around a central light sparkling prisms, each of which catches the glow at its own angle, and flashes it back of its own color, while the sovereign completeness of the perfect white radiance comes from the blending of all their separate rays; so they who stand around the starry throne receive each the light in his own measure and manner, and give forth each a true and perfect, and altogether a complete, image of Him who enlightens them all, and is above them all. Like the serene choirs of angels in the old pictures, each one with the same tongue of fire on his brow, with the same robe flowing in the same folds to the feet, with the same golden hair, yet each a separate self, with his own gladness, and a different instrument for praise in his hand, and his own part in that "undisturbed song of pure concert," we shall all be changed into the same image, and yet each heart grow great with its own blessedness and each spirit bright with its own proper luster of individual and characteristic perfection.

THE RIGHTEOUSNESS OF GOD

And the work of righteousness shall be peace, and the effect of righteousness
quietness and assurance forever—Is. 32:17

"Thy righteousness is like the great mountains" [Ps. 36:6]. Like these, its roots are fast and stable; like these, it stands firm forever; like these, its summits touch the fleeting clouds of human circumstance; like these, it is a shelter and a refuge, inaccessible in its steepest peaks, but affording many a cleft in its rocks [Ex. 33:22] where a man may hide and be safe. But, unlike these, it knew no beginning and shall know no end. Emblems of permanence as they are, though Olivet looks down on Jerusalem as it did when Melchizedek was its king, and Tabor and Hermon stand as they did before human lips had named them, they are wearing away by winter storms and summer heats. But, as Isaiah has taught us, when the earth is old, God's might and mercy are young; for "the mountains shall depart and the hills be removed, but my kindness shall not depart from thee" [Is. 54:10]. "The earth shall wax old like a garment . . . but . . . my righteousness shall not be abolished" [Is. 51:6]. It is more stable than the mountains, and firmer than the firmest things upon earth.

Here towers Vesuvius; there at its feet lie the waters of the bay. So the righteousness springs up like some great cliff, rising sheer from the water's edge, while its feet are washed by the "sea of glass mingled with fire" [Rev. 15:2]—the Divine judgments, unfathomable and shoreless. The mountains and the sea are the two grandest things in nature, and in their combination sublime; the one the home of calm and silence, the other in perpetual motion. But the mountain's roots are deeper than the depths of the sea; and though the judgments are a mighty deep, the righteousness is deeper, and is the bed of that ocean.

The metaphor, of course implies obscurity, but what sort of obscurity? The obscurity of the sea. And what sort of obscurity is that? Not that which comes from mud, or anything added; that which comes from depth. As far as a man can see down into its blue-green depths, they are clear and translucent; but where the light fails and the eye fails, there comes what we call obscurity. The sea is clear, but our sight is limited.

And so there is no arbitrary obscurity in God's dealings, and we know as much about them as it is possible for us to know; but we cannot see to the bottom. A man on the cliff can see much deeper down in the ocean than a man on the bank. The further you climb, the further you will see down into the "sea of glass mingled with fire" that lies placid before God's throne. Let us remember that it is a hazardous thing to judge of a picture before it is finished, of a building before the scaffolding is pulled down; and it is a hazardous thing for us to say about any deed or any revealed truth that it is inconsistent with the Divine character. Wait a bit; wait a bit! "Thy judgments are a great deep" [Ps. 36:6]. The deep will be drained off one day, and you will see the bottom of it.

THE TRUE OBJECT OF LOVE

He that loveth not knoweth not God; for God is love—1 John 4:8

We are made with hearts that need to rest upon an absolute love; we are made with understandings that need to grasp a pure, a perfect, and, as I believe, (paradoxical though it may sound), a personal Truth. We are made with wills that crave for an absolute perfect holiness. And we need all that love, truth, authority, purity to be gathered into one; for the misery of the world is that when we set out to look for treasures, we have to go into many lands and to many merchants to buy many goodly pearls. But we need One of great price [Matt. 13:46], in which all our wealth may be invested. We need that One to be an undying and perpetual possession. There is One to whom our love can ever cleave, and fear none of the sorrows or imperfections that make earthward-turned love a rose with many a thorn, One for whom it is a pure gain to lose ourselves, surrender of the heart [Phil. 1:21]. And that One is God, revealed and brought near to us in Jesus Christ. In that great Savior we have a love at once divine and human; we have the great transcendent instance of love leading to sacrifice. On that love and sacrifice for us Christ builds His claim on us for our hearts, and our all. Life alone can communicate life; it is only light that can diffuse light; it is only love that can kindle love; it is only sacrifice that can inspire sacrifice. And so He comes to us, and asks that we should just love Him back again as He has loved us. He first gives Himself utterly unto us, and then asks us to give ourselves wholly to Him. He first yields up His own life, and then He says, "He that loseth his life for my sake shall find it." The object, the true object, for all this depth of love which lies slumbering in our hearts, is God in Christ, the Christ that died for us.

God's love is Christ's love; Christ's love is God's love. And this is the lesson that we gather—that this Divine lovingkindness does not turn away from thee, my brother and my friend, because thou art a sinner, but remains hovering about thee, with wooing invitations and with gentle touches, if it may draw thee to repentance, and open a fountain of answering affection in thy seared and dry heart. The love of God is deeper than all our sins. "For His great love wherewith He loved us, even when we were dead in sins, hath quickened us" [Eph. 2:4, 5]. Sin is but the cloud behind which the everlasting Sun lies in all its power and warmth, unaffected by the cloud; and the light will yet strike, the light of His love will yet pierce through, with its merciful shafts bringing healing in their beams, and dispersing all the pitchy darkness of man's transgression. And as the mists gather themselves up and roll away, dissipated by the heat of that sun in the upper sky, and reveal the fair earth below, so the love of Christ shines in, melting the mist and dissipating the fog, thinning it off in its thickest places, and at last piercing its way through it, down to the heart of the man that has been lying beneath the oppression of his thick darkness, and who thought that the fog was the sky, and that there was no sun there above.

SHELTERING BENEATH GOD'S WING

How excellent is thy lovingkindness, O God! therefore the children of men put
their trust under the shadow of thy wings—Psalm 36:7

God's lovingkindness, or mercy, as I explained the word might be rendered, is *precious*, for it is the true meaning of the word translated "excellent." We are rich when we have that for ours; we are poor without it. The true wealth is to possess God's love, and to know in thought and realize in feeling and reciprocate in affection His grace and goodness, the beauty and perfectness of His wondrous character. That man is wealthy who had God on his side; that man is a pauper who has not God for his.

The word rendered, and accurately rendered, "put their trust," has a very beautiful literal meaning. It means to flee for refuge, as the manslayer might flee into the strong city, or as Lot did out of Sodom to the little city on the hill, as David did into the cave from his enemies. So says the Word. With such haste, with such intensity, staying for nothing, and with the effort of your whole will and nature, flee to God. That is trust. Go to him for refuge from all evil, from all harm, from your own souls, from all sin, from hell and death and the devil. Put your trust under "the shadow of His wing."

That is a beautiful image, drawn, probably, from the grand words of Deuteronomy, where the tenderness of God is likened to the eagle stirring upon her nest, fluttering over her young [32:11], with tenderness in her fierce eye and protecting strength in the sweep of her mighty pinion. So God spreads the covert of His wing, strong and tender, beneath which we may all gather ourselves and nestle. And how can we do that? By the simple process of fleeing unto Him, as made known to us in Christ our Savior; to hide ourselves there. For let us not forget how even the tenderness of this metaphor was increased by its shape on the tender lips of the Lord: "How often would I have gathered thy children together . . . as a hen gathereth her chickens under her wings" [Matt. 23:37]. The Old Testament took the emblem of the eagle, sovereign, strong, and fierce. The New Testament took the emblem of the domestic fowl, peaceable, gentle, and affectionate. Let us flee to that Christ, by humble faith, with the plea on our lips—

"Cover my defenseless head
With the shadow of Thy wings";

and then all the Godhead, in its mercy, its faithfulness, its righteousness, and its judgments, will be on our side, and we shall know how precious is the lovingkindness of the Lord, and find in Him the home and hiding place of our hearts forever.

VICTORY THROUGH THE BLOOD OF THE LAMB

Thanks be to God, which giveth us the victory through our Lord Jesus Christ—
1 Cor. 15:57

That victory is possible. The Apocalypse shows us that there are two opposing powers—the "beast" on the one side, and "the Lamb" on the other. These two divide the world between them in the seer's vision. That is to say, Jesus Christ has conquered the bestial tendencies of our nature; He has conquered the selfish godlessness which is apt to cast its spells and weave its chains over us all. The Warrior-Lamb, singular and incongruous as the combination sounds, is the victor. He conquers because He is the Lamb of sacrifice; He conquers because He is the Lamb of innocence; He conquers because He is the Lamb of meekness, the gentle and, therefore, the all-victorious. By Christ we conquer. Through faith, which lays hold on His power and victory, we too may conquer. "This is the victory that overcometh the world, even our faith" [1 John 5:4].

Young men and women! Do not let yourselves be led away captives to the shambles by the fascinations and seductions of this poor, fleeting present. Keep your heel on the neck of the animal that is within you; take care of that selfish godlessness into which we all are tempted to fall. Listen to the trumpet-call that ought to stir your hearts, that summons you to freedom and to victory through the blood of the Lamb. And do you, by humbly clasping Him as your sacrifice, your leader, and your power, enroll yourselves among those who, in His own good time, shall come victorious from the "beast" and from his image [Rev. 15:2].

Our Captain provides us with an inexhaustible strength, to which we may fully trust. We shall not exhaust it by any demands that we can make upon it. We shall only brighten it up, like the nails in a well-used shoe, the heads of which are polished by stumbling and scrambling over rocky roads. "Thy shoes shall be iron and brass; and as thy days so shall thy strength be" [Deut. 33:25].

Did you ever see that electric light which is made by directing a strong stream upon two small pieces of carbon? As the electricity strikes upon these and turns their blackness into a fiery blaze, it eats away their substance as it changes them into light. But there is an arrangement in the lamp by which a fresh surface is continually being brought into the path of the beam, and so the light continues without wavering, and blazes on. The carbon is our human nature, black and dull in itself; the electric beam is the swift energy of God, which makes us light in the Lord. God does not turn people out to scramble over rough mountains with thin-soled boots on. When an Alpine climber is preparing to go away into Switzerland for rock work, the first thing he does is to get a pair of strong shoes, with plenty of iron nails in the soles of them. Each of us may be sure that if God sends us on stony paths He will provide us with strong shoes, and will not send us out on any journey for which He does not equip us well.

MISDIRECTED ZEAL

I bear them record that they have a zeal of God, but not according to knowl-
edge—Rom. 10:2

There is nothing more tragic in this world than misdirection of man's capacity for love and sacrifice. It is like the old story in the book of Daniel, of how the heathen monarch made a great feast, and when the wine began to inflame the guests, sent for the sacred vessels taken from the Temple of Jerusalem, that had been used for Jehovah's worship, and, as the narrative says, with a kind of shudder at the profanation. "They brought the golden vessels that were taken out of the temple of the House of God, which was at Jerusalem, and the king and his princes, his wives and his concubines, drank in them. They drank wine and praised the gods" [Dan.5:3].

So this heart of mine, which has the Master's initials and His arms engraven upon it, in token that it is His cup—this heart of mine I too often fill with the poisonous and intoxicating draught of earthly pleasure and earthly affections; and, as I drink it, the madness goes through my veins, and I praise the gods of my own making instead of Him whom alone I ought to love. We should be our own rebukes in this matter, and the heroism of the world should put to shame the cowardice and the selfishness of the Church. Contrast the depth of your affection for your household with the tepidity of your love for your Savior. Contrast the willingness with which you sacrifice yourself for some dear one with the grudgingness with which you yield yourselves to Him. Contrast the rest and the sense of satisfaction in the presence of those you love, and your desolation when they are absent, with the indifference whether you have Christ beside you or not. And remember that the measure of your power of loving is the measure of your obligation to love your Lord; and that if you are all frost to Him and all fervor to them, in a very solemn sense "a man's foes shall be they of his own household. He that loveth father or mother more than me is not worthy of me!" [Matt. 10:36, 37].

I would beseech you to bring that power of uncalculating love and self-sacrificing affection which is in you, and fasten it where it ought to fix—on Christ, who died on the Cross for you. Such a love will bring blessedness to you. Such a love will ennoble and dignify your whole nature, and make you a far greater and fairer man or woman than you otherwise ever could be. Like some little bit of black carbon put into an electric current, my poor nature will flame into beauty and radiance when that spark touches it. So, love Him and be at peace; give yourselves to Him, and He will give you back yourselves, ennobled and transfigured by the surrender. Lay yourselves on His altar, and that altar will sanctify both the giver and the gift.

UNCONSCIOUS POWER FOR SERVICE

We know not with what we must serve the Lord—Ex. 10:26

The weakest and the lowest, the roughest and the hardest, the most selfishly-absorbed man and woman among us has lying in him and her dormant capacities for flaming up into such a splendor of devotion, and magnificence of heroic self-forgetfulness and self-sacrifice as is represented in many words of the Bible. A mother will do it for her child, and never think that she has done anything extraordinary; husbands will do such things for wives; wives for husbands; friends and lovers for one another. All who love the sweetness and power of the bond of affection know that there is nothing more gladsome than to fling one's self away for the sake of those whom we love. And the capacity for such love and sacrifice lies in all of us; prosaic, commonplace people as we are, with no great field on which to work out our heroism, yet it is in us all to love and give ourselves away thus if once the heart be stirred. If once the capacity is roused to action, it will make a man blessed and dignified as nothing else will. The joy of unselfish love is the purest joy that man can taste; the joy of perfect self-sacrifice is the highest joy that humanity can possess—and it lies open for us all.

And wherever, in some humble measure, these emotions of which I have been speaking are realized, there you get weakness springing up into strength, and the ignoble into loftiness. Astronomers tell us that, sometimes, a star that has shone inconspicuous, way down in their catalogues fifth of sixth magnitude, will all at once flame out, having kindled and caught fire somehow, and will blaze in the heavens, outshining Jupiter and Venus. And so some poor, vulgar, narrow nature, touched by this Promethean fire of pure love that leads to perfect sacrifice, will "flame in the forehead of the morning sky," an undying splendor, and a light forevermore. All have this capacity in them, and all are responsible for the use of it. What have you done with it? Is there any person or thing in this world that has ever been able to lift you up out of your miserable selves? Is there any magnet that has proved strong enough to raise you from the low levels along which your life creeps? Have you ever known the thrill of resolving to become the bondservant and the slave of some great cause not your own? Or are you, as so many are, like spiders living in the midst of your web, mainly intent upon what it can catch for you? Have you ever set a light to that inert mass of enthusiasm that lies in you? Have you ever awakened the sleeper? Learn the lesson that there is nothing that so ennobles and dignifies a common nature as enthusiasm for a great cause, self-sacrificing love for a worthy heart.

CHRIST THE TRUE OBJECT OF OUR ENDEAVOR

For to me to live is Christ, and to die is gain—Phil. 1:21

"Whose image and superscription hath it?" said Christ in Luke 20:24, looking at the roman *denarius* that they brought and laid in His palm. If the emperor's head is on it, why, then, *he* has a right to the tribute of it. And then He went on to say in verse 25, "Render, therefore, unto Caesar the things which be Caesar's, and unto God the things which be God's." So there are things that have God's head upon them, God's image and superscription stamped, and these are your hearts, your whole constitution and nature. As plainly as the penny had the head of Augustus on it, and therefore proclaimed that he was emperor where it was current, so plainly does every soul carry in the image of God the witness that He is its owner, and that it should be rendered in tribute to Him.

And among all these marks of a Divine possession and a Divine destination printed upon human nature, it seems to me that none are more plain than this fact, that we can all of us thus give ourselves away in the abandonment of a profound and all-commanding love. That capacity unmistakably proclaims that it is destined to be directed towards God, and to find its rest in Him. As distinctly as some silver cup, with its owner's initials and arms engraved upon it, declares itself to be "meet for the master's use" [2 Tim. 2:21], so distinctly does your soul, by reason of this faculty, proclaim that it is meant to be turned to Him in whom alone all love can find its perfect satisfaction; for whom alone it is blessed and great to shed life itself; and who only has the authority over our human spirits.

I will not say that such emotions, wherever expended on creatures, are ever wasted. For however unworthy may be the objects on which they are lavished, the man himself is the better and the higher for having cherished them. The mother for her child, though her love and self-forgetfulness and self-sacrifice may, in some respects, be called but an animal instinct, is elevated and ennobled by the exercise of them. The patriot and the thinker, the philanthropist, even—although I take it to be the lowest of the scale—the soldier, who, in some cause which he thinks to be a good one, and not merely in the tigerish madness of the battlefield, throws away his life, is lifted in the scale of being by the deed. And so I am not going to say that when men love each other passionately and deeply, and sacrifice themselves for one another, or for some cause of purpose affecting only temporal matters, the precious elixir of life is wasted. God forbid! But I do say that all these objects, sweet and gracious as some of them are, ennobling and elevating as some of them are, if they are taken apart from God, are insufficient to fill your hearts; and that if they are slipped in between you and God, as they often are, then they bring sin and sorrow.

THE BLESSEDNESS OF A RIGHT CHOICE

Butter and honey shall he eat, that he may know to refuse the evil, and choose the good—Is. 7:15

If you choose Christ, you choose all that your nature needs for its rest, for its peace, for its development, for its expansion, for its efflorescence into growing beauty through eternity. If you will take Christ for your Lord, your heart may fold its wings like the dove that came back from the flood, and may rest in His love, which is perfect and pure and wise and unalterable. If you will take Christ for your choice, and become His servant, and let Him save you and rule you, then all the seeking understanding will find in Him, and in the manifold and endless "treasures of wisdom and knowledge" [Col. 2:3] into which His name breaks—like the sunbeam when it strikes upon the mirror, and its shattered into a million dancing brightnesses—all that the intellect can require. If you will take Christ for your Savior and your King, then that mastering will which so often leads us astray, and those passions which so often plunge us into filth and mire, will own His guidance; and the lion shall lie down with the lamb, and the bear in the menagerie of your heart will eat straw like the ox, and you will be able to lay your hand on the cockatrice den and not be stung, and all the wild beasts will be tamed, and your feebleness as that of "a little child shall lead them" [Is. 11:6].

If you will take Christ for your Savior and your King, the disease of your natures will be healed, which He only can heal. For no man looks all the facts in the face, or has made a choice worthy of calling by that name, who has not looked the fact of sin in the face, and settled how he is going to get rid of the three-pronged dart which it flings—guilt, and punishment, and power—if he does not take Christ's way of getting rid of it. There is none that can touch the central corruption of humanity, none that can bring pardon, none that can enable us to shake the venomous beast that has fastened on our hands into the fire, and feel no harm, except Christ only. You may "cut yourselves with knives and lancets till the blood gush out" [see 1 Kgs. 18:28], and cry to all the gods besides, and to yourself, who are the Jupiter of them all, from morning to evening, to get rid of the fact of sin, and there will be no voice nor answer, "nor any that regarded" [1 Kgs. 18:29].

If you will take Christ as your Savior, and serve Him, you will find it possible to live more noble, helpful and manly lives for God and the world than by any other means. If you will take Christ for your Savior, and yourselves be enrolled as His obedient servants, then you will secure for yourselves a future without a cloud, in which ills have no power to harm, and all things are transmuted into good, and death has no bitterness and eternity no terror. Let Baal come and do the like. Till he does, I urge that no claims can for a moment be set by the side of Christ's.

ITTAI OF GATH

And Ittai answered the king, and said: As the Lord liveth, and as my lord the king liveth, surely in what place my lord the king shall be, whether in death or life, even there also will thy servant be—2 Sam. 15:21

Look at the picture of that Philistine soldier, as teaching us what grand, passionate self-sacrifice may be evolved out of the roughest natures. Here they are, "faithful among the faithless"; as foreign soldiers surrounding a king often are, notably, for instance, the Swiss guard in the French Revolution. Their strong arms might have been of great use to David, but his generosity cannot think of involving them in his fall, and so he says to them: "I am not going to fight; I have no plan. I am going where I can. You go back and 'worship the rising sun.' Absalom will take you in, and be glad of your help, And as for me, I thank you for your past loyalty. Mercy and peace be with you!"

It is a beautiful nature that, in the depth of sorrow, thinks more of dragging other people into it than of its own fate. Generosity breeds generosity, and this rough Philistine captain breaks out into a burst of passionate devotion, garnished in soldier fashion with an unnecessary oath or two, but ringing very sincere, and meaning a great deal. As for himself and his men, they have chosen their side. Whoever goes, they stay. Whatever befalls, they stick by David; and if the worst come to the worst, they can all die together, and their corpses lie in firm ranks around their dead king. David's heart is touched and warmed by their outspoken loyalty; he yields and accepts their service. Ittai and his noble six hundred tramp on, out of our sight, with all their households behind them. Analyze their words, and do you not hear, ringing in them, these three things, which are the seed of all nobility and splendor in human character—a passionate, personal attachment, issuing in spontaneous heroism of self-abandonment, and in supreme satisfaction in the beloved presence? And these may spring up in the rudest, roughest nature. A Philistine soldier was not a very likely man in whom to find refined and lofty emotion. He was hard by nature, hardened by his rough trade; and unconscious, at the moment here, that he was doing anything at all heroic or great. Something had smitten this rock, and out of it there came the pure refreshing stream. For Ittai and his men the one thing needful was to be beside him in whose eye they had lived, from whose presence they had caught inspiration; their trusted leader, before whom their souls bowed down. So then his vehement speech is the pure language of love.

The world knows nothing of its greatest men, but there is a day coming when the spurious mushroom aristocracy of power and the like, that the world has worshiped, will be forgotten—like the nobility of some conquered land, that is brushed aside and relegated to private life by the new nobility of the conquerors, and the true nobles, God's greatest—the righteous, who are righteous because they have trusted in Christ—shall shine forth like the sun "in the kingdom of My Father."

"IT PASSETH KNOWLEDGE"

To the acknowledgment of the mystery of God, and of Christ, in whom are hidden all the treasures of wisdom and knowledge—Col. 2:2, 3

I do not suppose that the paradox of knowing the love of Christ which "passeth knowledge" [Eph. 3:19] is to be explained by taking "know" and "knowledge" in two different senses, so as that it means mere understanding is incapable of grasping. That of course is an explanation which might be defended, but I take it that it is much truer to the Apostle's meaning to suppose that he uses the words "know" and "knowledge" both times in the same sense. And so we get two familiar thoughts. The understanding can grasp, but it can never grasp all around, the love of Jesus Christ. You and I believe, I hope, that Christ's love is not a man's love, or at least that it is more than a man's love. We believe that it is the flowing out to us of the love of God, that all the fullness of the Divine heart pours itself through that narrow channel of the human nature of our Lord, and therefore that the flow is endless and the Fountain infinite.

I suppose I do not need to show you that it is possible for people to have, and that in fact we do possess, a real, a valid, a reliable knowledge of that which is infinite, although we possess, as a matter of course, no adequate and complete knowledge of it. But I only remind you that we have before us in Christ's love something which, though the understanding is not by itself able to grasp, yet the understanding led by the heart can lay hold of, and can find in it infinite treasures. But we can only lay our poor hands, as a child might lay its tiny palm upon the base of some great cliff—we can lay our poor hands on his love, and hold it in a real grasp of a real knowledge and certitude, but we cannot put our hands around it, and feel that we *com*prehend as well as *ap*prehend. Blessed be His name—we cannot!

His love can only become to us a subject of knowledge as it reveals itself in its manifestations. Yet after even these manifestations, it remains unuttered and unutterable, even by the Cross and grave, even by the glory and the throne.

My friend, God hath loved us with an everlasting love. He has provided an eternal redemption and pardon for us. If you would know Christ at all, you must go to Him as a sinful man, or you are shut out from Him altogether. If you *will* go to Him as a sinful being, fling yourself down there, not try to make yourself better, but say, "I am all full of unrighteousness and transgression; let Thy love fall upon me and heal me"; you will get the answer, and in your heart there shall begin to live and grow up a root of love to him, which shall at last effloresce into all knowledge and into all purity of obedience; for he that hath had much forgiven, loveth much; and "he that loveth . . . knoweth God" [1 John 4:8], and "dwelleth in God, and God in him" [1 John 4:16].

THE BRUISED REED RESTORED

A bruised reed shall He not break—Is. 42:3

Here is the picture. A slender bulrush, growing by the margin of some tarn or pond; its sides crushed and dented in by some outward power, some gust of wind, some sudden blow, the foot of some passing animal. The head is hanging by a thread, but it is not yet snapped or broken off from the stem. It is "bruised," but the bruise is not irreparable. And so, says this text, there are reeds bruised and "shaken by the wind," but not yet broken. And the tender Christ comes, with His gentle, wise, skillful surgery, to bind these up and to make them strong again.

On no man has sin fastened its venomous claws so deeply but that these may be wrenched away. In none of us has the virus so gone through our veins but that it is capable of being expelled. The reeds are all bruised, the reeds are none of them broken. And so this text comes with its great triumphant hopefulness and gathers into one mass as capable of restoration the most abject, the most worthless, the most ignorant, the most sensuous, the most godless, the most Christ-hating of the race. And He looks on all the tremendous bulk of a world's sins with the confidence that He can move that mountain [Matt. 17:20] and cast it into the depths of the sea.

In accordance with other metaphors of Scripture, we may think of "the bruised reed" as expressive of the condition of men whose hearts have been crushed by the consciousness of their sins. "The broken and the contrite heart," bruised and pulverized, as it were, by a sense of evil, may be typified for us by this bruised reed. And then from the words of this text there emerges the great and blessed hope that such a heart, wholesomely removed from its self-complacent fancy of soundness, shall certainly be healed and bound up by His tender hand. Did you ever see a gardener dealing with some plant, a spray of which may have been wounded? How delicately and tenderly the big, clumsy hand busies itself about the tiny spray, and by stays and bandages brings it into an erect position, and then gives it water and loving care. Just so does Jesus Christ deal with the conscious and sensitive heart of a man that has begun to find out how bad he is, and has been driven away from all his foolish confidence. Christ comes to such a one and restores him, and, just because he is crushed, deals with him gently, pouring in His consolation. Wheresoever there is a touch of penitence, there is present a restoring Christ.

Brother and sister, suffering from any sorrow, and bleeding from any wound, there is balm and a physician! There is one hand that will never be laid with blundering kindness or with harshness upon our sore hearts, but whose touching will be healing and whose presence will be peace.

The Christ that knows our sins and sorrows will not break the bruised reed. The whole race of man may be represented in that parable that came from His own lips, as fallen among thieves that have robbed him and wounded him, and left him bruised, and blessed be God, only "half dead,"—sorely wounded, indeed, but not so sorely but that he may be restored. And there comes One with the wind and the oil, and pours them into the wounds [Luke 10:30–34].

CHRIST THE FOSTERER OF INCIPIENT AND IMPERFECT GOOD

The smoking flax (the dimly-burning wick) shall he not quench—Is. 42:3

In all men, just because the process of evil and the wounds from it are not so deep and complete as that restoration is impossible, therefore is there something in their nature which corresponds to this dim flame that needs to be fostered in order to blaze brightly abroad. There is no man out of hell but has in him something that wants but to be brought to sovereign power in his life in order to make him a light in the world. You have got consciences at least; you have convictions, you know you have, which, if you followed them out, would make Christians of you straight away. You have got aspirations after good, desires after purity and nobleness of living, which only needs to be raised to the height and the dominance in your lives which they ought to possess in order to revolutionize your whole course. There is a spark in every man which, fanned and cared for, will change him from darkness into light. Fanned and cared for it needs to be, and fanned and cared for it can only be by Divine power coming down upon it from without. He from whom all sparks of light have died out is not a man, but a devil. And for all of us the exhortation comes: "You have a law within testifying to God and to duty"; listen to it and care for it. In a narrower way, the words may be applied to a class. There are some of us who have in us a little spark, we believe, of a Divine life, the faint beginnings of a Christian character. We call ourselves Christ's disciples. We are; but oh, how dimly the flax burns! They say that where there is smoke there is fire. There is a deal more smoke than fire in most Christian people of this generation. And if it were not for such thoughts as this, about that dear Christ that will not lay a hasty hand upon some little tremulous spark, and by one rash movement extinguish it forever, there would be but little hope for a great many of us.

How do you make "smoking flax" burn? You give it oil, you give it air, and you take away the charred portions. And Christ will give you, in your feebleness, the oil of His Spirit, that you may burn brightly as one of the candlesticks in His temple; and He will let air in, and take away the charred portions by the wise discipline of sorrow and trial sometimes whatsoever means it may be, be sure of this, that He will neither despise nor neglect the feeblest inclination of good after Him, but will nourish it to perfection and to beauty.

The reason why so many Christian men's Christian light is so fuliginous and dim is just that they keep away from Jesus Christ. "Abide in me and I in you. As the branch cannot bear fruit of itself, except it abide in the vine, no more can ye except ye abide in me" [John 15:4]. How can the Temple lamps burn bright unless the Priest of the Temple tends them? Keep near Him, that His hand may nourish your smoking dimness into a pure flame, leaping heavenward and illuminating your lives.

OUR LORD'S PERFECT MANHOOD

He shall not fail nor be discouraged, till he have set judgment in
the earth—Is. 42:4

There are no bruises in this reed. That is to say, Christ's Manhood is free from all scars and wounds of evil or of sin. There is no dimness in this light. That is to say, Christ's character is perfect, His goodness needs no increase. There is no trace of effort in His holiness, no growth manifest in His God-likeness, from the beginning to the end. There is no outward violence that can be brought to bear upon Him that shall stay Him in His purpose. There is no inward failure of strength that may lead us to fear that His work shall not be completed. And because of all these things, because of His perfect exemption from human infirmity, because in Him was no sin, He is manifested to take away our sins. Because in Him there was goodness incapable of increase, being perfect from the beginning, therefore is He manifested to make us participants of His own unalterable and infinite goodness and purity. Because no outward violence, no inward weakness, can ever stay His course nor make Him abandon His purpose, therefore His Gospel looks upon the world with boundless hopefulness, with calm triumph; will not hear of there being any outcast and irreclaimable classes; declares it to be a blasphemy against God and Christ to say that any man or any nations are incapable of receiving the Gospel and of being redeemed by it, and comes with supreme love and a calm consciousness of infinite power to you, my brother, in your deepest darkness, in your moods most removed from God and purity, and declares to you that it will heal you, and will raise all that in you is feeble to its own strength. Every man may pray to that strong Christ who fails not nor is discouraged—

> "What in me is dark, illumine;
> What is low, raise and support"—

in the confidence that He will hear and answer. If you do that you will not do it in vain, but His gentle hand laid upon you will heal the bruises that sin has made. Out of your weakness, as of "a reed shaken with the wind" [Luke 7:24], the Restorer will make a pillar of marble in the temple of His God. And out of your smoking dimness of wavering light—a spark at the best, almost buried in the thick smoke that accompanies it—the fostering Christ will make a brightness which shall flame as the perfect light that "shineth more and more unto the noontide of the day."

A DARK CHAMBER IN EVERY HEART

He hath set me in dark places, as they that be dead of old—Lam. 3:6

Every man is a mystery to himself as to his fellows. With reverence, we may say of each other as we say of God—"Clouds and darkness are round about Him." After all the manifestations of a life, we remain enigmas to one another, mysteries to ourselves; for every man is no fixed somewhat, but a growing personality, with dormant possibilities of good and evil lying in him, which up to the very last moment of life may flame up in altogether unexpected and astonishing developments, so as that we have all to feel that after all self-examination there lie awful possibilities within us which we have not fathomed; and after all our knowledge of one another we yet do see but the surface, and each soul dwells alone.

There is in every heart a dark chamber. There are very, very few of us that dare to tell all our thoughts and show our inmost selves to the dearest ones. The most silvery lake that lies sleeping amid beauty, itself the very fairest spot of all, when drained off shows ugly ooze and filthy mud, and all manner of creeping abominations in the slime. I wonder what we should see if our hearts were, so to speak, drained off, and the very bottom layer of everything brought into the light? Do you think you would like it? Do you think you could stand it?

Well, then, go to God and ask Him to keep you from the unconscious sins. Go to Him and ask Him to root out of you the mischiefs that you do not know are there, and live humbly and self-distrustfully, and feel that your only strength is: "Hold Thou me up, and I shall be safe" [Ps. 119:17]. "Hast thou seen what they do in the *dark?*" [Ezek. 8:12].

Trust Christ, and so thy soul shall no longer be like "the sea that cannot rest" [Is. 57:20], full of turbulent wishes, full of passionate desires that come to nothing, full of endless moanings, like the homeless ocean that is ever working and never flings up any product of its work but yeasty foam and broken weeds—but thine heart shall become translucent and still, like some land-locked lake, where no winds rave nor tempests ruffle; and on its calm surface there shall be mirrored the clear shining of the unclouded blue, and the perpetual light of the sun that never goes down.

IMPERISHABLE HIEROGLYPHICS

The sin of Judah is written with a pen of iron, and with the point of a diamond: it is graven upon the table of their heart, and upon the horns of your altars—Jer. 17:1

You and I, by our memory, by that marvelous faculty that people call the imagination, by our desires, are forever painting the walls of the inmost chambers of our hearts with such pictures. It is an awful faculty that we possess of, so to speak, surrounding ourselves with the pictures of the things that we love, and have yielded ourselves in devotion and desire unto.

I do not dwell upon that, but I want to drop one very earnest caution and beseeching entreaty. Mind what you paint upon those mystic walls! Foul things, "creeping things and abominable beasts" [Ezek. 8:10], only too many of you are tracing there. Mind! They are ineffaceable. No repentance will obliterate them. I do not know whether even Heaven can blot them out. What you love, what you desire, what you think about, you are photographing, printing on the walls of your immortal nature. And just as today, thousands of years after the artists have been gathered to the dust, we may go into Egyptian temples and see the figures on their walls, in all the freshness of their first coloring, as if the painter had but laid down his pencil a moment ago; so, on your hearts, youthful evils, the sins of your boyhood, the prurience of your earliest days, may live ugly shapes, that no tears and no repentance will ever wipe out. Nothing can do away with "the marks of that which once hath been." What are you painting on the chambers of imagery in your hearts?—obscenity, foul things, mean things, low things? Is that mystic shrine within you painted with such figures as in some chambers in Pompeii, where the excavators had to cover up the pictures because they were so foul? Or, is it like the cells in the Covenant of San Marco at Florence, where Fra Angelico's holy and sweet genius painted on the bare walls, to be looked at, as he fancied, only by one devout brother, in each cell, angel imaginings, and noble, pure celestial faces that calm and hallow those who gaze upon them? What are you doing, my brother, in the dark, in the chambers of your imagery?

Everything which you do leaves its effect with you forever, just as long-forgotten meals are in your blood and bones today. Every act that a man performs has printed itself upon his soul; it has become a part of himself; and, though, like a newly-painted picture, after a little while the colors go in, why is that? Only because they have entered into the very fiber of the canvas, and have left the surface because they are incorporated with the substance, and they want but a touch of varnish to flash out again.

FALSE WORSHIP

They worship the work of their own hands, that which their fingers have made—
Is. 2:8

A man's true worship is not the worship that he performs in the public temple, but that which he offers down in that little private chapel where nobody goes but himself. Worship is the attribution of supreme excellence to, and the entire dependence of the heart upon, a certain person. And the people or the things to which a man attributes excellence, and on which he hangs his happiness and his well-being, these be his gods, no matter what his outward profession is. You can find out what these are for yourself, if you will honestly ask yourself one or two questions. What is it that I want most? What is it which makes my ideal of happiness? What is it which I feel that I should be desperate without? What do I think about most naturally and spontaneously, when the spring is taken off, and my thoughts are allowed to go as they will? And if the answer to none of these questions is "God!" then I do not know why you should call yourself a worshiper of God. It does not matter, though we pray in the temple, if we have the dark subterranean pit, where our true adoration is rendered. I am afraid there are a great many of us nominal Christians, connected with Christian churches, posing before men as orthodox religionists, who keep this private chapel where we do our devotions to an idol and not to God. If our real gods could be made visible, what a pantheon they would make! All the foul forms painted on that underground cell would be paralleled in the creeping things [Ezek. 8:10]—which crawl along the low earth, and never sour nor even stand erect, and in the vile, bestial forms of passion to which some of us really bow down. Honor, wealth, literary or other distinction, the sweet sanctities of human love dishonored and profaned by being exalted to the place which Divine love should hold, ease, family, animal appetites, lust, drink—these are the gods of some of us.

"Ephraim is joined to idols, let him alone" [Hos. 4:7]. What a contrast between that condition of mind and the gentle, gracious power which, like the dew, is distilled into the soul by the influences of the spirit of God. The one is like the frowning cliffs which front the wild Polar ocean, white with ice and black with barren rock; the other like the limestone walls that keep back the Mediterranean, green and flower to the water's edge—a barrier as complete, but all draped with beauty, and fruitful and sunny.

WORSHIP GOD

Give unto the Lord the glory due unto his name: bring an offering, and come be-
fore Him: worship the Lord in the beauty of holiness—1 Chr. 16:29

Ask yourselves, not whom do you worship before the eyes of men, but who is the
God that in your inmost heart you bow down before? What do you do in the dark
[Ezek. 8:12] ? That is the question. Whom do you worship there? The other thing is not
worship at all.

And do not forget that all such diversion of supreme love and dependence from
God alone is like the sin of the men in Ezekiel's vision (Ezek. 8), that it is sacrilege.
They had taken a chamber in the very Temple, and turned that into a temple of the
false gods. Who is your heart made to shrine? Why! Every stone, if I may so say, of the
fabric of our being bears marked upon it that it was laid in order to make a dwelling-
place for God. Who are you meant to worship, by the witness of the very constitution of
your nature and make of your spirits? Is there anybody but One that is worthy to get the
priceless gift of human love absolute and entire? Is there any but One to whom it is
aught but degradation and blasphemy for a man to bow down? Is there any being but
One that can still the tumult of my spirit, and that can satisfy the immortal yearnings of
my soul? We were made for God; and whenever we turn the hopes, the desires, the affections, the obedience, and that which is the root of them all, the confidence that ought
to fix and fasten upon Him, to other creatures, we are guilty, not only of idolatry, but of
sacrilege. We commit the sin of which that wild reveler in Babylon was guilty, when, at
his great feast, in the very madness of his presumption, he bade them to bring forth the
sacred vessels from the Temple at Jerusalem: "and the king and his princes and
his . . . concubines drank in them . . . and praised the gods" [Dan. 5:3, 4]. So we take the
sacred chalice of the human heart, on which there is marked the sign-manual of heaven,
claiming it for God's and fill it with the spiced and drugged draught of our own sensu-
alities and evils, and pour out a libation to vain and false gods. Render unto Him that
which is His; and see, even upon the walls, scrabbled all over with the deformities that
we have painted there, lingering traces, like those of some dropping fresco in a roofless
Italian church, which suggest the serene and perfect beauty of the image of the One
whose likeness was originally traced there, and for whose worship it was all built.

The imitation of the object of worship has always been felt to be the highest form
of worship. Many an ancient teacher, beside the Stoic philosopher, has said, "He who
copies the gods worships them adequately."

THOU GOD SEEST ME

And she called the name of the Lord that spake unto her, thou God seest me: for she said, Have I also here looked after him that seeth me?"—Gen. 16:13

In Ezekiel's vision of the "Chambers of Imagery" (Ezek. 8) we see the sudden crashing in upon the cowering worshipers of the revealing light. Apparently the picture suggests that these elders knew not the eyes that were looking upon them. They were hugging themselves in the conceit, "the Lord seeth not; the Lord hath forsaken the earth." And all the while, all unknown, God and His prophet stand in the doorway and see it all. Not a finger lifted, not a sign to the foolish worshipers, of His presence and inspection, but in stern silence He records and remembers.

And does that need much bending to make it an impressive form of stating a solemn truth? There are plenty of us to whom it is the least welcome of all thoughts that there in the doorway stand God and His Word. Why should it be, my brother, that the properly blessed thought of a Divine eye resting upon you should be to you like the thought of a policeman's bull's-eye to a thief? Why should it not be rather the sweetest and the most calming and strength-giving and companioning of all convictions? "Thou God seest me." The little child runs about the lawn perfectly happy as long as she knows that her mother is watching her from the window. And it ought to be sweet and blessed to each of us to know that there is no darkness where a Father's eye comes not. Do not think of His eye as the prisoner in a solitary cell thinks of the pinhole somewhere in the wall there, through which a jailer's jealous inspection may at any moment be glaring in upon him; but think of Him your Brother, who "knew what was in man" [John 2:25], and who knows each man, and see in Christ the all-knowing Godhood that loves yet better than it knows, and beholds the hidden evils of men's hearts, in order that it may cleanse and forgive all which it beholds.

One day a light will flash in upon all the dark cells. We must all be manifest before the judgment seat of Christ. Do you like that thought? Can you stand it? Are you ready for it? My friend, let Jesus Christ come to you with His light. Let Him come into the dark corners of your hearts. Cast all your sinfulness, known and unknown upon Him that died on the Cross for every soul of man, and He will come; and His light, streaming into your hearts, like the sunbeam upon foul garments, will cleanse and bleach them white by its shining upon them. Let Him come into your hearts by your lowly penitence, by your humble faith, and all these vile shapes that you have painted on its walls will, like phosphorescent pictures in the daytime, pale and disappear when the Sun of Righteousness, with healing on His beams, floods your soul, making no part dark, and turning all into a Temple of the living God.

THE LOVE THAT IS GIVEN

Behold what manner of love the Father hath bestowed upon us, that we should be called the sons of God—1 John 3:1

We are called upon to come with our little vessels to measure the contents of the great ocean, to plumb with our short lines the infinite abyss, and not only to estimate the quantity, but the quality, of that love, which, in both, surpasses all our means of comparison and conception.

Properly speaking, we can do neither the one nor the other, for we have no line long enough to sound the depths, and no experience which will give us a standard with which to compare its quality. But all that we can do, John would have us do—that is, work, and ever look at the workings of that love till we form some not wholly inadequate idea of it.

We can no more "behold what manner of love the Father has bestowed on us" than we can look with undimmed eyes right into the middle of the sun. But we can in some measure imagine the tremendous and beneficent forces that ride forth horsed on his beams to distances which the imagination faints in trying to grasp, and reach their journey's end unwearied and ready for their tasks as when it began. Here we are ninety odd millions of miles from the center of the system, yet warmed by its heat, lighted by its light, and touched for good by its power in a thousand ways. All that has been going on for no one knows how many *aeons*. How mighty the Power which produces these effects! In like manner, who can gaze into the fiery depths of that infinite Godhead, into the ardors of that immeasurable, incomparable, inconceivable love? But we can look at and measure its activities. We can see what it does, and so can in some degree understand it, and feel that after all we have a measure for the Immeasurable, a comparison for the Incomparable, and can thus "Behold what manner of love the Father hath bestowed upon us" [1 John 3:1].

We may gain another measure of the greatness of this love if we put an emphasis on one word, and think of the love given to *"us,"* such creatures as we are. Out of the depths we cry to Him, not only by the voice or our supplications, but even when we raise no call of entreaty, our misery pleads with His merciful heart, and from the heights there comes upon our wretchedness and sin the rush of this great love, like a cataract, which sweeps away all our sins, and floods us with its own blessedness and joy. The more we know ourselves, the more wonderingly and thankfully shall we bow down our hearts before Him, as we measure His mercy by our unworthiness.

THE CROSS THE PROOF OF GOD'S LOVE

But God commendeth his own love toward us, in that, while we were yet sinners, Christ died for us—Rom. 5:8

We have to turn to the work of Christ, and especially to His death, if we would estimate the love of God. The most wonderful revelation to every heart of man of the depths of that Divine heart lies in the gift of Jesus Christ. The Apostle bids me "behold what manner of love" [1 John 3:1]. And I turn to the Cross, and I see there a love which shrinks from no sacrifice, but gives "Him up to death for us all." I turn to the Cross, and I see there a love which is evoked by no loveableness on my part, but comes from the depth of His own Infinite Being, who loves because He must, and who must because He is God. I turn to the Cross, and I see there manifested a love which sighs of recognition, which desires nothing of me but the repayment of my poor affection; and I see there a love that will not be put away by all sinfulness and shortcomings and evil. So, streaming through the darkness of eclipse, and speaking to me even in the awful silence in which the Son of man died there for sin, I "behold," and I hear the "manner of love that the Father hath bestowed upon us." Undeserved and Infinite, boundless and endless, in its measure measureless, in its quality transcendent—the love of God to me in Jesus Christ my Savior.

In like manner we have to think, if we would estimate the "manner of this love," that through and in the great sacrifice of Jesus Christ there comes to us the gift of a Divine life like His own. Perhaps it might be a refinement of interpretation; but it certainly does seem to me that that expression, "To bestow His love upon" us, is not altogether the same as to love us, but that there is a greater depth in it. There may be some idea of that love itself being as it were infused into us, and not merely of its consequences or tokens being given to us; as Paul speaks of "the love of God shed . . . abroad in our hearts" [Rom. 5:5] by the spirit which is given to us. At all events this communication of Divine life, which is at bottom Divine love—for God's life is God's love—is His great gift to men.

Be that as it may, these two are the great tokens, consequences, and measures of God's love to us—the gift of Christ, and that which is the sequel and outcome thereof, the gift of the Spirit which is breathed into Christian spirits. These two gifts, which are one gift, embrace all that the world needs. Christ for us and Christ in us must both be taken into account if you would estimate the manner of the love that God has bestowed upon us.

FATHERHOOD AND SONSHIP

Beloved, now are we the sons of God, and it doth not yet appearwhat we shall be: we know that, when he shall appear, we shall be like him; for we shall see him even as he is—1 John 3:2

The doctrine of the New Testament about the Fatherhood of God and the sonship of man does not in the slightest degree interfere with these three great truths, that all men, though the features of the common humanity may be almost battered out of recognition in them, are all children of God because He made them; that they are children of God because still there lies in them something of the likeness of the creative Father; and, that they are all children of God because He loves and provides and cares for every one of them! All that is blessedly and eternally true; but it is also true that there is a higher relation than that to which the name "Children of God" is more accurately given, and to which in the New Testament that name is confined; and if you ask what it is, let me quote to you three passages in this Epistle which will answer the question: "Whosoever believeth that Jesus is the Christ is born of God" [5:1], that is the first; "Every one that doeth righteousness is born of him" [2:29], that is the second; "Every one that loveth is born of God" [4:7], that is the third. Or, to put them all into one expression, which holds them all, in the first chapter of John's Gospel you find this, in the great words of his prologue: "To as many as received him to them gave he power to become the sons of God." Believing in Christ with loving trust produces, and as the result of that belief, doing righteousness and loving the brethren prove, the fact of sonship, in its highest and its truest sense.

What is implied in that great name by which the Almighty gives us a name and a place as of sons and daughters? Clearly, first, a communicated life; therefore, second, a kindred nature which shall be "pure as He is pure" [1 John 3:3]; and, third, growth to full maturity.

This sonship, which is no mere empty name, is the aim and purpose of God's dealings, of all the revelation of His love, and most especially the great gift of His love in Christ. Has that purpose been accomplished in you? Have you ever looked at that great gift of love that God has given you on purpose to make you His child? If you have, why has it not made you one? Are you trusting to Jesus Christ, whom God has sent forth that we might receive the standing of sons in Him? Are you a child of God because a brother of that Savior? Have you received the gift of a Divine life through Him? My friend, remember the grim alternative: a child of God or a child of the devil! Bitter words, narrow words, uncharitable words—as people call them! And I believe, and therefore I am bound to say it, *true* words, which it concerns *you* to lay to heart.

OUR SONSHIP NO EMPTY TITLE

Let us not love in word, neither in tongue, but in deed and in truth . . . hereby we know that we are of the truth, and shall assure our hearts before Him—
1 John 3:18, 19

"And such we are" [1 John 3:1]. This is a kind of "aside," in which John adds the Amen for himself and for his poor brothers and sisters, toiling and moiling, obscure among the crowds of Ephesus, to the great truth. He asserts his and their glad consciousness of the reality of the fact of their sonship, which they know to be no empty title. He asserts, too, the present position of that sonship, realizing it as a fact today, amid all commonplace vulgarities and annoying cares and petty aims of life's little day. "Such we are"—the "Here am I, Father," of the child, answering the Father's call, "My Son." He turns doctrine into experience. He is not content with merely having the thought in his creed, but his heart clasps it, and his whole nature says Amen!—to the great truth. I ask you, do you do that? Do not be content with hearing the truth, or even with assenting to it, and believing it in your understandings. The truth is nothing to you, unless you have made it your very own by faith. Do not be satisfied with the orthodox confession; unless it has touched your heart, and made your whole soul thrill with thankful gladness and quiet triumph, it is nothing to you.

The mere belief of thirty-nine, or thirty-nine thousand, Articles of Christianity is nothing; but when a man has a true heart-faith in Him whom all articles are meant to make us know and love, then dogma becomes life, and the doctrine feeds the soul. Does it do so with you, my brother? Can *you* say, "And such are we"? Take another lesson. The Apostle was not afraid to say, "I know that I am a child of God." There are many very good people whose tremulous, timorous lips have never ventured to say "I know." They will say, "Well, I hope," or sometimes, as if that was not uncertain enough, they will put in an adverb or two, and say, "I humbly hope that I am." It is a far more robust kind of Christianity, a far truer one, and a humbler one, too, that throws all considerations of my own character and merits, and all the rest of that rubbish, clean behind me; and when God says "My son!" says "My Father"; and when God calls us His sons and daughters, leaps up and gladly answers, "And we are!" Do not be afraid of being too confident, if your confidence is built on God, and not on yourself; but be afraid of being too diffident, and be afraid of having a great deal of self-righteousness masquerading under the guise of such a profound consciousness of your own unworthiness that you dare not call yourself a child of God. It is not a question of worthiness or unworthiness; it is a question, in the first place and mainly, of the truth of Christ's promise and the sufficiency of Christ's Cross; and in a very subordinate degree of anything belonging to you.

THE NATURAL A TYPE OF THE SPIRITUAL

He that is spiritual judgeth all things—1 Cor. 2:15

The natural impulse of us all is to find shadows and symbols of spiritual life in natural existence. He who spake as never man spake, spake in parables, and, knowing all things, took bread and said, "This is My body." Surely, besides all the other purposes of that institution, there is this also to teach us to see everywhere emblems of Him. Every day we walk amid the "outward and visible signs of an inward and spiritual grace," and in that meaning of the word sacrament, the true and Christian view of this wonderful world is that it is all one great sacrament. All the elements stand as types of spiritual things. The sunshine is to speak to us of the "light of the world," the life of men. The wind blows— an emblem of that Spirit which, though He comes low and soft, as befits a "Comforter," can rise and wax into a tempest against all "the lofty and lifted up" [Is. 2:12]. The water speaks of the stream of life and the drink for thirsty souls; and the fire, of His purity and of His wrath. All *objects* are consecrated to Him. The trees of the field, in a thousand places, speak of the "root of David" [Rev. 5:5], and the vine of which we are all branches [John 15:5]. The everlasting mountains are His "righteousness"; the mighty deep, His "judgments." All the *processes* of nature have been laid hold of by Him. The gentle dew falls a promise, and the lashing rain forebodes another storm, when many a sand-built house shall be swept away. Every spring is a prophecy of the resurrection of the dead, every harvest a promise of the coming of His kingdom and the blessed issues of all service for Him. All *living things,* in like manner, testify of Him. In that sense, as in others, He is lord over the fish of the seas, and over the fowls of the air, and over the beasts of the field. The eagle stirring up its nest [see Deut. 32:11], the "hen gathering her chickens under her wings" [Matt. 23:37], speak of Him, His functions, and His relations to us. The "Lion of the tribe of Judah" [Rev. 5:5] and the "lamb of God" [John 1:29] were His names. All *occupations* of men, also, are consecrated to reveal Him. He laid His hand upon the sower and the vine-dresser, upon the plowman and the shepherd, upon the merchant and the warrior, upon the king and the prophet and the judge, upon the teacher and the lawgiver, as being emblems of Himself. All *relations* between men testify of Him. Father and mother, brother and friend, husband, parent, and children, they are all consecrated for this purpose.

CONTEMPLATION OF GOD'S LOVE TO US

Behold the Lamb of God, which taketh away the sin of the world—John 1:29

"Behold" is not the mere exclamation which you often find both in the Old and in the New Testaments, which is simply intended to emphasize the importance of what follows, but it is a distinct command to do the thing—to look and to ever look, and to look again, and live in the habitual and devout contemplation of that infinite and wondrous love of God.

I have but two remarks to make about that, and the one is this, that this habit of devout and thankful meditation upon the love of God, as manifested in the sacrifice of Jesus Christ, and the consequent gift of the Divine Spirit, joined with the humble, thankful conviction that I am a child of God thereby, lies at the foundation of all vigorous and happy Christian life. How can a thing which you do not touch with your hands and see with your eyes produce any effect upon you, unless you think about it? How can a religion which can only influence through thought and emotion do anything in you, or for you, unless you occupy your thoughts and your feelings with it? It is sheer nonsense to suppose it possible. Things which do not appeal to sense are real to us, and, indeed, we may say, *are* not at all for us, only as we think about them. If you had a dear friend in Australia, and never thought about him, he would even cease to be dear, and it would be all one to you as if he were dead. If he were really dear to you, you *would* think about him.

We may say—though, of course, there are other ways of looking at the matter—that, in a very intelligible sense, the degree in which we think about Christ, and in Him behold the love of God, is a fairly accurate measure of our Christianity.

Now, will you apply that sharp test to yesterday, and the day before, and the day before that, and tell me how much of your life was pagan and how much of it was Christian? You will never make anything of your professed Christianity, you will never get a drop of happiness or any kind of good out of it; it will neither be a strength, nor a joy, nor a defense to you, unless you made it your habitual occupation to "behold the manner of love" [1 John 3:1]; and look, and look, and look, ever look, until it warms and fills your heart.

February 16

A GLORIOUS EFFORT

For I determined not to know anything among you, save Jesus Christ, and him crucified—1 Cor. 2:2

We cannot keep the great sight of Christ's Cross before the eye of our minds without effort. You will have very resolutely to look away from something else, if, amid all the dazzling gauds of earth, we are to look over them all to the far-off luster of that heavenly love. Just as timorous people in a thunderstorm will light a candle that they may not see the lightning, so many Christians have their hearts filled with the twinkling light of some miserable tapers of earthly care and pursuits, which, though they be dim and smoky, are bright enough to make it hard to see the silent depths of heaven, though it blaze with a myriad stars. If you hold a sixpence close enough up to the pupil of your eye, it will keep you from seeing the sun; and if you hold the world close to mind and heart, as many of you do, you will only see, around the rim of it, the least tiny ring of the overlapping love of God. What the world lets you see you will see, and the world will take care that it will let you see very little—not enough to do you any good, not enough to deliver you from its chains. Wrench yourself away, my brother, from the absorbing contemplation of jewelry and treasure, and look at the true riches. If you have ever had some glimpses of that wondrous love, and ever been drawn by it to cry, Abba, Father!—do not let the trifles which belong not to your true inheritance fill your thoughts, but renew the vision, and by determined turning away of your eyes from beholding vanity, look away from the things that are seen, that you may gaze upon the things that are not seen [Heb. 11:3], and chiefest among them, on the love of God in Christ Jesus our Lord.

If you have never looked on that love, I beseech you now to turn aside and see this great sight. Do not let that brightness burn unnoticed while your eyes are fixed on the ground like men absorbed in gold-digging, while a glorious sunshine is flushing the eastern sky. Look to the unspeakable, incomparable, immeasurable love of God, in giving up His Son to die for us all. Look and be saved. Look and live. Behold what manner of love the Father hath bestowed on you, and beholding, you will become the sons and daughters of the Lord God Almighty [see 1 John 3:1].

PETER'S PENITENT LOVE
(PART ONE)

Jesus saith to Simon Peter, Simon, son of Jonah, lovest thou me more than these?
He saith unto him: Yea, Lord; thou knowest that I love thee. He saith unto him:
Feed my lambs—John 21:15.

In these words there is an obvious intention to recall various points in the past of the Apostle's history. In their emphatic dwelling on the human side of his character, they suggest that by his fall he has forfeited the name of the "man of rock" [see Matt. 16:18], and has proved himself, not stable, but uncertain as the shifting wind. And so they would pierce his heart. The fact of his risen Lord coming to him with a question about his love upon His lips would be a dagger in his soul; all the more because he knew that the question was a reasonable one, since he had so shamefully sinned against love. Now, all this deliberate raking up of the man's past sin looks to be very cruel. Is that like "not breaking the bruised reed nor quenching the smoking flax?" [Is. 42:3]. Does that seem like the generosity of love which is ashamed to recall the transgression that it forgives? Would not Christ have been nearer the ideal of Divine and perfect forgiveness if He had not put Peter through this torture of remembrance? No! For the happiest love and the deepest to Him must always rest upon the contrite remembrance of sins forgiven. Therefore the tenderest and most divine work of Christ is to help His penitent servant to a true penitence. He cannot give His love, nor honor with service, unless we acknowledge and abandon our sin before Him. He will make sure work. The keenest cut of the surgeon's knife is not cruel. The malignant humors have to be drained out, even squeezed out by a hand, the pressure of which (because it is firm), however gentle it may be, will always be painful. And it is poor surgery to begin with bandages and styptics, when what is wanted is that the ulcer shall be cut open and the putrescent matter gotten rid of. Therefore does Christ thus hold the man right up against his past, and make him, as the preliminary to the fullest communication and reception of His love, feel intensely and bitterly the reality of his transgression.

Peter's answer shows how he has learned some lessons, at any rate, by his fall and restoration. He will not hesitate one moment to avow his love. The consciousness of his treachery does not make his lips falter in the very least. He is ready at once with his "yes!" But, as many of you know, the love which he professes is not exactly the love which Christ asks about. The two words in the question in the answer, which are both translated—and rightly translated—"love," are not the same. And though this is not the place to try and draw the delicate lines of distinction that separate between them, it is important for the whole understanding of the story to notice that the love which Peter claims is, in some sense, inferior to the love which Christ asks. He will not say that he has climbed to the heights of that loftier, diviner emotion, but he will avow that he knows he has a hearty, human, natural affection for his Master, such as we cherish for those that are dear to us. So far he will go, but he had rather that his Master should judge him than that he should judge himself. "He knows nothing against himself" in this matter, yet he refers himself to the Lord: "Thou knowest all things; thou knowest that I love thee" [John 21:17].

PETER'S PENITENT LOVE (PART TWO)

He saith to him again the second time, Simon, son of Jonah, lovest thou me? He saith unto him, Yea, Lord; Thou knowest that I love thee. He saith unto him, Feed my sheep—John 21:16

The second question and the second answer are identical with the first. Again Christ craves the higher; again the Apostle, in his steadfast humility, will not go one step beyond what he feels he is sure about, nor pretend to have anything deeper or loftier than he knows he has. And so once more he answers word for word as he has answered before.

And then with the third question and answer, this struggle, if I may call it so, between Christ and Peter comes to an end. Christ accepts Peter's word, substitutes it in His question for the word which He had previously employed; and so, in one aspect, seems to yield to His apostle, as if He said, "Well then! If you cannot give me the higher I will take the lower, and be glad to have even that." But, in another aspect the change of the word sharpens the point of the question, and seems to fling a doubt over the genuineness even of the lower kind of affection which Peter was willing to profess. "Are you so sure, then, that even as men love one another, you love Me?" Did the denial look as "if you had *any* kind of love in your heart to Me?" And the question thus sharpened pierces deeper into the Apostle's heart, and gives rise to a little dash of impatience at being doubted, which is a better proof of his love than many words would have been. He will no more say "Yes!" But he will leave it to the Master to answer for him, as if he said, "Well, then! If you do not believe me, I will say nothing more; but look at me! Thou knowest all things. Here is my heart; take it and probe it! I say nothing; Thou seest that I love Thee." And so the questioning ends.

Now, take these two figures just as they stand before us. Look! There is Jesus Christ, fresh from the Cross, coming to you for a double purpose, to remind you of your unworthiness, your failures, your denials, your forgetfulness of Him; and to beg you for your love. What a depth of perfect placability and forgiveness there is in that, that He comes to the denier with only these gentle and delicate reminders, with no spoken rebuke, with no uttered word in reference to the past! His questions imply this: "Whatever the past has been, if you can only say in truth that you love Me now, it is all right, and there will never be another word said about your falls!" He does, in effect, what wise fathers and mothers do with their wayward children after some burst of naughtiness. Their question is, "Do you love me, then?" And if the answer to that is swift and real, then no more need be said about the fault. In a very deep sense, though not in the deepest, the love of the penitent effaces the sin. That which truly effaces it is the blood of Jesus Christ, and the love of the penitent comes after and not before forgiveness, which is the Divine act that blots out iniquity, and is the consequence, not its cause, of forgiveness. But when a penitent denier comes back to the Master, and in humble faith in His pardoning mercy clasps His feet and washes them with tears, the believing love is all that Christ asks, ere He reinstates in all the forfeited privileges.

PETER'S LOVE A TYPE OF OURS

He saith unto him the third time, Simon, son of Jonah, Lovest thou me? Peter was grieved because he said unto him the third time, Lovest thou me? And he said unto Him, Lord, thou knowest all things; thou knowest that I love thee—
John 21:17

Notice how we have here, not only that figure of Christ fresh from the Cross, with all the appeal that His sufferings for us ought to make in our hearts, smiting upon those hearts a deeper consciousness of our transgression, but we have also the figure, full of encouragement and of teaching for us, of the penitent rejoicingly acknowledging, notwithstanding his sin, his fervent love to the Master. Do not let any sense of unworthiness make you hesitate in saying, "I love Thee?" Do not try to find out whether you love Christ or not by inferences from your conduct.

You do not do that about your love to one another. You do not say, "I do so-and-so for my wife, or my husband, therefore I conclude that I love him, or her." You start with the feeling, with the consciousness of the feeling, with the glad avowal of it; and then, to the best of your power, you shape your conduct accordingly. It is beginning at the wrong end to begin with conduct, and to look to it for the answer to the questions, "do I love the Lord or not?" "Am I His, or am I not?" All of us have to bewail inconsistencies, but any Christian man or woman who seeks to answer the question whether they love Jesus Christ by inferences drawn from conduct is condemning himself or herself to a lifelong burden of weariness, and to a religion in which, because there will be little joy, there will be little power and freedom. Let us not be afraid, after the example of this man, howsoever dark and numerous may have been our faults, let us not be afraid to profess our love to Him.

The consciousness of our treachery and of His pardon should deepen our love to Christ. So out of our very falls we may rise to a close and more blessed experience, and come to understand for ourselves how the publicans and harlots may go into the Kingdom before the Pharisees. The only source from which a true love to Jesus Christ, warm enough to melt the ice of our hearts, and flowing with a powerful enough stream to sweep the corruption out of our natures, can ever flow is the sense of our pardon from Him. That sense will deepen as the consciousness of our manifold transgressions deepens. So the more we feel our evil and our guilt, the more let us cleave to that great Lord that has given Himself for us.

It was but a shallow conviction of sin that moved in Peter's breast at the other miraculous draught of fishes, when he said, "Depart from me, for I am a sinful man!" [Luke 5:8]. He has learned here a deeper knowledge of his own fault; he knows better how bad he has been and how weak he still is; and, therefore, instead of saying "Depart!" he says, "Let me cleave to Thee: Thou knowest that I love Thee."

THE SERVICE WITH WHICH LOVE IS HONORED

Jesus saith unto him, Feed my sheep—John 21:17

The threefold command to Peter, first of all to care for the sustenance of the least, then to guide and direct the more advanced, and then to open the deepest stores of God's truth, and impart wisdom as well as guidance to all, of all stages—these are the charges which love wins for its honor and its crown. Of course, these injunctions apply primarily to the Apostles, and subordinately to the teachers of the Church who still remain; but they also apply to all of us, in our measure and degree. The lesson is just this: the spring of all service to men is love to Christ. Historically it has been so.

A wider and a wiser philanthropy has sprung within the limits of the Christian Church than anywhere else. That love is the great antagonist of selfishness; that love imbues men with Christ's own spirit; that love leads me to care for all that Christ cares for. It is a poor affection that does not cherish the property of an absent friend. If one that is dear to us, going away to the other side of the world, says to us, "Will you take care of my dog till I come back again?" we shall care for it if we care for him. And when He says to us, "Care for My sheep," we shall not have much love for the Shepherd if we forget the flock.

Therefore, let us further learn, dear friend, that all so-called Christian service which does not rest on the basis of love to Jesus Christ is profitless. People complain that after all the preaching and Sunday-school teaching and the like, so few results should be found. My belief is that we get as much success as we work for, and that if some power could make inaudible every word of our preaching that had been spoken from other motives than love to Jesus Christ, many an eloquent sermon would have little left. And if every line in our religious books which had been written from other motives were expunged, what gaps on the page there would be! How many names would fade out of our subscription lists! How many of your Christian activities would disappear if that test were applied to them! And do you expect God to bless the work which is no Christian service at all—unless its foundation has been laid in love to the Master?

THE CROWN OF SERVICE

When thou wast young, thou girdedst thyself, and walkedst whither thou wouldest: but when thou shalt be old, thou shalt stretch forth thy hands, and another shall gird thee, and carry thee wither thou wouldest not. This spake he, signifying by what death he should glorify God—John 21:18, 19

The enigmatic words draw a contrast between the earlier days of independence, of self-will, of strength which is its own master and its own guide, and the latter days when some unwelcome necessity should be laid upon him, and the constraint of an external hand should lead him whither he would not. They would sound obscure to Peter at first. The whole depth and meaning of them, no doubt, was not originally disclosed to him, or to his brethren. But before the predicted end came, the Apostle had learned what was meant, and told his brethren that he knew that the putting off of his tabernacle could be a swift process, even as the Lord Jesus had showed him. But still, though they would not be understood in their full depth, these words, no doubt, would be felt to cast something of a somber shadow over the apostolic function and prospects of the future. And so, notice how all that shadow is irradiated with sunlight by the final words, "Follow me!" [v. 19] which, though no doubt it may have referred to a literal going apart with Jesus at the moment for some unknown purpose, yet is intended to gather up the injunction of service and the prophecy of suffering into one great, all-comprehensive command. Treading in Christ's footsteps, the path of toilsome service becomes easy, and martyrdom itself a trivial pain.

That last command puts the crown on the service of life and the suffering of death. He who, living or dying, is the Lord's and follows Him, can strenuously do and calmly die. It is the sum of all duty, the one all-sufficient command which absorbs into itself all law, and by its grand simplicity rules all life.

So this incident yields great truths for us all. The penitent can go back to his Lord and avow his love. Love is the foundation for service. We shall serve Him in the measure in which we love Him; and if thus drawn by His mighty love, and conscious of our own manifold weaknesses, and smitten with the sense of His pardoning mercy, we cleave close to His footsteps, life will be easy, service will be blessed, and that last moment, which to others is as if some bony hand was stretched out to take them away "whither they would not" into a dark land, will be to us like what it was to the Apostle Peter himself in the hour of his deliverance from the prison. The Lord Jesus Christ Himself will come to us and say to us, "Rise quickly and follow Me!" And the chains will drop from our hands, and we shall pass through the iron gate that opens of its own accord; and we shall find ourselves in the city, and know that it was not a vision, but the reality of the appearance of that Lord whom we love, though we have denied Him so often and served Him so ill.

THE CHRISTIAN'S CHARACTER

And the very God of peace sanctify you wholly; and I pray God your whole spirit and soul and body be preserved blameless, unto the coming of our Lord Jesus Christ—1 Thess. 5:23

A priest must be pure. And Christ washes us from all stain, and clothes us in priestly garments of holiness, which is better than innocence; for His blood cleanses from all sin [1 John 1:9], and the spirit which He puts within all who have faith in Him makes them love righteousness and hate iniquity.

Thus consecrated, admitted to the innermost shrine, appointed to offer the richest sacrifice of self, and clothed in purity, they who were captives of sin are made priests of the Most High God [Rom. 8:21; Rev. 1:6].

Their double dignity is but part of their assimilation to their Lord. Every one that is perfect shall be as his Master, and even here on earth the Christian life is the life of Christ in the soul, and consists in growing likeness to Him. Is He a King? So are we. Is He a Priest? So, therefore, are we. Is He a son? So are we. Is He the Heir? So are we. Is He the "Anointed?" "He that in Christ hath anointed us is God." His offices, His dignity, His character, His very life becomes ours, if we are His.

This royal diadem and priestly mitre are offered to us all. They are the prerogative of no class. Earthly royalties have no place within the church of the redeemed, where all are brethren; and not even an apostle has "dominion over" his brethren's "faith." There is no place in it for human priests who offer outward sacrifices and claim a special standing as channels of sacramental grace. We may all have Christ's hand laid on our heads, which will make us kings and priests to God by a true coronation and ordination. If we come to Him in penitence and faith, as knowing our sins and looking to Him to loose us from them by His own blood, He will set us on high to reign as the vassal kings of His great empire, and bring us near, that we may stand ministering before the Lord the sweet-savored offering of our ransomed selves. Thus we shall be kings and priests here, and look forward to dim glories yet to come, when we shall reign with Him as kings, and as His servants shall do priestly service in the Eternal Temple.

The one question for us all is, Do our eyes fix and fasten on that dear Lord, and is it the description of our whole lives, that we see Him and walk with Him? Oh, if so, then life will be blessed, and death itself will be but as "a little while," when we "shall not see Him," and then we shall open our eyes and behold Him close at hand, whom we saw from afar, and with wandering eyes, amid the mists and illusions of earth [John 16:16]. To see Him as He has become for our sakes is heaven on earth. To see Him as He is will be the heaven of heaven; and before that Face, as the sun shining in his strength, all sorrows, difficulties, and mysteries will melt as morning mists.

THE CHRISTIAN'S DIRECT ACCESS
TO GOD

*Let us therefore come boldly unto the throne of grace, that we may obtain mercy,
and find grace to help in the time of need—Heb. 4:16*

Christ, the great High Priest, gives those whom He has redeemed priestly access to
God [Rev. 1:6]. For them the veil of the temple is rent, and the holiest place is
patent to their reverent entrance. He has done it by His revelation of God, whereby He
has brought the whole depth and tenderness of the Father's heart close to our hearts. He
has done it by His death, which removes all obstacles to a sinful man's entrance into
the presence of that awful holiness, and brings us near through His blood. He does it by
putting within our hearts the Spirit which cries Father, the new life which sets towards
God as water rises to the level of its source. Thus every soul of man, however ignorant,
guilty, and weak, may come into the presence-chamber of God, needing no priest, no
hand to lead, no introducer to the present at the interview. Trusting Christ our Forerunner, who is for us entered within the veil, we may come boldly to the Throne, which
we shall find, when so approached, a throne of grace, and standing close beneath it,
may hold direct fellowship with the Father and with the Son. We may dwell in the secret place of the Most High, and depart not from the temple day or night, if we will go
with our hands in Christ's to the God whom Christ reveals, by the path which Christ
has opened for us.

It is needful that every priest should have something to offer. And this great High
Priest makes it possible that we should come, not empty-handed, but bringing the one
sacrifice acceptable to God—the offering of hearts set on fire by His love. Christ has offered the one all-sufficient sacrifice for the sins of the whole world. And on the footing
of that sole and perpetual expiatory sacrifice, we, weak and sinful as we are, can draw
near with our thank-offerings, the only sacrifices which we need or can render. Our of-
ferings can never purge away sin: that has been done once for all by the "one sacrifice for
sins forever" [Heb.10:10–12]. And whosoever is thereby loosed from his sins by the
blood of Christ is thereby made himself a priest, to offer up spiritual sacrifices of joyful
thanksgiving. The sacrifices we have to offer are ourselves—yielding ourselves up in the
blessed self-surrender of love, and placing ourselves unreservedly in God's hands, to live
to His praise, and be disposed of by His supreme will. With such sacrifices God is well
pleased.

GOVERNMENT OF SELF

I keep under my body, and bring it into subjection: lest that by any means, when I have preached to others, I myself should be a castaway—1 Cor. 9:27

The great love of Christ is not contented with simply breaking the bondage of the slaves. It has more to do for them before it reaches its end. Emancipation is not enough. It is only a step in the process, a means towards a more wonderful result. He liberates them that He may ennoble them. He sets them free from the tyrants who held them captive that He may crown them with a crown of glory [Rom. 8:21]. He brings them that were bound out of the prison-house, and causes them to have rule among princes. So far-reaching are His great purposes that to loose us from our sins seems inadequate to fulfill the counsel of His love, unless it be followed by the wonderful bestowal of kingly dignity.

And what does that imply? Are we to lose ourselves in dim, vague thoughts of some future millennial reign and vulgar outward glories? I think not. John believed—and any man that has learned the Christian view of life will say "Amen" to the belief—that every man who has become the servant of Christ is the king and lord of everything else; that to submit to Him is to rule all besides. "He hath made us kings" [Rev. 1:6] in the act of submission; and on the head that bends before His throne in grateful love and lowly confidence, He stoops to lay lightly a crown, to raise the man up and say, "Arise and reign!" [2 Sam. 3:21].

Reign over what? First of all, over the only kingdom that any man really has, and that is himself. We are meant to be monarchs of this tumultuous and rebellious kingdom within. Vice and lust, fancies, tastes, whims, purposes, desires, they all go boiling and seething in our natures. It is meant that we should keep a tight hand on them, and be lords over them, and not let them run away with us, and carry you "whither they would," as so many of us do in our hours of weakness. In our inmost heart and conscience we know that we are meant to be lords of ourselves. There is something in each of us that responds to the noble words—self-control, self-denial; but the difficulty is how to carry them out, how to reign and rule over this rebellious kingdom within us. Law has no power to get itself obeyed. Conscience shares in law's weakness. It is a voice, authoritative in speech, but without force to compel attention. We cannot curb ourselves. There must be a power without to reinforce our wavering wills and to hold down our rebellious desires. Christ does this for us, and no person or system or power but He can do it thoroughly for any man.

THE CHRISTIAN'S CONSECRATION

Who then is willing to consecrate his service this day unto the Lord?—*1 Chr. 29:5*

All things serve the soul that serves Christ. All are yours if ye are His; and the great old words of that wondrous psalm which sets forth God's purpose in making man so long unaccomplished, and, as it would seem in so many cases, hopelessly thwarted, will be fulfilled in us. "Thou madest him to have dominion over the works of Thy hands; thou hast put all things under his feet" [Ps. 8:6]. All things *are* beneath the feet of him who humbly lies at the feet of Jesus Christ. Obedience is sovereignty. Christ's brethren are every one the children of a King. He who looses us from our sins makes us kings [Rev. 1:6], and yet in all the dominion servants, for we become kings, not for ourselves, but "unto God."

A priest was consecrated by the anointing oil touching hand and foot and ear; nor was he set apart for his office without sacrifice. Christ's priests are consecrated, not without the willing surrender of their whole being to His service; wherefore they are called upon to yield or present themselves to God, and their members as instruments of righteousness. But their true consecration comes from the touch of the great High Priest's hand laid upon their spirits, and the anointing with that Spirit which dwelt in Him without measure, by whom He offered Himself to God, and which He gives to all that trust Him. For their sakes He consecrated Himself that they also might be consecrated. That Spirit dwelling in Him made Him the Messiah, the anointed of God, Prophet, Priest, and King; and that Spirit of Christ dwelling in His servants makes them His anointed, His prophets, kings, and priests. His anointing is a real, not a ceremonial, setting apart to God's service, the impartation of a real inward fitness to be a holy priesthood.

So long as we are joined to Christ, we partake of His life, and our lives become music and praise. The electric current flows from Him through all souls that are "in Him," and they glow with fair colors, which they owe to their contact with Jesus. Interrupt the communication, and all is darkness. We have as much of God as we can hold. All Niagara may roar past a man's door, but only as much as he diverts through his own sluice will drive his mill or quench his thirst. That grace is like the figures in the Eastern tales, that will creep into a narrow room no bigger than a nutshell, or will tower heaven high. Our spirits are like the magic tent whose walls expanded or contracted at the owner's wish; we may enlarge them to enclose far more of the grace than we have ever possessed.

THE RULE OF CHRIST

My yoke is easy, and my burden is light—Matt. 11:30.

If you want to rule yourselves, let Christ rule you. Put your trust in Him; leave yourself in His hand; lay yourselves at His feet; rest upon His great sacrifice; look to Him for forgiveness; and then look to Him for marching orders, and for pure living, and for everything else. He will give power to your will, however feeble it was before, and susceptibility to your conscience that it never had when it was case-hardened by your love of evil, and you will be able to subdue the passions which would sweep you away and would laugh at all other control. Put the reigns into His hands, and He will bridle and tame your wild desires. Submit to Him, and He will make you "lord of yourself, though not of lands"—man's noblest kingship.

We are like some of those little Rajahs whose states adjoin our British possessions, who have trouble and difficulty with revolted subjects, and fall back upon the great neighboring power, saying: "Come and help me; subdue my people for me, and I will put the territory into your hands." Go to Christ and say: "Lord! They have rebelled against me! These passions, these lusts, these follies, these weaknesses, these sinful habits of mine, they have rebelled against me! What am I to do with them? Do Thou come and bring peace into the land, and Thine shall be the authority." And He will come and loose you from your sins, and make you kings [Rev. 1:6].

And there is another realm over which we may rule; and that is, this bewitching and bewildering world of time and sense, with its phantasmagoria and its illusions and its lies, that draw us away from the real life and truth and blessedness. Do not let the world master you! It will, unless you have put yourself under Christ's control. He will make you king over all outward things, by enabling you to despise them in comparison with the sweetness which you find in Him, and so to get the highest good out of them. He will make you their lord by helping you to use all the things seen and temporal as means to reach a full possession of the things unseen and eternal. Their noblest use is to be the ladder by which we climb to reach the treasures which are above. They are meant to be symbols of the eternal, like painted windows through which our eye may travel to the light beyond, which gives them all their brilliancy. He rules the waves who, with a strong hand on the tiller, makes the currents serve to bear his ship to the harbor. And he rules outward things who bends and coerces them to be the servants of his spirit in its highest aspirations, and so turns them to their noblest use.

THE ROYALTY OF THE REDEEMED

And hath made us kings and priests unto God and his Father—Rev. 1:6

"He loveth us"; that is the eternal act that lies at the foundation of the universe. "He hath washed us from our sins in His own blood" [Rev. 1:5]; that is the great fact in Time, done once and needing no repetition [Heb. 10:10], and capable of no repetition, into which all the fullness and sweetness and pathos and power of that infinite love has been gathered and condemned.

And then there follows, in the words of this text, the ultimate consequence and lofty development, at once, of that eternal, timeless love, and of that redeeming act which "hath washed us from our sins," and, yet more wonderful, "hath made us kings and priests to God."

Every Christian man is a king and priest. Those who have been washed from their sins by the blood of Christ have thereby become members of that Kingdom of God which consists of all whose wills bow to His for His dear love's sake. But, inasmuch as such submission to His sway gives authority and mastership over all beside, that kingdom is a kingdom whose subjects are royal; and in this sense, too, Christ is King of kings. It would appear that the phrase in the old law was so used to express the double idea of a Kingdom of Kings, in other places of the New Testament, and probably, therefore, here. For instance, we have it quoted again in this book (5: 10), with a clause added which distinctly shows that there "kingdom" is, in the writer's mind, equivalent to "kings"—namely, "and we shall reign upon the earth." Again, Peter gives it in the form of "a royal priesthood" [1 Pet. 2:9], where the original force of "kingdom" has disappeared altogether, and the lone idea of the royalty of believers remains. It seems probable, then, that in the words before us, we are to see the same idea predominant, though no doubt the other must also be taken into account.

It is also to be remembered that both these high titles originally and properly belong to Christ, and are bestowed on believers by deviation or transference from Him. The wholesome usage of ancient times forbade the blending of these two offices in one person, but He is a priest after the order of Melchizedek [Ps. 110:4]. He wears the mitre and the crown, and, as the prophet Zechariah foretold, "shall be a priest upon His throne" [6:13]; what He is, He, in His love, raises all His servants to be.

"GIRD UP YOUR LOINS"

Let your loins be girded about, and your lights burning; And ye yourselves like unto men that wait for their Lord—Luke 12:35, 36

The five foolish virgins [Matt. 25:1, 2] did not go away into any forbidden paths. No positive evil is alleged against them. They were simply asleep. The other five were asleep, too. I do not need to enter, here and now, into the whole interpretation of the parable, or there might be much to say about the difference between these two kinds of sleep. But what I wish to notice is that there was nothing except negligence darkening into drowsiness, which caused the dying out of the light. This process of gradual extinction may be going on, and may have been going on, for a long while, and the people that carried the lamp be quite unaware of it.

How could a sleeping woman know whether her lamp was burning or not? How can a drowsy Christian tell whether his spiritual life is bright or not? To be unconscious of our approximation to this condition is, I am afraid, one of the surest signs that we are in it. I suppose that a paralyzed limb is quite comfortable. At any rate, paralysis of the spirit may be going on without our knowing anything about it.

So do not put these poor words of mine away from you, and say, "Oh! They do not apply to me." I am quite sure that the people to whom they do apply will be the last people to take them to themselves. And while I quite believe (thank God!), that there are many of us who may feel and know that our lamps are not going out, sure I am that there are some of us whom everybody but themselves knows to be carrying a lamp that is so far gone out that it is smoking and stinking in the eyes and noses of the people that stand by.

Be sure that nobody was more surprised than were the five foolish women when they opened their witless, sleepy eyes, and saw the state of things.

There is only one road, with well-marked stages, by which a back-sliding or apostate Christian can return to his Master. And that road has three halting-places upon it, through which our heart must pass if it has wandered from its early faith and falsified its first professions. The first of them is the consciousness of the fall, the second is the resort to the Master for forgiveness, and the last is the deepened consecration to Him. When the patriarch Abraham, in a momentary lapse from faith to sense, thought himself compelled to leave the land to which God had sent him, because a famine threatened; when he came back from Egypt, as the narrative tells us with deep significance, he went to the "place where he had been at the beginning . . . unto the place of the altar which he had made there at the first" [Gen. 13:3, 4]. Yes! My friend; we must begin over again, tread all the old paths, enter by the old wicket-gate, once more take the place of the penitent, once more make acquaintance with the pardoning Christ, once more devote ourselves in renewed consecration to His service. No man that wanders into the wilderness but comes back by the King's highway, if He comes back at all.

LOST BY DOING NOTHING

The foolish said unto the wise, Give us of your oil—Matt. 25:8

It was not of set purpose that the foolish five took no oil with them. They merely neglected to do so, not having the wit to look ahead and provide against the contingency of a long time of waiting for the bridegroom. Their negligence was the result, not of deliberate wish to let their lights go out, but of their heedlessness; and because of that negligence they earned the name of "foolish." If we do not look forward, and prepare for possible drains upon our powers, we shall deserve the same adjective. If we do not lay up stores for future use, we may be sent to school to learn from the harvesting ant and the bee. That lesson applies to all departments of life; but it is eminently applicable to spiritual life, which is sustained only by communications from the spirit of God. For these communications will be imperceptibly lessened, and may be altogether intercepted, unless diligent attention is given to keep open the channels by which they enter the spirit. If the pipes are not looked to, they will be choked by masses of matted trifles, through which the "rivers of living water" [John 7:38], which Christ took as a symbol of the Spirit's influences, cannot force away. The thing that makes shipwreck of the faith of most professing Christians that do come to grief is no positive wickedness, no conduct which would be branded as sin by the Christian conscience, or even by ordinary people, but simply inactivity. If the water in a pond is never stirred, it is sure to stagnate, and green scum to spread over it, and a foul smell to rise from it. A Christian man has only to do what I am afraid a good many of us are in great danger of doing—that is, nothing—in order to ensure that his lamp shall go out. Do you try to keep yours alight? There is only one way to do it—that is, to go to Christ and get Him to pour His sweetness and His power into our open hearts.

The punishment for shirking work is to be denied work. Just as the converse is true, that in God's administration of the world and of His Church, the reward for faithful work is to get more to do, and the filling a narrow sphere is the sure way to have a larger sphere to fill. So, if a man abandons plain duties, then he will get no work to do. And that is why so many Christian men and women are idle in this world, and stand in the marketplace, with a certain degree of truth, saying, "No man hath hired us." No! Because so often in the past, tasks have been presented to you, forced upon you, almost pressed into your unwilling hands, that you have refused to take; and you are not going to get any more. You have been asked to work—I speak now to professing Christians—duties have been pressed upon you, fields of service have opened plainly before you, and you have not had the heart to go into them. And so you stand idle all day now, and the work goes to other people that can do it; and God honors them, and passes you by.

HE WILL NEVER LEAVE US

He hath said, I will never leave thee, nor forsake thee—Heb. 13:5

When one of the old patriarchs had committed a great sin, and had unbelievingly twitched his hand out of God's hand, and gone away down into Egypt, to help himself, instead of trusting to God, he was commanded, on his return to Palestine, to go to the place where he dwelt at the first, and begin again at that point where he began when he first entered the land [Gen. 3:3, 4]; which, being translated, is just this: the only way to keep our spirits vital and quick is by having recourse, again and again, to the same power which first imparted life to them, and that is done by the same means, the means of simple reliance upon Christ, in the consciousness of our own deep need, and believingly waiting upon him for the repeated communication of the gifts which we, have so often misimproved. Negligence is enough to slay. Doing nothing is the sure way to quench the Holy Spirit.

And, on the other hand, keeping close to him is the sure way to secure that He will never leave us. You can choke a lamp with oil, but you cannot have in your hearts too much of that Divine grace. And you get all that you need if you choose to go and ask it from him. Remember the old story about Elisha and the poor woman [2 Kgs. 4]. The cruse of oil began to run. She brought all the vessels that she could rake together, big and little, pots and cups, of all shapes and sizes, and set them, one after the other, under the jet of oil. They were all filled; and when she brought no more vessels, the oil stayed. If you do not take your empty hearts to God, and say, "Here, Lord! Fill this cup, too; poor as it is, fill it with thine own gracious influences," be very sure that no such influences will come to you. But if you do go, be as sure of this, that so long as you hold out your emptiness to Him, He will flood it with His fullness, and the light that seemed to be sputtering to its death will flame up again. He will not quench the smoking wick, if only we carry it to Him; but as the priests in the Temple walked all through the night to trim the golden lamps, so He who walks amid the seven candlesticks will see to each [Rev. 1:12, 13, 20].

"Looking unto Jesus" [Heb. 12:2] is the secret triumph over the fascinations of the world. And if we habitually so look, then the sweetness that we shall experience will destroy all the seducing power of lesser and earthly sweetness, and the blessing, the light of the sun will dim and all but extinguish the deceitful gleams that tempt us into the swamps where we shall be drowned. Turn away, then, from these things; cleave to Jesus Christ; and though in ourselves we may be as weak as a hummingbird before a snake, or a rabbit before a tiger, He will give us strength, and the light of His face shining down upon us will fix our eyes and make us insensible to the fascinations of the sorcerer. So we shall not need to dread the question, "Who hath bewitched you?" [Gal. 3:1], but ourselves challenge the utmost might of the fascinators with the triumphant question, "Who shall separate us from the love of Christ?" [Rom. 8:35].

Help us, O Lord! We beseech Thee, to live near Thee. Turn away our eyes from beholding vanity, and enable us to set the Lord always before us, that we be not moved.

THE GRADUAL EXTINCTION OF GOD'S LIGHT IN THE SOUL

Our lamps are gone out—Matt. 25:8

All spiritual emotions, and vitality, like every other kind of emotion and vitality, die unless nourished. Let no theological difficulties about "the final perseverance of the saints" [Eph. 6:18], or "the indefeasibleness of grace," and the impossibility of slaying the Divine life that has once been given to a man, come in the way of letting this parable have its full, solemn weight. These foolish virgins had oil and had light; the oil gave out by their fault, and so the light went out, and they were startled, when they awoke from their slumber, to see how, instead of brilliant flame, there was smoking wick.

Let us take the lesson. There is nothing in our religious emotions which has any guarantee of perpetuity in it, except upon certain conditions. We may live, and our life may ebb. We may trust, and our trust may tremble into unbelief. We may obey, and our obedience may be broken by the mutinous risings of self-will. We may walk in the paths of righteousness, and our feet may falter and turn aside. There is certainty of the dying out of all communicated life, unless the channel of communication with the life from which it was first kindled be kept constantly clear. The lamp may be "a burning and a shining light" [John 5:35], or, more accurately translating the phrase of our Lord, "a light kindled and" (therefore) "shining," but it will only be light "for a season," unless it is fed from that from which it was first set alight—and that is, from God Himself.

"Our lamps are gone out." What a slow process! The flame does not all die into darkness in a minute. There are stages in the process. The white portion of the flame becomes smaller and the blue part extends; then the flame flickers, and finally shudders itself, as it were, off the wick; then nothing remains but a charred red line along the top; then that line breaks up into little points, and one after another these twinkle out, and then all is black, and the lamp is gone out. And so, slowly, like the ebbing away of the tide, like the reluctant long-protracted dying of summer days, like the dropping of the blood from some fatal wound, by degrees the process of extinction creeps, creeps, creeps on, and the lamp that was going is finally gone out.

The infinite mercy of God is not mere weak indulgence, which so deals with a man's failures and sins as to convey the impression that these are of no moment whatsoever. And the severity which said, "No! Such work is not fit for such hands until the heart has been 'broken and healed,'" is of a piece with the severity which is love. "Thou wast a God that forgavest them, though thou tookest vengeance of their inventions" [Ps. 99:8]. Let us learn the difference between a weak charity which loves too foolishly, and therefore too selfishly, to let a man inherit the fruit of his doings, and the large mercy which knows how to take the bitterness out of the chastisement, and yet knows how to chastise.

BEARING FRUIT

I am like a green olive tree in the house of God—Psalm 52:8

The God-bedewed soul, beautiful, pure, strong, will bear fruit. "His beauty shall be as the olive tree" [Hos. 14:6]. Anybody that has ever seen a grove of olives knows that their beauty is not such as strikes the eye. If it was not for the blue sky overhead, that rays down glorifying light, they would not be much to look at or talk about. The tree has a gnarled, grotesque trunk, which divides into insignificant branches, bearing leaves mean in shape, harsh in texture, with a silvery underside. It gives but a quivering shade, and has no massiveness, nor sympathy. But there are olives on the branches. And so the beauty of the humble tree is in what it grows for man's good. After all, it is the outcome in fruitfulness which is the main thing about us. God's meaning, in all his gifts of dew, and beauty, and purity, and strength, is that we should be of some use in the world.

The olive is crushed into oil, and the oil is used for smoothing and suppling joints and flesh, for nourishing and sustaining the body as food, for illuminating darkness as oil in the lamp. And these three things are the three things for which we Christian people have received all our dew, and all our beauty, and all our strength—that we may give other people light, that we may be the means of conveying to other people nourishment, that we may move gently in the world as lubricating, sweetening, soothing influences, and not irritating and provoking, and leading to strife and alienation. *The* question, after all, is, does anybody gather fruit off *us*, and would anybody call *us* "trees of righteousness, the planting of the Lord, that He may be glorified" [Is. 61:3]? May we all open our hearts for the dew from heaven, and then use it to produce in ourselves beauty, purity, strength, and fruitfulness!

Union with Christ is the condition of all fruitfulness. There may be plenty of activity and yet barrenness. Works are not fruit. We can bring forth a great deal "of ourselves," and because it is of ourselves it is naught. Fruit is possible only on condition of union with Him. He is the productive glory of it all. We are not to be content with a little fruit—a poor shriveled bunch of grapes that are more like marbles than grapes, here and there, upon the half-nourished stem. The abiding in Him will produce a character rich in manifold graces. "A little fruit" is not contemplated by Christ at all. God forbid that I should say that there is no possibility of union with Christ and a little fruit! A little union will have a little fruit. Why is it that the average Christian man of this generation bears only a berry or two here and there, like such as are left upon the vines after the vintage, when the promise is that if he will abide in Christ, he will bear *much* fruit?

ALL STRENGTH IN CHRIST

As ye have therefore received Christ Jesus the Lord, so walk ye in him: Rooted and built up in him, and established in the faith—Col. 2:6

Speak we of strength? Christ is the type of strength. Of beauty? He is the perfection of beauty. And it is only as we keep close to Him that our lives will be all fair with the reflected loveliness of His, and strong with the communicated power of His grace—"strong in the Lord, and in the power of His might" [Eph. 6:10]. If we are to set forth anything, in our daily lives, of this strength, remember our lives must be rooted in, as well as bedewed by, God. Hosea's emblems, beautiful and instructive as they are, do not reach to the deep truth set forth in still holier and sweeter words. "I am the Vine, ye are the branches" [John 15:5]. The union of Christ and His people is closer than that between dew and plant. Our growth results from the communication of His own life to us. Therefore is the command stringent and obedience to it blessed, "Abide in Me—for apart from Me, ye can do"—and are—"nothing" [John 15:5].

Let us remember that the loftier the treetop the wider the spread of its sheaves of dark foliage; if it is steadfastly to stand, immovable by the loud winds when they call, the deeper must its roots strike into the firm earth. If your life is to be a fair temple-palace, worthy of God's dwelling in, if it is to be impregnable to assault, there must be quite as much masonry underground as above, as is the case in great old buildings and palaces. And such a life must be a life "hid with Christ in God" [Col. 3:3]. Then it will be strong. When we strike our roots deep into Him, our branches also shall not wither, and our leaves shall be green, and all that we do shall prosper. The wicked are not so. They are like chaff—rootless, fruitless, lifeless, which the wind driveth away [Ps.1:4].

"Apart from Me ye can do nothing." *There* is the condemnation of all the busy life of men which is not lived in union with Jesus Christ. It is a long row of figures which, like some other long rows of figures added up, amount just to *zero*. "Without Me—nothing." All your busy life, when you come to sum it up, is made up of *plus* and *minus* quantities, which precisely balance each other; and the net result, unless you are in Christ, is just nothing; and on your gravestones the only right epitaph is a great round zero next to the words: "He did not do anything. There is nothing left of his toil; the whole thing has evaporated and disappeared." That is life apart from Jesus Christ. Separate from Christ the individual shrivels, and the possibilities of fair buds wither and set into no fruit. And no man is the man he might have been unless he holds on to Jesus Christ and lets His life come into him.

STRENGTH OF CHARACTER

And cast forth his roots as Lebanon—Hos. 14:5

A God-bedewed soul that has been made fair and pure, by communion with God, ought also to be strong. He shall cast forth his roots "as Lebanon." I take it that simile does not refer to the roots of that giant range that slope away down under the depths of the Mediterranean. That is a beautiful emblem, but it is not in line with the other images in the context. As these are all dependent on the promise of the dew, and represent different phases of the results of its fulfillment, it is natural to expect thus much uniformity in their variety, that they shall all be drawn from plant life. If so, we must suppose a condensed metaphor here, and take "Lebanon" to mean the forests which another prophet calls "the glory of Lebanon" [Is. 35:2]. The characteristic tree in Lebanon, as we all know, is the cedar.

It is named in Hebrew by a word which is connected with that for "strength." It stands as the very type and emblem of stability and vigor. Think of its firm roots by which it is anchored deep in the soil; think of the shelves of massive dark foliage; think of its unchanged steadfastness in storm; think of its towering height; and thus arriving at the meaning of the emblem, let us translate it into practice in our own lives. "He shall . . . cast forth his roots as Lebanon." Beauty? Yes! Purity? Yes! And braided in with them, if I may so say, the strength which can say "No!", which can resist, which can persist, which can overcome; power drawn from communion with God. "Strength and beauty" should blend in the worshipers, as they do in the "sanctuary" in God Himself. There is nothing admirable in mere force; there is often something sickly and feeble, and therefore contemptible, in mere beauty. Many of us will cultivate the complacent and the amiable sides of the Christian life, and be wanting in the manly "muscles that throw the world," and can fight to the death. But we have to try and bring these two excellences of character together, and it needs an immense deal of grace and wisdom and imitation of Jesus Christ, and a close clasp of His hand, to enable us to do that.

Many a stately elm that seems full of vigorous life, for all its spreading boughs and clouds of dancing leaves, is hollow at the heart, and when the storms comes goes down with a crash, and men wonder, as they look at the ruin, how such a mere shell of life, with a core of corruption, could stand so long. It rotted within, and fell at last because its roots did not go deep down to the rich soil, where they would have found nourishment, but ran along near the surface, among gravel and stones. If we would stand firm, be sound within, and bring forth much fruit, we must strike our roots deep in Him who is the anchor of our souls and the nourisher of all our being.

THE PURITY AND BEAUTY OF THE CHRISTIAN LIFE

He shall grow as the lily . . . and his beauty shall be as the olive tree, and his smell as Lebanon—Hosea 14:5, 6

A soul bedewed by God will spring into purity and beauty. Ugly Christianity is not Christ's Christianity. Some of us older people remember that there used to be a favorite phrase to describe unattractive saints, that they had "grace grafted on a crab stick." There are a great many Christian people whom one would compare to any other plant rather than a lily. Thorns and thistles and briars are a good deal more like what some of them appear to the world. But we are bound, if we are Christian people, by our obligations to God, and by our obligations to men, to try and make Christianity look as beautiful in people's eyes as we can. That is what Paul said. "Adorn the doctrine" [Titus 2:10]; make it look well, inasmuch as it has made you look attractive to men's eyes. Men have a fairly accurate notion of beauty and goodness, whether they have any goodness or any beauty in their own characters or not. Do you remember the words, "Whatsoever things are pure; whatsoever things are lovely, whatsoever things are of good report . . . if there be any praise"—from men—"think on these things" [Phil. 4:8]. If we do not keep that as the guiding star of our lives, then we have failed in one very distinct duty of Christian people—namely, to grow more like a lily, and to be graceful in the lowest sense of that word, as well as *grace-full* in the highest sense of it. We shall not be so in the lower, unless we are so in the higher. It may be a very modest kind of beauty, very humble, and not at all like the flaring reds and yellows of the gorgeous flowers that the world admires. These are often like a great sunflower, with a disc as big as a cheese. But the Christian beauty will be modest and unobtrusive and shy, like the violet half-buried in the hedge-bank, and unnoticed by careless eyes, accustomed to see beauty only in gaudy, flaring blooms. But unless you, as a Christian, are in your character arrayed in the "beauty of holiness" [Ps. 29:2], and the holiness of beauty, you are not quite the Christian that Jesus Christ wants you to be; setting forth all the gracious and sweet and refining influences of the Gospel in your daily life and conduct.

GOD'S PROMISE OF GRACE

His favor is as dew upon the grass—Prov. 19:12

The prose of this sweet old promise, that God will be as the dew unto His people, is, "If I depart I will send Him unto you." If we are Christian people, we have the perpetual dew of that Divine Spirit, which falls on our leaves and penetrates to our roots, and communicates life, freshness, and power, and makes growth possible—more than possible, certain—for us. "I"—Myself through My Son, and in My Spirit—"I will be"—an unconditional assurance—"as the dew unto Israel" [Hos. 14:5].

Yes! That promise is in its depth and fullness applicable only to the Christian Israel, and it remains true today and forever. Do we see it fulfilled? One looks around our congregations, and into one's own heart, and we behold the parable of Gideon's fleece acted over again—some places soaked with the refreshing moisture, and some as hard as a rock and as dry as tinder, and ready to catch fire from any spark from the devil's forge and be consumed in the everlasting burnings some day. It will do us good to ask ourselves why it is that, with a promise like this for every Christian soil to build upon, there are so few Christian souls that have realized its fullness and its depth. Let us be quite sure of this—God has nothing to do with the failure of His promise. And let us take all the blame to ourselves.

"I will be as the dew unto Israel." Who was Israel? The man that wrestled all night in prayer with God, and took hold of the Angel, and prevailed, and wept, and made supplication to Him [Gen. 32]. So Hosea tells us, and, as he says in the passage where he describes the Angel's wrestling with Jacob at Peniel, "there He spake with us" [12:4]—when He spake He spake with him who first bore the name. Be you Israel, and God will surely be your dew, and life and growth will be possible.

The dew, formed in the silence of the darkness, while men sleep, falling as willingly on a bit of dead wood as anywhere, hanging its pearls on every poor spike of grass, and dressing everything on which it lies with strange beauty, each separate globule tiny and evanescent, but each flashing back the light, and each a perfect sphere, feeble one by one, but united mighty to make the pastures of the wilderness rejoice—so, created in silence by an unseen influence, feeble when taken in detail, but strong in their myriads, glad to occupy the lowliest place, and each bright with something of celestial light, Christian men and women are to be in the midst of many people as a dew from the Lord.

THE DEW OF GOD'S GRACE

I will be as the dew unto Israel—Hos. 14:5

Scholars tell us that the kind of moisture that is meant in these words about the dew is not what we call dew, of which, as a matter of fact, there falls little or none at the season of the year referred to in this text, in Palestine, but that the word really means the heavy night-clouds that come upon the wings of the south-west wind, to diffuse moisture and freshness over the parched plains in the very height and fierceness of summer. The metaphor of "the dew" becomes more beautiful and striking if we note that, in the previous chapter, where the prophet was in his threatening mood, he predicts that "an east wind shall come, the wind of the Lord shall come up from the wilderness" [Hos. 13:5]—the churning storm, with death upon its wings—"and his spring shall become dry, and his fountain shall be dried up." We have, then, to imagine the land gaping and parched, the hot air having, as with an invisible tongue of flame, licked streams and pools dry, and having shrunken fountains and springs. Then, all at once, there comes down upon the baking ground, and the faded, drooping flowers that lie languid and prostate on the ground in the darkness, borne on the wings of the wind, from the depths of the great unfathomed sea, an unseen moisture. You cannot call it rain, so gently does it diffuse itself; it is more like a mist, but it brings life and freshness; and everything is changed. The dew, or the night mist, as it might more properly be rendered, was evidently a good deal in Hosea's mind; you may remember that he uses the image again in a remarkably different aspect, where he speaks of men's goodness as being like a morning cloud and the early dew that passes away [13:3]. The natural object which yields the emblem was all inadequate to set forth the Divine gift which is compared to it, because as soon as the sun has risen, with burning heat, it scatters the beneficent clouds, and the "sunbeams like swords" threaten to slay the tender green shoots. But this mist from God, that comes down to water the earth, is never dried up. It is not transient. It may be ours, and live in our hearts.

THE INDWELLING LIFE OF CHRIST

He that abideth in me, and I in him, the same bringeth forth much fruit: for
without me ye can do nothing—John 15:5

Like most writers and speakers, John had favorite expressions, which exercised a fascination over him, and were always ready to trickle from his pen or drop from his lips. He has a vocabulary of his own. Life and death, light and darkness, love and hatred, are antitheses constantly recurring in his writings, and in which he states the deepest things he has to say. These repetitions are not redundancy. He turns the jewels every way, and lets the many-colored light flash from them at all angles. One of his pet words is this "abide," significant of the quiet, contemplative temper of the man, but significant of a great deal more. He uses it, if I deem correctly, somewhere between sixty and seventy times in the Gospels and Epistles, far more than all the other instances of its use in the rest of the New Testament put together. To John, one great characteristic of the Christian life was that it was the abiding life. The Christian life is a life of dwelling in Christ.

I have said that this is one of John's favorite words. He learned it from his Master. It was in the upper room where it came from Christ's lips [Luke 24:29], with a pathos which was increased by the shadow of departure that lay over His heart and theirs. It was when He was on the eve of leaving them, as far as outward presence was concerned, that He said to them so tenderly, "Abide in Me, and I in you" [John 15:4]. No doubt the old apostle had meditated long on the words, and experience and age had done their best work for him, not in carrying him beyond his Master's utterances, but in showing him how these were elastic, and widened out to contain far more of wisdom, of comfort, and of guidance than he had at first suspected them to hold.

Heaven must bend to earth before earth can rise to heaven. The skies must open and drop down love before love can spring in the fruitful fields. And it is only when we look with true trust to that great unveiling of the heart of God which is in Jesus Christ that our hearts are melted, and all their snows are dissolved into sweet waters, which, freed from their icy chains, can flow, with music in their ripple and fruitfulness along their course, through our otherwise silent and barren lives. With unworn and fresh heart we may bring forth fruit in old age, and have the crocus in the autumnal fields as well as in the springtime of our lives.

"ABIDE IN ME, AND I IN YOU"

As the branch cannot bear fruit of itself, except it abide in the vine; so neither can ye, except ye abide in me—John 15:4

"Abide in Me, and I in you." That is the ideal of the Christian life, a reciprocal mutual dwelling of Christ in us and of us in Christ. These two thoughts are but two sides of the one truth, the interpenetration, by faith and love, of the believing heart and the beloved Savior, and the community of spiritual life as between them. The one sets forth more distinctly Christ's gracious activity and wondrous love, by which He condescends to enter into the narrow room of our spirits, and to communicate their life and all the blessings He can bestow. The other sets forth more distinctly our activity, and suggests the blessed thought of a home and a shelter, an inexpugnable fortress and a sure dwelling place, a habitation to which all generations may continually resort. He dwells in us as the spirit or the life in the body communicated to every part, and vitalizing every part. We dwell in Him as the limb dwells in the frame, or, as He Himself has put it, as the branch dwells in the vine.

Now this thought, in its two sides, as seems to me, is far too little present to the consciousness and to the experience, to the doctrinal belief and to the personal verification of that belief in our own lives, of the mass of Christian people. To me it is the very heart of Christianity, for which that which, in the popular apprehension, has all but crowded it out of view—namely, Christ *for* us—is the preface and introduction. I do not want that this great truth should be in any measure obscured, but I do want that, inseparably connected with it in our belief and in our experience, there should be far more than there is, the companion sister-thought, Christ *in* us and we in Christ.

You may call that "mystical," if you like. I am not frightened at a word. There is a good and there is a bad mysticism. And there is no grasp of the deepest things of religion without that which the irreligious mind thinks that it has disposed of by the cheap and easy sneer that it is "mystical." If it is true that we can only speak of spiritual experiences in the terms of analogies drawn from material things; if it is true that where a man's treasure is there his heart is [Luke 12:34], wherever his body may be; if it is true that loving hearts, even in the imperfect unions of earth, do interpenetrate and enclose one another—then the mysticism which says "Christ in me and I in Christ" is abundantly vindicated. And your Christianity will be a shallow one, unless the truths which these two great complementary thoughts suggest be truths verified in your experience.

A MUTUAL INDWELLING

That life which I now live in the flesh I live by the faith of the Son of God who loved me, and gave himself for me—Gal. 2:20

I need not remind you how the great thought of mutual indwelling is, through John's writings particularly, extended not only to our relation to God, but to our relations to God the Father and God the Spirit. The Apostle almost as frequently speaks about our dwelling in God and God's dwelling in us. And he reports to us that Christ spoke about the Spirit dwelling with us, and being in us, and that forever. So it is the "whole fullness of the Godhead" [Col. 2:9], in all the phases of its manifestation and possible relation to humanity, that is thus conceived of as entering into this deep and most real relation to Christian souls. Into that fire of God we may pass, and walk in the midst of the flame unharmed, with nothing consumed except the bonds that hold us.

Let me say one word about the ways by which this mutual indwelling may be procured and maintained. You talk about the doctrine as being mystical. Well, the way to realize it as a fact is plain and unmystical enough to suit anybody. There are two streams of representation in John's writings about this matter. Here is a sample of one of them: "He that eateth My flesh and drinketh My blood abideth in Me, and I in him." Similarly, he says: "If that which ye have heard from the beginning abide in you, ye also shall abide in the Son and in the Father." And, still more definitely, "Whosoever shall confess that Jesus is the Son of God, God dwelleth in him, and he in God" [1 John 4:15]. So, then, the acceptance, by our understandings and by our hearts, of the truth concerning Jesus Christ, and the grasping of these truths so closely by faith that they become the nourishment of our spirits, so that we eat His flesh and drink His blood, is the condition of that mutual indwelling.

And if that seems to be too far removed from ordinary moralities to satisfy those who will have no mysteries in their religion, and will not have it anything else than a repetition of the plain dictates or conscience, take the other stream of representations: "If we love one another, God dwelleth in us" [1 John 4:12]. "He that dwelleth in love dwelleth in God" [1 John 4:16]. "If ye keep my commandments, ye shall abide in my love" [John 15:10]. The harm of mysticism of Christianity enjoins the punctilious discharge of plain duties. "He that keepeth His commandments dwelleth in him and he in him" [1 John 3:24].

THE CHRISTIAN LIFE ONE OF STEADFAST PERSISTENCE

Be thou faithful unto death, and I will give thee a crown of life—Rev. 2:10

I am afraid that there are few things which the average Christian man of this generation needs more than the exhortation to steadfastly continue in the course which he says he has adopted. Most of us have our Christianity by fits and starts. It is spasmodic and interrupted. We grow, as the vegetable world grows, in the favorable months only, and there are long intervals in which there is no progress. Far too many of us have seasons of quickened consciousness and experience, and then dreary winters in which there is no life, and nothing but black frost binding the ground.

Take the lesson of this constantly recurring word "abide," and let there be in your Christianity the homely virtue of perseverance, for heaven is won and character is built up by homely virtues. "No day without a line," said the great author, as the secret of success. I look around upon our Christian communities, and I see many whose Christian experience is like some of the tropical rivers, bank full and foaming this month, and next, when the hot sunshine comes out, a stagnant pond here and another one there, and between them a ghastly stretch of white boulders. When the meteorologist puts his sensitized paper out to record the hours of brilliant sunshine in the day, there will come, in our climate and city, most often, a line where the sun has had its power, and then a long stretch of unchanged paper, where it had gone behind a cloud. That is a picture of the Christian experience of a disastrously large number of us. Let us learn this lesson, "Abide in my word; let my word abide in you." A Christian life should be one of steadfast, unbroken persistence.

Oh! But you say, "that is an ideal that nobody can get to." Well! I am not going to quarrel with anybody as to whether such an ideal is possible or not. It seems to me a woeful waste of time to be fighting about possible limits when we are so far short of the limits that are known. Until our lives approximate a great deal more closely to a continuous line, do not let us take each other by the throat because we may differ as to whether the line can ever be absolutely closed up into unbroken continuity.

How beautiful it is to see a man, below whose feet time is crumbling away, holding firmly by the Lord whom he has loved and served all his days, and finding that the pillar of cloud, which guided him while he lived, begins to glow in its heart of fire as the shadows fall, and is a pillar of light to guide him when he comes to die.

THE CHRISTIAN LIFE ONE OF ABIDING BLESSEDNESS

Blessed are the pure in heart, for they shall see God—Matt. 5:8

Our Lord, in that same discourse in which He spoke about abiding in us and we in Him, used the word very frequently in a great variety of aspects, and among them He said, "These things have I spoken unto you, that my joy might remain in you" [John 15:11]. And in other places we read about "abiding in the light" [1 Tim. 6:16], or having eternal life abiding in us. And in all these various places of the use of this expression there lies the one thought that it is possible for us to make, here and now, our Christian lives are one long series of conscious enjoyment of the highest blessings. There will be ups and downs, there will be circumstances that agitate and disturb. It will sometimes be hard for us to keep hold of our Lord, when tempests are sweeping us away from Him, and the sea is running hard and high. But, "My joy may remain in you." And, even if there be a circumference of sorrow, joy and peace may be the center, and not be truly broken by the incursions of calamities. There are springs of fresh water that dart up from the depths of the salt sea, and spread themselves over its waves. It is possible, in the inmost chamber, to be still while the storm is raging without. Oh, if we are keeping our hold on Christ, and dwell in that strong fortress, no matter what enemies may assail us, we shall be kept in perfect peace. It is our own fault if ever external things have power over us enough to shake our inmost and central blessedness. "As sorrowful, yet always rejoicing" [2 Cor. 6:10].

Amid all the tragical changes to which all things around us, and we ourselves, are exposed, let us grasp and keep our hold on the abiding Christ, "The same yesterday, and today, and forever" [Heb. 13:8], and in Him we, too, fleeting as we are, shall endure forevermore.

May I add one word? John says about another king of abiding: "He that loveth not his brother abideth in death" [1 John 3:14]; and he quotes John the Baptist as saying, "He that believeth not on the Son shall not see life, but the wrath of God abideth on him" [John 3:36]. There is a permanence heavy with all loss and tragical with all despair. "Abide in Me," for, severed from Me, ye are nothing.

Christ is all in all to His people. He is all their strength, wisdom, and righteousness. They are but the clouds irradiated by the sun, and bathed in its brightness. He is the light which flames in their gray mist and turns it to a glory. They are but the belt, and cranks, and wheels, He is the power. They are but the channel, muddy and dry; He is the soul dwelling in every part to save it from corruption and give movement and warmth.

"Thou art the organ, whose full breath is thunder,
I am the keys, beneath Thy fingers pressed."

THE PERMANENT LIFE OF THE CHRISTIAN

He that doeth the will of God abideth forever—1 John 2:17

These words imply, not so much dwelling, or persistence, or continuity, during our earthly career, as, rather, the absolute and unlimited permanence of the obedient life. It will endure when all things else, "the world, and the lust thereof" [1 John 2:17], have slid away into obscurity, and have ceased to be. Now, of course, it is true that Christian men, temples of Christ, are subject to the same law of mutation and decay as all created things are; and it is true, on the other hand, that men whose lives are "cribbed, cabined, and confined" within the limits of the material and visible have these lives as permanent, in a very solemn and awful sense, inasmuch as their fruit continues, though it is fruitless fruit, and inasmuch as they have to bear forever the responsibility of their past. The lives that run parallel with God's will last, and when everything that has been against that will, or negligent of it, is summed up, and comes to naught, and is abolished, these lives continue. The life that is in conformity with the will of God lasts in another sense, inasmuch as it persists through all changes, even the supreme change that is wrought by death, in the same direction, and is substantially the same. For the man that was doing God's will here, down among cotton bales, and ledgers, and retorts, and dictionaries, will do God's will yonder, amid the glories; and it will be the same life, with the same guiding principles, with the same root for its activities. So it will last forever.

If we grasp the throne of God, we shall be co-eternal with the throne that we grasp. We cannot die, nor our work pass and be utterly abolished, as long as He lives. Some trees that, like sturdy Scotch firs, have strong trunks, and obstinate branches, and unfading foliage, looking as if they would defy any blast or decay, run their roots along the surface, and down they go before the storm; others, far more slender in appearance, strike theirs deep down, and they stand whatever winds blow. So strike your roots into God and Christ. "He that doeth the will of God abideth forever" [1 John 2:17]. And, "In my Father's house are many mansions" [John 14:2]. They that have here dwelt in Christ, persistently seeking to have His truth dwelling in them and wrought out by them, will pass into the permanence of the heavenly home.

THE EVER-PRESENT LOVE OF JESUS CHRIST

Unto him that loved us, and washed us from our sins in his own blood—Rev. 1:5

The foundation of all our hopes, and all our joys, and all our strength in the work of the world, should be this firm conviction, that we are wrapped about by, and evermore in, an endless ocean, so to speak, of a present Divine love, of a present loving Christ. He loves *us*, says John; and he speaks to all ages and people. The units of each generation and of every land have a right to feel themselves included in that word, and every human being is entitled to turn the "us" into "me." For no crowds block the access to His heat, nor empty the cup of His love before it reaches the thirsty lips on the furthest outskirts of the multitude. He does with all the multitude who hang on Him as He did when He fed the thousands. He ranks them all on the grass, and in order ministers to each his portion in due season. We do not jostle each other. There is room in that heart of Christ for us all.

"The glorious sky, embracing all,
Is like its Maker's love;
Wherewith encircled, great and small
In peace and order move."

Every star has its separate place in the great round, and "He calleth them all by their names" [Ps. 147:4], and holds them in His mind. So we, and all our brethren, have each our own orbit and our station in the Heaven of Christ's heart, and it embraces, distinguishes, and sustains us all, "Unto Him that loved us."

Another thought may be suggested, too, of how this present timeless love of Christ is unexhausted by exercise, pouring itself ever out, and ever full notwithstanding. They tell us that the sun is fed by impact, from objects from without, and that the day will come when its furnace-flames shall be quenched into gray ashes. But this love is fed by no contributions from without, and will outlast the burnt-out sun, and gladden the ages of ages forever.

All generations, all thirsty lips and ravenous desires, may slake their thirst and satisfy themselves at that great fountain, and it shall not sink one inch in its marble basin. Christ's love, after all creatures have received from it, is as full as at the beginning, and unto us upon whom the ends of the earth are come, this precious and sweet, all-sufficing love pours as full a tide as when first it blessed that little handful that gathered around Him on earth. Other rivers run shallow as they broaden, but this "river of God" is as deep when it wraps the world as if it were poured through the narrows of one heart.

THE UNCHILLED LOVE OF THE CHRIST

Who loved me, and gave himself for me—Gal. 2:20

The love of Christ is unchilled by the sovereignty and glory of His exaltation. There is a wonderful difference between the Christ of the Gospels and the Christ of the Revelation. People have exaggerated the difference into contradiction, and then, running to the other extreme, others have been tempted to deny that there was any. But there is one thing that is not different. The nature behind the circumstances is the same. The Christ of the Gospels is the Christ in His lowliness, bearing the weight of man's sins; the Christ of the Apocalypse is the Christ in His loftiness, ruling over the world and time—but it is the same Christ. The one is surrounded by weakness and the other is girded with strength, but it is the same Christ. The one is treading the weary road of earth, the other is sitting at the right hand of God the Father Almighty; but it is the same Christ. The one is the "Man of sorrows and acquainted with grief" [Is. 55:3], the other is the Man glorified and a companion of Divinity; but it is the same Christ. The hand that holds the seven stars [Rev. 2:1] is as loving as the hand that was laid in blessing upon the little children [Matt. 19:14]; the face that is as the sun shining in its strength beams with as much love as when it drew publicans and harlots to His feet. The breast that is girt with the golden girdle is the same breast upon which John leaned his happy head. The Christ is the same, and the love is unaltered. From the midst of the glory and the sevenfold brilliancy of the light which is inaccessible, the same tender heart bends down over us that bent down over all the weary and the distressed when He Himself was weary; and we can lift up our eyes above stars and systems and material splendors, right up to the central point of the universe, where the enthroned Christ is, and see "Him that loveth us"—even *us!*

When He was here on earth, the multitude thronged Him and pressed Him, but the wasted forefinger of one poor timid woman could reach the garment's hem for all the crowd [Matt. 9:20]. He recognized the difference between the touch that had sickness and supplication in it and the jostlings of the mob, and His healing power passed at once to her who needed and asked it, though so many were surging around Him. So still He knows and answers the silent prayer of the loving and the needy heart. However tremulous and palsied the finger, however imperfect and ignorant the faith, His love delights to answer and to over-answer it, as He did with that woman, who not only got the healing which she craved, but bore away besides the consciousness of His love and the cleansing of her sins.

THE TYRANNY OF SIN

Whosoever committeth sin is the servant of sin—John 8:34

Every wrong thing that we do tends to become our master and our tyrant. We are held and bound in the chains of our sins. The awful influence of habit, the dreadful effect upon a nature of a corrupted conscience, the power of regretful memories, the pollution arising from the very knowledge of what is wrong—these are some of the strands out of which the ropes that bind us are twisted. We know how tight they grip. I am speaking now, no doubt, to people who are as completely manacled and bound by evils of some sort—evils of flesh, of sense, of lust; of intemperance in some of you; of pride and avarice and worldliness in other of you; of vanity and frivolity and selfishness in others of you—as completely manacled as if there were iron shackles upon your wrists and fetters upon your ankles.

You remember the old story of the prisoner in his tower, delivered by his friend, who sent a beetle to crawl up the wall, fastening a silken thread to it, which had a thread a little heavier attached to the end of that, and so on, and so on, each thickening in diameter until they got to a cable. That is how the devil has got hold of a great many of us. He weaves around us silken threads to begin with, slight, as if we could break them with a touch of our fingers, and they draw after them, as certainly as destiny, "at each remove" a thickening "chain," until, at last, we are tied and bound, and our captor laughs at our mad plunges for freedom, which are as vain as a wild bull's in the hunter's nets. Some of you have made an attempt at shading off sin—how have you got on with it? As a man would do who, with a file made out of an old soft knife, tried to work through his fetters. He might make a little impression on the surface, but he would mostly scratch his own skin, and wear his own fingers, and to very little purpose.

But the chains can be removed. Christ looses them by "His blood." Like a drop of corrosive acid, that blood, falling upon the fetters, dissolves them, and the prisoner goes free, emancipated by the Son. That death has power to deliver us from the guilt and penalty of sin. The Bible does not give us the whole theory of an atonement, but the fact is seen clear in its passages that Christ died for us [Rom. 5:8], and that the bitter consequences of sin in their most intense bitterness, even that separation from God which is the true death, were borne by Him for our sakes, on our account, and in our stead.

His blood looses the fetters of our sins [Rev. 1:5], inasmuch as His death, touching our hears, and also bringing to us new powers through His Spirit, which is shed forth in consequence of His finished work, frees us from the power of sin, and brings into operation new powers and motives which free us from our ancient slavery. The chains which bind us shrivel and melt as the ropes that bound the Hebrew youths in the fire [Dan. 3:23], before the warmth of His manifested love and the glow of His Spirit's power.

THE GRATITUDE OF REDEEMED SOULS

Thou art worthy, O Lord, to receive glory and honor and power—Rev. 4:11

Worthy is the Lamb that was slain—Rev. 5:12

Irrepressible gratitude bursts into doxologies from John's lips, even here at the beginning of the book, as the seer thinks of the love of Christ; and all through the Apocalypse we hear the shout of praise from earth or heaven. The book which closes the New Testament "shuts up all" "with a sevenfold chorus of hallelujahs and harping symphonies," as Milton says in his stately music, and may well represent for us, in that perpetual cloud of incense rising up fragrant to the Throne of God and of the Lamb, the unceasing love and thanksgiving which should be man's answer to Christ's love and sacrifice.

Such love and praise, which is but love speaking, is all which He asks. Love can only be paid by love. Any other recompense offered to it is coinage of another currency, that is not current in its kingdom. The only recompense that satisfies love is its own image reflected in another heart. That is what Jesus Christ wants of you. He does not want your admiration, your outward reverence, your lip service, your grudging obedience; His heart hungers for more and other gifts from you. He wants your love, and is unsatisfied without it. He desired it so much that He was willing to die to procure it, as if a mother might think, "My children have been cold to me while I lived; perhaps, if I were to give my life to help them, their hearts might melt." All the awful expenditure of love stronger than death is meant to draw forth our love. He comes to each of us, and pleads with us for our hearts, wooing us to love Him by showing us all He has done for us and all He will do. Surely the Cross borne for us should move us! Surely the throne prepared for us should touch us into gratitude!

That Lord who died and lives dwells now in the heavens, the center of a mighty chorus and tempest of praise which surges around His throne, loud as the voice of many waters, and sweet as harpers harping on their harps. The main question for us is, Does He hear our voice in it? Are our lips shut? Are our hearts cold? Do we meet His fire of love with icy indifference? Do we repay His sacrifice with unmoved self-regard, and meet His pleadings with closed ears? "Do ye thus requite the Lord, O foolish people and unwise?" [Deut. 32:6].

Take this question home to your heart, How do you owe unto the Lord? He has loved thee, has given Himself for thee, and His sacrifice will unlock thy fetters and set thee free. Will you be silent in the presence of such transcendent mercy? Shall we not rather, moved by His dying love, and joyful in the possession of deliverance through His Cross, lift up our voices and hearts in a perpetual song of praise, to which our lives of glad obedience shall be as perfect music accompanying noble words, "Unto Him that loveth us, and washed us from our sins by His own blood?"

A GOOD REASON FOR CONFIDENCE

And now, my little children, abide in him; that, when he shall appear, we may
have confidence, and not be ashamed before him at his coming—1 John 2:28

The happy assurance of the love of God resting upon me, and making me His child
through Jesus Christ, does not dissipate that darkness that lies beyond.

"We are the sons of God, *and,*" just because we are, "it doth not yet appear what we
shall be" [1 John 3:2]. Or, as the words are rendered in the Revised Version, "it is not yet
made manifest what we shall be." The meaning of that expression, "It doth not appear,"
or, "It has not been manifested," may be put into very plain words, I think, thus: John
would simply say to us, "There has never been set forth before men's eyes in this earthly
life of ours an example or an instance of what the sons of God are to be in another state
of being." And so, because men have never had the instance before them, they do not
know much about that state.

In some sense there has been a manifestation through the life of Jesus Christ. Christ
has died; Christ is risen again. Christ has gone about among men upon earth after resurrection. Christ has been raised to the right hand of God, and sits there in the glory of
the Father. So far it has been manifested what we shall be. But the risen Christ is not
the glorified Christ; and although He has set forth before man's senses the irrefutible
fact of another life, and to some extent some glimpses and gleams of knowledge with regard to certain portions of it, I suppose that the "glorious body" of Jesus Christ was not
assumed by Him till the cloud received Him out of their sight, nor indeed could He,
even while He moved among the material realities of this world, and did eat and drink
before them. So that, while we thankfully recognize that Christ's resurrection and ascension have brought life and immortality to light, we must remember that it is the fact,
and not the manner of the fact, which they make plain, and that, even after His example, it has not been manifested what is the body of this glory which He now wears, and
therefore it has not yet been manifested what we shall be when we are fashioned after its
likeness. There has been no manifestation, then, to sense or to human experience, of
that future, and therefore there is next to no knowledge about it.

"When He shall appear." To what period does that refer? It seems most natural to
take the appearance here as being the same as that spoken of only a verse or two before.
"And now, little children, abide in Him; that when He shall *appear,* we may have confidence, and not be ashamed before Him at His coming." That "coming," then, is the "appearance" of Christ; and it is at the period of His coming in His glory that His servants
"shall be like him, and see him as he is" [1 John 3:2].

CHRISTIAN GLADNESS

With joy shall ye draw water out of the wells of salvation—Is. 12:3

There are better things than joy. Indeed, there are few things of smaller account than it, if taken by itself. A life framed on purpose to secure it is contemptible and barren of nobility or beauty. It is certain to be a failure, as it deserves to be. To pursue it is to lose it. The only way to get it is to follow steadily the path of duty, without thinking of joy, and then, like sleep, it comes most surely unsought, and we "being in the way" [Gen. 24:27], the angel of God, bright-haired Joy, is sure to meet us.

The best in a man recoils from any system which makes much of joy as a motive to action, and Christian teachers have sometimes done unwitting harm by preaching a kind of gospel which has come to little more than this: "Be Christians that you may be happy." No doubt the natural result of every right and pure course of life is to bring a real joy; and lightness of heart follows goodness as certainly as fragrance is breathed from the opened flowers. With every pure action pure joy is bound up. Men have staggered at the inequalities of outward fortune, and been driven by them to doubt whether there was any God. But it would be a far more overwhelming difficulty if there were not connection between goodness and happiness; if a man could love and serve God, and not find joy in proportion to his love and service; if a pure and sober-suited Joy were not one of the "virgins following" Religion, the Queen, it would be doubly hard to believe in God.

So, though it is by no means the highest reason for being a Christian, nor the loftiest view to take of the effects of Christianity, it would be folly to refuse to recognize the fact that a true Christian life is a joyful life, or to neglect to use it as a real, though subsidiary, motive to such a life. It is quite possible to be beset all about with cares and troubles and sorrows, and yet to feel, in spite of loss and disappointment and loneliness, a pure foundation of joys Divine and celestial gladness welling up in our inmost hearts, sweet amid bitter waters. There may be life beneath the snow; there may be fire burning, like the old Greek fire, below the water; we may pour oil on the stormiest waves, and it will find its way to the surface, and do something to smooth the billows; while "in heaviness through manifold temptations" [1 Pet. 1:6] we may yet have a "joy unspeakable and full of glory" [1 Pet. 1:8]. For I suppose that a man has this power, that if he have two objects of contemplation, to one or other of which he may turn his mind, he can choose which of the two he will turn to. Like a railway signalman, you may either flash the light through the pure white glass or the darkly colored one. You may either choose to look at everything through the medium of the sorrows that belong to time or through the medium of the joys that flow from eternity. The question is, which of the two we choose shall be uppermost in our hearts and give the color to our experience.

JOY UNSPEAKABLE AND FULL OF GLORY

Whom not having seen, ye love; in whom, though now ye see Him not, yet believing, ye rejoice with joy unspeakable and full of glory: receiving the end of your faith, even the salvation of your souls—1 Pet. 1:8, 9

It is a proof of the low average of Christian life that this language seems to most commentators all too wide and exuberant to describe the ordinary Christian. But the Apostle is speaking about the ideal type, about the possibility; and if the reality of an average Christian experience does not come up to that, so much the worse for the experience. It does not affect the possibility in the very slightest degree. I admit the language is strong. But, as we have already remarked, it is not so difficult to explain the strong epithets as applied to the possibilities of Christian joy, even here, as it is to break up a sentence so compactly knit as this into two halves, one referring to this side of the grave and the other to the world beyond.

But notice that, whatever may be the depth and greatness of this joy, Peter clearly anticipates that it is to be simultaneous with the "heaviness through manifold temptations" [1 Pet. 1:6].

The two emotions may subsist side by side, neither neutralizing the other, nor the bright and the dark so blending as to make a monotonous gray. But the occasions for sorrow may be keenly felt, and the joy which comes from higher springs may none the less possess the soul. The separate existence of the two extremes rather than their coalescence in an apathetic middle state is best. Paul's apparent paradox is a deep truth, "as sorrowful, yet always rejoicing" [2 Cor. 6:10].

And then the language of Peter reminds us that the gladness which thus belongs to the Christian life is silent and a transfigured "joy unspeakable and glorified," as the word might be rendered. "He is a poor man who can count his flock," said the old Latin proverb. Those joys are on the surface that can be spoken. The deep river goes silently, with equable flow, to the great ocean; it is the little shallow brook that chatters among the pebbles. And so all great emotion, all deep and noble feeling is quiet, as Cordelia, in Shakespeare's *King Lear*, says, she can "love and be silent," so we at our happiest must be glad and silent. If we can speak our joy, it is scarcely worth speaking. The true Christian gladness does not need laughter nor many words; it is calm and grave, and the world would say severe. "The gods approve the depth and not the tumult of the soul."

The true Christian joy is glorified, says Peter. The glory of Heaven shines upon it and transfigures it. It is suffused and filled with the glory for which the Christian hopes, like Stephen when God's glory smote him on the face and made it shine as an angel's [see Acts 6:15]. Joy may easily become frivolous and contemptible, and there is nothing more difficult in the conduct of life than to keep gladness from degenerating and from corrupting the character. But the effect of Christianity, even on the common human joys, is to exalt and dignify them, besides the effect in giving the joys proper to itself which are in their very nature exalted and exalting. It changes, if I may so say, the light, fluttering Cupids of earthly joys, with flimsy butterfly wings, into calm, grave angels with mighty plumes.

JOY THE RESULT OF FAITH

Hitherto have ye asked nothing in my name: ask, and ye shall receive, that your joy may be full—John 16:24

The act of faith is the condition of joy. Joy springs from the contemplation or experience of something calculated to excite it; and the more real and permanent and all-sufficient that object, the fuller and surer the joy. But where can we find such an object as Him with whom we are brought into union by our faith? Jesus Christ is all-sufficient, full of pity, full of beauty and righteousness, all that we can desire—and all this forever. Union with Him provides an object on which all the fervor of the heart may pour itself out. In Him our faith grasps the absolutely good and perfect. Confidence is joy. But when confidence fastens on such a Christ, it is joy heightened and glorified. If we have the certain knowledge that the dear Lord died for us, and live realizing His power and sanctifying Spirit, His constant tenderness and more than womanly sympathy and affection, then nothing can come to us that will deprive us of our gladness as long as our hearts are anchored upon Him only. Our gladness will be accurately co-temporaneous with our trust. As long as we are exercising faith, so long shall we experience joy; not one instant longer. It is like a piano, whose note ceases the moment you lift your finger from the key; not like an organ, in which the sound persists for a time after.

The moment you turn your eyes away from Jesus Christ, that moment does the light fade from your eyes. It is like a landscape lying bathed in the sunshine; a little white cloud creeps across the face of the sun, and all the brightness is gone from leagues of country in an instant. As long as, and not a hair's breadth longer than, our faith in Christ is exercised, so long have we gladness. You cannot live upon yesterday's faith nor furbish up again old experience to produce new joy. Ever and ever you must draw afresh from the fountain, and secure constant joy by continuance of renewed confidence in Him.

There is a sufficient reason for the failure of most Christian lives to attain this perfection of joy as their habitual possession, in the interrupted and fragmentary character of their faith. If we are only exercising it by fits and starts, we shall have only short and far-between visits of gladness in our lives. The measure of our faith is the measure of our joy. He that soweth sparingly of the former shall reap sparingly of the latter. And the duration of our joy depends on the duration of our faith. What wonder, then, that instead of its continual sunshine, we should have but occasional glimpses of its brightness, and that our skies should mostly be weeping or gray with clouds? The reason for such imperfect and interrupted joy is simply our imperfect and interrupted faith.

THE GIFT WHICH ENHANCES JOY

The God of hope fill you with all joy and peace in believing, that ye may abound in hope, through the power of the Holy Ghost—Rom. 15:13

The exercise of faith is itself joy, apart from what faith secures. We stretch out our hands to Christ, and the act is blessedness. But we lay hold of His hand, and in it there is a blessing which, when we take it, makes us glad. Faith is the condition of joy; and the salvation of our souls, which we receive as its end, is the great reason for joy.

If my heart is humbly, and even tremulously, resting upon Him, I have, in the measure of my faith, the real origin of all salvation. What are the elements of which salvation consists? The fact and the sense of forgiveness to begin with. Well, I have that, have I not, if I trust Christ? A consciousness of favor, a sense of the friendship of God in Christ?—I have these, if I trust Him. A growing possession of pure desires, heaven-wrought tastes, of all that is called in the Bible "the new man" [Eph. 4:24]—well! I have that, surely, if I trust Him. My soul is saved when it is delivered from its sin, and filled with the love of God, and when the will is set in glad accord with His will. Such progressive salvation is given to me if I am trusting in Him, "Whom having not seen, ye love." All these will tend to joy. The consciousness of forgiveness will make me glad. The sense of His love will make me glad. The consciousness of union with Jesus will make me glad. Increasing deliverance from the burden of my self-will will make me glad. A growing obedience to Him will make me glad. It is joy to the just to do judgment. Brightening hopes will make me glad; and, in a thousand other ways, joy unspeakable and full of glory will attend the reception in our souls of that salvation which begins here and is perfected hereafter.

Surely, if we can find a power which will thus ennoble and calm our joy, and make it the ally of all things lovely and of good report, we shall have found a treasure indeed.

Such a power we can find in fellowship with Jesus Christ, through whom our joys, which have too long trailed along the ground, may be lifted high above the frivolities, and sometimes criminalities and hollownesses, which, with so many of us, do duty for gladness. "As the crackling of thorns under a pot" [Eccl. 7:6], so is much of the world's mirth. Make sure, my friend, that your joy is deep and still, noble and glorified, being drawn from Christ.

THE PERFECT JOY OF A PRESENT SALVATION

In thy presence is fulness of joy: at thy right hand there are pleasures forevermore—Psalm 16:11

The present salvation points onward to its own completion, and in that way becomes further a source of joy. In its depths we see reflected a blue heaven with many a star. The salvation here touches the soul alone; but salvation in its perfect form touches the body, soul, and spirit, and transforms all the outward nature to correspond to these and make a worthy dwelling for perfected men. That prospect brings joy beyond the reach of anything else to afford. The glory of that perfect salvation gleams already, and touches the Christian joy into nobleness and solemn greatness. And as the salvation is eternal, so the joy may be abiding. "Joys are like poppies spread," and when the opiate petals swiftly drop, an ugly brown head like a skull is left, full of poisonous seeds. But this joy blooms amaranthine flowers, and being the reflex of Christ's own eternal joy, endures according to His promise, "that my joy might remain in you, and that your joy might be full" [John 15:11].

That perfect salvation heightens our joy here by the hope of a perfect joy hereafter. We dare to look forward to a state when sorrow and joy shall no more be in strange juxtaposition, the white and the black dog in the same leash, but joy shall reign alone and sorrow be dethroned. Our partial experience of salvation here warrants that anticipation.

Here we are, like the Laplanders in their winter huts, pitched upon the snowy plain. Desolation and white death outside, but inside light and warmth, food and companionship. Without our hut are sorrow, and loss, and change, and care, and loneliness, and anxiety, and perplexity, and all the discipline that is needful for us, though within we have Christ. But then we shall journey south to the lands of the sun, where no storms rage and winter never comes. Here our joy is like an exotic plant, stunted and struggling with an ungenial sky and unkindly soil; there in its native place it spreads a broader leaf and bears a sweeter fruit. Here we taste of the river of His pleasures, there we shall drink from the fountain. All comes from Christ, the incomplete salvation and sorrow-shaded joy of the present, the perfect salvation and unmingled gladness of the future. The nearer we are to Him, the more of both shall we possess, till we reach His presence, where there is fullness of joy, and sit at His right hand, where there are pleasures forevermore.

OUR LORD'S DIVINE NATURE

And without controversy great is the mystery of godliness: God was manifested in the flesh, justified in the Spirit, seen of angels, preached unto the Gentiles, believed on in the world, received up into glory—1 Tim. 3:16

The Divine nature of the Lord Jesus Christ is woven through the whole of the Book of Revelation, like a golden thread, and manifestly is needed to explain the fact of this solemn ascription of praise (*see* Revelation 1:5, 6) to Him, as well as to warrant the application of each clause of it to His will. For John to lift up his voice in this grand doxology to Jesus Christ was blasphemy, if it was not adoration of Him as Divine. He may have been right or wrong in his belief, but surely the man who sang such a hymn to his Master believed Him to be the Incarnate Word, God manifest in the flesh. If we share that faith, we can believe in Christ's present love to us all. It is no misty sentiment or rhetorical exaggeration to believe that every man, woman, and child that is or shall be on the earth till the end of time has a distinct place in His heart, is an object of His knowledge and of His love.

This one word, then, is the revelation to us of Christ's love, as unaffected by time. Our thoughts are carried by it up into the region where dwells the Divine nature, above the various phases of the fleeting moments which we call past, present, and future. These are but the lower layer of clouds which drive before the wind, and melt from shape to shape. He dwells above in the naked, changeless blue.

As of all His nature, of His love we can be sure that time cannot bind it. We say, not, "It was," or, "It will be," but we can proclaim the changeless, timeless, majestic present of that love which burns and is not consumed, but glows with as warm a flame for the latest generations as for those men who stood within the reach of its rays while He was on earth. "I am the First and the Last," says Christ, and His love partakes of that eternity. It is like a golden fringe which keeps the web of creation from raveling out. Before the earliest of creatures was this love. After the latest it shall be. It circles them all around, and locks them all in its enclosure. It is the love of the Divine heart, for it is the same yesterday, and today, and forever. It is the love of a human heart, for that heart could shed its blood to loose us from our sins. Shall we not take this love for ours? The heart that can hold all the units of all successive generations, and so love each that each may claim a share in the grandest issues of its love, must be a Divine heart, for only there is there room for the millions to stand, all distinguishable and all enriched and blessed by that love. Is there any meaning but exaggerated sentiment in this word of Revelation, any meaning that will do for a poor heart struggling with its own evil, and with the world's miseries and devilries, to rest upon, unless we believe that Christ is Divine, and loves us with an everlasting love because He is God manifest in the flesh?

THE SIN OF SINS

And he did not many mighty works there because of their unbelief—Matt. 13:58

There is but one sin in the world, properly speaking, and that is the sin of not loving God. The sins we commonly speak of are but different manifestations of this one sin—different in degree, diverse in various respects, diverse in enormity, but the enormity is chiefly to be determined by the measure of the revelation made of the character of God unto us. God becomes manifest in Christ; and lo, this unknown God is found to be a Being of most amazing love, humbling Himself to the meanest of mankind, bearing all things, suffering long, seeking not His own, answering the insults and contradictions of sinners with words and act of incredible blessing.

Thus does the glorious Being, who upholds all things by the word of His power, draws near to you with papers of emancipation, whereby you may escape the captivity of sin and Satan, the liability to death and hell; with hands pierced in the conflict with him who has the power of death, winning for you a path to life and glory; and now the universe looks on to see how you will receive the words of this Redeemer. It is possible for you to commit a sin of greater magnitude than you conceive of by simply neglecting the words of Christ. How fearful the alienation of the heart from God when such a surpassing embodiment of Divine love fails to overcome the indifference of that heart!

The terrible thing about the sin of unbelief is that its life is a life of slumber. It makes no noise in the heart. It has no visible shape. An angry word that falls from your lips has a reverberation in the depth of your heart; but unbelief is simply a state, and does not ordinarily reveal itself by any overt symptom. It is the atmosphere in which you move; and, as you never moved in any other, it does not shock you. But it is the sin of sins, and until you learn to hate it above all sins, there is little hope of your deliverance from sin.

A warmer tone of spiritual life would change the atmosphere which unbelief needs for its growth. It belongs to the fauna of the glacial epoch; and when the rigors of that wintry time begin to melt, and warmer days to set in, the creatures of the ice have to retreat to Arctic wildernesses, and leave a land no longer suited for their life. Dig down to the living Rock, Christ and His infinite love to you, and let *it* be the strong foundation, built into which you and your love may become living stones, a holy temple, partaking of the firmness and nature of that on which it rests.

CHRISTIAN JOY A DUTY

Although the fig-tree shall not blossom, neither shall fruit be in the vines; the labor of the olive shall fail, and the fields shall yield no meat; the flock shall be cut off from the fold, and there shall be no herd in the stalls; yet I will rejoice in the Lord, I will joy in the God of my salvation—Hab. 3:17, 18

It is a plain positive duty to cultivate true Christian joy. "Rejoice in the Lord always" [Phil. 4:4] is a command. The true ideal of Christian character gives a very prominent place to gladness, and they who do not in some measure attain to a joyous religion fail in a very important part of Christian duty. Of course there are many experiences in Christian life, and there are sides of Christian truth which are calculated to produce a sobered solemnity and sadness. But while all that is perfectly true, it is also true that it is incumbent upon us Christian people so to gather into our hearts the far more abounding joys of Divine communion, quiet trust, and bright hope, as that there shall be no room in our lives for despondency or despair, and not much room in our lives for tears. Christian gladness is Christian duty.

Ah! But you say: "I cannot help my circumstances, and they hinder joy." No! But God's Gospel is given to us to make us think less of our circumstances, and to say, as the prophet said of old, "Though the fig tree shall not blossom, and there be no fruit in the vine," or, in modern language, "Though trade be bad, and the profits of my business be decreasing; though I have but a poor outlook for the future, and do not know what I am to turn to next; though my home be desolate compared with what it was, and faces that used to be beside me have gone into the dust forever, yet will I experience joy in the Lord, and rejoice in the God of my salvation."

Has it come to this, that our Christianity is the kind of thing that the devil suggested Job's religion was—that we are only going to trust when there is not much need for it, and to believe in Him and love Him when He is doing well with us? If we are at the mercy of circumstances, then we need to look to the reality of our Christianity.

But you may say: "I cannot control my temperament. I am not naturally sanguine or buoyant in my disposition." No! Well, God's Gospel was given to us to control our temperaments, and to make it possible by reason of its great gifts and motives, that characters which were not naturally inclined to be joyful should be made so. And if our Christianity does nothing for us in the way of helping us to appropriate alien virtues, I do not know what difference there is between "nature" and "grace"; and I think we had better see to it whether we have any higher power than our own working in our hearts.

March 28

THE GREATNESS OF TRIFLES

And they compel one, Simon of Cyrene, coming out of the country, the father of Alexander and Rufus, to go with him, to bear his cross—Mark 15:21

How little these people knew that they were making this man immortal! What a strange fate that is which has befallen those persons in the Gospel narrative, who for an instant come into contact with Jesus Christ. Like ships passing across the white splendor of the moonlight on the sea, they gleam silvery pure for a moment as they cross the track, and then are lost and swallowed up again in the darkness.

This man Simon, fortuitously, as men say, meeting the little procession at the gate of the city, for an instant is caught in the radiance of the light, and stands out visible forevermore to all the world; and then sinks into the blackness, and we know no more about him. This brief glimpse tells us very little, and yet the man and his act and its consequences may be worth thinking about. If that man had started from the little village where he lived five minutes earlier or later, if he had walked a little faster or slower, if he had happened to be lodging on the other side of Jerusalem, or if the whim had taken him to go in at another gate, or if the centurion's eye had not chanced to alight on him in the crowd, or if the centurion's fancy had picked out somebody else to carry the cross—then all his life would have been different. And so it is always. You go down one turning rather than another, and your whole career is colored thereby. You miss a train, and you save your life. Our lives are like the Cornish rocking stones, pivoted on little points. The most apparently insignificant things have got such a strange knack of suddenly developing unexpected consequences, and turning out to be, not small things at all, but great and decisive and fruitful.

And so let us draw from that thought such lessons as these. Let us look with ever fresh wonder on this marvelous contexture of human life, and on Him that molds it all to His own perfect purposes. Let us bring the highest and largest principles to bear on the smallest events and circumstances, for you never can tell which of these is going to turn out a revolutionary and formative influence in your life. And if the highest and the holiest Christian principle is not brought to bear upon the trifles, depend upon it it will never be brought to bear upon the mighty things.

Indeed, in one sense life is made up of trifles; and if the highest religious motives are not brought to bear upon the trifles of life, they will very seldom be brought to bear at all, and life, which is divided into grains like the sand, will have gone by with him while he is preparing for the big events which he thinks worthy of being regulated by lofty principles. Take care of the pennies and the pounds will take care of themselves. Look after the trifles, for the law of life is like that which is laid down by the psalmist about the kingdom of Jesus Christ: "There shall be a handful of corn in the earth" [Ps. 72:16], a little seed sown in an apparently ungenial place "on the top of the mountains." But this will come of it, as the verse continues: "the fruit thereof shall shake like Lebanon" and the great harvest of benediction or of curse, of joy or of sorrow, will come from the minute seeds that are sown in the *great* trifles of your daily life.

THE BLESSEDNESS AND HONOR OF HELPING JESUS CHRIST

Helpers in Christ Jesus—Rom. 16:3

There are plenty of men in this day that scoff at Jesus, that mock Him, that deny His claims, that seek to cast Him down from His throne, that rebel against His dominion. It is an easy thing to be a disciple when all the crowd is crying "Hosanna!" It is a much harder thing to be a disciple when the crowd, or even when the influential cultivated opinion of a generation, is crying "Crucify Him! Crucify Him!" And some of you Christian men and women have to learn the lesson that if you are to be Christians you must be Christ's companions when His back is at the wall as well as when men are exalting and honoring Him; that it is your business to confess Him when men deny Him, to stand by Him when men forsake Him, to avow Him when the avowal is likely to bring contempt upon us with some people; and thus, if not to bear our own cross, yet in a very real sense to bear His Cross after Him. Let us go forth unto Him without the camp, bearing His reproach; the tail end of His Cross, it is the lightest! He has got the heaviest on His own shoulders, but we have to ally ourselves with that suffering, and if it be, with that despised Christ, if we are to be His disciples.

There will be hostility, alienation, a comparative coolness, and absence of a full sense of sympathy in many people, with you, if you are a true Christian. There will be a share of contempt from the wise and the cultivated of this generation, as in all generations. The mud that is thrown after the Master will spatter your faces too, to some extent; and if we are walking with Him, we shall share to the extent of our communion with Him in the feelings with which many men regard Him. Stand to your colors! Do not be ashamed of the Master in the midst of a crooked and perverse generation.

Christ needs nothing, and yet He needs us. He needs nothing, and yet He needed that donkey that was tethered at the place where two ways met, in order to ride into Jerusalem upon it. He does not need man's help, and yet He does need it, and He asks for it. And though He bore Simon the Cyrenean's sins "in His own body on the tree" [1 Pet. 2:24], he needed Simon the Cyrenean to help Him to bear the tree.

And He needs us to help Him to spread throughout the world the blessed consequences of that Cross and bitter passion. So for us all there is granted the honor, and from us all there is required the sacrifice and the service of helping the suffering Savior.

THE HUMBLEST CHRISTIAN
SERVICE REWARDED

*Wheresoever the gospel shall be preached throughout the whole world, this also
that she hath done shall be spoken of for a memorial of her—Mark 14:9*

The lesson drawn from the story of Simon of Cyrene is that of the perpetual recompense and record of humblest Christian work. There were different degrees of criminality, and different degrees of sympathy with Him, if I may use the word, in that crowd that stood around the Master. The criminality varied from the highest degree of violent malignity in the Scribes and Pharisees, down to the lowest point of ignorance, and therefore innocence, on the part of the Roman legionaries who were merely the mechanical instruments of the order given, and stolidly "watched Him there" [Matt. 27:36] with eyes which saw nothing.

And, on the other hand, all grades of service, and help and sympathy, from the vague emotions of the crowd who beat their breasts, and the pity of the daughters of Jerusalem, the kindly-meant help of the soldiers who would have moistened the parched lips, and the heroic love of the women at the Cross, whose ministry was not ended even with His life. But surely the most blessed share in that day's tragedy was reserved for Simon the Cyrene, whose bearing of the Cross may have been compulsory at first, but became, before it was ended, willing service.

But, whatever were the degrees of recognition of Christ's character, and of sympathy with the meaning of His sufferings, yet the smallest and the most transient impulse of loving gratitude that went out towards Him was rewarded then, and is rewarded forever, by blessed results in the heart that feels it. Besides these, service for Christ is recompensed, as in the instance before us, by a perpetual memorial: "How little Simon knew that wherever in the whole world this gospel was preached, there also this that *he* had done should be told for a memorial of him" How little he understood when he went back to his rural lodging that night that he had written his name high up on the tablet of the world's memory, to be legible forever.

Why, men have fretted their whole lives away to get what this man got, and knew nothing of one line in that chronicle of fame.

And so we may say it shall be always, "I will never forget any of their works." We may not leave them on any records that men can read. What of that, if they are written in letters of light in that "Lamb's Book of Life," to be read out by Him before His Father and the holy angels in that last great day? We may not leave any separable traces of our service, any more than the little brook that comes down some gully on the hillside flows separate from its sisters, with whom it has coalesced in the bed of the great river or in the rolling, boundless ocean. What of that, so long as the work, in its consequences, shall last? Men that sow some great prairie broadcast cannot go into the harvest field and say, "I sowed the seed from which that ear came, and you the seed from this." But the waving abundance belongs to them all, and each may be sure that his work survives and is glorified there; "that he that soweth and he that reapeth may rejoice together" [John 4:36]. So a perpetual remembrance is sure for the smallest Christian service.

THE BLESSEDNESS OF CONTACT WITH THE SUFFERING CHRIST

The fellowship of his sufferings—Phil. 3:10

Simon the Cyrenean apparently knew nothing about Jesus Christ when the Cross was laid on his shoulders. He would be reluctant to undertake the humiliating task, and would plod along behind Him for a while, sullen and discontented, but by degrees be touched by more of sympathy and get closer and closer to the Sufferer. And if he stood by the Cross when it was fixed, and saw all that transpired there, no wonder if, after a longer or a shorter examination, he came to understand who He was that he had helped, and to yield himself to Him wholly.

Yes! Christ's great saying, "I, if I be lifted up, will draw all men unto me" [John 12:32], began to be fulfilled when He began to be lifted up. The centurion, the thief, and Simon of Cyrene, by looking on the Cross, recognized the Crucified.

And it is the only way by which any of us will ever learn the true mystery and miracle of Christ's great and loving Being and work. I beseech you, take your places there behind Him, near His Cross, gazing upon Him till your hearts melt, and you, too, learn that He is your Lord, and your Savior, and your God. The Cross of Jesus Christ divides men into classes, as the Last Day will. It, too, parts men—sheep to the right hand, goats to the left. If there was a penitent, there was an impenitent, thief; if there was a convinced centurion, there were gambling soldiers; if there were hearts touched with compassion, there were mockers who took His very agonies and flung them in His face as a refutation of His claims. On the day that Cross was reared on Calvary it began to be what it has been ever since, and is at this moment to every soul that reads this, "a savor of life unto life, or of death unto death" [2 Cor. 2:16]. Contact with the suffering Christ will either bind you to His service, and fill you with His Spirit, or it will harden your hearts, and make you tenfold more selfish—that is to say, tenfold more a child of hell than you were before you saw and touched and handled that Divine meekness of the suffering Christ. Look to Him, I beseech you, who bears what none can help Him to carry, the burden of the world's sin. Let Him bear yours, and yield to Him your grateful obedience, and then take up your cross daily [see Luke 9:23] and bear the light burden of self-denying service to Him who has borne the heavy load of sin for you and all mankind.

THE CRY FROM THE DEPTHS

Out of the depths have I cried unto thee, O Lord. Lord, hear my voice: let thine ears be attentive to the voice of my supplications—Psalm 130:1, 2

The depths are the place for us all. Every man has to go down there, if he takes the place that belongs to him. Unless you have cried to God out of these depths, you have never cried to Him at all. Unless you come to Him as a penitent, sinful man, with the consciousness of transgression awakened within you, your prayers are shallow. The beginning of all true personal religion lies in the sense of my own sin and my lost condition. Why, the difference between the tepid, superficial religion, that so many have, and the true thing consists a great deal more in this than in anything else—that in the one case a sense of sin has been awakened, and in the other it has not. I believe, for my part, that as far as creed is concerned, the reason of the larger number of the misapprehensions and watering-down, of the full-toned Christian truth which we see around us comes from this, that men have not appreciated the importance, as a factor in their theology, of the doctrine of sin. And so far as practice is concerned, one main reason why the religion that prevails is such a poor, flabby, powerless thing is the same. If a man does not think much about sin, he does not think much about a Divine Savior. Wherever you find practically men and women with a Christianity that lies very lightly upon them, that does not impel them to any acts of service and devotion, that seldom breaks out into any heroism of self-surrender, and never rises into the heights of communion with God, depend upon it that the roots of it are to be found here, that the man has never been down there into the pit, and never sent his voice up from it as some man that has tumbled down a coalpit might fling a despairing voice up to the surface, in the hope that somebody stumbling past the mouth of it might hear the cry. "Out of the depths" he has not cried unto God.

You want nothing more than a cry to get you out of the depths. If out of the depths you cry, you will cry yourself out of the depths. Here is a man at the foot of a cliff that rises beetling like a black wall behind him; the sea in front; the bare, upright rock at his back; not a foothold for a mouse between the tide at the bottom and the grass at the top there. What is he going to do? There is only one thing—he can shout. Perchance somebody will hear him; a rope may come dangling down in front of him; and, if he has got nerve, he may shut his eyes and make a jump and catch it. There is no way for you up out of the pit but to cry to God, and that will bring a rope down; nay, rather, the rope is there—your grasping the rope and your cry are one. "Ask, and ye shall receive" [John 16:24]. God has let down the fullness of His forgiving love in Jesus Christ, and all that we need is the call, which is likewise faith, which accepts while it desires, and desires in its acceptance; and then we are lifted up there "out of a horrible pit, out of the miry clay, and set my feet upon a rock, and established my goings" [Ps. 40:2].

A DARK FEAR

If thou, Lord, shouldest mark iniquities, O Lord, who shall stand?—Psalm 130:3

To "mark iniquities" is to impute them to us. The word in the original means to watch—that is to say, to remember in order to punish. If a man be regarded by God's eye through the mist of his own sins, they turn the bright sun of God's own light into a red-hot flaming ball of fire. Like a man having to yield ground to an eager enemy, or to bend before the blast, every man has to bow before that flashing brightness, and to own that retribution would be destruction.

Do we not all know that our characters and our lives have been, as it were, distorted; that our moral nature has been marred with animal lusts, and that ambitions and worldly desires have come in and prevented us from following the law of conscience? Is not that very conscience, more or less distorted, drugged and dormant? And is not all this largely voluntary? Do we not feel, in spite of all pleas about circumstances and "heredity," that we could have helped being what we are? And do we not feel that, after all, if there be such a thing as God's judgment and retribution, it must come on us with terrible force? That is what the Psalmist means when he says that if God be strict to mark iniquities there is not one of us that can stand before Him; and we know it is true. You may be a very respectable man; that is not the question. You may have kept your hands clear from anything that would bring you within the sweep of the law; that has nothing to do with it. You may have subdued animal passions, been sober, temperate, chaste, generous—a hundred other things. Granted, of course! Gross, palpable sin slays its thousands; and that clean, white, respectable, ghastly purity of a godless, self-complacent morality, I do believe, slays its tens of thousands. And you, not because your goodness is not goodness of a sort, but because you are building upon it, and think that such words as those of the Psalmist, go clean over your heads—you are in this perilous position.

Oh, dear friend! Will you take ten minutes quietly to think over that verse, "If Thou, Lord, shouldest mark iniquities, O Lord, who shall stand?" Can I? CAN I?

Is it not true that, deep below the surface, contentment with the world and the things of the world, a dormant, but lightly slumbering, sense of want and unsatisfied need, lies in your souls? Is it not true that it wakes sometimes at a touch; that the tender, dying light of sunset, or the calm abysses of the mighty heavens, or some strain of music, or a line in a book, or a sorrow in your heart, or the solemnity of a great joy, or close contact with sickness and death, or the more direct appeals of Scripture and of Christ, astir a wistful yearning and a painful sense of emptiness in your hearts, and of insufficiency in all the ordinary pursuits of your lives?

A BRIGHT ASSURANCE

But there is forgiveness with thee, that thou mayest be feared—Psalm 130:4

"Forgiveness?" The word so translated has for its literal meaning "cutting-off," "excision." And so it suggests the notion of taking a man's soul and his sin, that great black deformity that has grown upon it, feeding upon it, and cutting it clean out with a merciful amputating knife. You know that doctors sometimes say, "Well, the only salvation of him would be an operation, but the tumor has got so implicated with the vital tissues that it would scarcely be possible to apply the knife." And that is what the world says, and that is what philosophy says, and modern pessimism says, about my sin, and your sin, and the world's sin. "No! We cannot operate; we cannot cut out the cantankerous tumor." And Christianity says, "Miserable physicians are ye all; stand aside!" And it does it by a mighty and wondrous act.

God's Divine mercy and infinite power and love are in that Cross of Jesus Christ, which separates between man and his disease, and cuts out the one and leaves the other more living after the amputation of that which was killing him, and which the world thinks to be a bit of himself. It is not a bit of himself, says the Gospel; it can all be swept away through His forgiveness.

Men may say, "There cannot be forgiveness; you cannot alter consequences." But forgiveness has not to do only with consequences; forgiveness has to do with the personal relation between me and God. And that can be altered. The Father forgives as well as the judge; the Father forgives, though he sometimes chastises.

If a man has sinned, his whole life thereafter will be different from what it would have been if he had not sinned. I know that well enough. You cannot, by any pardon, alter the past, and make it not to be. I know that well enough. The New Testament doctrine and the Old Testament hope of forgiveness does not assert that you can, but it says that you and God can get right with one another. A person can pardon. We have not merely to do with impersonal laws and symbols; we have not only to do with "the mill of God that grindeth slowly," but with God Himself. There is such a thing as the pardon of God, and forgiveness is possible. His love will come to men free, unembittered, undammed back by transgressions, if the man will go and say, "Father! I have sinned! Forgive! For Thy dear Son's sake. There is forgiveness with Thee!" And that forgiveness lies at the root of all true godliness. "There is forgiveness with Thee, *that Thou mayest be feared.*" No man reverences, and loves, and draws near to God so rapturously, so humbly, as the man that has learned pardon through Jesus Christ. My dear friend, believe this: your religion must have for its foundation the assurance of God's pardoning mercy in Christ, or it will have no foundation at all worth speaking about. I press that upon you, and ask you this one question: Is the basis of your religion the sense that God has forgiven you freely all your iniquities?

GOD'S INEXHAUSTIBLE MERCY

Let Israel hope in the Lord; for with the Lord there is mercy, and with him is
plenteous redemption. And he shall redeem Israel from all his iniquities—
Ps. 130:7, 8

There is nothing which isolates a man so severely as a consciousness of sin and of his relation to God. But there is nothing that so knits him to all his fellows, and brings him into such wide-reaching bonds of amity and benevolence, as the sense of God's forgiving mercy for his own sin. So the call bursts from the lips of the pardoned man, inviting all to taste the experience and exercise the trust which have made him glad: "Let Israel hope in the Lord." Look at the broad Gospel he has come to preach. "For with the Lord there is mercy, and with Him is redemption." Not only forgiveness; but redemption—and that from every form of sin. It is "plenteous"—multiplied, as the word might be rendered. Our Lord has taught us to what a sum that Divine multiplication amounts. Not once, nor twice, nor thrice, but "seventy times seven" is the prescribed measure of human forgiveness; and shall men be more placable than God? The perfect numbers, seven and ten multiplied together, and that again increased sevenfold, to make a numerical symbol for the Innumerable, and to bring the Infinite within the terms of the Finite. It is inexhaustible redemption, not to be provoked, not to be overcome by any obstinacy of evil—available for all, available for every grade and every repetition of transgression. That forgiving grace is older and mightier than all sins, and is able to conquer them all. As when an American prairie for hundreds of miles is smoking in the autumn fires, nothing that man can do can cope with it. But the clouds gather, and down comes the rain, and there is water enough in the sky to put out the fire. And so God's inexhaustible mercy, streaming down upon the lurid smoke-pillars of man's transgression, and that alone, is weight enough to quench the flame of man's and of a world's, transgressions, heated from the lowest hell. "With him is plenteous redemption; And he shall redeem Israel from *all* his iniquities." That is the Old Testament prophecy. Let me leave on your hearts the New Testament fulfillment of it. The Psalmist said, "He shall redeem Israel from all his iniquities." He was sure of that, and his soul was at "peace in believing" [Rom. 15:13] it. But there were mysteries about it which he could not understand. He lived in the twilight dawn, and he and all his fellows had to watch for the morning, of which they saw but the faint promise in the Eastern sky. The sun is risen for us—"Thou shalt call His name JESUS, for He shall save His people from their sins" [Luke 1:31]. That is the fulfillment, the vindication, and the explanation of the Psalmist's hope. Lay hold of Christ, and He will lift you out of the depths, and set you upon the sunny heights of the mountain of God.

April 5

THE ONE HELPER

A very present help in trouble—Psalm 46:1

Many of us are trying to make up for not having the One by seeking to stay our hearts on the many. But no accumulation of insufficiencies will ever make a sufficiency. You may fill the heaven all over with stars bright and thick as those in the whitest spot in the galaxy, and it will be night still. Day needs the sun, and the sun is one, and when it comes the twinkling lights are forgotten. You cannot make up for God by any extended series of creatures, any more than a row of figures that stretched from here to *Sirius* and back again would approximate to infinitude.

The very fact of the multitude of helpers is a sign that none of them are sufficient. There are no end of "cures" for toothache—that is to say, there is none. There are no end of helps for men that have abandoned God—that is to say, every one in turn, when it is tried, and the stress of the soul rests upon it, gives, and is found to be a broken staff that pierces the hand that leans upon it.

Consult your own experience. What is the meaning of the unrest and distraction that marks the lives of most of the men in this generation? Why is it that you hurry from business to pleasure, from pleasure to business, until it is scarcely possible to get a quiet breathing time for thought at all? Why is it but because one after another of your gods have proved insufficient, and so fresh altars must be built for fresh idolatries, and new experiments made, of which we can safely prophecy the result will be the old one. We have not gotten beyond St. Augustine's saying: "Oh, God! My heart was made for Thee, and in Thee only doth it find repose." The many idols, though you multiply them beyond count, all put together, will never make the one God. You are seeking what you will never find. The many pearls that you seek will never be enough for you. The true wealth is One, One pearl of great price [Matt. 13:46].

The Lord may seem to sleep on His hard, wooden pillow on the stern of the little fishing-boat, and even while the frail craft begins to fill may show no sign of help, but before the waves have rolled over her, the cry of fear that yet trusts, and of trust that yet fears, wakes Him who knew the need, even while He seemed to slumber, and one mighty word, as of a master to some petulant slave, "Peace, be still" [Mark 4:39], hushes the confusion, and rebukes the fear, and rewards the faith. We on whom the ends of the earth are come have the same Helper, the same Friend, that "the world's gray patriarchs" had. They that go before do not prevent them that come after. The river is full still. The van of the pilgrim host did, indeed, long, long ago, drink, and were satisfied, but the bright waters are still as transparent, still as near, still as refreshing, still as abundant as they ever were.

THE PROOF OF GOD'S LOVE

God commendeth his love toward us, in that, while we were yet sinners, Christ died for us—Rom. 5:8

"God *commendeth* His love." That is true and beautiful, but that is not all that the Apostle means. The idea of commendation is certainly in it, but there is also another idea which in order precedes the commendation—namely, that of confirmation, or establishing as a certainty. Now these two things are ordinarily separated. We first of all prove a fact, and then we press it upon people, or "commend" it to their feelings; but in regard of the love of God these two are one. You cannot prove God's love as you can a mathematical problem, as a bare intellectual process. You must prove it by showing it in operation; and the confirmation of its existence which is derived from the witness of its energy is at once the demonstration of it to the understanding and the commending of it to the heart and the feelings.

So, says Paul, God in one and the same act establishes the certainty of His love, for our understanding, and presses it upon our hearts and consciences. "He commends His love toward us." It must be kept in mind that Paul was writing to Roman Christians, a good many years after the death of Jesus Christ—to men and women that had never seen Christ, and whom Christ had never seen in the flesh. And to these people he says, "Christ died for *us*." You Roman believers that never heard about Him till long after His Crucifixion—He died for *you*. And God, not *commended*, but "*commendeth*, His love toward us" in that death—which, put into other words, is this: the Cross of Jesus Christ is for all the world, for every age, the standing and ever-present demonstration of the boundless love of God. God not merely "commends," but "proves," His love by Christ's death. It is the one evidence which makes that often doubted fact certain. By it alone is it possible to hold the conviction that, in spite of all that seems to contradict the belief, God *is* love [1 John 4:8].

If this be the summing-up of all religion, a practical conclusion follows. When we feel ourselves defective in the glow and operative driving power of love to God, what is the right thing to do? When a man is cold he will not warm himself by putting a clinical thermometer into his mouth, and taking his temperature, will he? Let him go into the sunshine and he will be warmed up. You can pound ice in a mortar, and except for the little heat generated by the impact of the pestle, it will keep ice still. But float the iceberg down into the tropics, and what has become of it? It has all run down into sweet warm water, and mingled with the warm ocean that has dissolved it. So do not think about yourself and your own loveless heart so much, but think about God, and the infinite welling up of love in His heart to you, a great deal more. "We love him because He first loved us." Therefore, to love Him more, we must feel more that He does love us.

Then let me say, too, that if we love Him, it will be the motive power and spring of all manners of obedience and glad services. It is the mother color, so to speak, which you can color, and to which you can add in various ways, and produce variously tinted and tasted and perfumed commixtures. Love lies at the foundation of all Christian goodness. It will lead to the subjugation of the will. And that is the thing that is most of all needed to make a man righteous and pure. So St. Augustine's paradox, rightly understood, is a magnificent truth, "Love! And do what you will." For then you will be sure to will what God wills, and you ought.

❋

FOR HIS SAKE

I do not this for your sakes . . . but for mine holy name's sake—Ezek. 36:22

Do you not think that the Cross of Jesus Christ speaks to the world of a love which is not drawn forth by any merit of goodness in us? Men love because they dimly discern, or think they do, that there is something worthy of their love. God loves because we need Him; God loves because He is God. His love is not evoked by anything in me, except my dependence and necessity; but God's love wells up from the infinite depth of His own nature, undrawn forth by anything in His creatures. "I Am that I Am" [Ex. 3:14] is His name. He is His own cause, His own motive; and as His being, so His love, which is His being, is automatic, self-originated, and pouring out forever, in obedience to the impulse of His own heart, the inexhaustible treasures of His love. "Not for your sakes, O house of Israel, but for Mine own Name's sake."

But if that love revealed by the Cross be a love which is not drawn forth by any merit or goodness of ours, then, not being contingent upon our goodness, it is not turned away by our badness. We cannot sin it away. It was not bestowed on us at first, any more than His sunshine falls on us, because we deserve it, but because He is God, and He made us. And so it will encircle us forever, and cleave to us to the very end, and never let us go.

The Cross of Christ preaches to us a love that has no cause, motive, reason, or origin except Himself.

That is what is meant by the theological phrase "free grace"—an expression which has often been regarded as the byword of a narrow school, but which, rightly understood, is no hard piece of technical theology, but throbbing with life—the very grandest conception of the heart of God which men can grasp. Such grace, the gift of such love, does the Christ commend to us.

"For our behalf,"—bending over us in order that the benefit might come to us—that is the picturesque metaphor that lies in the little word "for." Observe, too, the significant present tense, "God commend*eth* His love," and the emphatic repetition three separate times in the verse (Rom. 5:8) of "us" and "we." Both peculiarities bring out the great truth that Christ's death is a death, "not for an age, but for all time"; not for this, that, or the other man; not for a section of the race, but for the whole of us—in all generations. The power of that death, as the sweep of that love, extends over all humanity, and holds forth benefits to every man of woman born.

IS CHRIST'S DEATH A REAL BENEFIT TO ME?

Lord, to whom shall we go? thou hast the words of eternal life—John 6:68

Now, I want to ask a question very earnestly: In what conceivable way *can* Christ's death be a real benefit to me? How can it do me any good? A sweet, a tender, an unexampled, beautiful story of innocence and meekness and martyrdom which will shine in the memory of the world, and on the pages of history, as long as the world shall last! It is all that; but what good does it do me? Where does the benefit to me individually come in? There is only one answer, and I urge you to ask yourselves, if, in plain, sober, common sense, the death of Jesus Christ means anything at all to anybody, more than other martyrdoms and beautiful deaths, except upon one supposition, that He died *for* us, because He died *instead of* us. The two things are not identical; but, as I believe, and venture to press upon you, in this case they are identical. I do not know where you will find any justification for the rapturous language of the whole New Testament about the death of Christ and its benefits flowing to the whole world, unless you take the Master's own words, "The Son of Man . . . came to minister, and to give His life a ransom *for* many" [Matt. 20:28; Mark 10:45].

Ah! Dear friend, there we touch the bed-rock. That is the truth that flashes up the Cross into lustre, before which the sun's light is but darkness. He who bore it died for the whole world, and was the eternal Son of the Father. If we believe that, then we can understand how Paul here blends together the heart of God and the heart of Christ, and sets high above Nature and her ambiguous oracles, high above Providence and its many perplexities, and in front of all the shrinkings and the fears of a reasonably alarmed conscience, the one truth, "God commendeth his love for us, in that, while we were yet sinners, Christ died for us." Is that your faith, your notion of Christ's death, and of its relation to the love of God?

There are two passages of Scripture which contain the whole secret of God, and the whole secret of a noble, blessed, human life. And here they are: "God so loved the world that he gave his only begotten Son, that whosoever believeth in him shall not perish, but have everlasting life." [John 3:16]. If that is your thought about God, you know enough about Him for time and eternity. "We love Him because He first loved us" [1 John 4:19]. If you can say that about yourself, all is well.

Dear friend, do you believe the one? Do you affirm the other?

SLEEPING THROUGH JESUS

For if we believe that Jesus died and rose again, even so them also asleep in Jesus will God bring with him—1 Thess. 4:14

They "sleep through Him." It is by reason of Christ and His work, and by reason of that alone, that death's darkness is made beautiful, and death's grimness is softened down to this. Now, in order to grasp the full meaning of such words as these of the Apostle, we must draw a broad distinction between the physical fact of the ending of corporeal life and the mental condition which is associated with it by us. What we call death, if I may say so, is a complex thing—bodily phenomenon *plus* conscience; the sense of sin, the certainty of retribution in the dim beyond. And you have to take these two apart. The former remains; but if the other is removed, the whole has changed its character, and is become another thing, and a very little thing. The death of Jesus Christ takes all the—I was going to say the *nimbus* of apprehension and dread arising from conscience and sin, and the forecast of retribution—takes all that away. There is nothing left for us to face except the physical fact; and any poor soldier, with a coarse red coat upon him, will face that for eighteenpence a day, and think himself well paid. Jesus Christ has abolished death, leaving the mere shell, but taking all the substance out of it. It has become a different thing to men, because in that death of His He has exhausted the bitterness, and has made it possible that we should pass into the shadow, and not fear either conscience or sin or judgment.

So, dear "brethren, I would not have you to be ignorant concerning them which are asleep, that ye sorrow not even as others which have no hope" [1 Thess. 4:13]. And I would have you to remember that while Christ by His work has made it possible that the terror may pass away, and death may be softened and minimized into slumber, it will not be so with you—unless you are joined to Him, and by trust in the power of His death, and the overflowing might of His resurrection, have made sure that what He has passed through, you will pass through, and where He is, and what He is, you will be also.

Two men die by one railway accident, sitting side by side upon one seat, smashed in one collision. But though the outward fact is the same about each, the reality of their deaths is infinitely different. The one falls asleep through Jesus, in Jesus; the other dies indeed, and the death of his body is only a feeble shadow of the death of the spirit. Do you knit yourself to the Life, which is Christ, and, then, "He that believeth on Me shall never die" [see John 11:26]!

April 10

REST AND CONSCIOUSNESS

As for me, I will behold thy face in righteousness: I shall be satisfied, when I awake, with thy likeness—Ps 17:15

The "sleeper in Christ" is not unconscious. He is parted from the outer world; he is unaware of externals. When Stephen knelt below the old wall, and was surrounded by howling fanatics that slew him, one moment he was gashed with stones and tortured, and the next "he fell asleep" [Acts 7:60]. They might howl, and the stones fly as they would, and he was all unaware of it. Like Jonah sleeping in the hold, what did the howling of the storm matter to him? But separation from externals does not mean suspense of life or of consciousness; and the slumberer often dreams, and is aware of himself persistently throughout his slumber. Nay! Some of his faculties are set at liberty to work more energetically because his connection with the outer world is for the time suspended.

Scripture, as it seems to me, distinctly carries this limitation of the emblem. For what does it mean when the Apostle says, "to depart . . . to be with Christ . . . is far better" [Phil. 1:23]? Surely he that thus spoke conceived that these two things were contemporaneous, "the departing and the being with Him." And surely he who thus spoke could not have conceived that a millennium-long parenthesis of slumberous unconsciousness was to intervene between the moment of his decease and the moment of his fellowship with Jesus. How could a man prefer that dormant state to the state here, of working for and living with the Lord? Surely, being with Him must mean that we know where we are and who is our companion.

And what does that text mean, "Ye are come . . . to the spirits of just men made perfect" [Heb. 12:22, 23], unless it means that one of these two classes of persons who are thus regarded as brought into living fellowship, each is aware of the other? Does perfecting of the spirit mean the smiting of the spirit into unconsciousness? Surely not, and surely in the face of such words as these we must recognize the fact that, however limited and imperfect may be the present connection with the disembodied dead, who sleep in Christ, with external things—they know themselves, they know their home and their companions, and they know the blessedness in which they are lapped.

We have also the idea of awaking. The pagans said, as indeed one of their poets has it, "Suns can sink and return, but for us, when our brief light sinks, there is but one perpetual night of slumber." The Christian idea of death is that it is transitory as a sleep in the morning, and sure to end. As St. Augustine says somewhere, "Wherefore are they called sleepers but because in the day of the Lord they will be re-awakened."

"THEM THAT SLEEP"

So he giveth to his beloved sleep—Ps. 127:2

Sweetest, deepest, most appealing to all our hearts is that emblem of death, "Them that sleep" [Dan. 12:2]. It is used, if I count rightly, some fourteen times in the New Testament, and it carries with it large and plain lessons, on which I touch but for a moment. What, then, does this metaphor say to us?

Well, it speaks first of rest. That is not altogether an attractive conception to some of us. If it be taken exclusively, it is by no means wholesome. I suppose that the young, and the strong, and the eager, and the ambitious, and the prosperous rather shrink from the notion of their activities being stiffened into slumber. But, dear friend, there are some of us, like tired children in a fair, who would gladly do away with the weariness, who have made experience of the distractions and bewildering changes, whose backs are stiffened with toil, whose hearts are heavy with loss. And to all of us, in some moods, the prospect of shuffling off this weary coil of responsibilities and duties, and tasks and sorrows, and of passing into indisturbance and repose, is appealing. I believe, for my part, that after all the deepest longing of men, though they search for it through toil and effort, the deepest longing is for repose. As the poet has taught us, "there is no joy but calm." Every heart is weary enough, and heavy laden, and laboring enough, to feel the sweetness of a promise of rest—

"Sleep, full of rest from head to foot,
    Lie still, dry dust, secure of change."

Yes! But the rest of which our emblem speaks is, as I believe, only applicable to the bodily frame. The word "sleep" is a transcript of what sense enlightened by faith sees in that still form, with the folded hands and the quiet face and the closed eyes. But let us remember that this repose, deep and blessed as it is, is not, as some would say, the repose of unconsciousness. I do not believe, and I would not have you to believe, that this emblem touches the vigorous spiritual life, or that the passage from out of the toil and moil of earth into the calm of the darkness beyond has any power in limiting or suspending the vital force of the man.

THE SLEEP OF DEATH

Our friend Lazarus sleepeth; but I go, that I may awake him out of sleep—
John 11:11

It is to Jesus primarily that the New Testament writers owe their use of this gracious emblem of sleep. For, as you remember, the word was twice upon our Lord's lips; once when, over the twelve-years-old maid, from whom life had barely ebbed away, he said, "She is not dead, but sleepeth" [Luke 8:52]; and once when, in regard of the man Lazarus, from whom life had removed further, he said, "Our friend sleepeth, but I go that I may awake him out of his sleep." But Jesus was not the originator of the expression. You find it in the Old Testament, where the prophet Daniel, speaking of the end of the days and the bodily resurrection, designates those who share in it as "them that sleep in the dust of the earth" [Dan. 12:2]. And the Old Testament was not the sole origin of the phrase. For it is too natural, too much in accordance with the visibilities of death, not to have suggested itself to many hearts and been enshrined in many tongues. Many an inscription of Greek and Roman times speaks sadly of death under this figure. But almost always it is with the added, deepened note of despair, that it is a sleep which knows no waking, but lasts through eternal night.

Now, the Christian thought associated with this emblem is the precise opposite of the pagan one. The pagan heart shrank from the ugly thing because it was so ugly. So dark and deep a dread coiled around the man as he contemplated it that he sought to drape the grimness in some kind of thin transparent veil, and to put the buffer of a word between him and its ugliness. But the Christian's motive for the use of the word is the precise opposite. He uses the gentler expression because the thing has become gentler.

You find one class of representations in the New Testament which speak of death as being a departing and a being with Christ; or which call it, as one of the Apostles does, an "exodus," where it is softened down to be merely a change of environment, a change of locality. Then another class of representations speak of it as "putting off this my tabernacle," or, the dissolution of the "earthly house" [2 Cor. 5:1]—where there is a broad, firm line of demarcation drawn between the inhabitant and the habitation, and the thing is softened down to be a mere change of dwelling. Again, another class of expressions speak of it as being an "offering" [2 Tim. 4:6], where the main idea of that of a voluntary surrender, a sacrifice or libation of myself, and my life poured out upon the altar of God.

A LOVE THAT SHRINKS FROM NO SACRIFICE

He that spared not his own Son, but delivered him up for us all, how shall he not with him also freely give us all things?—Rom. 8:32

I cannot venture to use words of my own about such a subject, but I read in this very Epistle of Romans of a wonderful comparison, which to me is most beautiful and most instructive, and wakens thoughts that are perhaps too blessed and too mystic to be put into words, when I read, "He that spared not his own Son, but freely delivered him up to the death for us all"; and recognize there an allusive reference to that old story, surely the most touching in the pages of the Old Testament history, of the father and son going up the mountain side together to the mysterious sacrifice, and of the sorrow that passed over the heart of Abraham when he had to give up Isaac at the command of the Divine voice. Some shadow of what men call "giving up" and "loss" may be conceived to have passed across the mirror of the Divine experience when Christ died. I know not; I dare not speak about such things, but I do say that Christ's Cross preaches to you and me of a love on the part of our Father God which shrinks from no sacrifices. "God so loved the world that he gave his only begotten Son" [John 3:16]. That Cross proves to you and presses upon you a love which wants nothing but your love; which hungers, if I may so say, for the return of your love and of your thankfulness. A great poet of our own generation has described, with an allowable boldness, God as sitting amid His angels, praising Him as with a voice of many thunders, and of harpers with their harps, and saying about one poor man's voice that had for awhile become silent, "I miss my little human praise." It is true. He wants your love. "The Father seeketh," said Christ—how strange and beautiful!—"the Father seeketh such to worship him" [John 4:23]. "My son, give me thine heart" [Prov. 23:26], is the inmost meaning of Christ's Cross. Yield your love to Him, and then your Father will say as you come back, "It was meet that we should be glad, for this my son was dead, and is alive again" [see Luke 15:24, 32].

GOD'S LOVE DEMONSTRATED

In this was manifested the love of God toward us, becauase that God hath sent his only begotten Son into the world, that we might live through him—1 John 4:9

What is the connection between God's love and Christ's death? How does any, even the most extreme, love and regard and self-sacrifice on the part of Jesus—how does that demonstrate *God's* love? Is it not obvious that we must conceive the relation between God and Christ to be singularly close in order that Christ's death should prove God's love?

Suppose it had been said, "*Paul's* death proves the love of God?"—there would have been no probative force in that fact. But when we read "Christ's death proves it," I would press this question: Does the assertion hold water, and is there any common sense in it at all except upon one supposition—that the man who said that God's love was proved by Christ's propitiatory death believed that the heart of Christ was the revelation of the heart of God; and that what Christ did, God did in His well-beloved Son?

If you believe, as I believe, that Jesus Christ was God manifest in the flesh, then it is reasonable to say, "God commendeth *His* love to us in that . . . *Christ* died for us" [Rom. 5:8].

Let us remember, too, that God's love is all-embracing, because it embraces each. It can only be true that Christ died for us all if every man on earth has a right to say, "Christ died for me."

That is what I pray you will do. Do not take shelter in the crowd. God does not deal with men in a crowd. And Christ's death was not for men in a crowd, it was not for the abstraction "humanity," "the world," "the race"; it was for men, one by one, each singly, as if there had not been another human being in existence except just that one. I believe that we were all in Christ's heart all in His purpose, when He gave Himself up to the death for us all; and that, therefore, His cross—on which He died that you and I, and all of us, might live; on which He yielded Himself up to the outward penalty of sin in order that none of its inward penalty might ever fall upon them that trust in Him—is the manifestation of the love of God to the whole world; because Christ's death embraced in its purpose the whole world, and every unit that is in it, and, therefore, thee, and thee, and thee, my brother! Do you believe that?

April 15

ALL TRUTH BASED UPON CHRISTIANITY

Every good gift and every perfect gift is from above, and cometh down from the Father of lights, with whom is no variableness, neither shadow of turning—James 1:17

There never was, and there is not, any religion untouched by Christianity that has any firm grip of that truth, "God is Love" [1 John 4:16]. There have been all kinds of deities in the world, outside the limits of the circle in which the influence of the Gospel has been felt. You have had cruel, capricious, good-natured, savage, vicious, revengeful, and impure deities. You have had the deification of lust and passion and favoritism and caprice, as well as of lofty and pure things; but there is no God of *Love* anywhere that ever I heard of, except where some faint rays of Christianity and its blessed message have come. And the people that now-a-days are kicking down the ladder by which they have climbed, and, in the name of this conviction which they owe to the Gospel of Jesus Christ, are turning around and rejecting that Gospel, are committing intellectual suicide, and strike away the very basis upon which the truth that they value so much rests. The fact remains that men have never been able to raise themselves up to, and maintain themselves at, the lofty level of the lofty belief that God is Love, when they have turned their backs on the Cross of Jesus Christ. Let history answer if they have!

I believe that the course of thought in cultivated Europe is coming to this plain alternative—that a mere bare theism cannot keep its hold, and that the choice is between Christ and His Cross on the one hand, and black disbelief in the love of God, and in God at all, on the other. These two will divide the field. There will either be a happy calm, triumphant hold of God's love manifest in Jesus Christ, or there will be a despairing sense that we walk in darkness as orphan creatures here, knowing not whether we have a Father and a home.

Oh, dear brother! Our own conscience may tell us, and the world's history may tell us, and men-made religions may tell us, that it is not an easy thing for a man to say, nor to believe in his heart, that God is Love.

And when God's love is proved, it needs to be pressed upon us; does it not? How we all forget it, and turn away from it, are careless about it; oppose ice to His flame, are selfish to His love, indifferent to His pleadings! Do not you, dear brother? Do we not need something that shall touch our hearts, and shall press upon us, as well as prove to us, the endless love of our Father God? I think we do.

THE DIVINE REDEEMER

God so loved the world that he gave his only begotten Son, that whosoever believeth in him should not perish, but have everlasting life—John 3:16

Christ's death proves God's love, because Christ is Divine. How else do you account for that extraordinary shifting of the persons in these words of Paul, "God commendeth his love to us, in that, while we were yet sinners, Christ died for us" [Rom. 5:8]? *God* proves His love because *Christ* died? How so? God proved His love because Socrates died? God proved his love because some self-sacrificing doctor went into a hospital, and died in curing others? God proved His love because some man sprang into the sea and rescued a drowning woman, at the cost of his own life? Would such talk hold? Then I want to know how it comes that Paul ventures to say that God proved His love because Jesus Christ died?

Unless we believe that Jesus Christ is the Eternal Son of the Father, whom the Father sent, and who willingly came for us and for our redemption; unless we believe that in Him dwelt all the fullness of the Godhead bodily; unless we believe that, as He Himself said, "He that hath seen me hath seen the Father" [John 14:19]; unless we believe that His death was the act, the consequence, and the revelation of the love of God, who dwelt in Him as in none other of the sons of men, I, for one, venture to think that Paul is talking nonsense, and that his argument is not worth a straw. You must come to the full-toned belief which, as I think, permeates and binds together every page of the New Testament—God so loved the world, and sent His Son to be the propitiation for our sins [1 John 2:2]; that Son who in the beginning was with God, and was God [John 1:1, 2]. And then a flood of light is poured on the words of Paul, and we can adoringly bow the head and say "Amen! God hath to my understanding, and to my heart, proved and commended His love, in that Christ died for us"

The death on the Cross was on our behalf, therefore it was the spontaneous outgush of an infinite love. It was for us, in that it brought an infinite benefit. And so it was a token and a manifestation of the love of God such as nothing else could be.

GOD PROVES HIS OWN LOVE

Herein is love, not that we loved God, but that he loved us, and sent his Son to be the propitiation for our sins—1 John 4:10

Let us think for a moment of the fact which is thus the demonstration of the love of God, and try to realize what it is that this Cross says to us, as we gaze upon the silent Sufferer meekly hanging there. I know that my words must fall far beneath the theme, but I can only hope that you will read them charitably, and try to better them for yourselves in your own thoughts.

I look, then, to the dying Christ, and I see there the revelation, because the consequence, of a love which is not called forth by any loveableness on the part of its objects. The Apostle emphasizes that thought, if we render his words fully, because he says, "God commendeth *his* love" [Rom. 5:8]—a love which, like all that belongs to that timeless, self-determining Being, has its reason and its roots in Himself alone! We love because we discern the object to be loveable. God loves by what I may venture to call the very necessity of His nature. Like some artesian well that needs no pumps nor machinery to draw up the sparkling waters to flash in the sunlight, there gushes up from the depths of His own heart the love which pours over every creature that He has made. He loves because He is God.

It is only the Gospel of a dying Christ that can calm the reasonable consciousness of discord and antagonism that springs in a man's heart when he lets his conscience speak. It is because He died for us that we are sure now that the black mountain wall of our sin, which, to our own apprehension, rises separating us and our God, is, if I may say so, surged over by the rising flood of His love. The Cross of Christ teaches me that, and so it is the gospel for men that know themselves to be sinners. Is there anything else that teaches it? I know not where it is, if there be.

That dying Christ, hanging there, in the silence and the darkness of eclipse, speaks to me, too, of a Divine love which, though not turned away by man's sin, is rigidly righteous. There is a current easy-going religion which says, "Oh! We do not want any of your evangelical contrivances for forgiveness. God is Love. That is enough for us." I venture to say that the thing which that form of thought calls love is not love at all, but pure weakness; such as in a king or in a father would be immoral. It is not otherwise in God. My brother! Unless you can find some means whereby the infinite love of God can get at and soothe the sinner's heart without periling God's righteousness, you have done nothing to the purpose. Such a one-eyed, lopsided gospel will never work, has not worked, and it never will. But, when I think of my Christ bearing the sins of the world, I say to myself, "Herein is love." "By his stripes we are healed" [1 Pet. 2:24], and in Him love and righteousness are both crowned as distinctive attributes in harmonious oneness. Is there anything else that will do that? If there be, I, for one, know not what it is.

A SUMMARY OF CHRISTIAN GRACES

Add to your faith virtue, and to virtue knowledge; and to knowledge temperance; and to temperance patience; and to patience godliness; and to godliness brotherly kindness; and to brotherly kindness charity—2 Pet. 1:5-7

All the excellences which precede godliness are of the more stern, the more severe, and self-regarding kind, and those which follow it are of the gentler sort, and refer to others. Before it stand strength, discrimination, self-control, patience, all having reference to myself alone, and mainly to the difficulties and antagonisms which I meet with in life. There follow it "brotherly kindness and charity"; having reference to others, and being gentle and sweet. If I might so say, it is as in some Alpine range, where the side that faces the north presents rugged cliffs and sparse vegetation, and close-knit strength to breast the tempest, and to live amid the snows; while the southern side has gentler slopes, and a more fertile soil, a richer vegetation, and a sunnier sky. So here: on the one side you get these severe and self-regarding graces, fronting a world full of antagonism and evil; and on the other side you get the gentler graces, fronting a world full of men that need care and help; while above them all towers the great summit that points to the stars, and lives up among the blue, from which flow down on the one side the streams of love and pity, and on the other run down the cliffs that front the stormy north. In the beginning faith; at the end love; in the center godliness; which will blend into one harmonious whole the virtues of strength and of gentleness, even as the type and example of both are found in the Christ of whom long ago it was said: "He shall come with a strong hand; . . . and shall carry the lambs in His bosom, and gently lead those that are with young" [Is. 40:10, 11].

And in like manner, the great difficult problem of how far I am to carry my own cultivation of Christian excellence apart from regard to others, and how far I am to let my obligations to help and succor others overcome the necessity for individual cultivation of Christian character; that difficulty which presses practically upon some of us with great force is best solved as Peter solves it here. Put godliness in the middle, let that be the center, and from it will flow on the one side all needful self-discipline and tutoring, and on the other all wise and Christlike regard to the needs and the sorrows of the men around us.

TRUE GREATNESS

He shall be great in the sight of the Lord—Luke 1:15

So spake the angel who foretold the birth of John the Baptist. "In the sight of the Lord." Then men are not on a dead level in His eyes. Though He is so high and we are so low, the country beneath Him that He looks down upon is not flattened to Him, as it is to us from an elevation, but there are greater and smaller men in His sight, too. No epithet is more misused and misapplied than that of "a great man." It is flung about as indiscriminately as ribbons and orders are by some petty state. Every little man that makes a noise for awhile gets it hung around his neck. Think what a set they are that are gathered in the world's paradise, and honored as the world's great men! The mass of people are so much on a level, and that level is so low that an inch above the average looks gigantic. But the tallest blade of grass gets mowed down by the scythe, and withers as quickly as the rest of its green companions, and goes its way into the oven as surely. There is the world's false estimate of greatness and there is God's estimate. If we want to know what the elements of true greatness are, we may well turn to the life of this man, of whom the prophecy went before him, that he should be "great in the sight of the Lord." That is gold that will stand the test.

We may remember, too, that Jesus Christ, looking back on the career to which the angel was looking forward, endorsed the prophecy, and declared that it had become a fact, and that "among them that are born of woman there hath not arisen a greater than John the Baptist" [Matt. 11:11]. There is no characteristic which may not be attained by any man, woman, or child among us. "The least in the Kingdom of Heaven" [Matt. 5:19] may be greater than he. It is a poor ambition to seek to be *called* "great." It is a noble desire to *be* "great in the sight of the Lord." And if we will keep ourselves close to Jesus Christ that will be attained. It will matter very little what men think of us if at last we have praise from the lips of Him who poured such praise on His servant. We may, if we will. And then it will not hurt us though our names on earth be dark, and our memories perish from among men.

"Of so much fame in Heaven expect thy reward."

COURAGE UNWAVERING AND IMMOVABLE

What went ye out into the wilderness for to see? A reed shaken with the wind?—
Luke 7:24.

"What went ye out into the wilderness for to see? A reed shaken with the wind?" Nay! An iron pillar that stood firm whatsoever winds blew against it. This, as I take it, is in some true sense the basis of all moral greatness, that a man should have a grip which cannot be loosened—like that of the cuttlefish with all its tentacles around its prey—upon the truths that dominate his being and make him a hero. "If you want me to weep," said the old artist-poet, "there must be tears in your own eyes." If you want me to believe, you yourself must be aflame with conviction which has penetrated to the very marrow of your bones. And so, as I take it, the first requisite, either for power upon others, or for greatness, in a man's own development of character, is that there shall be this unwavering firmness of grasp of clearly-apprehended truths, and unflinching boldness of devotion to it.

No doubt there is much to be laid to the account of temperament; but whatever their temperament may be, the way to this unwavering courage, and firm, clear ring of indubitable certainty, is open to every Christian man and woman; and it is their own fault, their own sin and their own weakness, if they do not possess these qualities. Temperament! What on earth is the good of our religion if it is not to modify and govern our temperament? Has a man a right to examine on one side, and give up the attempt to clear the fence, because he feels that in his own natural disposition there is little power to take the leap? Surely not! Jesus Christ came here for the very purpose of making our weakness strong; and if we have a firm hold upon Him, then, in the measure in which His love has permeated our whole nature, will be our unwavering courage, and out of weakness we shall be made strong.

Then let our closeness to Jesus Christ, and our experience of His power, kindle in us the fiery enthusiasm with which He baptizes all His true servants, and let it, because we know the sweetnesses that excel, deprive us of all liability to be tempted away by the vulgar and coarse delights of earth and of sense. Let us keep ourselves clear of the babble that is around us, and be strong because we grasp Christ's hand.

THE HIGHEST TYPE OF COURAGE

And when they beheld the boldness of Peter and John, and had perceived that
they were unlearned and ignorant men, they marveled, and they took knowledge
of them, that they had been with Jesus—Acts 4:13

Moral characteristics do not reach a climax unless there has been much underground building to bear the lofty pinnacle. And no man, when great occasions come to him, develops a courage and an unwavering confidence which are strange to his habitual life.

There must be the underground building; and there must have been many a fighting down of fears, many a curbing of tremors, many a rebuke of hesitations and doubts in the gaunt, desert-loving prophet, before he was man enough to stand before Herod and say, "It is not lawful for thee to have her" [Matt. 14:4].

Of course, the highest type of this undaunted boldness and unwavering firmness of conviction is not in John and his like. He presented strength in a lower form than did the Master from whom his strength came. The willow has a place as well as the oak. Firmness is not obstinacy; courage is not rudeness. It is possible to have the iron hand in the velvet glove, not of etiquette—observing politeness, but of a true considerateness and gentleness. They who are like Him that was "meek and lowly in heart" [Matt. 11:29] are surest to possess the unflinching resolve which set His face like a flint, and enabled Him to go unhesitatingly and unrecalcitrant to the Cross itself.

Do not let us forget, either, that John's unwavering firmness wavered; that over the clear heaven of his convictions there *did* steal a cloud; that he from whom no violence could wrench his faith, felt it slipping out of his grasp when his muscles were relaxed in the dungeon; and that he sent "from the prison"—which was the excuse for the message—to ask the question, "After all, '*Art* Thou He that should come?'" [Luke 7:20].

Nor let us forget that it was that very moment of tremulousness which Jesus Christ seized in order to pour an unstinted flood of praise for the firmness of his convictions on the wavering head of the Forerunner. So if we feel that though the needle of our compass points true to the pole, yet when the compass frame is shaken the needle sometimes vibrates away from its true goal, do not let us be cast down, but believe that a merciful allowance is made for human weakness. This man was great because he had such dauntless courage and firmness that over his headless corpse in the dungeon at Machaerus might have been spoken what the Regent Murray said over John Knox's coffin, "Here lies one that never feared the face of man."

EXALTATION ABOVE WORLDLY GOOD

I know both how to be abased, and I know how to abound: everywhere and in all things I am instructed both to be full and to be hungry, both to abound and to suffer need. I can do all things through Christ which strengtheneth me—
Phil. 4:12, 13

"What went ye out into the wilderness for to see? A man clothed in soft raiment?" [Luke 7:25]. You would have gone to a palace if you had wanted to see that, not to the reed beds of Jordan. As we all know, in his life, in his dress, in his food, in the aims that he set before him, John rose high above all regard for the debasing and perishable sweetnesses that hold of flesh, and are ended in time. He lived conspicuously for the Unseen. His asceticism, which belonged to his age, was not the highest type of the virtue which it expressed. As the might of gentleness is greater than the might of such strength as John's, so the asceticism of John is lower than the self-government of the Man that comes eating and drinking.

But while that is true, I seek to urge this old threadbare lesson, always needed, never needed more than amid the senselessly luxurious habits of this generation, that one indispensable element of true greatness and elevation of character is that every one of us should live high above these temptations of gross and perishable joys; should

"Scorn delights and live laborious days."

No man has a right to be called "great" if his aims are small. And the question is, not as modern idolatry of intellect, or, still worse, modern idolatry of success, often makes it out to be, has he great capacities, or, "has he won great prizes," but has he greatly used himself and his life? If your aims are small, you will never be great; and if your highest aims are but to get a good slice of this world's pudding, no matter what powers God may have given you to use, you are essentially a small man.

I remember a vigorous and contemptuous illustration of St. Bernard's: he likens a man that lives for these perishable delights which John spurned to a spider spinning a web out of his own substance, and catching in it nothing but a wretched prey of poor little flies. Such a one has no right to be called a great man surely! Our aims rather than our capacity determine our character, and they who greatly aspire after the greatest things within the reach of men, which are faith, hope, charity [1 Cor. 13:13]; and who, for the sake of effecting these aspirations, put their heels upon the head of the serpent, and suppress the animal in their nature—these are the men "great in the sight of the Lord" [Luke 1:15].

ENTHUSIASM FOR RIGHTEOUSNESS

And was clad with zeal as a cloke—Is. 59:17

You may think that fiery enthusiasm has little to do with greatness; I believe it has everything to do with it, and that the difference between men is very largely to be found here, whether they flame up into the white heat of enthusiasm for the things that are right, or whether the only things that can kindle them into anything like earnestness remind you how, all through John the Baptist's career, there burnt, unflickering and undying, that steadfast light; how he brought to the service of the plainest teaching of morality a fervor of passion and of zeal almost unexampled and magnificent. I need not remind you how Jesus Christ Himself laid His hand upon this characteristic, when He said of him, "he was a light kindled and shining." But I would lay upon all our hearts the plain practical lesson that if we keep in that tepid region of lukewarmness which is the utmost approach to tropical heat that moral and religious questions are capable of raising in many of us, goodbye to all chance of being "great in the sight of the Lord" [Luke 1:15]. We hear a great deal about the "blessings of moderation," the "dangers of fanaticism," and the like. I venture to think that the last thing which the moral consciousness of England wants today is a refrigerator, and that what it needs a great deal more than that is, that all Christian people should be brought face to face with this plain truth—that their religion has, as an indispensable part of it, "a spirit of burning," and that if they have not been baptized in fire, there is little reason to believe that they have been baptized with the Holy Ghost.

"Full of the Holy Ghost" [Acts 6:3], as a vessel might be to its brim of golden wine! Full! A dribbling drop or two in the bottom of the jar: whose fault is it? Why, with that rushing mighty wind to fill our sails if we like, should we be lying in the sickly calms of the tropics, with the pitch oozing out of the seams, and the idle canvas flapping against the mast? Why, with those tongues of fire hovering over our heads, should we be cowering over gray ashes in which there lives a little spark? Why, with that great rushing tide of the river of the water of life, should we be like the dry watercourses of the desert, with bleached and white stones baking where the streams should be running? "Thou that art named the house of Jacob, is the Spirit of the Lord straitened? Are these his doings?" [Mic. 2:7]. But if we stay ourselves on God, amid struggle and change here, He will gladden us further with perpetual joys. "Because he is at my right hand I shall not be moved" [Ps. 16:8]. Every one of us knows that to be kept unmoved will demand the exercise of power far beyond the limitations of humanity. We are swept by such surges of passion; we are swayed by such storms of temptation; we are smitten by such shocks of destiny, that to stand steadfast is beyond our power. And there is only one thing that will make us steadfast, and that is that we should be, if I might use such a figure, bolted and lashed on to, or rather incorporated into, the changeless steadfastness of the unmoved God.

I long that you and myself may be a flame for goodness; may be enthusiastic over plain morality; and may show that we are so by our daily life, by our rebuking the opposite, if need be, even if it took us into Herod's chamber and made Herodias our enemy for life [Matt. 14].

April 24

SELF-DENIAL BEFORE JESUS CHRIST

He must increase, but I must decrease—John 3:30

There is nothing that I know in biography anywhere more beautiful, more striking, than the contrast between the two halves of the character and demeanor of the Baptist: how, on the one side, he fronts all men undaunted and recognizes no superior, and how neither threats nor flatteries nor anything else will tempt him to step one inch beyond the limitations of which he is aware, nor to abate one inch of the claims which he urges; and, on the other hand, like some tall cedar, touched by the lightning's hand, he falls prone before Jesus Christ and says, "He must increase, and I must decrease." "A man can receive nothing except it be given him of God" [John 3:27]. He is all boldness on one side; all submission and dependence on the other.

You remember how, in the face of many temptations, this attitude was maintained. The very message which he had to carry was full of temptations to a self-seeking man to assert himself. You remember the almost rough "No!" with which, reiteratively, he met the suggestions of the deputation from Jerusalem, that sought to induce him to say that he was more than he knew himself to be, and how he stuck by that infinitely humble and beautiful saying, "I am the voice"—that is all [John 1:19–23]. You remember how the whole nation was in a kind of conspiracy to tempt him to assert himself, and was ready to break into a flame if he had dropped a spark, for "all men were musing in their heart whether he was the Christ or not," and all the lawless and restless elements would have been only too glad to gather around him if he had declared himself the Messiah. Remember how his own disciples came to him, and tried to play upon his jealousy, and to induce him to assert himself. "Master! He whom thou didst baptize," and so didst give Him the first credentials that sent men on His course, has outstripped thee, and "all men cometh to him" [John 3:26]. And you remember the lovely answer that opened such depths of unexpected tenderness in the rough nature. "He that hath the bride is the bridegroom. The friend of the bridegroom heareth the voice; and that is enough to fill my cup with joy to the very brim" [John 3:29].

And what conceptions of Jesus Christ had John that he thus bowed his lofty crest before Him, and softened his heart into submission almost abject? He knew Him to be the coming Judge, with the fan in His hand, who could baptize with fire, and he knew Him to be "the Lamb of God which taketh away the sin of the world" [John 1:29]. Therefore he fell before Him. We shall not be "great in the sight of the Lord" [Luke 1:15] unless we copy that example of utter self-denial before Jesus Christ. Thomas á Kempis says somewhere, "He is truly great who is small in his own sight and thinks nothing of the giddy heights of worldly honor." You and I know far more of Jesus Christ than John the Baptist did. Do we bow ourselves before Him as he did? The Source from which he drew his greatness is open to us all. Let us begin with the recognition of the Lamb of God that takes away the world's sin, and with it ours. Let the thought of what He is and what He has done for us bow us in unfeigned submission. Let it shatter all dreams of our own importance or our own desert. The vision of the Lamb of God, and it only, will crush in our hearts the serpent's eggs of self-esteem and self-regard.

April 25

DEATH AND LIFE

The law of the Spirit of life in Christ Jesus hath made me free from the law of sin and death—Rom. 8:2

The blood of the first martyr spoke of death; the blood of Christ speaks of life. The former, as I have said, was the first death. We can partly understand how awful must have been the experience of those who stood by and saw, for the first time, that mystery before their eyes—a dead man. How there comes from this first incident the dark foreboding of all the dim subsequent events of a like kind. It heads a great series stretching away into the darkness; the first of millions like itself, the first experience of that which saddens all hearts sooner or later, of that which lays its hand upon all joys one time or another, of that which comes to each man as a fear, even when the better man within him reaches out towards it as a hope and a deliverance. Abel's death [Gen. 4] speaks of the beginning of the fulfillment of the solemn law which wraps us all. The veil is spread over all nations, and we walk beneath its black folds.

"The blood of sprinkling . . . speaketh better things" [Heb. 12:24]. The blood is the life; the blood shed is the life given up; the blood received is the life incorporated. You can live on the blood of Jesus Christ. You can have it, if I may so say, transfused into your veins. The spirit of life which was in Him may be yours. It was shed that it might be partaken of by all the world.

And so, while the stark corpse of the first martyr lying there, pale and bloody in its gore [Acts 7], proclaims the beginning of the reign of death, the blood of Jesus Christ proclaims the beginning of life, and is the means of the communication of His own eternal and Divine life to all that love Him and believe upon Him. The alabaster box of His manhood is broken that the house of the world may be filled with the odor of the ointment. "He that eateth my flesh and drinketh my blood dwelleth in me, and I in him" [John 6:56].

In that life is also given purity like its own. Abel "being dead yet speaketh" [Heb. 11:4], and proclaims the nobleness of goodness, of righteousness, and of faith; but Christ living, not only proclaims the nobleness of goodness and righteousness and faith, but gives us His own purity; and "the law of the Spirit of life in Christ Jesus makes us free from the law of sin and of death" [Rom. 8:2].

So, dear brother, one voice speaks of hatred, the other of all-embracing love; one voice speaks of retribution, the other of pardon; one voice prophesies a dolorous prophecy of universal death, the other proclaims a glad evangel of all-conquering life. Listen, then, to the solemn warning with which, as with uplifted finger and grave look of admonition, the writer in Hebrews speaks; "See that ye refuse not Him that speaketh" [12:25]. Let not your ears be dumb to the infinite mercy and gracious pardon which speak to you from the shed blood of Christ. God hears its voice, and forgives all our hate. Do you hearken to its voice, and accept the love that speaks its tenderest message in the blood shed for you.

VENGEANCE AND PARDON

Lord, shall we smite with the sword? . . . Jesus answered . . . Suffer ye thus far. And
he touched his ear, and healed him — Luke 22:49, 51

"What hast thou done? The voice of thy brother's blood crieth unto me from the ground" say the grand words of Genesis 4:10. There it lies—the earth will not drink it in; there it lies, pleading, appealing to Divine justice to smite the evildoer. A vehement figure, representing a solemn truth, that every evil has a tongue which calls to Heaven against the iniquity of the evildoer; or, to put it into plainer words, all sin necessarily appeals to God for punishment of the sinner. It does so from the very nature of things and the constitution of the universe. Whatsoever is contrary to the Divine will calls upon God to smite, and smiting to avenge. And that is true, and will be true through all eternity. And there is no gospel that does not base and found itself upon that. And the first sin of man against man, this first murder and first martyrdom, proclaims to earth, as it appeals to Heaven, the solemn fact that the law of the Divine nature and the necessity of the universe is that evil shall be punished, and that retribution shall follow upon wrongdoing.

Christ's death comes under that law too. "His blood be on us, and on our children" [Matt. 27:25], shouted the frenzied mob, lightly incurring the awful burden; and His blood *was* on them and on their children." And the dissolution of their national existence, and the sweeping away of their special privileges, and the destruction of Temple and worship, and their continuance till this day a hissing and a byword upon the face of the earth, show us how the blood of Christ spoke what the blood of Abel spoke, and cried to God for vengeance; and the vengeance came, and is here today.

And yet the cry for retribution is not the predominant tone. There is a deeper voice than that. Christ's blood, meaning thereby the fact of Christ's death, is present in the Divine mind—not only as the consequence of man's sin, and therefore a crime, but as the consequence of its own infinite love, and therefore an atonement and a propitiation. And while in one aspect it did bring down, as it ought to bring down, judgments upon the wicked hands that crucified and slew, in the other aspect it has brought down upon all the world, and upon us if we will accept it, the blessing of that pardoning grace that sweeps away all sin and makes us pure and holy. The blood of Jesus Christ cries to God for pardon—that is to say, is an element ever present before the Divine mind, conditioning and modifying the incidence of His judgments, and His punishment for sin. Here is the center of Christianity. The one thing which makes it a power to bless and to help is the Cross, on which the Sacrifice for the sins of the world has died. Is your Christianity a Christianity which is founded on the fact of Christ's death for the sins of the world, and from that draws all your hope, all your knowledge of God and of man, as well as all your power for holiness and obedience? I beseech you, let that voice speak to your hearts and consciences, that they may be sprinkled from dead works by the blood that "speaketh better things than that of Abel" [Heb. 12:24].

THE TWO VOICES

The voice of thy brother's blood crieth unto me from the ground—Gen. 4:10
Speaketh better things than that of Abel—Heb. 12:24

We have the blood that speaks of man's hate, and the other blood that speaks of God's love. The former was shed simply because the milk of brotherly affection was all curdled into hate through the working of jealousy and of envy. So that first dismal story rises up on the very threshold of history as a solemn revelation of the possibilities of diabolical and murderous hatred that lie in all human relationships and in all men's hearts; and speaks to every one of us the warning that we shall not cherish the tiny seeds of jealousy and envy of a brother's good, which may ripen and fructify into the devilish fruit of murder, as it did there.

Christ's death was also caused by man's sins, by the antagonism which was raised in man by His very beauty and purity. Eternal goodness came into the world, and the world hated the light, because its deeds were evil.

But we have to go deeper than that. The blood of Abel proclaimed man's hate, the blood of Christ proclaims God's infinite love. For He died, not because men hated Him, but because He loved men. He did not die because Pharisees and Scribes, with all the others who were roused in antagonism against Him, carried out their schemes, but He died because He allowed Himself to die. It was not their hostility that nailed Him to the Cross, it was His purpose to save. It was not because men willed it that He perished from the life of earth, but because He would give Himself for us. And so, while from that old dim incident far away there, low down on the horizon of history, there streams out, as it were, a baleful light that speaks of man's sin and hatred, from this other there rays out a celestial brightness, which proclaims the infinite love of the Father who gave His Son, and the infinite love of the Son who gave Himself. The one is reeking with hatred, the other is fragrant with love. The one shows the depths of possible evil in men's hearts, and how all human affection may be embittered and turned to its opposite; the other shows how the infinite lovingkindness of God lives on and on, like the patient sunshine upon the glaciers, notwithstanding all the coldness and the alienation of man's nature, and how that infinite and wondrous love shrinks not from even the death which the hate it would win to love can inflict. "The blood of sprinkling speaketh better things than that of Abel," in that against the blackness of man's hate it lifts the sevenfold luster of the infinite love of God.

THE SIGNIFICANCE OF THE BLOOD OF CHRIST

The blood of sprinkling, that speaketh better things than that of Abel—Heb. 12:24

That dim figure, standing on the very horizon of time, has a tragic significance. Abel's was the first death, the first murder, the first fratricide, the first martyrdom. And so, according to the energetic phrase of the Book of Genesis, his blood had a mournful voice. It cried to God from the ground for retribution [4:10]. It prophesied of much more to follow. It proclaimed the hatred of the evil against the good, and so it was a voice of lamentation and of woe.

The blood of Jesus Christ has a significance broadly distinguished from that of all innocent martyrs. Abel is the first of the class, the type of the whole, and "in his hand a glass which showed many more" to follow; for the same causes will produce the same effects. The death of Christ belongs to that class. He, too, is an innocent Victim; He, too, dies because bad men hate the good with a murderous hatred; He, too, dies because He bears witness to the truth, and for the truth to which He bears witness. He is a Martyr.

And is that all? Does the blood of Christ speak the same things as the blood of Abel, only more tenderly and more loudly? Nay; there are some of us, I am afraid, to whom it does; to whom it only reiterates the old lesson of the world's wages to the world's teachers; to whom it is nothing more than the highest, the most touching, the most tragic example of what the good man has to meet with when he asserts the principles of his own life against the principles on which the world's lives are mostly regulated. Let me urge upon you that if Christ's blood says nothing more to you than that He is the foremost of the martyrs and the innocents, who have died because the world hated them and their goodness, Christ's blood is dumb to you.

It speaks other lessons altogether than these, dear brother; does it speak them to you? Have you penetrated beneath that surface significance which, blessed as it is, is only surface, and have you come down to the characteristic thing, the something more, which makes Christianity all that it is, of blessing and power? And do you hear another proclamation altogether from the shed blood than the proclamation of innocent martyrdom, as over the fate of the good and the pure?

"We love him, because he first loved us" [1 John 4:19]. Very simple words! But they go down into the depths of God, lifting burdens off the heart of humanity, turning duty into delight, and changing the aspect of all things. He who knows that God loves him needs little more for blessedness; he who loves God back again offers more than all burnt offering and sacrifices.

MUTUAL FRIENDSHIP

A friend loveth at all times, and a brother is born for adversity—Prov. 17:17

Mutual confidence is the mortar which binds the stones of society together into a building. It makes the difference between the herding together of beasts and the association of men. No community could keep together for an hour without mutual confidence, even in regard of the least intimate relationships of life. But it is the very lifeblood of friendship. You cannot say, "A. B. is my friend, but I do not trust him." If suspicion creeps in, like the foul malaria of tropical swamps, it kills all friendship. Therefore "he was called the friend of God" [James 2:23] is by James deduced from the fact that he believed God, "and it was imputed to him for righteousness" [Rom. 4:22]. You cannot make a friend of a man that you do not know where to have. There may be some vague reverence of, or abject reluctant submission to, "the unknown God" [Acts 17:23], the something outside of ourselves that perhaps makes for righteousness; but for any vivid, warm throb of friendship there must be, first a clear knowledge, and then a living grappling of that knowledge to my very heart, by my faith. Unless I trust God I cannot be a friend of God's. If you and I are His friends, we trust Him, and He will trust us. For this friendship is not one-sided; and the word, though it may be ambiguous as to whether it means one whom I love or one who loves me, really includes both persons to the compact, and there are analogous, if not identical, emotions in each. So that, if I trust God, I may be sure that God trusts me, and, in His confidence, leaves a great deal to me, and so ennobles and glorifies me by His reliance upon me.

And so we come to this, that the heavenly and the earthly friend, like friends on the low levels of humanity, love each other because they trust each other. I have said that the words "my friend" may either mean one whom I love or one who loves me, but that the two things are, in the present connection, inseparable. Only let us remember where the sweet reciprocation and interchange of love begins: "We love him because he first loved us" [1 John 4:19]. "When we were enemies, we were reconciled to God by the death of his Son" [Rom. 5:10]. And so we have to turn to that heavenly Friend, and feel that as life itself, so the love which is the life of life, has its beginning in Him, and that never would our hearts have turned themselves from their alienation unless there had poured down upon them the attractive outflow of His great love. It was an old fancy that, wherever a tree was struck by lightning, all its tremulous foliage turned in the direction from which the bolt had come. When the merciful flash of God's great love strikes a heart, then all its tendrils turn to the source of the life-giving light, and we love back again in sweet reverberation to the primal and original love.

THE PERFECT VISION AND THE PERFECT LIKENESS

As for me, I shall behold thy face in righteousness: I shall be satisfied, when I awake, with thy likeness—Ps. 17:15

To behold Christ will be the condition and the means of growing like Him. That way of transformation by beholding, or of assimilation by the power of loving contemplation, is the blessed way of ennobling character, which even here, and in human relationships, has often made it easy to put off old vices and to clothe the soul with unaccustomed grace. Men have learned to love and gaze upon some fair character till some image of its beauty has passed into their ruder natures. To love such and to look on them has been an education. The same process is exemplified in more sacred regions, and quickened by Divine powers, as men learn to love and look upon Christ, and so become like Him, as the sun stamps a tiny copy of its blazing sphere on the eye that looks at it. But all these are but poor, far-off hints and low preludes of the energy with which that blessed vision of the glorified Christ shall work on the happy hearts that behold Him, and of the completeness of the likeness to Him which will be stamped in light upon their faces.

It matters not, though it does not yet appear what we shall be, if to all the questionings of our own hearts we have this for our all-sufficient answer, "We shall be like him" [1 John 3:2]. As Richard Baxter has it:

"My knowledge of that life is small,
 The eye of faith is dim;
But, 'tis enough that Christ knows all,
 And I shall be like Him!"

It is enough for the servant that he be as his Lord.

There is no need to go into the dark and difficult questions about that vision. "We shall see him as he is" [1 John 3:2]. For He Himself prayed, in that great intercessory prayer, "Father, I will that they also which thou hast given me be with me where I am; that they may behold my glory" [John 17:24]. And that vision of the glorified manhood of Jesus Christ—certain, direct, clear, and worthy, whether it come through sense or through thought, to be called vision—is all the sight of God that men in Heaven through eternity will have. "No man hath seen God at any time" [John 1:18]. And through the millenniums of a growing glory, Christ, as He is, will be the manifested Deity. Then, as a bit of glass, when the light strikes it, flashes into sunny glory, as every poor little muddy pool on the pavement, when the sunbeam falls upon it, has the sun mirrored even in its shallow mud, so into your poor heart and mine the vision of Christ's glory will come, molding and transforming you to its own beauty. Those rays of His beauties will pour right down upon us, "as with open face," reflecting as glass does, the glory of the Lord, we "shall be changed into the same image" [2 Cor. 3:18].

THE PEACE OF FORGIVENESS

I wait for the Lord, my soul doth wait, and in His word do I hope. My soul waiteth for the Lord, more than they that watch for morning; I say, more than they that watch for morning—Psalm 130:5, 6

This is what I call permanent, peaceful attitude of the spirit that has tasted the sweet consciousness of forgiving love, a continual dependence upon God. Like a man that has just recovered from some illness, but still leans upon the hand, and feels his need of seeing the face, of that kindly physician that has helped him through, there will be still, and always, the necessity for the continual application of that pardoning love. But they that have tasted that the Lord is gracious can sit very quietly at His feet and trust themselves to His kindly dealings, resting their souls upon His strong word, and looking for the fuller communication of light from Himself. This is a beautiful picture of a tranquil, continuous, ever-rewarded, and ever-fresh waiting upon Him, and reliance upon His mercy.

"More than they that watch for the morning." That is beautiful! The consciousness of sin was the dark night. The coming of His forgiving love flushed all the eastern heaven with diffused brightness that grew into the perfect day. And so the man waits quietly for the dawn, and his whole soul is one absorbing desire that God may dwell with him, and brighten and gladden him.

The thundering side of the sky makes all the more tender the sapphire blue of the other side:—"But there is forgiveness with thee, that thou mayest be feared" [Ps. 130:4]. No man ever comes to that confidence that has not sprung to it, as it were, by a rebound from the other thought. It needs, first of all, that the heart should spring into the relief and the gladness of the counter truth. It must first have felt the shudder of the thought, "If Thou, Lord, shouldst," in order to come to the gladness of the thought, "But there is forgiveness with Thee!"

Do you know what *Bethesda* means? "House of Mercy"; perhaps so named to commemorate some benefactor that had built the portico; more probably to suggest to the poor sick creatures a gleam of hope from the thought that God had love and care for them. There seemed a sharp contradiction between the condition of the people and the name. But we are gathered, as they were, in the House of Mercy. That is to say, though we have all departed from the right way, God's love encompasses us still, and this earth, seamed and stained as it has been by man's sin, is, notwithstanding, the chosen field in which He will manifest the tenderness of His compassion and the love of His heart. If any of you ever saw St. Peter's in Rome, you will remember the great sweeping colonnades which extend from its front and reach out their arms as though they would embrace the city and the world; and in the midst there springs and sparkles a pure fountain. So God's love compasses all us sick folk, and in the midst there rises the fountain which will heal. We are in the House of Mercy. The world is gathered around the fountain opened for sin and for uncleanness. It is not intermittent, but evermore His blood avails for us. It is not exhausted by one cure, or by two or three; but there is enough for each and enough for all; enough for thee and me and all our fellows. Christ is coming to you by my poor unworthy words, and saying, "Wilt thou be made whole?" [John 5:6]. Take Christ for your Healer, for your healing, and for your health.

DELIVERANCE FOR THE CAPTIVES

He hath sent me . . . to proclaim liberty to the captives, and the opening of the
prison to them that are bound—Is. 61:1

Many of us know not the bondage in which we are held. We are held in it all the more really and sadly because we conceit ourselves to be free. Those poor, light-hearted people, in the dreadful days of the French Revolution, used to keep up some ghastly mockery of society and cheerfulness in their prisons; and festooned the bars with flowers, and made believe to be carrying on their life freely, as they used to do; but for all that, day after day the wagons came to the gates, and morning after morning the jailer stood at the door of the dungeons with the execution list in his hand, and one after another of the triflers were dragged away to death.

And so men and women are living a life which they fancy is free, and all the while they are in bondage, held in a prison house. You, my brother, are chained by guilt; you are chained by sin, you are chained by the habit of evil with a strength of which you never know till you try to shake it off.

And there comes to each of us a mighty Deliverer, who breaks the gates of brass, and who cuts the bars of iron in sunder [Ps. 107:16]. Christ comes to us. By His death He has borne away the guilt; by His living Spirit He will bear away the dominion of sin from our hearts; and if the Son will make us free, we shall be free indeed. Oh! Ponder that deep truth, I pray you, which the Lord Christ has spoken in words that carry conviction in their very simplicity to every conscience. "He that committeth sin is of the devil." [1 John 3:8]. And as you feel sometimes—and you all feel sometimes—the catch of the fetter on your wrists when you would desire to stretch out your hands to good, listen as to a true Gospel to this old word which, in its picturesque imagery, carries a truth that should be life. To us all "the breaker is gone up before us, the prison gates are open." Follow His steps, and take the freedom which He gives: and beware that you "stand fast . . . in the liberty wherewith Christ hath made us free, and be not entangled again with any yoke of bondage" [Gal. 5:1].

Some of you are the slaves of your own lusts. Some of you are the slaves of the world's maxims. Some of you are held in bondage by some habit that you abominate, but cannot get away from. Here is freedom for you. The dark walls of the prison are around us all. "For God hath concluded them all in unbelief, that he might have mercy upon all" [Rom. 11:32]. Blessed be His Name! As the angel came to the sleeping Apostle [Acts 12:7–10], and to his light touch the iron gates swing obedient on their hinges, and Roman soldiers who ought to have watched their prey were lulled to sleep, and fetters that held the limbs dropped as if melted; so, silently, in His meek and merciful strength, the Christ comes to us all, and the iron gate which leadeth out into freedom opens of its own accord at His touch, and the fetters fall from our limbs, and we go forth free men.

THE NEW AND THE LIVING WAY

By a new and living way, which he hath consecrated for us, through the veil, that is to say, his flesh—Heb. 10:20

If we rightly understand our natural condition, it is not only one of bondage to evil, but it is of separation from God. Parts of the Divine character are always beautiful and sweet to every human heart when it thinks about them. Parts of the Divine character stand frowning before a man who knows himself for what he is; and conscience tells us that between Him and us there is a mountain of impediment piled up by our own evil. And Christ comes, the Pathfinder and the Path; the Pioneer who breaks the way for us through all the hindrances, and leads us up to the presence of God.

For we do not know God as He is except by Jesus Christ. We see fragments, and often distorted fragments, of the Divine nature and character apart from Jesus, but the real Divine nature as it is, and as it is in its relation to me, a sinner, is only made known to me in the face of Jesus Christ. When we see Him we see God. Christ's tears are God's pity, Christ's gentleness is God's meekness, Christ's tender drawing love is not only a revelation of a most pure and sweet brother's heart, but a manifestation through that brother's heart of the deepest depths of the Divine nature. Christ is the heart of God. Apart from Him, we come to the God of our own consciences, and we tremble; we come to the God of our own fancies, and we presume; we come to the God dimly guessed at and pieced together from out of the hints and indications of His works, and He is little more than a dead name to us. Apart from Christ, we come to a fact established beyond any doubt which we call a God—a shadow through which you can see the stars shining. But we know the Father when we believe in Christ. And so all the clouds rising from our own hearts and consciences and fancies and misconceptions which we have piled together, between God and ourselves, Christ clears away; and in this way He opens the path to God. It is only the God manifest in Jesus Christ that draws men's hearts to Him. The God that is in Christ is the only God that humanity ever loved. Other gods they may have worshiped with cowering terror and with far-off lip-reverence, but this God has a heart, and wins hearts because He has, and so Christ opens the way to Him. He not only makes God known to us, and not only makes Him so known to us as to draw us to Him, but in that likewise He, by the fact of His Cross and Passion, has borne, and borne away, the impediments of our own sin and transgression which rise forever between us and Him.

May 4

OUR CAPTAIN

The breaker is come up before them; they have broken up, and have passed through the gate, and are gone out by it: and their king shall pass before them, and the Lord on the head of them—Mic. 2:13

Our Lord is the breaker, going up before us in the sense that He is the Captain of our life's march. The prophet knew not that the Lord their King, of whom it is enigmatically said that he, too, as well as "the breaker," is to go before them, was, in mysterious fashion, to dwell in that breaker; and that those two, whom he sees separately—are yet in a deep and mysterious sense—one. The host of the captives, returning in triumphant march through the wilderness and to the promised land is, in the prophet's words, headed both by the breaker and by the Lord. We know that the breaker is the Lord, the Angel of the Covenant whose name is Jehovah. Christ breaks the prison of our sins, and leads us forth on the path to God, marches at the head of our life's journey, and is our example and commander, and Himself present with us through all life's changes and sorrows. Here is the great blessing and peculiarity of Christian morals that they are all brought down to that sweet obligation: "Do as I did." Here is the great blessing and strength for the Christian life in all its difficulties—you can never go where you cannot see in the desert the footprints, haply spotted with blood, that your Master left there before you, and, planting your trembling feet in the prints, as a child might imitate his father's strides, learn to recognize that all duty comes to this: "Follow Me" [Matt. 4:19]; and that all sorrow is calmed, ennobled, made tolerable and glorified by the thought that He has borne it.

The Roman matron of the legend struck the knife into her bosom, and handed it to her husband with the words, "It is not painful!" Christ has gone before us in all the dreary solitude, and in all the agony and pains of life. He has hallowed them all, and has taken the bitterness and the pain out of each of them for them that love Him. If we feel that the breaker is before us, and that we are marching behind Him, then wherever He leads us we may follow, and whatever He has passed through we may pass through. We carry in His life the all-sufficing pattern of duty. We have in His companionship the all-strengthening consolation. Let us leave the direction of our road in His hands who never says "Go!" but always "Come!" This general marches in the midst of His battalions, and sets His soldiers on no enterprises or forlorn hopes which He has not Himself dared and overcome. So Christ goes as our companion before us, the true pillar of fire and cloud [Ex. 13:21] in which the present Deity abode, and He is with us in real companionship. Our joyful march through the wilderness is directed, patterned, protected, companioned by Him; and when He "putteth forth His own sheep," blessed be His Name! "He goeth before them" [John 10:4].

JESUS THE FORERUNNER

Within the veil, whither the forerunner is for us entered, even Jesus, made a high priest forever after the order of Melchisedek—Heb. 6:19, 20

Christ's resurrection is the only solid proof of a future life. Christ's present resurrection life is the power by partaking in which, "though we were dead, yet shall we live" [John 11:25]. He has trodden that path, too, before us. He has entered into the great prison into which the generations of men have been hounded and hurried, and where they lie in their graves, as in their narrow cells; He has entered there. With one blow He has driven the gates from their hinges, and has passed out, and no soul can any longer be shut in as forever into that ruined and opened prison. Like Samson, He has taken the gates which from of old barred its entrance, and borne them on His strong shoulders to the city on the hill. And now death's darts are blunted, his fetters are broken, and his jail has its doors wide open. And there is nothing for him to do now but to fall upon his sword and to kill himself, for the prisoners are gone. "Oh, death! I will be thy plague; oh, grave! I will be thy destruction." "The breaker is come up before us" [Mic. 2:13]; therefore it is not possible that we should be holden of the ineffective chains that He has broken.

The Forerunner is for us entered, passed through the heavens, and entered into the holiest of all. We are too closely knit to Him, if we love Him and trust Him, to make it possible that we shall be where He is not, or that He shall be where we are not. Where He has gone we shall go—in Heaven, blessed be His Name! He will still be the leader of our progress and the captain at the head of our march. For He crowns all His other work by this, that, having broken the prison house of our sins, and opened for us the way to God, and been the leader and the captain of our march through all the pilgrimage of life, and the opener of the gate of the grave, for our joyful resurrection, and the opener of the gate of Heaven for our triumphal entrance, He will still, as the Lamb that is in the midst of the Throne, go before us, and lead us into green pastures and by the still waters. This shall be the description of the growing blessedness and power of the saints' life above, "These are they which follow the Lamb withersoever He goeth" [Rev. 14:4].

This Master, Christ, works in front of His men. The farmer that goes first among all the sowers, and heads the line of reapers in the yellowing harvest-field, may well have diligent servants. Our Master went forth, weeping, bearing precious seed, and has left it in our hands to sow in all furrows [Ps. 126:6]. Our Master is the Lord of the harvest, and has borne the heat of the day before His servants. Let it be our life's work to show forth Christ's praise. Let the very atmosphere in which we move and have our being be prayer. Let two great currents set ever through our days, which two, like the great movements in the ocean of the air, are but the upper and under halves of the one movement—that beneath with constant energy of desires rushing in from the cold poles to be warmed and expanded at the tropics, where the all-moving sun pours his direct rays; that above charged with rich gifts from the Lord of light, glowing with heat drawn from Him, and made diffusive by His touch, spreading itself out beneficent and life-bringing into all colder lands, swathing the world in soft, warm folds, and turning the polar ice into sweet waters.

DIVINE WISDOM

If any of you lack wisdom, let him ask of God, that giveth to all men liberally, and
upbraideth not—James 1:5

What does James mean by "wisdom"? He means the sum of practical religion. With him, as with the Psalmist, sin and folly are two names for the same thing, and so are religion and wisdom. He, and only he, has wisdom who knows God with a living heart-knowledge which gives a just insight into the facts of life and the bounds of right and wrong, and which regulates conduct and shapes the whole man with power far beyond that of knowledge, however wide and deep, illuminating intellect, however powerful. "Knowledge" is poor and superficial in comparison with this wisdom, which may roughly be said to be equivalent to practical religion.

The use of this expression to indicate the greatest deficiency in the average Christian character simply suggests this thought, that if we had a clear, constant, certain God-regarding insight into things as they are, we should lack little. Because, if a man habitually kept vividly before him the thought of God, and with it the true nature and obligation and blessedness of righteous-loving obedience, and the true foulness and fatality of sin—if he saw these with the clearness and the continuity with which we may all see the things that are unseen and eternal; if he saw life steadily, and saw it whole; if he saw the rottenness and the shallowness of earthly things and temptations, and if he saw the blessed issue of every God-pleasing act—the perfecting of conduct would be secured.

It would be an impossibility for him, with all that illumination blazing in upon him, *not* to walk in the paths of righteousness with a glad and serene heart. I do not believe that all sin is a consequence of ignorance, but I do believe that our average Christian life would be revolutionized if we each carried clearly before us, and continually subjected our lives to the influence of, the certain verities of God's Word. The thing that we want most is clearer and more vivid conceptions of the realities of the Christian revelation and of the facts of human life. These will act as tests, and up will start in his own shape the fiend that is whispering at our ears, when touched by the spear of this Divine wisdom. So here is our root-deficiency; therefore, instead of confining ourselves to trying to cure isolated and specific faults, or to attain isolated and specific virtues, let us go deeper down, and realize that the more our whole natures are submitted to the power of God's truth, and of the realities of the future and of the present, of Time and Eternity, the nearer shall we come to being "perfect and entire," lacking nothing [James 1:4].

※

HOW TO GET WISDOM

Let him ask in faith, nothing wavering: For he that wavereth is like a wave of the sea driven with the wind and tossed—James 1:6

"Let him ask." This direction might at first sight strike one as being like the specification of the thing lacking, scarcely what we should have expected. Does James say, If any of you lack "wisdom" [1:5], let him sit down and think? No! "If any of you lack wisdom," let him go to pundits and rabbis, and get it from them? No! "If any of you lack wisdom, let him ask." A strange apparent disconnection between the issue and the means suggested! Very strange, if *wisdom* lives only up in the head! Not so strange if it has its seat in the depths of the human spirit. If you want to learn theology, you have to study. If you seek to master any science, you have to take yourself to the appropriate discipline. It is of no use to pray to God to make you a good geologist, or botanist, or lawyer, or doctor, unless you also take the necessary means to become one. But if a man wants the Divine wisdom, let him get down on his knees. That is the best place to secure it. "Let him ask"; because that insight, so clear, so vivid, so constant, and so perfectly adequate for the regulation of the life, is of God. It comes to us from the Spirit of God that dwells in men's hearts. And to receive that spirit of wisdom the one thing necessary is that we should want it. That is all. Nothing more, but nothing less. I doubt very much whether hosts of the average Christian people of this generation do want it, or would know what to do with it if they had it; or whether the gift of a heart purged from delusions, and of eyes made clear always to behold the God who is ever with us, and the real importance of the things around us, is the gift that most of us pray for most. "If any man lack wisdom, let him ask." It is a gift, and it is to be obtained from that Holy Spirit who dwells and works in all believers. The measure of their desire is the measure of their possession. That wisdom can be had for the asking, and is not to be won by proudly self-reliant effort. But let us not think that any kind of "asking" suffices to put that great gift in our hearts. The petition that avails must be sincere, intense, constant, and accompanied by corresponding conduct.

Wisdom is not exactly what we should have expected to be named as the main thing lacking in the average Christian. James uses this venerable word with all the associations of its use in the Old Testament, and in all the solemn depth of meaning which he had learned to attach to it, on the lips of psalmists, prophets, and teachers of the true wisdom. If that were at all doubtful, it is made certain by his own subsequent description of "wisdom." He says that it is "from above", and then goes on to ascribe all manner of moral and spiritual good to its presence and working on a man. It is "pure, peaceable, gentle, and easy to be entreated, full of mercy and good fruits" [James 3:17]. You cannot say such glowing things about the wisdom which has its seat in the understanding only, can you? These characteristics must apply to something a great deal more august and more powerful in shaping and refining character.

THE CONSCIOUSNESS OF GOD'S PRESENCE

I will dwell in the house of the Lord forever—Psalm 23:6

What the psalmist desires is that he should be able to keep up unbroken consciousness of being in God's presence, and should be always in touch with Him. That seems hard, and people say, "Impossible! How can I get above my daily work, and be perpetually thinking of God and His will, and realizing consciously communion with Him?" But there is such a thing as having an under-current of consciousness running all through a man's life and mind; such a thing as having a melody sounding in our ears perpetually, "so sweet we know not we are listening to it" until it stops, and then, by the poverty of the naked and silent atmosphere, we know how sweet were the sounds that we scarcely knew we heard, and yet did hear so well high above all the din of earth's noises.

Every man that has ever cherished such an aspiration as this does know the difficulties all too well. And yet, without entering upon thorny and unprofitable questions as to whether the absolute, unbroken continuity of consciousness of being in God's presence is possible for men here below, let us look at the question, which has a great deal more bearing upon our present condition—namely, whether a greater continuity of that consciousness is not possible than we attain to today. It does seem to me to be a foolish and miserable waste of time and temper and energy for good people to be quarreling about whether they can come to the absolute realism of this desire in this world when there is not one of them that is not leagues below the possible realization of it, and knows that he is. At all events, whether or not the line can be drawn without a break at all, the breaks may be a great deal shorter and a great deal less frequent than they are. An unbroken line of conscious communion with God is the ideal; and that is what this singer wanted and worked for. How many of my feelings and thoughts today, or of the things that I have said and done since I woke this morning, would have been done and said and felt exactly the same if there were not a God at all, or if it did not matter in the least whether I ever came into touch with Him or not? Oh, dear friend, it is no vain effort to bring out lives a little bit nearer unbroken continuity of communion with Him. And God knows, and each for himself knows, how much and how sore our need is of such a union. "One thing have I desired of the Lord, that will I seek after; that I," in my study; I, in my shop; I, in my parlor, kitchen, or nursery; I, in my studio; I, in my lecture hall—"may dwell in the house of the Lord all the days of my life" [Ps. 27:4]. In our "Father's house are many mansions" [John 14:2]. The room that we spend most of our lives in, each of us at our tasks or our work-tables, may be in our Father's house, too; and it is only we that can make certain that it shall be.

DESIRE FOR GOD

We shall be satisfied with the goodness of thy house, even of thy temple—
Ps. 65:4

The inmost meaning of the Psalmist's desire is that the consciousness of God shall be diffused throughout the whole of a man's days, instead of being coagulated here and there at points. The Australian rivers in a drought present a picture of the Christian life of far too many of us—a stagnant, stinking pool here, a stretch of blinding gravel there; another little drop of water a mile away, then a long line of foul-smelling mud, and then another little pond. Why? It ought to run in a clear stream—that has a scour in it, and that will take all filth off the surface.

The Psalmist wanted to break down the distinction between sacred and secular; to consecrate work, of whatsoever sort it was. He had learned what so many of us need to learn far more thoroughly, that if our religion does not drive the wheels of our daily business, it is of little use; and that if the field in which our religion has power to control and impel is not that of the trivialities and secularities of our ordinary life, there is no field for it at all.

"All the days of my life" [Ps. 23:6]—Not only on Sundays; not for five minutes in the morning, when I am eager to get to my daily work, and less than five minutes at night, when I am half asleep, but through the long day doing this, that, and the other thing for God, and by God, and with God, and making Him the motive and the power of my course, and the companion to heaven! And if we have, in our lives, things over which we cannot make the sign of the Cross, the sooner we get rid of them the better. And if there is anything in our daily work, or in our characters, about which we are doubtful, here is a good test: does it seem to check our continual communion with God as a band around the wrist might do the continual flow of the blood? Or does it help us to realize His presence? If the former, let us have no more to do with it; if the latter, let us seek to increase it.

Modern teachers tell us that the religious emotions may be exercised, and all the blessing and all the advantage of them secured, although they are not directed to a personal God. The God of this religion without a God is, according to some, collective humanity; according to others, a vague unknowable; according to others, nature, or the physical universe, which can call forth the admiration and dependence and submission, which are the constituents of "religion." But all that is nonsense. The only real religion is the religion which lays a believing hand on Jesus Christ as the Revealer of the Father and the Savior of the world; and sees in Him a God near enough to be known, tender enough to be loved, mighty enough to succor, compassionate enough to answer and to forgive. There can be no substitute for the living God. Reverence, worship, the consecration of heart and life, need a living person to evoke them, and deep beneath all other necessities and cries of the human spirit lies this, so tragically misinterpreted by many of us: "My soul thirsteth for God, for the living God" [Ps. 42:2], who is made known to us in the fullness of His gentleness and His power in the person and face of Jesus Christ.

DWELLING IN GOD'S HOUSE

This is my rest forever: here will I dwell; for I have desired it—Ps. 132:14

This is an allusion not only, as I think, to the Temple, but also to the Oriental habit of giving a man who took refuge in the tent of the sheikh guest-rites of protection and provision and friendship. The habit exists to this day, and travelers among the Bedouin tell us lovely stories of how even an enemy with the blood of the closest relative of the owner of the tent on his hands, if he can once get in there and partake of the salt of the host, is safe, and the first obligation of the owner of the tent is to watch over the life of the fugitive as over his own.

So the Psalmist says in one place, "I desire to have guest-rites in Thy tent; to lift up its fold, and shelter there from the heat of the desert. And although I be dark, and stained with many evils and transgressions against thee, yet I come to claim the hospitality and provision and protection and friendship which the laws of the house do bestow upon a guest." Carrying out substantially the same idea, Paul tells the Ephesians, as if it were the very highest privilege that the gospel brought to the Gentiles: "Ye are no more strangers, but fellow citizens with the saints, and *of the household of God";* incorporated into His household, and dwelling safely in His pavilion as their home. That is to say, the blessedness of keeping up such a continual consciousness of touch with God is, first and foremost, the certainty of infallible protection. Oh, how it minimizes all trouble, and brightens all joys, and calms amid all distractions, and steadies and sobers in all circumstances, to feel ever the hand of God upon us! He who goes through life finding that, when he has trouble to meet, it throws him back on God, and that, when bright mornings of joy drive away nights of weeping, these wake morning songs of praise and are brightest because they shine with the light of a Father's love, will never be unduly moved by any vicissitudes of fortune. Like some inland and sheltered valley, with great mountains shutting it in, that "heareth not the loud winds when they call" beyond the barriers that enclose it, our lives may be tranquilly free from distraction, and may be full of peace, of nobleness, and of strength, on condition of our keeping in God's house all the days of our lives.

Trust brings rest, because it casts all our burdens on another. Every act of reliance, though it does not deliver from responsibility, delivers from anxiety. We see that even when the object of our trust is but a poor creature like ourselves. Husbands and wives who find settled peace in one another, parents and children, patrons and protected, and a whole series of other relationships in life, are witnesses to the fact that the attitude of reliance brings the actuality of repose. A little child goes to sleep beneath its mother's eye, and is tranquil, not only because it is ignorant, but because it is trustful. So, if we will only get behind the shelter, the blast will not blow about us, but we shall be in what they call on the opposite side of the Tweed—in a word that is music in the ears of some of us—a "lown place," where we hear not the loud winds when they call. Trust is rest; even when we lean upon an arm of flesh, though that trust is often disappointed. What is the depth of the repose that comes not from trust that leans against something supposed to be a steadfast oak, that proves to be a broken reed, but against the Rock of Ages! We which have "believed do enter into rest" [Heb. 4:3].

UNION WITH GOD

Whoso hearkeneth unto me shall dwell safely, and shall be quiet from fear of evil—Prov. 1:33

The God whom men know, or think they know, outside of the revelation of Divinity in Jesus Christ, is a God before whom they sometimes tremble, who is far more often their terror than their love, who is their "ghastliest doubt" still more frequently than He is their dearest faith. But the God that is in Christ woos and wins men to Him, and from His great sweetness there streams out, as it were, a magnetic influence that draws hearts to Him. He has made "the rough places plain" [Is. 40:4] and the "crooked things straight" [Is. 42:16]; leveled the mountains and raised the valleys, and cast up across all the wilderness of the world a highway along which "the wayfaring man" [Is. 33:8], though a fool, may travel. Narrow understandings may know, and self-ish hearts may love, and low-pitched confessions may reach the ear of, the God who comes near to us in Christ, that we in Christ may come near to Him. The breaker is come up before us [Mic. 2:13]. "Having therefore, brethren, boldness to enter into the holiest of all . . . by a new and living way, which he hath consecrated for us . . . let us draw near with true hearts" [Heb. 10:19–22].

One of the blessings that come to the dweller in God's house, and not a small one, is that, by the power of this one satisfied longing, driven like an iron rod through all the tortuosities of my life, there will come into it a unity which otherwise few lives are ever able to attain, and the want of which is no small cause of the misery that is great upon men. Most of us seem, to our own consciousness, to live amid endless distractions all our days, and our lives to be a heap of links parted from each other rather than a chain. But if we have that one constant thought with us, and if we are, through all the variety of occupations, true to the one purpose of serving and keeping near God, then we have a charm against the frittering away of our lives in distractions, and the misery of multiplicity, and we enter into the blessedness of unity and singleness of purpose; and our lives become, like the starry heavens in all the variety of their motions, obedient to one impulse. For unity in a life does not depend upon the monotony of its tasks, but upon the simplicity of the motive which impels to all varieties of work. So it is possible for a man harassed by multitudinous avocations, and drawn here and there by some-times apparently conflicting and always bewildering, rapidly-following duties, to say, "This one thing I do" [Phil. 3:13], if all his doings are equally acts of obedience to God.

GUESTS OF GOD

One thing have I desired of the Lord, that will I seek after; that I may dwell in the house of the Lord all the days of my life—Psalm 27:4

"One thing have I *desired* . . . that will I *seek* after." There are two points to be kept in view to that end. A great many people say, "One thing have I desired," and fail in persistent continuity of the desire. No man gets rights of residence in God's house for a longer time than he continues to seek for them. The most advanced of us, and those that have longest been like Anna, who "departed not from the temple" day nor night [Luke 2:37], will certainly eject ourselves, unless, like the Psalmist, we use the verb in both tenses, and say, "One thing *have* I desired . . . that *will* I seek after." John Bunyan saw that there was a back door to the lower regions close by the gates of the Celestial City. There may be men who have long lived beneath the shadow of the sanctuary, and at the last shall be found outside the gates.

But the words not only suggest by the two tenses of the verbs the continuity of the desire which is destined to be granted, but also by the two verbs themselves—*desire* and *seek after*—the necessity of uniting prayer and work. Many desires are unsatisfied because conduct does not correspond to desires. Many a prayer for greater holiness and closer communion with God remains unanswered because the people who pray these prayers never do a thing to fulfill their prayers. I do not say they are hypocrites; certainly they are not consciously so, but I do say that there is a large measure of conventionality that means nothing in the prayers of average Christian people for more holiness and likeness to Jesus Christ.

If we want this desire of dwelling in the house of the Lord to be fulfilled, the day's work must run in the same direction as the morning's petition, and we must, like the psalmist say, "I *have desired* it of the Lord, and I, for my part, *will seek after it.*" Then, whether or not we reach absolutely to the standard, which is none the less to be aimed at, though it seems beyond reach, we shall draw nearer and nearer to it, and God helping our weakness and increasing our strength, quickening us to "desire," and upholding us to "seek after," we may hope that, when the days of our life are past, we shall but remove into an upper chamber, more open to the sunrise and flooded with light, and shall go no more out, but "dwell in the house of the Lord forever" [Ps. 23:6].

TRUE AND FALSE SORROW FOR SIN

Godly sorrow worketh repentance to salvation, not to be repented of: but the sorrow of the world worketh death—2 Cor. 7:10

There is a broad distinction between the right and the wrong kind of sorrow for sin. "Godly sorrow" is literally rendered "*sorrow according to God*," which may either mean sorrow which has reference to God, or sorrow which is in accordance with His will; that is to say, which is pleasing to Him. If it is the former, it will be the latter. I prefer to suppose that it is the former sorrow, which has reference to God.

And then, opposite to that, there is another king of sorrow, which the Apostle calls the "sorrow of the world," which is devoid of that reference to God. Here we have the characteristic difference between the Christian way of looking at my own faults and shortcomings, and the sorrow of the world, which has got no blessing in it, and will never lead to anything like righteousness and peace. It is just this—one has reference to God, puts its sin by His side, sees its blackness relieved against the "fierce light" of the Great White Throne, and the other way has not that reference.

To expand that for a moment, there are plenty of us that, when our sin is behind us, and its bitter fruits are in our hands, are sorry enough for our faults. A man that is lying in the hospital, a wreck, with the sin of his youth gnawing the flesh off his bones, is often sorry that he did not live more soberly and chastely and temperately in his past. That fraudulent bankrupt man that has not received his annulment, and has lost his reputation, and can get nobody to lend him enough money to start himself in business again, as he hangs about the streets slouching in his rags, is sorry enough that he did not keep the straight road. The "sorrow of the world" has no thought about God in it at all. The consequences of sin set many a man's teeth on edge that does not reel any compunction for the wrong that he did. My brother, is that your position?

And then we can come a step further. Crime means the transgression of man's law; wrong means the transgression of conscience's law. Some of us would perhaps have to say, "I have done crime." We are all of us quite ready to say, "I have done wrong many a time"; but there are some of you that hesitate to take the other step, and say, "I have done sin," which is the transgression of God's law.

SIN AND GOD

I will be merciful to their unrighteousness, and their sins . . . will I remember
no more—Heb. 8:12

Sin has, for its correlative, God. If there is no God, there is no sin. There may be faults, there may be failures, there may be transgression, breaches of the moral law, things done inconsistent with man's nature and constitution, and so on; but if there be a God, then we have personal relations to that Person and His law; and when we break His law, it is more than crime; it is more than fault; it is more than transgression; it is more than wrong; it is sin; and it is when you lift the shutter off conscience, and let the light of God rush in upon your hearts and consciences, that you have the wholesome sorrow that worketh repentance and salvation and life.

Oh, dear friend, I do beseech you to lay these simple thoughts to heart! Remember, I am urging no rigid uniformity of experience or character, but I am saying that unless a man has learned to see his sin in the light of God, and in the light of God to weep over it, he has yet to know "the straight gate that leadeth unto life" [Matt. 7:14].

I believe that a very large amount of the superficiality and easygoingness of the Christianity of today comes just from this, that so many who call themselves Christians, that profess it, have never once received a glimpse of themselves. I remember once holding on by the ground on the top of Vesuvius, and looking full into the crater, all swirling with sulphurous fumes. Have you ever looked into your hearts like that, and seen the wreathing smoke and the flashing fire that are there? If you have, you will cleave to that Christ who is your sole deliverance from sin.

But, remember, there is no prescription about depth or amount or length of time during which this sorrow shall be felt. If, on the one hand, it is essential, on the other hand there are a great many people that ought to be walking in the light and the liberty of God's gospel who bring darkness and clouds over themselves by the anxious scrutinizing question, "Is my sorrow deep enough?"

Deep enough! What for? What is the use of sorrow for sin? It is to lead a man to repentance and to faith. If you have received as much sorrow as leads you to penitence and trust, you have received enough. It is not your sorrow that is going to wash away your sin; it is Christ's blood. So let no man trouble himself about the question, Do I have enough sorrow? The one question is, "Has my sorrow led me to cast myself on Christ?"

SORROW ACCORDING TO GOD

And David said unto Nathan, I have sinned against the Lord. And Nathan said unto David, The Lord also hath put away thy sin—2 Sam. 12:13

In 2 Corinthians 7:10 the Apostle Paul takes it for granted that a recognition of our own evil and a consequent penitent regretfulness lies at the foundation of all true Christianity. Now, I do not want to insist upon any uniformity of experience in people, any more than I should insist that all their bodies should be of one shape or of one proportion. Human lives are infinitely different, human dispositions are subtly varied; and because both one and the other are never reproduced exactly in any two people, therefore the religious experience of no two souls can ever be precisely alike.

We have no right to ask—and much harm has been done by asking—for an impossible uniformity of religious experience. You can print off as many copies as you like, for instance, of a drawing of a flower, on a printing press, and they shall all be alike, petal for petal, leaf for leaf, shade for shade; but no two hand-drawn copies will be so precisely alike, still less will any two of the real buds that blow on the bush there. Life produces resemblance with differences; it is machinery that makes facsimilies.

So we insist on no pedantic or unreal uniformity; and yet, while leaving the widest scope for diversity of individual character and experience, and not asking that a man all diseased and blotched with the leprosy of sin for half a lifetime, and a little child that has grown up at his mother's knee, "in the nurture and admonition of the Lord" [Eph. 6:4], and so has been saved innocent of much transgression, shall have the same experience—yet Scripture, as it seems to me, and the nature of the case do unite in asserting that there are certain elements which, in varying proportions indeed, will be found in all true Christian experience, and of these an indispensable one—and in a very large number, if not in the majority of cases, a fundamental one—is this which Paul calls "godly sorrow."

Surely a reasonable consideration of the facts of our conduct and character point to that as the attitude that becomes you and me! Does it not? I do not charge you with crimes, as the law interprets them. I do not suppose that many who read these lines are living in flagrant disregard of the elementary principles of common everyday morality. There are some, no doubt. There are, no doubt, unclean men; there are, no doubt, men and women that are living in avarice and worldliness, and things that the ordinary consciences of the populace point to as faults and blemishes. But I appeal to the so-called respectable people, that can say: "I am not as other men are . . . unjust, adulterers, or even as this publican" [Luke 18:11]. I come to you, and I have this one question to put to you: Looking at your character all around, in the light of the purity and righteousness and love of God, how say ye—guilty or not guilty, sinful or not sinful?

Be honest with yourself, and the answer will not be far to seek.

THE LAW OF LIFE

Walk worthy of God, who calleth you into his own kingdom and glory—
1 Thess. 2:12

Here we have the whole law of Christian conduct in a nutshell. There may be many detailed commandments, but they can all be deduced from this one. We are lifted up above the region of petty prescriptions, and breathe a bracing mountain air. Instead of regulations, very many and very dry, we have a principle which needs thought and sympathy in order to apply it, and is to be carried out by the free action of our own judgments. The whole sum of Christian duty lies in conformity to the character of a Divine Person with whom we have loving relations.

The Old Testament says: "Be ye holy, for I the Lord your God am holy" [Lev. 19:2]. The New Testament says: "Be ye followers of God . . . and walk in love" [Eph. 5:1, 2]. So then, whatever in that Divine nature of flashing brightness and infinite profundity is far beyond our apprehension and grasp, there are in that Divine nature elements—and those the best and most divine in it—which are perfectly within the power of every man to copy.

Is there anything in God that is more Godlike than righteousness and love? And is there any difference in essence between a man's righteousness and God's—between a man's love and God's? The same gases make combustion in the sun and on the earth, and the spectroscope tells you that it is so. The same radiant brightness that flames burning in the love, and flashes white in the purity of God, that may be reproduced in man.

Love is one thing all the universe over. Other elements of the bond that unite us to God are rather correspondent in us to what we find in Him. Our concavity, so to speak, answers to His convexity; our hollowness to His fullness; our emptiness to his all-sufficiency. So our faith, for instance, lays hold upon His faithfulness, and our obedience grasps, and bows before, His commanding will. But the love with which I lay hold of Him is like the love with which He lays hold on me; and righteousness and purity, howsoever different may be their accompaniments in an Infinite and uncreated Nature from what they have in our limited and bounded and progressing being, in essence are one. So, "Be ye holy, for I am holy" [1 Pet. 1:16]; "Walk in the light, as he is in the light" [1 John 1:7], is the law available for all conduct; and the highest Divine perfections, if I may speak of preeminence among them, are the imitable ones, whereby He becomes our Example and our Pattern.

THE CHRISTIAN IDEAL

Only let your conversation be as it becometh of the gospel of Christ—Phil. 1:27

Let no man say that such an injunction is vague or hopeless. You must have a perfect ideal if you are to live at all by an ideal. There cannot be any flaws in your pattern if the pattern is to be of any use. You aim at the stars, and if you do not hit them you may progressively approach them. We need absolute perfection to strain after, and one day—blessed be His Name!—we shall attain it. Try to walk worthy of God, and you will find out how tight that precept grips, and how close it fits.

The love and the righteousness which are to become the law of our lives are revealed to us in Jesus Christ. Whatever may sound impracticable in the injunction to imitate God assumes a more homely and possible shape when it becomes an injunction to follow Jesus. And just as that form of the precept tends to make the law of conformity to the Divine nature more blessed and less hopelessly above us, so it makes the law of conformity to some mere ideal of goodness less cold and unsympathetic. It makes all the difference to our joyfulness and freedom whether we are trying to obey a law of duty, seen only too clearly to be binding, but also above our reach, or whether we have the law in a living Person whom we have learned to love. In the one case there stands upon a pedestal above us a cold perfection, white, complete, marble; in the other case there stands beside us a living law in pattern, a Brother, bone of our bone and flesh of our flesh, whose hand we can grasp, whose heart we can trust, and of whose help we can be sure. To say to me, "follow the ideal of perfect righteousness," is to relegate me to a dreary, endless struggling; to say to me, "Follow your Brother, and be like your Father," is to bring warmth and hope and liberty in to all my effort. The word that says, "Walk worthy of God" is a royal law, the perfect law of perfect freedom.

When we say, "Walk worthy of God," we mean two things—one, "Do after His example," and the other, "Render back to Him what He deserves for what He has done for you." And so this law bids us measure, by the side of that great love that died on the Cross for us all, our poor, imperfect returns of gratitude and of service. He has lavished all His treasure on you; what have you brought Him back? He has given you the whole wealth of His tender pity, of His forgiving mercy, of His infinite goodness. Do you adequately repay such lavish love? Has He not "sown much and reaped little" in your heart? Has He not poured out the fullness of His affection, and have we not answered Him with a few grudging drops squeezed from our hearts?

THE ONE RULE OF CONDUCT

Be ye therefore followers of God, as dear children; and walk in love, as Christ also hath loved us, and gave himself for us—Eph. 5:1, 2

People have always been apt to think of the gospel more as a message of deliverance than as a practical guide. And we all need to make an effort to prevent our natural indolence and selfishness from making us forget that the gospel is quite as much a rule of conduct as a message of pardon.

It is both by the same act. In the very facts on which our redemption depends lies the law of our lives. Do not always be looking at Christ's Cross only as your means of acceptance. Do not only be thinking of Christ's Passion as that which has barred you from the gates of punishment, and has opened for you the gates of the Kingdom of Heaven. It has done all that; but if you are going to stop there, you have only grabbed hold of a very maimed and imperfect edition of the Gospel. The Cross is your *pattern*, as well as the anchor of your hope and the ground of your salvation—if it is anything at all to you. And it is not the ground of your salvation and the anchor of your hope unless it is your pattern. It is the one in exactly the same degree in which it is the other.

So all self-pleasing, all harsh insistence on your own claims, all neglect of suffering and sorrow and sin around you, comes under the lash of this condemnation. If Christian men and women would only learn to take away the scales from their eyes and souls—not looking at Christ's Cross with less absolute trustfulness, as that by which all their salvation comes, but also learning to look at it as closely and habitually as yielding the pattern to which their lives should be conformed—and would let the heart-melting thankfulness which it evokes when gazed at as the ground of our hope prove itself true by its leading them to an effort at imitating that great love, and so walking worthy of the Gospel, how their lives would be transformed! It is far easier to fetter your life with yards of red-tape prescriptions—do this, do not do that; far easier to out-pharisee the Pharisees in punctilious scrupulosities, than it is honestly, and for one hour, to take the Cross of Christ as the pattern of your lives, and to shape yourselves by that.

One looks around upon a lethargic, a luxurious, a self-indulgent, a self-seeking, a world-intoxicated professing Church, and asks, "Are these the people on whose hearts a cross is stamped?" Do these men—or rather let us say, do *we* live as becometh the gospel [Phil. 1:27] which proclaims the divinity of self-sacrifice, and that the law of a perfect human life is perfect self-forgetfulness, even as the secret of the Divine nature is perfect love? Walk "worthy of the gospel of Jesus Christ" [Phil. 1:27].

May 19

A WORTHY CALLING

By this shall all men know that ye are my disciples, if ye have love one to another—John 13:35

Men that are called to high functions prepare themselves therefore. If you knew that you were going away to Australia in six months, would you not be beginning to get your outfit ready? You Christian men profess to believe that you have been called to a condition in which you will absolutely obey God's will, and be the loyal subjects of His Kingdom, and in which you will partake of God's glory. Well then, obey His will here, and let some scattered sparkles of that uncreated light that is one day going to flood your soul lie upon your face today. Do not go and cut your lives into two halves, one of them all contradictory to that which you expect in the other, but bring a harmony between the present, in all its weakness and sinfulness, and that great hope and certain destiny that blazes on the horizon of your hope, as the joyful state to which you have been invited. "Walk worthy of the vocation wherewith ye are called" [Eph. 4:1]. That same thought of the destiny should feed our hope, and make us live under its continual inspiration. A walk worthy of such a calling and such a Caller should know no despondency, nor any weary, heartless lingering, as with tired feet on a hard road. Brave good cheer, undimmed energy, a noble contempt of obstacles, a confidence in our final attainment of that purity and glory which is not depressed by consciousness of present failure—these are plainly the characteristics which ought to mark the advance of the men in whose ears such a summons from such lips rings as their marching orders. And a walk worthy of our calling will turn away from earthly things. If you believe that God has summoned you to His Kingdom and glory, surely, surely, that should deaden in your heart the love and the care for the trifles that lie by the wayside! Surely, surely, if that great Voice is inviting, and that merciful Hand is beckoning you into the light, and showing you what you may possess there, it is not walking according to that summons if you go with your eyes fixed upon the trifles at your feet, and your whole heart absorbed in this present fleeting world! Unworldliness, in its best and purest fashion—by which I mean not only a contempt for material wealth and all that it brings, but the setting loose by everything that is beneath the stars—unworldliness is the only walk that is "worthy of the vocation wherewith ye are called."

And if you hear that voice ringing like a trumpet call, or a commander's shout on the battlefield, into your ears, ever to stimulate you, to rebuke your lagging indifference; if you are ever conscious in your inmost hearts of the summons to His kingdom and glory, then, no doubt, by a walk worthy of it, you will make your calling sure; and there "an entrance shall be ministered unto you abundantly into the everlasting kingdom" [2 Pet. 1:11].

"CALLED TO BE SAINTS"

Beloved of God: called to be saints—Rom. 1:7

In the last chapter of the Epistle to the Romans (verse 2), we read about a very small matter, that it is to be done "as becometh saints." It is only about the receiving of a good woman that was traveling from Corinth to Rome, and extending hospitality to her in such a manner as should be expected of professing Christians; but the very minuteness of the details to which the great principle is applied points a lesson. The biggest principle is not too big to be brought down to the narrowest details, and that is the beauty of principles as distinguished from regulations. Regulations try to be minute, and however minute you make them, some case always starts up that is not exactly provided for in them. And so the regulations come to nothing. A principle does not try to be minute, but it casts its net wide, and it gathers various cases into its meshes. Like the fabled tent in the old legend, that could contract so as to have room for but one man, or extend wide enough to hold an army; so this great principle of Christian conduct can be brought down to giving "Phebe our sister, which is a servant of the Church which is at Cenchrea" [Rom. 16:1], good food and a comfortable lodging, and any other little kindnesses, when she comes to Rome. And the same principle may be widened out to embrace and direct us in the largest tasks and most difficult circumstances.

"As becometh saints"—the name is an omen, and carries in it rules of conduct. The root idea of "saint" is "one separated to God," and the secondary idea which flows from that is "one who is pure." All Christians are "saints." They are consecrated and set apart for God's service, and in the degree in which they are conscious of and live out that consecration, they are pure. So their name, or rather the great fact which their name implies, should be ever before them, a stimulus and a law. We are bound to remember that we are consecrated, separated as God's possession, and that therefore purity is indispensable. The continual consciousness of this relation and its resulting obligations would make us recoil from impurity as instinctively as the sensitive plant shuts up its little green fingers when anything touches it; or as the wearer of a white robe will draw it up high above the mud on a filthy pavement. Walk worthily of saints is another way of saying, Be true to your own best selves. Work up to the highest ideal of your character. That is far more wholesome than to be always looking at our faults and failures, which depress and tempt us to think that the actual is the measure of the possible, and the past or present of the future. There is no fear of self-conceit or of a mistaken estimate of ourselves. The more clearly we keep our best and deepest self before our consciousness, the more shall we learn a rigid judgment of the miserable contradictions to it in our daily outward life, and even in our thoughts and desires. It is a wholesome exhortation, when it follows these others of which we have been speaking (and not else), which bids Christians remember that they are saints and live up to their name.

THE ALL-COMPREHENSIVE LAW

Except your righteousness shall exceed the righteousness of the Scribes and Pharisees, ye shall in no case enter into the kingdom of heaven—Matt. 5:20

A Christian's inward and deepest self is better than his outward life. We all have convictions in our inmost hearts which we do not work out, and beliefs that do not influence us as we know they ought to do, and sometimes wish that they did. By our own fault our lives but imperfectly show their real inmost principle. Friction always wastes power before motion is produced.

So then we may well gather together all our duties in this final form of the all-comprehensive law, and say to ourselves, "Walk worthily of saints." Be true to your name, to your best selves, to your deepest selves. Be true to your separation for God's service, and to the purity which comes from it. Be true to the life which God has implanted in you. That life may be very feeble, and covered by a great deal of rubbish, but it is Divine. Let it work, let it out! Do not disgrace your name!

These are the phrases of the law of Christian conduct. They reach far, they fit close, they penetrate deeper than the needlepoints of minute regulations. If you will live in a manner corresponding to the character, and worthy of the love of God as revealed in Christ, and in conformity with the principles that are enthroned upon His Cross, and in obedience to the destiny held forth in your high calling, and in faithfulness to the name that He Himself has impressed upon you; then your righteousness shall exceed the righteousness of the painful and punctilious pharisaical obedience to outward commands, and all things lovely and of good report will spring to life in your hearts and bear fruit in your lives.

All these exhortations go on the understanding that you are a Christian; that you have taken Christ for your Savior, and are resting upon Him, and recognizing in Him the revelation of God, and in His Cross the foundation of your hope; that you have listened to, and yielded to, the Divine summons, and that you have a right to be called a saint. Is that presumption true about you, my friend? If it is not, Christianity thinks that it is of no use wasting time talking to you about conduct.

The first message which Christ sends to you is, to trust your sinful selves to Him as your only, all-sufficient Savior. When you have accepted Him, and are leaning on Him with all your weight of sin and suffering, and loving Him with your ransomed heart, then, and not till then, will you be in a position to hear His law for your life, and to obey it; then, and not till then, will you appreciate the Divine simplicity and breadth of the great command to walk worthy of God [1 Thess. 2:12], and the Divine tenderness and power of the motive which enforces it, and prints it on yielding and obedient hearts, even the dying love and Cross of His Son. Till then, listen to and accept the great answer of our Lord's to those who came to Him for a rule of conduct, instead of for the gift of Life: "This is the work of God, that ye should believe on him whom he hath sent" [John 6:29].

BLIND TO OUR OWN FAULTS

And [David] said to Nathan, As the Lord liveth, the man that hath done this thing shall surely die . . . because he did this thing, and because he had no pity. And Nathan said to David, Thou art the man—2 Sam. 12:5-7

If a man's own sin is held up before him a little disguised, he says, "How ugly it is!" And if only for a moment he can be persuaded that it is not his own conduct, but somebody else's, that he is judging, the instinctive condemnation comes. We have got two sets of names for vices: one set which rather mitigates and excuses them, and another set which puts them in their real hideousness. We keep the palatable set for home consumption, and liberally distribute the plainspoken, ugly set among the vices and faults of our friends.

The same thing which I call in myself prudence, I call in you meanness. The same thing which you call in yourself generous living, you call in your friend filthy sensualism. That which, to the doer of it, is only righteous indignation, to the onlooker is passionate anger. That which, in the practicer of it, is no more than a due regard for the interests of his own family and himself in the future, is, to the envious lookers-on, shabbiness and meanness in money matters. That which, to the liar, is only prudent diplomatic reticence, to the listener is falsehood. That which, in the man that judges his own conduct, is but "a choleric word," is, in his friend, when he judges him, "flat blasphemy."

And so we go all around the circle, and condemn our own vices, when we see them in other people. So the King who had never thought, when he stole away Uriah's one ewe lamb, and did him to death by traitorous commands, setting him in the front of the battle, that he was lacking in compassion, blazes up at once, and righteously sentences the other "man" to death, "because he had no pity." He had never thought of himself or of his crime as cruel, as mean, as selfish, as heartless. But when he sees a partially disguised picture of it, he knows it for the devil's child that it is. Robert Burns in his poem "To a Louse," writes in his Scottish dialect: "Oh! wad some power the giftie gie us, To see oursels as ithers see us; It wad frae many an error free us". And so it would, to see ourselves as we see others. We judge our brother and ourselves by two different standards.

For godliness, we need to cultivate the habit of discrimination between good and evil, right and wrong, because the world is full of illusions, and we are very blind. We need to cultivate the habit of self-control, and rigid repression of passions, and lusts, and desires, and tastes, and inclinations before His calm and sovereign will, because the world is full of fire, and our hearts and natures are tinder. And we need to cultivate the habit of patience in all its three senses of endurance in sorrow, of persistence in service, and of hope of the future, because the more a man cultivates that habit, the larger will be his stock of proofs of the lovingkindness and goodness of his God, and the easier and more blessed it will be for him to live in continual communion with Him. There is no way by which your religion can become deep, all-pervasive, practical, or sovereign in your lives, but the old road of effort and of prayer. "Exercise thyself" [1 Tim. 4:7], as a gymnast does in the arena—exercise thyself unto godliness—and do not fancy that the Christian life comes as a matter of course on the back of some one initial act of a long-forgotten faith in Jesus Christ.

FAMILIARIZATION OF HABIT

Who is he that saith, and it cometh to pass, when the Lord commandeth it not?—
Lam. 3:37

Let me remind you how a strong wish for a thing that seems desirable always tends to confuse to a man the plain distinction between right and wrong; and how passions once excited, or the animal lusts and desires once kindled in a man, go straight to their object without the smallest regard to whether that object is to be reached by the breach of all laws, human and Divine, or not. If a man is hungry, and bread is before him, his mouth waters, whether it is his own or other people's. Excite any passion, and the passion is but a blind propensity towards certain good, and has no question or consideration of whether right or wrong is involved at all. Habit familiarizes with evil, and diminishes our sense of it as evil. A man that has been for a half-a-day, in some ill-ventilated room does not notice the poisonous atmosphere; if you go into it, you are half-suffocated at first, and breathe more easily as you get used to it. A man can live amid the foulest poison of evil; and, as the Styrian peasants get fat upon arsenic, his whole nature may seem to thrive by the poison that it absorbs. They tell us that the breed of fish that live in the lightless caverns in the bowels of some mountains, by long disuse have had their eyes atrophied out of them, and are blind because they have lived out of the light. And so men that live in the love of evil lose the capacity of discerning the evil. And he that walketh in darkness becomes blind, blind to his sin, and blind to all the realities of life.

Then is it not also true, that many of us systematically and of set purpose continually avoid all questions as to the moral nature of our conduct? How many a man and woman never sits down to think whether what they have been doing is right or wrong, because they have, deep down, an uneasy suspicion as to what the answer would be. So, by reason of fostering passion, by reason of listening to wishes, by reason of the habit of wrong doing, by reason of the systematic avoidance of all careful investigation of our character and of our conduct, we lose the power of fairly deciding upon the nature of our own acts.

In order to secure habitual godliness, you will want manly strength and vigor, because you can get no hold of an unseen God except by a definite effort of thought, which will require resolute will. There we touch on one of the reasons why much modern Christianity is so feeble. We do not screw ourselves up to think about God and Christ in our daily life. So the truths which we believe slip from our slack grasp before we know that they are gone. A majician will put a coin in a man's palm, and shut his hand upon it, and say, "Are you sure you have it?" "Open your hands." It is not there. That is how a good many of your lose your religion; you think you have it; you once had it. The last time you looked at it, it was there. It is not there now. Why? Because you have not added to your faith strength, and made the efforts of mind and will which are needed in order to keep hold of the things which have been freely given to you of God. Do not spend your time merely trying to cultivate special graces of the Christian character, however needful they may be for you, and however beautiful they may be in themselves. Seek to have that which sanctifies and strengthens them all. Faith is the foundation, godliness the apex and crown.

GOD'S GREAT DESIRE

God our Savior, who will have all men to be saved, and to come unto the
knowledge of the truth—1 Tim. 2:3, 4

God wants to save the world, but God can only save men one at a time. There must be an individual access to Him, as I have said about the conviction of sin, just as if He and I were the only two beings in the whole universe. There is no wholesale reception into God's Church or into God's kingdom; God's mercy is not given to crowds, except as composed of individuals who have individually received it. There must be the personal act of faith; there must be my solitary coming to Him. As the old mystics used to define prayer, so I might define the whole process by which men are saved from their sins, "the flight of the lonely soul to the lonely God." My brother, it is not enough for you to say, "We have sinned"; say, "I have sinned." It is not enough that from a gathered congregation there should go up the united litany, "Lord, have mercy upon us!" "Christ, have mercy upon us!" "Lord, have mercy upon us!" You must make the prayer your own: "Lord have mercy upon *me!*" It is not enough that you should believe, as I suppose most of you fancy that you believe, that Christ has died for the sins of the whole world. That belief will give you no share in His blessedness. You must come to closer grips with Him than that; and you must be able to say, "Who loved *me*, and gave Himself for *me*." Let us have no running away into the crowd. Come out, and stand by yourself, and for yourself stretch out your own hand, and take Christ for yourself.

A man may die of starvation in a granary. You may be lost in the midst of this abundance that Christ has supplied for you. And the difference between really possessing salvation and losing it lies very largely in the difference between saying "us" and "me." "Thou art the man" in regard of the general accusation of sin; "Thou art the man" [2 Sam. 12:7] in regard of the solemn law which proclaims "the soul that sinneth it shall die" [Ezek. 18:20]. And—blessed be God!—"Thou art the man" in regard of the great promise that says, "If any man thirst, let him come unto me and drink" [John 7:37].

Christ gives you a blank check in this world: "Whoso cometh unto me, I will in no wise cast out" [John 6:37]. Write your own name in, and by thy personal faith in the Lamb of God that died for thee, your sins shall pass away; and all the fullness of God shall be your very own forever. "If thou be wise, thou shalt be wise for thyself; and if thou scornest, thou alone shalt bear it" [Prov. 9:12].

A MESSAGE OF MERCY

The sacrifices of God are a broken spirit: a broken and a contrite heart, O God, thou wilt not despise—Psalm 51:17

One indispensable characteristic and certain criterion of a true message and gospel from God is that it pierces the conscience and kindles the sense of sin. There is a great deal of so-called Christian teaching, both from pulpits and books, in this day, which, to my mind, is altogether defective by reason of its under-estimate of the cardinal fact of sin, and its consequent failure to represent the fundamental characteristic of the gospel as being deliverance and redemption. I am quite sure that the root of nine tenths of all the heresies that have ever afflicted the Christian Church, and of the weaknesses of so much popular Christianity, is none other than this failure adequately to recognize the universality and the gravity of the fact of transgression. If a thing comes to you, calls itself God's message, and does not start with man's sin, nor put in the forefront of its utterances the way by which the dominion of that sin in your own heart can be broken, and the penalties of that sin in your present and future life can be swept away, *ipso facto*, it is condemned, as not a gospel from God, or fit for man. Oh, my brother, it sounds harsh; but it is the truest kindness, when Nathan stands before the King, and with his flashing eye, and stern, calm voice says, "Thou art the man" [2 Sam. 12:7]. Was not that nobler, truer, tenderer, worthier of God, than if he had smoothed him down with soft speeches that would not have roused his conscience? Is it not the truest benevolence that keeps the surgeon's hand steady while his heart is touched by the pain he inflicts, as he thrusts his gleaming instrument of tender cruelty into the poisonous sore? And is not God's mercy and love manifest for us in this, that He begins all His work with us with the grave, solemn indictment of each soul by itself, "Thou art the man." "He showed me all the mercy, for He taught me all the sin."

Sin is a universal disease. Humanity is bound in one because all of us are among the multitude of powerless folk. Like the boils and sores that broke out in Egypt when Moses tossed the dust in the air, whether it is Pharaoh or the slave grinding at the millstone, or the outcast on the dunghill, the sore is there on every skin. Does not the assurance that God's great love is not turned away from men by their transgressions feed the hope—nay, rather, inspire the certainty—that for all the sick there is healing? It seems to me that any man that believes in a God who is not a devil ought to believe in a God who revels Himself. Here is the very weakness of what nowadays is called "theism," that, asserting the existence of a Supreme Being who is love and righteousness, it maintains that that Being has never said a single word to men, and never done a single thing, to lift them out of the mire. Whosoever may believe that, I cannot; and it seems to me that the doctrine of Christianity is far more in consonance with the assurance that He is love than that dreary creed that the infinite and loving God has not spoken, and never will nor can speak, to His world. Carlyle, in one of his bursts of melancholy, said, speaking about the Deity as he conceived Him, "And He has done nothing!" He *has* done something. He has opened "a fountain . . . for sin and for uncleanness" [Zech. 13:1].

THE NEED OF A DIVINE REVELATION

Search the Scriptures, for in them ye think ye have eternal life; and they are they which testify of me—John 5:39

We want another than our own voice to lay down the law of conduct, and to accuse and condemn the breaches of it. Conscience is not a wholly reliable guide, nor either an impartial nor an all-knowing judge. Unconsciousness of evil is not innocence. It is not the purest of women that wipes her mouth and says, "I have done no harm." My conscience says to me, "It is wrong to do wrong"; but when I say to my conscience, "Yes, and tell me what is wrong?" there is a large variety of answers possible. A man may sophisticate his conscience, and bribe his conscience, and throttle his conscience, and sear his conscience. And so the man that is worst, who, therefore, ought to be most chastised by his conscience, has most immunity from it; and where, if it is to be of use, it ought to be most powerful, there it is weakest.

What then? Why this, then—a standard that varies is not a standard; men are left with a leaden rule. My conscience, your conscience, is like the standard measures which we at present possess, which by their very names—foot, handbreadth, nail, and the like— tell us that they were originally but the length of one man's limb. And so your measure of right and wrong, and another man's measure, though they may substantially correspond, yet have differences due to your differences of education, character, and a thousand other things. So also the individual man's standard needs to be rectified. You have to send all the weights and measures up to the Tower now and then, to get them stamped and certified. And, as I believe, this fluctuation of our moral judgments shows the need for a fixed pattern and firm, unchangeable standard, external to our mutable selves. A light on deck which pitches with the pitching ship is no guide. It must flash from a white pillar founded on a rock and immovable amid the restless waves. Our need of such a standard raises a strong presumption that a good God will give us what we need, if He can. Such a standard He has given, as I believe, in the revelation of Himself which lies in this book of God, and culminates in the life and character of Jesus Christ our Lord. There, and by that, we can set our watches. There we can read the law of morality, and by our deflections from it we can measure the amount of our guilt.

THE EMPIRE OF FEAR

Who is among you that feareth the Lord, that obeyeth the voice of His servant, that walketh in darkness, and hath no light? let him trust in the name of the Lord—Is. 50:10

Fear is a shrinking apprehension of evil as befalling us, from the person or thing which we dread. We are sometimes brought face to face with that solemn thought that there are conditions of human nature in which the God who ought to be our dearest joy and most ardent desire becomes our ghastliest dread. The root of such an unnatural perversion of all that a creature ought to feel towards its loving Creator lies in the simple consciousness of discordance between God and man, which is the shadow cast over the heart by the face of sin. God is righteous; God righteously administers His universe. God enters into relations of approval or disapproval with His responsible creature. Therefore there lies, dormant for the most part, but present in every heart, and active in the measure in which that heart is informed as to itself, the slumbering cold dread that between it and God things are *not* as they ought to be.

I believe, for my part, that such a dumb, dim consciousness of discord attaches to all men, though it is often smothered, often ignored, and often denied. But there it is; the snake hibernates, but it is coiled in the heart all the same; and warmth will awake it. Then it lifts its crested head, and shoots out its forked tongue, and venom passes into the veins. A dread of God—the ghastliest thing in the world, the most unnatural but universal, unless expelled by perfect love!

Arising from that discomforting consciousness of discord there come, likewise, other forms and objects of dread. For if I am not in harmony with Him, what will be my fate in the midst of a universe administered by Him, and in which all are His servants? I sometimes wonder how it is that godless men front the facts of human life, and do not go mad! For here are we, naked, feeble, alone, plunged into a whirlpool, from the awful vortices of which we cannot extricate ourselves. There foam and swirl all manner of evils, some of them certain, some of them probable, any of them possible, since we are at discord with Him who wields all the forces of the universe, and wields them all with a righteous hand. "The stars in their courses fight against" [Judg. 5:20] the man that does not fight for God. While all things serve the soul that serves Him, all are embattled against the man that is against, or not for, God and His will.

Then there arises up another object of dread, which, in like manner, derives all its power to terrify and to hurt from the fact of our discordance with God; and that is "the shadow feared of man," that stands shrouded by the path, and waits for each of us.

FEAR GOD

Fear God, and keep his commandments: for this is the whole duty of man—
Eccl. 12:13

God; God's universe; God's messenger, Death—these are facts with which we stand in relation, and if our relations with Him are out of gear, then He, and all of these, are legitimate objects of dread to us.

But there is something else that casts out fear than perfect love, and that is—perfect levity. For it is the explanation of the fact that so many of us know nothing about what I am saying, and fancy that I am exaggerating or putting forward false views. There is a type of men who are below both fear and love, directed towards God; for they never think about Him, or trouble their heads concerning either Him or their relations to Him, or anything that flows therefrom. It is a strange faculty that we all have, of forgetting unwelcome thoughts and shutting our eyes to the things that we do not want to see, like Nelson when he put the telescope to his blind eye at Copenhagen, because he would not obey the signal of recall. But surely it is an ignoble thing that men should ignore or shuffle out of sight with inconsiderateness the real facts of their condition, like boys whistling in a churchyard, to keep their spirits up, and saying, "Who's afraid?" just because they are so very much afraid. Dear friend, do not rest until you face the facts, and, having faced them, have found the way to reverse them! Surely, surely, it is not worthy of men to turn away from anything so certain as that between a sin-loving man and God there must exist such a relation as will bring evil and sorrow to that man, as surely as God is! And He is. I urge you to take to heart these things, and do not turn away from them with a shake of your shoulders, and say, "He is preaching the narrow, old-fashioned doctrine of a religion of fear." No! I am not. But I am preaching this plain fact, that a man who is in discord with God has reason to be afraid, and I come to you with the old exhortation of the prophet, "Be troubled, ye careless ones" [Is. 32:11]. For there is nothing more ignoble or irrational than security which is only possible by covering over unwelcome facts. "Be troubled!" and let the trouble lead you to the Refuge.

THE MISSION OF FEAR

Every man hath his sword upon his thigh, because of fear in the night—Song 3:8

John uses a rare word when he says, "Fear hath *torment*" [1 John 4:18]. "Torment" does not convey the whole idea of the word. It means suffering, but suffering for a purpose; suffering which is correction; suffering which is disciplinary; suffering which is intended to lead to something beyond itself. Fear, the apprehension of personal evil, has the same function in the moral world as pain has in the physical. It is a symptom of disease, and is intended to bid us look for the remedy and the Physician. What is an alarm bell for but to rouse the sleepers, and to hurry them to the refuge? And so this wholesome, manly dread of the certain issue of discord with God is meant to do for us what the angels did for Lot; lay a mercifully violent hand on the shoulder of the sleeper, and shake him into aroused wakefulness, and hasten him out of Sodom before the fire bursts through the ground, and was met by the fire from above. The intention of fear is to lead to that which shall annihilate it and take away its cause.

There is nothing more ridiculous, nothing more likely to betray a man, than the indulgence in an idle fear which does nothing to prevent its own fulfillment. Horses in a burning stable are so paralyzed by dread that they cannot stir, and they get burnt to death. And for a man to be afraid—as every man ought to be who is conscious of unforgiven sin—for a man to be afraid, and there an end, is absolute insanity. I fear; then what do I do? Nothing! And that is true about hosts of us.

What should I do? Let the dread direct me to its source, my own sinfulness. Let the discovery of my own sinfulness direct me to its remedy, the righteousness and the Cross of Jesus Christ. He, and He alone, can deal with the disturbing element in my relation to God. He can "deliver me from my enemies" [Ps. 59:1]. It is Christ and His work, Christ and His sacrifice, Christ and His indwelling Spirit, that will comfort and overcome sin and all its consequences in any man and every man; taking away its penalty, lightening the heart of the burden of its guilt, delivering from its love and dominion— all three of which things are the barbs of the arrows with which fear riddles heart and conscience. So my fear should proclaim to me the merciful Name that is above every name [see Eph. 1:21], and drive me as well as draw me to Christ, the Conqueror of sin and the Antagonist of all dread. I am not preaching the religion of fear; but I think we shall scarcely understand the religion of love unless we recognize that dread is a legitimate part of an unforgiven man's attitude towards God. My fear should be to me like the misshapen guide that may lead me to the fortress where I shall be safe. Oh, do not tamper with the wholesome sense of dread. Do not let it lie, generally sleeping, and now and then awaking in your hearts, and bringing about nothing. Sailors that crash on with all sails set—stunsails and all—while the barometer is rapidly falling, and the boding clouds are on the horizon, and the line of the approaching gale is ruffling the sea yonder, have themselves to blame if they sink. Look to the falling barometer, and make ready for the coming storm, and remember that the mission of fear is to lead you to the Christ who will take it away.

THE EXPULSION OF FEAR

There is no fear in love, but perfect love casteth out fear: because fear hath torment. He that feareth is not made perfect in love—1 John 4:18

You cannot love and fear the same person, unless the love is of a very rudimentary and imperfect character. But just as when you pour pure water into a bladder, the poisonous gases that it may have contained will be driven out before it, so when love comes in dread goes out. The river, turned into the foul sewers of the heart, will sweep out all the filth before it, and leave everything clear. The black, greasy smoke-wreath, touched by the fire of Christ's love, will flash out into ruddy flame like that which has kindled them. And Christ's love will kindle in your hearts, if you accept it, and apprehend it aright, a love which will burn up and turn into fuel for itself the now useless dread.

Inconsistent as the two emotions are in themselves, in practice, they may be united by reason of the imperfection of the nobler. And in the Christian life they are united with terrible frequency. There are many professing Christian people who live all their days with a burden of shivering dread upon their shoulders, and an icy-cold fear in their hearts, just because they have not got close enough to Jesus Christ, and kept their hearts with sufficient steadfastness under the quickening influences of His love, to have shaken off their dread as a sick man's distempered fancies. A little love has not mass enough in it to drive out thick, clustering fears. There are hundreds of professing Christians who know very little indeed of that joyous love of God which swallows up and makes impossible all dread, who, because they have not a loving present consciousness of a loving Father's loving will, tremble when they front in imagination, and still more when they meet in reality, the evils that must come, and who cannot face the thought of death with anything but shrinking apprehension. There is far too much of the old leaven of selfish dread left in the experiences of many Christians. "I feared thee because thou art an austere man—and so, because I was afraid, I went and hid my talent, and did nothing for thee" [see Luke 19:21]—is a transcript of the experience of far too many of us. The one way to get deliverance is to go to Jesus Christ and keep close by Him.

There is only one wise thing to do, and that is to make clean work of getting rid of the occasion of dread, which is the fact of sin. Take all your sin to Jesus Christ; He will—and He only can—deal with it. He will lay His hand on you, as He did of old, with the characteristic word that was so often upon His lips, and which He alone is competent to speak in its deepest meaning. "Fear not, it is I," and He will give you the courage that He commands.

God hath not given us the spirit of fear, but of "power, and of love, and of a sound mind" [2 Tim. 1:7]. "Ye have not received the spirit of bondage again to fear, but ye have received the Spirit of adoption whereby we cry Abba! Father" [Rom. 8:15], and cling to Him as a child who knows his father's heart too well to be afraid of anything in his father, or of anything that his father's hand can send.

THE PROMISE OF THE PENTECOST

Is the Spirit of the Lord straitened?—Micah 2:7
And they were all filled with the Holy Spirit—Acts 2:4

What did the Pentecost declare and hold forth for the faith of the Church? I need not dwell at any length upon this thought. The facts are familiar to you, and the inferences drawn from them are commonplace and known to us all. But let me just enumerate them as briefly as may be. "Suddenly there came a sound . . . as of a rushing mighty wind, and it filled all the house where they were sitting. And there appeared . . . cloven tongues as of fire, and it sat upon each of them; and they were all filled with the Holy Ghost" [Acts 2:2–4]. What lay in that? First, the promise of a Divine Spirit whose symbols express some, at all events, of the characteristics and wonderfulness of His work. The "rushing of a mighty wind" spoke of a power which varied in its manifestations from the gentlest breath that scarce moves the leaves on the summer trees to the wildest blast that casts down all which stands in its way. The natural symbolism of the wind, the least material to the popular apprehension of all material forces, and of which the connection with the immaterial part of a man's personality has been expressed in all languages, point to a Divine, to an immaterial, to a might, to a life-giving power which is free to blow whither it listeth, and of which men can mark the effects, though they are all ignorant of the force itself. The twin symbol, the fiery tongues which parted and sat upon each of them, speak in like manner of the divine influences, not as destructive, but full of quick rejoicing energy and life, the power to transform and to purify. From wherever the fire comes, it changes all things into its own substance. From wherever the fire comes, there the ruddy spires shoot upward toward the heavens. From wherever the fire comes, there all bonds and fetters are melted and consumed. And so this fire transforms, purifies, ennobles, quickens, sets free; and where the fiery spirit is, there is energy, swift life, rejoicing activity, transforming and transmuting power which changes the recipient of the flame into flame himself.

In the fact of Pentecost there is the promise of a Divine Spirit which is to influence all the moral side of humanity. This is the great and glorious distinction between the Christian doctrine of inspiration and all others which have, in heathen lands, partially reached similar conceptions, that the Gospel of Jesus Christ has laid emphasis upon the *Holy* Spirit, and has declared that holiness of heart is the touchstone and test of all claims of Divine inspiration. Gifts are much, graces are more; and inspiration which makes wise is to be coveted, and inspiration which makes good is transcendently better. And there we find the safeguard against all the fanaticisms which have sometimes invaded the Christian Church, that the Spirit which dwells in men, and makes them free from the obligations of outward law and cold morality, is a Spirit that works a deeper holiness than law dreamed, and a more spontaneous and glad conformity to all things that are fair and good than any legislation and outward commandment can ever enforce.

THE GIFT OF THE SPIRIT

*And there appeared unto them cloven tongues, like as of fire; and it sat upon each
one of them—Acts 2:3*

The Spirit that came at Pentecost is not merely a Spirit of rushing might and of swift-flaming energy, but it is a Spirit of holiness whose most blessed and intimate work is all the homely virtues and sweet, unpretending goodnesses which can adorn and gladden humanity. And then the early story carried in it the promise and prophecy of a Spirit granted to all the Church. "They were all filled with the Holy Ghost" [Acts. 2:4].

There is the true democracy of Christianity, that its very basis is laid in the thought that every member of the body is equally close to the Head, and equally recipient of the life. There are none now who have a spirit which others do not possess. The ancient aspiration of the Jewish Lawgiver, "Would God that all the Lord's people were prophets, and that the Lord would put His Spirit upon them," is fulfilled in the experience of Pentecost; and the handmaiden and the children, as well as the old men and the servants, receive of that universal gift. Therefore pontifical claims, special functions, privileged classes, are alien to the spirit of Christianity, and blasphemies against the inspiring God. If "one is your master . . . all ye are brethren" [Matt. 23:8]. And if we have all been made to drink into one Spirit, then no longer hath any man dominion over our faith for power for us to intervene and to intercede with God. The promise of the early history was that of a spirit of swift energy, of transforming power, acting upon the moral nature granted to the whole Church, and filling the whole humanity of the men to whom He was granted; filling in the measure, of course, of their receptivity; filling, as the great sea does, all the creeks and the indentations along the shore. The deeper the creek, the deeper the water in it; the further inland it runs, the further will the refreshing sea water penetrate the bosom of the continent. And so each man, according to his character, stature, circumstances, and all the varying conditions which determine his power of receptivity, will receive a varying measure of that gift; and yet it is meant that all shall be full. The little vessel, the tiny cup, as the great cistern and the enormous vat, each contains according to its capacity. And if all are filled, then this quick Spirit must have the power to influence all the provinces of human nature, must touch the intellectual, must touch the moral, must touch the spiritual. The temporary manifestations and extraordinary signs of His power may well drop away as the flower drops away when the fruit has set. The operations of the Divine Spirit are to be felt thrilling through all the nature, and every part of the man's being is to be recipient of the power. Just as when you take a candle and plunge it into a jar of oxygen it blazes up, so my poor human nature, immersed in that Divine Spirit, baptized in the Holy Ghost, shall flame in all its parts into unsuspected and hitherto inexperienced brightness, Such are the elements of the promise of Pentecost.

THE REWARD OF CHRIST'S CONFLICT

Who for the joy that was set before him, endured the cross, despising the shame, and is set down at the right hand of the throne of God—Heb. 12:2

Our Lord's whole life is represented as being shaped and influenced by a vivid realization of an unseen reward; which vivid realization He owed to His faith. What was this unseen reward? The "joy that was set before Him." The image of the race is carried on here from the previous verses. At the finish line hangs the glittering crown, in the full view of the runners; so shining afar, and ever in the eye of that fighting, struggling Captain of our salvation, hung the gleaming glories of the "joy that was set before Him."

And what was the joy? I think the subsequent words must be taken as being the answer to it: "for the joy that was set before Him" was the joy into which He has entered—namely, His session at the right hand of God, or, in other words, the lifting up of His manhood into a participation with Divinity.

Along with the strong impulse of obedience to the will of the Father, and in perfect harmony with self-forgetting and supreme love to the whole world, another strand of the gold cord which bound our great sacrifice to the horns of the altar was the thought of the joy that was to come to Himself. That joy was to sit at the right hand of the Throne.

And if this seems to introduce an element of self-regard into our Lord's passion, which strikes cold on our hearts, let us not forget that all that exaltation is for our sakes, that it was all left for our sakes by the Incarnate Word, and that all which He won by His Cross and Passion was but the entrance of His manhood into the glory which was His own before the world was. Nor are we to forget that He is *"for us* entered" [Heb. 6:20] within the veil, nor that His exaltation is in order to His saving to the uttermost with God, before His incarnation, as a thing to be eagerly retained, so He did not look upon His sitting on the Father's Throne, after His passion, as a thing to be eagerly desired for Himself alone, but chiefly because by it He could carry on and complete His great work. So that we may allowably say, "The joy of the Lord is the salvation of His servants." "He shall see of the travail of His soul and . . . be satisfied" [Is. 53:11], and the joy of the shepherd when he bears the lost sheep on his shoulders, and the joy of the householder when the lost treasure is recovered, and the joy of a true elder brother when the prodigal comes home—are all blended in that great motive which nerved Jesus for His Cross, and form part, and the chief part, of the joy that was set before Him.

THE PATH OF SUFFERING

For in that he himself hath suffered being tempted, he is able to succor them that are tempted—Heb. 2:18

This issue of our Lord's life He had to keep before Himself by a constant effort. He trod the same path which others have to tread. He, too, like Abraham and Moses, and the others of the host of the faithful, had to keep His conviction of an unseen good, bright and powerful, by an effort of will, while surrounded by the illusions of time and sense. His faith grasped the unseen, and in the strength of that conviction impelled Him to do and suffer.

We have the same path to tread. We, too, if we are to do anything in this world befitting or like our Master, must rule our lives in the same fashion as our Master ruled His. That is to say, we must subordinate rigidly the present, and all its temptations, fascinations, cares, joys, and sorrows, to that far-off issue discerned by faith and by faith alone, but by faith clearly ascertained to be the one real substance, the one thing for which it is worthwhile to live and blessed to die. A life of faith, a life of effort to keep ever before us the unseen crown, will be a life noble and lofty. We are ever tempted to forget it. The "Man with the Muckrake," in John Bunyan's homely parable, was so occupied with the foul-smelling dung-heap that he thought a treasure, that he had no eyes for the crown hanging a hair's breadth over his head. A hair's breadth? Yes! And yet the distance was as great as if the universe had lain between.

Every man's life is ennobled in the measure in which he lives for a future. Even if it be a shabby and near future, in so far as it is future, such a life is better than a life that is lived for the present. A man that gets his wages once in a year will generally be, in certain respects, a higher type of man than he who gets them once a week. To take far-off views is, *pro tanto*, as far as it goes—an elevation of humanity. To be absorbed in the present moment is to be degraded to the level of the beasts.

The Christian "prize," which faith makes clear to us, has this great advantage over all other objects of pursuit—that it is too far off ever to be reached and left behind. Men in this world win their objects or lose them; but in either case they pass them and leave them in the rear. Whether it is better to creep, like the old mariners, from headland to headland, altering your course every day or two, or strike boldly out into the great deep, steering for an unseen port on the other side of the world that you never beheld, though you know it is there? Which will be the nobler voyage?

If one looks at the lives of most professing Christians, it looks as if we had but a very dim vision of this glory. And surely, if there is one thing that needs to be rung into our ears, compassed about as we are by the fascinations, temptations, and occupations of this life, it is that old exhortation, never more needed than by the worldly-minded Christians of this day, "Set your affection on things above, not on things on the earth" [Col. 3:2]. Take Christ for your example, and live, having "respect unto the recompense of the reward" [Heb. 11:26].

"HE ENDURED THE CROSS"

Ought not Christ to have suffered these things, and to enter into his glory?—
Luke 24:26

"Endured the Cross" [Heb. 12:2] does not merely mean "experienced the pain," but it means *stood steadfast under*, endured in the fullest and noblest sense of the word. Many a man endures suffering in the lower sense who does not endure it in the higher; but Christ did in both. And, of course, that endurance of the Cross was not confined to the moments of His life when the actual physical pain of the Crucifixion was upon Him, not confined to that last day, but stretched through His whole career. Therefore we may apply this "endurance," not only to the moment of actual physical sufferings, but to the whole of our Lord's earthly career, the patient, heroic steadfastness with which He bore them.

That is an aspect of our Lord's character that is not often enough presented to our minds. "The velvet glove has hidden the iron hand," in popular apprehension. Temptations which shatter feeble resolutions, as the waves some feeble dike, broke like the vain spray against that breakwater; His fixed will—that will like adamant, that could not be moved, that could not be broken, that never faltered—led Him to tread, from the beginning to the end of His career, a path every step of which was strewed with hot plowshares and sharp swords. He trod it with bleeding and with seared feet, but without a quiver and without a falter; and, as the hour drew near, we read that "he steadfastly set his face" [Luke 9:51]—made it hard as a flint—to go to Jerusalem, impelled by that threefold, mighty force of obedience to the Father, love to man, and vision of the glory, so that His disciples were struck with wonder and awe at the fixed determination stamped on the settled countenance, and manifested in the eager steps which outran them on the rocky road to the Cross. That heroic endurance must be ours too, if we are not to rot in selfish and inglorious ease. Life at first may seem happy and brilliant, a place for recreation or profit or pleasure, but we very soon find out that it is a sand-strewn wrestling-ground. Many flowers cannot grow where are the feet of the runner and the strife of the combatants. The first thing done to make an area for wrestlers is to take away the turf and the daisies, then to beat the soil down hard and flat. And so our lives get flattened, stripped of their beauty and their fragrance, because they are not meant to be gardens, they are meant to be wrestling-grounds. There comes to every life that is worth living hours of sacrifice when duty can only be done at the cost of a bleeding heart. Every man that is not the devil's servant has to carry a cross, and to be fastened to it, if he will do his Master's work. Besides which crucifixion in service, there are all the other common sorrows storming in upon us, so that sometimes it is as much as a man can do not to be swept away by the current, but to keep his footing in mid-channel.

NO CROSS, NO CROWN

Be thou faithful unto death, and I will give thee the crown of life—Rev. 2:10

The way to endure the cross is to look unto the crown, and the Christ. On the Cross He proclaimed, "It is finished." But the ending of the work on the Cross was but the beginning of a form of His work for us, which shall never cease until the trumpet of victory shall sound "It is done!" when the world has yielded to His love. He works for us, with us, and in us, as Lord of Providence and King of Grace, sustaining and upholding us in all our weakness, and tending the smoky flame of our dim faith till it bursts into clear radiance. The Captain has gone up from the field, and His soldiers are still in it. But He has not left them to struggle alone. He sits on high, looking down on us still fighting in the arena with wild beasts; but He does not only behold, but also helps our conflict, as Stephen, looking up, saw Him "standing" [Acts 7:55], not sitting, at the right hand of God, as if He had sprung to His feet to succor and receive the martyr-spirit. Nor is He exalted only to work for and in us, or to shed on our hearts the plenteous rain of His heavenly influences. He has entered within the veil as our Great High Priest, to make intercession for us, so making us confident that His great sacrifice is ever present to the Divine mind, as determining its acts towards those who trust in Christ. Nor is our share in His exaltation limited by these great privileges, for He has gone to prepare a place for us; and dimly as we may know what that means, we know, at all events, that but for Christ's presence there Heaven would be no place for us. Nor is this all; for, if we have given our hearts to Him, and are joined to the Lord by faith, we are, in a very profound sense, one spirit with Him.

So real is the union between us and Jesus that it cannot be that the Head shall be glorified and the members have no share in the glory. The Captain of Salvation is laureled and crowned, and all His soldiers, the weakest and the most sinful among them, if only they are knit to Him by humble faith, share in His victory, receive from His Throne showers of grace and blessing, which He pours down upon them, are inspired by His continual presence who teaches their hands to war and their fingers to fight, [see Ps. 144:1], and will be brought at last by Him coming for them again, that "where he is there his servants may be also" [John 14:3].

And so each of us, if only we take Christ for our Lord and Commander, may say in the calmness of a confident hope what David's soldier said to him in the heroism of his self-devotion, "As my Lord the King liveth, surely in what place my Lord the King shall be, whether in death or life, there also will thy servant be" [2 Sam. 15:21].

❋

"DESPISING THE SHAME"

They departed from the presence of the council, rejoicing that they were counted worthy to suffer shame for his name—Acts 5:41

The struggles of the Captain of our salvation are the pattern for His people, in what I may call the wholesome and wise contempt for the ills that bar His progress: "Despising the shame."

Contempt is an ugly word, but there are things which deserve it; and though we do not often associate the idea of it with the meek and gentle Christ, there were things in His life on which it was exercised. He despised arrogance. That is to say, He reduced it to its true insignificance by taking the measure of it, and looking at it as it was. And that is what I want you to feel we all have in our power. There are hosts of difficulties in our lives as Christian men, which will be big or little just as we choose to make them. You can either look at them through a magnifying or a diminishing glass. The magnitude of most of the trifles that affect us may be altered by our way of looking at them.

Learn the practical wisdom of minimizing the hindrances to your Christian career, pulling them down to their true smallness. Do not let them come to you and impose upon you with the notion that they are big and formidable; the most of them are only white sheets, and a rustic curmudgeon behind them, like a vulgar ghost. You go up to them, and they will be small immediately! Despise the shame and it disappears. And how is that to be done? In two ways. Go up the mountain, and the things in the plain will look very small; the higher you rise, the more insignificant they will seem. Hold fellowship with God, and live up beside your Master, and the threatening foes here will seem very, very unformidable.

Another way is: pull up the curtain, and gaze on what is behind it. The low foothills that lie at the base of some Alpine country may look high when seen from the plain, as long as the snowy summits are wrapped in mist; but when a little puff of wind comes and clears away the fog from the lofty peaks, nobody looks at the little green hills in front. So the world's hindrances, and the world's difficulties and cares, they look very lofty till the cloud lifts. And when we see the great white summits, everything lower does not seem so very high after all. Look to Jesus, and that will dwarf all difficulties.

TRIUMPH THROUGH CHRIST

We have such a high priest, who is set down on the right hand of the throne of the Majesty in the heavens—Heb. 8:1

The new thing which accrued because of Christ's Incarnation and sacrifice was that, as this text puts it with great emphasis, "*Jesus* sat at the right hand of the Throne"; or, to put it into other words, that the humanity of our Lord and Brother was lifted up to a participation in Divinity and the rule of the universe. That "sitting" expresses Rest, as from a finished and perfect work, a Rest which is not inactivity; Dominion, extending over all the universe; and Judgment. These three—Rest, Dominion, Judgment—are the prerogatives of the Man Jesus. That is what He won by His bloody passion and sacrifice.

And now what has that to do with us? We are to think of this triumph of the commander as being a revelation and a prophecy for us. Nobody knows anything about the future life except by means of Jesus Christ. We have no knowledge of another world except as we believe in the Resurrection of Jesus Christ from the dead and His Ascension up on high. We may have dreams, we may have hopes, we may have forebodings, we may argue from analogy, we may get the length of saying "peradventure," "probably"; but we cannot say we *know*, unless we will consent to take all our light, and all our knowledge, and all our certitude, and all hope from that great Lord whose death and resurrection are to the whole world the only guarantee of the future, whose presence there is the only light in all the darkness.

In His exaltation to the Throne a new hope dawns on humanity. If we believe that the Man Jesus sits on the throne of the universe, we have a new conception of what is possible for humanity. If a perfect human nature has entered into the participation of the Divine, our natures, too, *may* be perfect, and what He is and where He is, there, too, we may hope to come [see John 14:3]. So this Epistle in the second chapter, quoting the grand words of the psalm, which sometimes and in some moods seems more like irony than revelation: "Thou hast crowned him with glory and honor. . . . Thou hast put all things under his feet" [Ps. 8:5, 6], comments: "We see not yet all things put under Him." Nay, much the contrary. Look at all this weary world, with its miseries and its cares. What has become of the grand dream of the psalm? Has it all gone into moonshine and vapor? "We see not *yet* all things put under him" [Heb. 2:8]. Weary centuries have rolled away, and it does not seem a bit nearer. "But we see Jesus crowned with glory and honor" [Heb. 2:9]. He, and not all these failures and abortions of existing manhood—He is the type that God means us to be, and what we all may one day come to.

WATCHFULNESS AND WORK

Blessed is that servant whom his Lord, when he cometh, shall find so doing. Of a truth I say unto you, that he will make him ruler over all that he hath—
Luke 12:43, 44

The temptation for anyone who is much occupied with the hope of some great change and betterment in the near future is to be restless and unable to settle down to his work, and to yield to distaste of the humdrum duties of every day. If some man that kept a little chandler's shop in a back street was expecting to be made a king to-morrow, he would not be likely to look after his poor trade with great diligence. So we find in the Apostle Paul's second letter—that to the Thessalonians—that he had to en-counter, as well as he could, the tendency of hope to make men restless, and to insist upon the thought—which is the same lesson as is taught us by this passage—that if a man hoped, then he had with quietness to work and eat his own bread, and not be shaken in mind [see 2 Thess. 2:2].

"Blessed is that servant whom his Lord, when he cometh, shall find so doing" [Luke 12:43]. It may seem humble work to serve out hunches of bread and pots of black broth to the family of slaves, when the steward is expecting the coming of the master of the house, and every nerve is tingling with anticipation. But it is steadying work, and it is blessed work. It is better that a man should be found doing the homeliest duty as the outcome of his great expectations of the coming of his Master, than that he should be fidgeting and restless and looking only at that thought till it unfits him for his com-mon tasks. Who was it who, sitting playing a game of chess, and being addressed by some scandalized disciple with the question, "What would you do if Jesus Christ came, and you were playing your game?" answered, "I would finish it"? The best way for a steward to be ready for the Master, and to show that he is watching, is that he should be "found so doing" the humble tasks of his stewardship. The two women that were stoop-ing on either side of the millstone, and helping each other to whirl the handle around in that night, were in the right place, and the one that was taken had no cause to regret that she was not more religiously employed. The watchful servant should be a working servant.

REST AND RULE

Blessed is that servant whom, when he cometh, shall find so doing. Verily, I say unto you, That he shall make him ruler over all his goods—Matt. 24:46, 47

Verily I say unto you, He shall "gird Himself, and make them to sit down to meat, and will come forth and serve them" [Luke 12:37]. I do not know that there is a more wonderful promise, with more light lying in its darkness, in all Scripture than that. Jesus Christ continues in the heavens to be found in "the form of a servant" [Phil. 2:7]. As here He girded Himself with the towel of humiliation in the upper room, so there He girds Himself with the robes of His Imperial Majesty, and uses all His powers for the nourishment and blessedness of His servants. His everlasting motto is, "I am among you as he that serveth" [Luke 22:27]. On earth His service was to wash His disciples' feet; in heaven the pure foot contracts no stain and needs no basin. But in heaven He still serves, and serves by spreading a table, and, as a king might do at some ceremonial feasts, waiting on the astonished guests. Repose, in contrast with the girded loins and the weary waiting of the midnight watch; nourishment and the satisfaction of all desires; joy; society—all these things, and who knows how much more, that we shall have to get there to understand, lie in that metaphor, "Blessed is that servant" who is served by the Master and nourished by His presence. It is a wonderful confession of "the weariness, the fever, and the fret," the hunger and loneliness of earthly experience, that the thought of heaven as the opposite of all these things should have almost swallowed up the other thought with which our Lord associates it here. He would not have us think only of repose. He unites with that representation, so fascinating to us weary and heavy-laden, the other of administrative authority. He will set him "over all that He hath." The relation between earthly faithfulness and heavenly service is the same in essence as that between the various stages of our work here. The reward for work here is more work; a wider field, greater capacities. And what depths of authority, of new dignity, of royal supremacy, lie in these solemn and mysterious words I know not: "He will set him over all that He hath." My union with Christ is to be so close as that all His is mine; and I am master of it. But at all events this we can say, that the faithfulness here leads to larger service yonder; and that none of the aptitudes and capacities which have been developed in us here on earth will want a sphere when we pass yonder.

So let watchfulness lead to faithfulness, and watchful faithfulness and faithful watchfulness will lead to repose which is activity, and rule which is rest.

MEMORY AND HOPE

When my soul fainted within me, I remembered the Lord—Jon. 2:7

Memory and Hope are twins. The latter can only work with the materials supplied by the former. Hope could paint nothing on the blank canvas of the future unless its palette was charged by Memory. Memory brings the yarn which Hope weaves.

Our thankful remembrance of a past which was filled and molded by God's perpetual presence and care ought to make us sure of a future which shall, in like manner, be molded. "Thou hast been my help" [Ps. 63:7]: if we can say that, then we may confidently pray, and be sure of the answer, "Leave me not, neither forsake me, O God of my salvation" [Ps. 27:9]. And if we feel, as memory teaches us to feel, that God has been working for us, and with us, we can say with another psalmist, "Thy mercy, O Lord, endureth forever. Forsake not the works of thine own hands"; and we can rise to His confidence: "The Lord will perfect that which concerneth me" [Ps. 138:8].

Our remembrance, even of our imperfections, and our losses, and our sorrows, may minister to our hope. For surely the life of every man on earth, but most eminently the life of a Christian man, is utterly unintelligible, a mockery and a delusion and an impossibility, if there be a God at all, unless it prophesies of a region in which imperfection will be ended, aspirations will be fulfilled, desires will be satisfied. We have so much that unless we are to have a great deal more, we had better have had nothing. We have so much that if there be a God at all, we must have a great deal more. The new moon with a ragged edge, even in its imperfection beautiful, is a prophet of the complete resplendent orb. "On earth the broken arc, in heaven the perfect round."

The memory of defeat may be the parent of the hope of victory. The stone Ebenezer, "Hitherto hath the Lord helped us" [1 Sam. 7:12], was lifted to commemorate a victory that had been won on the very site where Israel, fighting the same foes, had once been beaten. There is no remembrance of failure so mistaken as that which takes the past failure as certain to be repeated in the future. Surely, though we have fallen seventy times seven—that is 490, is it not?—at the 491st attempt we may, and if we trust in God we shall, succeed [Matt. 18:22].

GOD'S GIFT OF HIMSELF TO US

I will be their God, in truth and in righteousness—Zech. 8:8

These words go far deeper than the necessary Divine relation to all His creatures. He is a God to every star that burns, and to every worm that creeps, and to every gnat that dances for a moment. But there is a close relation, and more blessed, than that. He is a God to every man that lives, lavishing upon him manifestations of His Divinity, and sustaining him in life. But within these great and wondrous universal relations which spring from the very fact of creative power and creatural dependence, there is a tender, a truer relationship of heart to heart, of spirit to spirit, which is set forth as the prerogative of the men that trust in Jesus Christ. The special does not contradict or deny the universal, the universal does not exclude the special: "I will be a God to them" [Heb. 8:10], in a deeper, more blessed, soul-satisfying, and vital sense than to others around them.

And what lies in that great promise passes the wit of man and the tongues of angels fully to conceive and tell. All that lies in that majestic monosyllable, which is shorthand for life and light and all perfectness, lived in a living person who has a heart, that word *God*—all that is included in that, God will be God to you and me if we like to have Him for such. "I will be a God to them"—then around them shall be cast the bulwark of the everlasting arm and the everlasting purpose. "I will be a God to them"—then in all dark places there will be a light, and in all perplexities there will be a path, and in all anxieties there will be quietness, and in all troubles there will be a hidden light of joy, and in every circumstance life will be saturated with an Almighty Presence which shall make the rough places plain and the crooked things straight. "I will be a God to them"—then their desires, their hungering after blessedness, their seeking after good need no longer roam open-mouthed and empty throughout a waste world, where there is only scanty fodder, enough to keep them from expiring, and never enough food to satisfy them; but in Him longings and hopes will all find their appropriate satisfaction. And there will be rest in God, and whatsoever aspirations after loftier goodness, and whatsoever base hankerings still lingering may have to be cherished and fought, the strength of a present God will enable us to aspire, and not to be disappointed, and to cast ourselves into the conflict, and be ever victorious. "I will be to them a God" is the same as to say that everything which my complex nature can require I shall find in Him.

OUR GOD FOREVER AND EVER

I will be to them a God, and they shall be to me a people—Heb. 8:10

God's gift of Himself to me teaches that all that Godhood, in all the incomprehensible sweep of its attributes, is on my side, if I will. They tell us that there are rays in the spectrum which no eye can see, but which yet have mightier chemical and other influences than those that are visible. The spectrum of God is not all visible, but beyond the limits of comprehension there lie dark energies which are full of blessedness and of power for us. "I will be to them a God." We must understand something of what that name signifies that we do not understand; and all that, too, is working on our side.

Now, remember that this giving of God to us by Himself is all concentrated in one historical act. He gave Himself to us when He spared not His only begotten Son. This text is one of the articles of the New Covenant. And what sealed and confirmed all the articles of that Covenant? The blood of Jesus Christ. It was when God "spared not His own Son" [Rom. 8:32], and when the Son spared not Himself on that Cross of Calvary, that there came to pass the ratifying and filling out and perfecting of the ancient typical promise, "I will be to them a God." There was the unspeakable gift in which God was given to humanity.

Here is a treasure—of gold lying in the road. Anybody that picks it up may have it; the man that does not pick it up does not get it, though it is there for him to lay his fingers on. Here is a river flowing past your door. You may put a pipe into it, and bring all its wealth and refreshment into your house, and use it for the quenching of your thirst, for the cleansing of your person, for the cooking of your victuals, for the watering of your gardens. And here is all the fullness of God welling past us. But Niagara may thunder close by a man's door, and he may perish of thirst. "I will be to them a God." What does that matter if I do not turn around and say, "O Lord! Thou art my God?" Nothing! Beggars come to your door, and you give them a bit of bread, and they go away, and you find it flung around the corner into the mud. God gives us Himself. I wonder how many of us have tossed the gift over the first hedge, and left it there. Yet all the while we are dying for lack of it, and do not know that we are.

Brother! You have to enclose a bit of the prairie for your very own, and put a hedge around it, and cultivate it, and you will get abundant fruits. You have to translate "their" into the singular possessive pronoun, and say "mine," and put out the hand of faith, and make Him in very deed yours. Then, and only then, is this giving perfected.

MYSELF FOR GOD

My beloved is mine, and I am his—Song 2:16

God enters into loving relations with me, and it is only when I am melted and encouraged by the perception and reception of these relations that there comes the answering throb in my heart. The mirror in our spirit has the other one reflected upon it; then it flings back its own reflection to the parent glass. God comes first with the love that He pours over us poor creatures; and when "we have known and believed the love that God hath to us" [1 John 4:16], then, and only then, do we throb back the reflected aye, the kindred, kindred love. For love is the same thing in the Divine heart and in my heart. In the other bonds that unite men to what is man's corresponds to what is God's. My faith corresponds to His faithfulness. My dependence corresponds to His sufficiency. My weak clinging answers to His strong grasp; my obedience to His commanding. But my *love* not only corresponds to, as the concave does to the convex, but it assimilates to, and is the likeliest thing in the creature to the infinitude of the Creator. And so there is a parallel, wonderful and blessed, between the giving love which says, "I will be to them a God," and the recipient love which responds, "We are to Thee a people."

Remember, too, that not only is there this general resemblance, but that our love manifests itself to God—I was going to say, just as God's love manifests itself to us, though, of course, there are differences that I do not need to touch upon here, in the act of self-surrender. He gave Himself to us. And we may use another form of speech still more emphatic, and say, He gave up Himself. For, surely, difficult as it may be for us to keep our footing in those lofty heights where the atmosphere is so rare, the gift of Jesus Christ was surrender; when the Father spared not His own Son, but delivered Him up for us all!

Not only is there this mutual possession, but each half, when cleft and analyzed, reveals the necessity for a similar reciprocity. For God's giving of Himself to us is nothing to us without our taking of God for ours; and, in like manner, of giving our ourselves to God would be all incomplete unless, in His strange love, He stooped from amid the praises of Israel to accept the poor gifts that we bring.

THE SAINT'S GIFT TO HIS LORD

And they shall be mine, saith the Lord of hosts, in the day when I make up my jewels; and I will spare them—Mal. 3:17

What is the surrender of the man that receives the love of God? In what region of my nature is that giving up of myself most imperative and blessed? In my will. The will is the man. The center-point of every human being is the will, and it is no use for us to talk about our having given ourselves to God, in response and in thankfulness to His gift of Himself to us, unless we come and say, "Lord, not my will, but thine" [Luke 22:42]; and bow ourselves in unreluctant and constant submission to His commandments and to His will. We give ourselves to God when, moved by His giving of Himself to us, we yield up our love to Him; and love never rests until it has yielded up its will to the Beloved. He indeed gives, asking for nothing; but He gives in a still deeper sense, asking for everything—and that everything is myself. And I yield myself to Him in the measure in which I cast my thankful love upon Him, and then bow myself as His servant, in humble consecration, to Himself, with all my heart and soul and mind and strength.

"They shall be my people" [Jer. 24:7]. That is wonderful! It is strange that we can imitate God, in a certain fashion, in the gift of self; but it is yet more strange and blessed that God accepts that gift, and counts it as one of His treasures to possess us. One of the psalmists had a deep insight into the miracle of the Divine condescension when he said, "He was extolled with *my* tongue" [Ps. 66:17]. It is strange that the loftiest of creatures should be lifted higher by the poor, tremulous lever of *my* praises; and yet it is so. He takes as His such poor creatures, full of imperfection and tremulous faith and disproved love, as you and I know ourselves to be, and He says, "My people." "They shall be mine" [Gen. 48:5]; my jewels, says He, "in the day which I make." Oh! It sometimes seems to me that it is more wonderful that God should take me for His than that He should give me Himself for mine.

Have you given yourself to Him? Have you begun where He begins, taking first the gift that is freely given to you of God, even Jesus Christ, in whom God dwells, and who makes all the Godhead yours, for your very own? Have you taken God for yours, by faith in that Lord "who loved me, and gave Himself for me" [Gal. 2:20]? And then, smitten by His love, and having the chains of self melted by the fire of His great mercy, have you said: "Truly I am thy servant . . . thou hast loosed my bonds" [Ps. 116:16]? You never own yourself till you give yourself away; and you never will give yourself to God, to be His, unless, with all your heart and strength, you cling to the rock-truth, that God has given Himself to every man that will take Him, in Jesus Christ, to be that man's God forever and ever.

THE NEW COVENANT

This is the covenant that I will make with them after those days, saith the Lord—
Heb. 10:16

We can scarcely estimate the shock to a primitive Hebrew Christian when he discovered that Judaism was to fade away. Such an earthquake might seem to leave nothing standing. Now, the great object of this Epistle to the Hebrews is to insist on that truth, and to calm the early Hebrew Christians under it, by showing them that the disappearance of the older system left them no poorer, but infinitely richer, inasmuch as all that was in it was more perfectly in Christ's Gospel. The writer has accordingly been giving his strength to show that all along the line Christianity is the perfecting of Judaism, in its Founder, in its priesthood, in its ceremonies, in its Sabbath. Here he touches the great central thought of the Old Covenant between God and man, and he falls back upon the strange words of one of the old prophets. Jeremiah had declared as emphatically as he, the writer, has been declaring, how the ancient system was to melt away and be absorbed in a new covenant between God and man. Is there any other instance of a religion which on the one side proclaims its own eternal duration, "the word of the Lord endureth forever" [1 Pet. 1:25], and on the other side declares that it is to be abrogated, antiquated, and done away? The writer of the Epistle had learned from more sacred lips than Jeremiah's the same lesson, for the Master said at the most solemn hour of His career, "This is the blood of the New Testament, which is shed for many for the remission of sins" [Matt. 26:28]. These articles of the New Covenant go very deep into the essence of Christianity, and may well be thoughtfully pondered by us all, if we want to know what the specific differences between the ultimate revelation in Jesus Christ and all other systems are.

The earliest Christian confession, the simplest and sufficient creed, was, Jesus is the Christ. What do we mean by that? We mean that He is the realization of the dim figure which arose, majestic and enigmatic, through the mists of a partial revelation. We mean that He is, as the word signifies etymologically, "anointed" with the Divine Spirit for the discharge of all the offices which, in old days, were filled by men who were fitted and designated for them by outward anointing—prophet, priest, and king. We mean that He is the substance of which ancient ritual was the shadow. We mean that He is the goal to which all that former unveiling, in part, of the mind and will of God steadfastly pointed. This, and nothing less, is the meaning of the declaration that Jesus is the Christ. The true presence of God, the true lustrous emanation from, and manifestation of, the abysmal brightness, is in Jesus Christ, "the brightness of his glory, and the express image of his person" [Heb. 1:3], for the central blaze of God's glory is God's love, and that rises to its highest degree in the name and mission of Jesus Christ our Savior. If we would see God, our faith must grasp the Man, the Christ, the Lord—as Climax of all names—the Incarnate God, the Eternal Word who has come among us to reveal to us all the glory of the Lord. So let us make sure that the fleshly tables of our hearts are not like the moldering stones that antiquarians dig up on some historical site, bearing half-obliterated inscriptions, with fragmentary names of mighty kings of long ago, but with the many-syllabled Name written firm, clear, legible, complete upon them, as on some granite block fresh from the stonecutter's chisel.

GOD'S WRITING ON THE HEART

I will put my law in their inward parts, and write it in their hearts—Jer. 31:33

I will put my laws into their mind, and write them in their hearts—Heb. 8:10

It seems to me that the two clauses in each of these passages are not precisely parallel, but parallel with a difference. I take it that "mind" here means very much what we make it mean in our popular phraseology—a kind of synonym for the understanding, or the intellectual part of a man's nature; and that "heart," on the other hand, means something a little wider than it does in our popular phraseology, and indicates not only the affections, but the center of personality in the human will as well as the seat of love. So these two clauses will mean, you see, if we carry that distinction with us, two things—the clear perception of the will of God and the coincidence of that will with our inclinations and desires. In men's natural consciences there is the law written on their minds; but, wait! We all know that there is an awful chasm between perception and inclination, and that it is one thing to know our duty and quite another to wish to do it. So the heart of this great promise is that these two things shall coincide in a Christian man, shall cover precisely the same ground, as two of Euclid's triangles, with the same angles, will, if laid upon each other, coincide line for line and angle for angle. Thus it is possible—and, if we observe the conditions, it shall be actual in us—that knowledge and will shall cover absolutely and exactly the same ground. Inclination shall be duty and duty shall be inclination and delight.

And how is that wonderful change upon men to be accomplished? *"I* will put, *I* will write." Only He can do it. We all know, by our own experience, the schism that gapes between the two things. *Every* man in the world knows a vast deal more of duty than *any* man in the world does. The worst of us has a standard that rebukes his evil, and the best of us has a standard that rebukes his evil, and the best of us has a standard that transcends his goodness, and, often transcends his inclination. But the Gospel of our Lord and Savior comes armed with sufficient power to make this miracle an actuality for us all; for it comes to substitute for all other motives to obedience the one motive of love. They but half understand the Gospel who dwell upon its sanctions of reward and punishment, and would seek to frighten men into goodness; and they misinterpret it almost as much who find the chief motive for Christian obedience in the glories of the heavenly state. The gospel appeals to men, not merely nor chiefly on the ground of self-interest, but it comes to them with one appeal, "If ye love me, keep my commandments" [John 14:15]. That is how the law is written on the heart. Wherever there is love, there is a supreme delight in divining and in satisfying the wish and will of the Beloved. His lightest word is law to the loving heart; His looks are spells and commandments. And if it is so in regard of our poor, imperfect human loves, how infinitely more so is it where the heart is touched by true affection for His own infinite love's sake, of that "Jesus" who is "most desired"! The secret of Christian morality is that duty is changed into choice, because love is made the motive for obedience.

DELIGHT IN GOD'S WILL

I delight to do thy will, O my God: yea, thy law is within my heart—Psalm 40:8

To have Christ shrined in the heart is the heart of Christianity, and Christ Himself is our law. So, in another sense than that which I have been already touching, the law is written on the heart on which, by faith and self-surrender, the name of Christ is written. And when it becomes our whole duty to become like Him, then He, being enthroned in our hearts, our law is within, and Himself to His "darlings" shall be, as the poet writes about another matter, "both law and impulse." Write His name upon your hearts, and your law of life is thereby written there. The very specific gift of Christianity to men is the gift of a new nature, which is "created in righteousness and holiness that flows from truth." The communication of a Divine life kindred with, and percipient of, and submissive to, the Divine will, is the gift that Christianity—or, rather, let us put away the abstraction and say that Christ—offers to us all, and gives to every man who will accept it. And thus, and in other ways on which I cannot dwell now, this great article of the New Covenant lies at the very foundation of the Christian life, and gives its peculiar tinge and cast to all Christian morality, commandment, and obligation.

But let me remind you how this great truth has to be held with caution. The evidence of this letter (Hebrews) itself shows that, while the writer regarded it as a distinctive characteristic of the Gospel, that by it men's wills were stamped with a delight in the law of God, and a transcript thereof, he still regarded these wills as unstable, as capable of losing the sharp lettering, of having the writing of God obliterated, and still regarded it as possible that there should be apostasy and departure. So there is nothing in God's promise which suspends the need for effort and for conflict. Still "the flesh lusteth against the spirit" [Gal. 5:7]. Still there are parts of the nature on which that law is not written. It is the final triumph, that the whole man, body, soul, and spirit, is, through and through, penetrated with and joyfully obedient to the commandments of the Lord. There is need, too, not only for continuous progress, effort, conflict, in order to keep our hearts open for His handwriting, but also for much caution, lest at any time we should mistake our own self-will for the utterance of the Divine voice. "Love, and do what thou wilt," said a great Christian teacher. It is an unguarded statement; but, profoundly true as in some respects it is, it is only absolutely true if we have made sure that the "thou" that "wills" is the heart on which God has written His law.

Only God can do this for us. One Man has transcribed the Divine will on His will without blurring a letter or omitting a clause. One Man has been able to say, in the presence of the most fearful temptations, "Not my will, but thine, be done" [Luke 22:42]. One Man has so completely written, perceived, and obeyed the law of His Father, that, looking back on all His life, He was conscious of no defect or divergence, either in motive or in act, and could affirm on the Cross, "It is finished" [John 19:30]. He who thus perfectly kept that divine law will give to us, if we ask Him, His Spirit, to write it upon our hearts, and "the law of the spirit of life in Christ Jesus hath made me free from the law of sin and death" [Rom. 8:2].

THE IMPASSABLE GULF BETWEEN CHRISTIANITY AND OTHER RELIGIOUS SYSTEMS

Their rock is not as our Rock, even our enemies themselves being judges—
Deut. 32:31

Christianity is a *new* covenant, undoubtedly, an altogether new thing in the world. For whatever other laws have been promulgated among men have had this in common, that they have stood over against the will with a whip in one hand and a box of sweets in the other, and have tried to influence desires and inclinations, first by the setting forth of duty, then by threatening, and then by promises to obedience. There is the inherent weakness of all, which is merely law. You do not make men good by telling them what goodness consists in, nor yet by setting forth the bitter consequences that may result from wrong-doing. All that is surface work. But here is a system that says that it deals with the will as from within, and moves and molds and revolutionizes it. "You cannot make men sober by Act of Parliament," people say. Well! I do not believe the conclusion which is generally drawn from that statement, but it is perfectly true in itself. To tell a man what he ought to do is very, very little help towards his doing it. I do not underestimate the value of a clear perception of duty, but I say that, apart from Christianity, in ninety-nine cases out of a hundred, that clear perception of duty is like a clear opening of a great gulf between a man and safety, which only makes him recoil in despair with the thought, "How can I ever leap across and clear *that?*" But the peculiarity of the gospel is that it gives both the knowledge of what we ought to be, and with and in the knowledge the desire, and with and in the knowledge and the desire the power to be what God would have us to be.

All other systems, whether the laws of a nation, or the principles of a scientific morality, or the solemn voice that speaks in our minds proclaiming some version of God's law to every man—all these are comparatively inadequate. They are like bill-stickers going about a rebellious province posting the king's proclamation—unless they have soldiers at their back, the proclamation is not worth the paper it is printed upon. But Christianity comes, and gives us that which it requires from us. So, in his succinct way, Saint Augustine penetrated to the very heart of this truth when he prayed, "Give what Thou commandest, and command what Thou wilt."

THE FREEDOM AND BLESSEDNESS
OF CHRIST'S SERVICE

*This is the love of God, that we keep his commandments: and his commandments
are not grievous—1 John 5:3*

Not to do wrong may be the mark of a slave's timid obedience. Not to wish to do
wrong is the charter of a son's free and blessed service. There is a higher possibility
yet, reserved for Heaven—not to be able to do wrong. Freedom does not consist in
doing what I like—that turns out, in the long run, to be the most abject slavery, under
the most severe tyrants—but it consists in liking to do what I ought. When my wishes
and God's will coincide, then, and only then, am I free. That is no prison, out of which
we do not wish to go. Not to be confined against our wills, but voluntarily to elect to
move only within the sacred, charmed, sweet circle of the discerned will of God, is the
service and liberty of the sons of God.

There are a great many Christians, so-called, who know very little about such
blessedness. To many of us religion is a burden. It consists of a number of prohibitions
and restrictions and commandments equally unwelcome. "Do not do this," and all the
while I would like to do it. "Do that," and all the while I do not want to do it. "Pray, because it is your duty; go to chapel, because you think it is God's will; give money that
you would much rather keep in your pockets; abstain from certain things that you
hunger for; do other things that you do not a bit desire to do, nor find any pleasure in
doing." That is the religion of hosts of people. They have need to ask themselves
whether their religion is Christ's religion. "My yoke is easy and my burden is light"
[Matt. 11:30]. Not because the things that He bids and forbids are less or lighter than
those which the world's morality requires of its followers, but because, so to speak, the
yoke is padded with the velvet of love, and inclination coincides in the measure of our
true religion with the discerned will of God. This is ever so far ahead of the experience
of crowds of professing Christians. There are still great numbers of professing Christians, and I doubt not that I speak to some such, on whose hearts only a very few of
the syllables of God's will are written, and these very faintly and blotted. But remember
that the fundamental idea of a covenant implies two people, and duties and obligations
on the part of each. If God is in covenant with you, you are in covenant with God. If He
makes a promise, there is something for you to do in order that that promise may be fulfilled to you.

"WHAT WILT THOU HAVE ME TO DO?"

And the people asked him, saying, What shall we do then?—Luke 3:10

What is there to do? First, and last, and midst, keep close to Jesus Christ. In the measure in which we keep ourselves in continual touch with Him will His law be written upon our hearts. If we are forever twitching away the paper; if we are forever flinging blots and mud upon it, how can we expect the transcript to be clear and legible? We must keep still that God may write. We must keep near Him that He may write. We must wait habitually in His presence. When the astronomer wishes to get the image of some far-off star, invisible to the naked eye, he regulates the motion of his sensitive plate, so that for hours it shall continue right beneath the invisible beam. So we have to still our hearts, and keep their plates—the fleshly tables of them—exposed to the heavens; then the likeness of God will be stamped there.

Be faithful to what is written there, which is the Christian shape of the heathen commandment, "Do the duty that lies nearest thee; so shall the next become plainer." Be faithful to the line that is "written," and there will be more on the tablet tomorrow.

Now this is a promise for us all. However blotted and blurred and defaced by crooked, scrawling letters, like child's copybook, with its first pothooks and hangers, our hearts may be, there is no need for any of us to say despairingly, as we look on the smeared page, "What I have written I have written." He is able to blot it all out, to take away the handwriting—our own—"that was against us, nailing it to his cross" [Col. 2:14], and to give us, in our inmost spirits, a better knowledge of, and a glad obedience to, His discerned and holy will. So that each of us, if we like, and will observe the conditions, may be able to say with all humility, "Lo! I come, in the volume of the book it is "written of *me*" [Heb. 10:7]. "I delight to do Thy will. Yea! thy law is within *my* heart" [Ps. 40:8].

Two mirrors set one against each other reflect one another, and themselves in each other, in long perspective. Two hearts that love, with similar reciprocation of influence, mirror back to each other their own affections. "I am thine; thou art mine," is the very mother-tongue of love, and of blessedness the source. All loving hearts know that. This mutual surrender, and, in surrender, reciprocal possession, is lifted up here into the highest regions. "I . . . will be their God . . . they shall be my people" [Jer. 31:33].

REPENTANCE AND FAITH

Repentance toward God, and faith toward our Lord Jesus Christ—Acts 20:21

Very near the close of his missionary career the Apostle Paul summed up his preaching as being all directed to two points, "Repentance towards God, and faith in our Lord Jesus Christ." These two, repentance and faith, ought never to be separated in thought, as they are inseparable in fact. Genuine repentance is impossible without faith; true faith cannot exist without repentance.

And yet the two are separated very often, in this day especially, even by earnest Christian teachers who have a great deal to say about faith, and not nearly enough in proportion about repentance; and the effect is to obscure the very idea of faith, and not seldom to preach, "Peace! peace! when there is no peace" [Jer. 8:11]. A gospel which is always talking about faith, and scarcely ever talking about repentance, is dispossessed indeed of some of its most unwelcome characteristics, but is also deprived of most of its power, and it may very easily become an ally of all righteousness and an indulgence to sin.

Some of the most formidable objections to the Christian doctrine of forgiveness—namely, that it is immoral in its substance—arise chiefly from forgetting that repentance towards God is as real a condition of salvation as is faith in our Lord Jesus Christ. We have here the Apostle's deliverance about one of these twin thoughts. We have three stages—the root, the stem, the fruit; sorrow, repentance, salvation. But there is a right and a wrong kind of sorrow for sin. The right kind breeds repentance, and thence reaches salvation; the wrong kind breeds nothing, and so ends in death. Look at this ladder, which the Apostle sets up "from a horrible pit and the miry clay" [Ps. 40:2] of evil, up to the sunny heights of salvation, and trace its stages; not forgetting that it is not a complete statement of the case, and needs to be supplemented, in the spirit of the words already quoted, by the other part of the inseparable whole, "faith toward our Lord Jesus Christ."

It would be an interesting study to examine the two letters of the Apostle Peter, in order to construct from them a picture of what he became, and to contrast it with his own earlier self, when full of self-confidence, rashness, and instability. It took a lifetime for Simon, the son of Jonas to grow into Peter; but it was done. And the very faults of the character became strength. What he had proved possible in his own case he commands and commends to us; and from the height to which he has reached he looks upwards to the infinite ascent which he knows he will attain when he puts off this tabernacle, and then downwards to his brethren, bidding them, too, climb and aspire. He is like some trumpeter on the battlefield who spends his last breath in sounding an advance. Immortal hope animates his dying injunction: "Grow in grace, and in the knowledge of our Lord and Savior" [2 Pet. 3:18].

THE BEGGAR'S PETITION

And when he heard that it was Jesus of Nazareth, he began to cry out, and say,
Jesus, thou Son of David, have mercy on me—Mark 10:47

Jesus was now on His last journey to Jerusalem. That night He would sleep at Bethany: Calvary was but a week off. He had paused to save Zacchaeus, and now He has resumed His march to His Cross. Popular enthusiasm is surging around Him, and for the first time He does not try to repress it. A shouting multitude are escorting Him out of the city. They have just passed the gates, and are in the act of turning towards the mountain gorge through which ran the Jerusalem road. A long file of beggars is sitting, as beggars do still in Eastern cities, outside the gate; well accustomed to lift their monotonous wail at the sound of passing footsteps. Bartimaeus is among them. He asks, according to Luke, what is the cause of the bustle, and is told that "Jesus of Nazareth is passing by." [see Luke 18:37]. The name wakes strange hope in him, which can only be accounted for by his knowledge of Christ's miracles done elsewhere. It is a witness to their notoriety that they had filtered down to the talk of beggars at city gates. And so, true to his trade, he cries, "Jesus . . . have mercy upon me!" In the cry there throbs the sense of need, deep and urgent; in it there is also the realization of the possibility that the widely flowing blessings of which Bartimaeus had heard might be concentrated and poured, in their full flood, upon himself. He individualizes himself, his need, Christ's power and willingness to help *him*. And, because he has heard of so many who have, in like manner, received His healing touch, he comes with the cry, "Have mercy upon *me*."

All this is upon the low level of physical blessings, need, and desire. But let us lift it higher. It is a mirror in which we may see ourselves, our necessities, and the example of what our desire ought to be. The deep consciousness of inadequacy, need, emptiness, blindness, lies at the bottom of all true crying to Jesus Christ. If you have never—knowing yourself to be a sinful man, in peril, present and future, from your sin, and stained and marred by reason of it—gone to Jesus Christ, you never have gone to Him in any deep sense at all. Only when I know myself to be a sinful man am I driven to cry, "Jesus! Have mercy on me." And I ask you not to answer it to me, but to press the question on your own consciences—"Have I any experience of such a sense of need; or am I groping in the darkness and saying, I see; weak as water, and saying I am strong?" "Thou knowest not that thou art poor, and naked, and blind" [Rev. 3:17]; and so that Jesus of Nazareth should be passing by has never moved thy tongue to call, "Son of David, have mercy on me."

THE SON OF DAVID

What think ye of Christ? whose son is he? They say unto him, The Son of David—
Matt. 22:42.

The cry of blind Bartimaeus expressed a clear insight into something at least of our Lord's unique character and power. Unless we know Him to be all that is involved in that august title, "the Son of David," I do not think our cries to Him will ever be very earnest. It seems to me that they will only be earnest when, on the one hand, we recognize our need of a Savior, and, on the other hand, behold in Him the Savior that we need. I can quite understand—and ever see plenty of illustrations of it all around us—a kind of Christianity, real as far as it goes, but in my judgment very superficial, which has no adequate conception of what sin means, in its depth, in its power upon the subject of it, or in its consequences here and hereafter; and, that sense being lacking, the whole scale of Christianity, as it were, is dropped, and Christ comes to be, not, as I think, the New Testament tells us He is, the Incarnate Word of God, who for us men and for our salvation bore our sins in His own body on the tree, and was made sin for us, that we might be made the righteousness of God in Him, but an Example, a Teacher, or a pure Model, or a Social Reformer, or the like. If men think of Him only as such, they will never cry to Him, "Have mercy upon me" [Ps. 31:9].

Oh! I pray you, whether you begin with looking into your own hearts and recognizing the crawling evils that have made their home there, and thence pass to the thought of the sort of Redeemer that you need and find in Christ—or whether you begin at the other side, and looking upon the revealed Christ in all the fullness in which He is represented to us in the Gospels, and from thence go back to ask yourselves the question, "What sort of man must I be if that is the kind of Savior that I need?"—I pray you ever to blend these two things together, the consciousness of your own need of redemption in His blood, and the assurance that by His death we are redeemed, and then to cry, "Lord! Have mercy upon me," and claim your individual share in the wide-flowing blessing, to turn all the generalities of His grace into the particularities of your own possession. We have to go one by one to His Cross, and one by one to pass through the wicket-gate. We have not cried to Him as we ought if our cry is only, "Christ! Have mercy upon us. Lord! Have mercy upon us. Christ! Have mercy upon us." We must be alone with Him, that into our own hearts we may receive all the fullness of His blessing; and our petition must be, "Thou Son of David, have mercy on *me*" [Mark 10:47]. Have you said that?

JESUS AND THE BLIND MAN

Blind Bartimaeus, the son of Timaeus, sat by the highway side begging—
Mark 10:46

The blind beggar had a clear insight into Christ's place and dignity. The multitude said to him, "Jesus of *Nazareth* passeth by." That was all they cared for or knew. He cries, "Jesus, Thou *Son of David*" [Mark 10:47], distinctly recognizing our Lord's Messianic character, His power and authority, and on that power and authority he built a confidence; for he says not as some other suppliants had done, either, "If thou wilt thou canst" [Matt. 8:2; Mark 1:40; Luke 5:12], or, "If thou canst do anything, have compassion on us" [Mark 9:22]: he is sure of both the power and the will.

Now, it is interesting to notice that this same clear insight other blind men in the Evangelist's story are also represented as having had. Blindness has its compensations; it leads to a certain steadfast brooding upon thoughts, free from disturbing influences. *Seeing* Jesus did not work faith; not seeing Him seems to have helped it. It left imagination to work undisturbed, and He was all the loftier to these men because the conceptions of their minds were not limited by the vision of their eyes. At all events, here is a distinct piece of insight into Christ's dignity, power, and will to which the seeing multitudes were blind.

The disciples attempted to stifle the cry. No doubt it was in defense of the Master's dignity, as they construed it, that the people sought to silence the persistent, strident voice piercing through their hosannas. They did not know that the cry of wretchedness was far sweeter to Him than their shallow hallelujahs. Christian people of all churches very especially, have been a great deal more careful of Christ's dignity than He is, and have felt that their formal worship was indecorously disturbed when by chance some earnest voice forced its way through it with the cry of need and desire. But this man had been accustomed for many a day, sitting outside the gate, to reiterate his petition when it was unattended to, and to make it heard amid the noise of passersby. So he was persistently bold and importunate and shameless, as the shallow critics thought, in his crying. The more they silenced him the louder he cried. Would God that we had more crying like that; and that Christ's servants did not so often seek to suppress it, as some of them do. If there are any of you who, by reason of companions, or cares, or habits, or sorrows, or a feeble conception of your own need, or a doubtful recognition of Christ's power and mercy, have been tempted to stop your supplications, do like Bartimaeus, and the more these, your enemies, seek to silence the deepest voice that is in you, the more let it speak.

THE MASTER'S CALL

The master is come, and calleth for thee—John 11:28

"Jesus stood still, and commanded him to be called" [Mark 10:49]. Remember that. He was on His road to His Cross, and the tension of spirit which the Evangelists notice as attaching to Him then, and which filled the disciples with awe as they followed Him, absorbed Him, no doubt, at this hour, so that He heard little of the people's shouts. But He did hear the blind beggar's cry, and He arrested His march in order to attend to it. That pause of the King, and the quick ear which discerned the difference between the unreal shouts of the crowd and the terrible sincerity in the cry of the beggar is still open. He is in the heavens, surrounded by its glories, and, as I think Scripture teaches us, wielding providence and administering the affairs of the universe. He does not need to pause in order to hear you and me. If He did, He would—if I may venture upon such an impossible supposition—bid the hallelujahs of heaven hush themselves, and suspend the operations of His providence if needs were, rather than you or I, or any poor man who cries to Him, should be unheard and unhelped. The living Christ is as tender a friend, has as quick an ear, is as ready to help at once, today, as He was outside the gate of Jericho. And every one of us may lift his or her poor, thin voice, and it will go straight up to the throne, and not be lost in the clamor of the hallelujahs that echo around His seat. Christ still hears and answers the cry of need. Send it up, and you will find that true. Notice the suppliant's response. That is a very characteristic right-about-face of the crowd, who one moment were saying, "Hold your tongue, and do not disturb Him," and the next moment were all eager to encumber him with help, and to say, "Rise up! Be of good cheer! He calleth thee." No thanks to them that He did. And what did the man do? "Sprang to his feet" [see Mark 10:49]—as the words rightly rendered would be—and flung away the sloppy rags that he had around himself for warmth and softness of seat, as he waited at the gate; "and came to Jesus" [Mark 10:50]. "Lay aside every weight, and the sin that doth so easily beset us, let us run" [Heb. 12:1] to the same refuge. You have to abandon something if you are to go to Christ to be healed. I daresay you know well enough what it is. I do not, but certainly there is something that entangles your legs and keeps you from finding your way to Him. And if there is nothing else there is yourself, and your trust in self, and that is to be put away. Cast away the garment spotted with the flesh, and go to Christ, and you will get relief.

THE ALL-ENCOMPASSING LOVE OF CHRIST

If you abide in me, and my words abide in you, ask whatsoever ye will, and it shall be done unto you—John 15:7

"What wilt thou that I should do unto thee?" [Mark 10:51]. A very few hours before He had asked the same question, with an entirely different significance, when the sons of Zebedee came to Him, and tried to get Him to walk blindfolded into a promise. He upset their scheme with the simple question, "What is it that you want?" And that meant, "I must know and judge before I commit Myself." But when He said the same thing to Bartimaeus, He meant exactly the opposite. It was putting the key of the treasure house into the beggar's hand. It was the implicit pledge that whatever he desired he should receive. He knew that the thing this man wanted was the thing that He delighted to give.

But the tenderness of the words, and the gracious promise that is hived in them, must not make us forget the singular authority that speaks in them. Think of a man doing as Jesus Christ did, standing before another and saying, "I will give you anything that you want." Either a madman, or a blasphemer, or "God . . . manifest in the flesh" [1 Tim. 3:16]; almighty power guided by infinite love!

And what said the man? He had no doubt what he wanted most: the opening of these blind eyes of his. And, dear brother, if we knew ourselves as well as Bartimaeus knew his blindness, we should have as little doubt what it is that we need most. Suppose you had this wishing-cap that Christ put on Bartimaeus's head put on yours, what would you ask? It is a penetrating question if men will answer it honestly. Think what you consider to be your chief need. Suppose Jesus Christ stood where I stand, and spoke to you: "What would ye that I should do for you?" [Mark 10:36]. If you are a wise man, if you know yourself and Him, your answer will come as swiftly as the man's—"Lord! heal me of my blindness, and take away my sin, and give me Thy salvation." There is no doubt about what it is that every one of us needs most. And there should be no doubt as to what each of us would ask first. The supposition that I have been making is realized. That gracious Lord is here, and is ready to give you the satisfaction of your deepest need, if you know what it is, and will go to Him for it. "Ask, and ye shall receive" [John 16:24].

THE HEALER AND THE HEALED

And Jesus said unto him, Go thy way; thy faith hath made thee whole—Mark 10:52

Bartimaeus had scarcely ended speaking when Christ began. He was blind at the beginning of Christ's little sentence; he saw at the end of it. "Go thy way; thy faith hath saved thee." The answer came instantly, and the cure was as immediate as the movement of Christ's heart in answer.

I here and now proclaim the possibility of an immediate passage from weakness to light. Some folk look askance at us when we talk about sudden conversions, but these are perfectly reasonable; and the experience of thousands asserts that they are actual. As soon as we desire we have, and as soon as we have we see. Whenever the lungs are open the air rushes in; sometimes the air opens the lung that it may. The desire is all but contemporaneous with the fulfillment, in Christ's dealings with men. The message is flashed along the wire from earth to heaven in an incalculably brief space of time, and the answer comes swift as thought and swifter than light. So, dear friend, there is no reason whatever why a similar instantaneous change should not pass over you now. You are unsaved; you may be saved. It is for yourself to settle whether you are or are not.

Here we have a clear statement of the path by which Christ's mercy rushes into a man's soul. "Thy faith hath saved thee." But it was Christ's power that saved him. Yes! it was; but it was faith that made it possible for Christ's power to make him whole. Physical miracles indeed did not always require trust in Christ, as a preceding condition, but the possession of Christ's salvation does, and cannot but do. There must be trust in Him in order that we may partake of the salvation which is owing solely to His power, His love, His work upon the Cross. The condition is for us; the power comes from Him. My faith is the hand that grasps His. It is His hand, not mine, that holds me up. My faith lays hold of the rope. It is the rope, and the person above that holds it, that lifts me out of the horrible pit and the miry clay [Ps. 40:2]. My faith flees for refuge to the City. It is the City that keeps me safe from the Avenger of Blood. Brother, exercise that faith, and you will find that vision. If you will fling away your hindrances, and grope your path to His feet, and fall down before Him, knowing your deep necessity, and trusting in Him to supply it, He will save you. Your new sight will gaze upon your Redeemer, and you will follow Him in the way of loving trust and glad obedience.

Jesus Christ was passing by. He was never to be in Jericho any more. If Bartimaeus did not get his sight then, he would be blind all his days. Christ and His salvation are offered to thee, my friend, now. Perhaps if you let Him pass you will never hear Him call again, and may abide in the darkness forever. Do not run the risk of such a fate.

KNOWING GOD

Thou shalt know that I the Lord am thy Savior, and thy Redeemer, the Mighty One of Jacob—Is. 60:16

We all know the difference between *hearsay* and *sight.* We may have read books of travel that tell of some scene of great natural beauty or historic interest, and may think that we understand all about it, but it is always an epoch when our own eyes look for the first time at the snowy summit of an Alp, or for the first time at the Parthenon on its rocky height. We all know the difference between *hearsay* and *experience.* We read books of the poets that portray love and sorrow, and the other emotions that make up our throbbing, changeful life; but we need to go through the mill ourselves before we understand what the grip of the iron teeth of the harrow of affliction is; and we need to have had our own hearts dilated by a true and blessed affection before we know the sweetness of love. Men may tell us about it, but we have to feel it ourselves before we know.

To come still closer; we all know the difference between hearing about a man and making his acquaintance. We may have been told much about him, and be familiar with his character, as we think; but, when we come face to face with him, and actually for ourselves experience the magnetism of his presence, or come under any of the influences of his character, then we know that our former acquaintance with him, by means of hearsay, was but superficial and shadowy. "I have heard of thee by the hearing of the ear, but now mine eyes seeth thee" [Job 42:5]. Can you say that? If so, you understand the text. "They shall teach no more every man . . . his brother, saying, Know the Lord"—as if He were a stranger—for "they shall all know me, from the least . . . to the greatest" [Jer. 31:34].

There is all the difference between knowing *about* God and knowing God; just the difference that there is between dogma and life, between theology and religion. We may have all the articles of the Christian creed clear in our understandings, and may owe our possession of them to other people's teaching; we may even, in a sense, believe them—and yet they may be absolutely outside of our lives. And it is only when they pass into the very substance of our being, and influence the springs of our conduct—it is only then that we know God.

ACQUAINTANCE WITH GOD

Acquaint now thyself with him, and be at peace: thereby good shall come unto thee—Job 22:21

Acquaintance with God may not include any more intellectual proposition about Him than the man had before he knew Him, but it has turned doctrines into fact, and instead of the mere hearsay and traditional religion, which is the only religion of millions, it has brought the true heart-grasp of Him, which is the only thing worth calling a knowledge of God. For let me remind you that while we may know a science or proposition by the exercise of our understandings in appropriate ways, that is not how we know people. And God is a Person, and to know Him does not mean to understand *about* Him, but to be on speaking terms with Him, to have a familiar acquaintance with Him, to "summer and winter" with Him, and so, by experience, to verify the things that before were mere doctrines. I want you to ask yourself, and I would ask myself, whether my religion is knowing *about* God or knowing Him; whether it is all made up of a set of truths which I assent to mainly because I am not sufficiently interested in them to contradict them, or whether these truths have become the very substance of my life. I do not believe in a religion without a dogma—I was going to say, I believe still less in a dogma without religion; and that is the Christianity of scores of professing Christians. It is as useless as are the dried seeds that rattle in the withered head of a poppy in the autumn, or as the shrivelled kernel that sounds in the hollowness of a half-empty nut.

Remember that to know God is to become acquainted with Him, and that only on the path of such familiar, friendly, loving fellowship and communion with Him can men find the confirmation of the truths about Him which make up the eternal revelation of Him in the Gospel. "We know"—that is a valid certainty, arising from experience, and it has as good a right to call it self knowledge as any of the processes by which men come to be sure about the physical facts of this material universe. I would even go further, and say that the fact that such a continual stream of witnesses, through all the generations, have been able to say, "I have tasted and I have seen that God is good" [Ps. 34:8], is to be taken into account by all impartial searchers after truth. And if men want to square their creeds with all the facts of humanity, let them not omit, in their consideration of the claims of Christian evidence, this fact, that from generation to generation men have said, and their lives have witnessed to its truth, "I know whom I have believed . . . and that He is able to keep" us [2 Tim. 1:12]. We know that we are of God. The whole case for Christianity *cannot* be appreciated from outside. "Taste and see."

"ALL SHALL KNOW ME"

They shall not teach every man his neighbor, and every man his brother, saying,
Know the Lord: for all shall know me, from the least to the greatest—Heb. 8:11

"They all, from the least to the greatest, shall know." There is to be no distinction of rank or age, or endowment, which shall result in some of the people of God having a position from which any of the others are altogether shut out. The writer is, of course, contrasting in his mind, though he does not express the contrast, the condition of things of old, when the spiritual aristocracy of the nation received communications which they then imparted to their fellows. In the morning dawn the highest summits catch the rays first, but as the sun rises it floods the lower levels, and at midday shines right down into the depths of the cavities. So the world is now flooded with the light of Christ; and every Christian man and woman, by virtue of their Christian character, does possess the unction from the Holy One, in which lie the potency and the promise of the knowledge of all things that are needful to be known for life and godliness. This is the true democracy of the gospel—the universal possession of the life of Christ by the Spirit.

Now, if that be so, then it is by no means a truth to be kept simply for the purpose of fighting against ecclesiastical or clerical encroachment and denials of it, but it ought to be taken as the candle of the Lord, by each of us, and in the light of it we ought to search very rigidly and very often our own Christian character and experiences. Do you know anything about that inward knowledge of God which comes from friendship with Him, and speaks irrefutable certainties in the heart which receives it? "If any man have not the Spirit of Christ, he is none of His" [Rom. 8:9]. If you owe all your knowledge of, and your faith in, the great verities of the Gospel, and the loving personality of God, to the mere report of others, if you cannot verify these by your own experience, if you cannot say, "Many things I know not; you can easily puzzle me with critical and philosophical subtleties, but this one thing I do know, that whereas I was blind, now I see" [see John 9:41]—if you cannot say that, I pray you, examine yourself whether your religion is not mainly a form, and how far it has any life in it at all.

✤
INDIVIDUAL RESPONSIBILITY

Therefore to him that knoweth to do good, and doeth it not, to him it is sin—
James 4:17

The recognition of the universality of the knowledge of God in all Christian people has great revolutionary work to do among the churches of Christendom yet. For I do not know that there are any of them that have sufficiently recognized this principle. Not only in a church where there is a priesthood and an infallible head of the Church on earth, nor in churches only that are bound by human creeds imposed on them by men, but also in churches like ours, where there is no formal recognition of either of these two errors, the practical contradiction of this universality is apt to creep in. It is a great deal more the fault of the people than of the priest; a great deal more the fault of the congregation than of the pastor, when they are lazily contented to take all their religion at second-hand from him, and to shuffle all the responsibility off their own shoulders on to his. If this truth obliges me, and all men who stand in my position, to say with the Apostle, "Not for that we have dominion over your faith, but are helpers of your joy" [2 Cor. 1:24], it obliges you to take nothing from me, or any man, on our bare words, nor to exalt any of us into a position which would contradict this great principle, but yourself, at first hand, to go to God, and get straight from Him the teaching which He only can give. Dominion and subjection, authority and submission to men, in any office in the church, are shut out by such words as these.

But brotherly help is not shut out. If a party of men are climbing a hill, and one is in advance of his fellows when he reached the summit, he may look down and call to those below, and tell them how fair and wide the view is, and beckon them to come and give them a helping hand up. So, because Christian men vary in the extent to which they possess and utilize the one gift of knowledge of God, and some of them are in advance of the others, it is all in accordance with this principle, that they that are in advance should help their brethren, and give them a brotherly hand. Not as if my brother's word can give me the inward knowledge of God, but it may help me to get that knowledge for myself. We can but do what the friend of the bridegroom does: he brings the bride to her lover, and then he shuts the door and leaves the two to themselves. That is all that any of us can do. You must yourself draw the water from the well of salvation. We can only tell you, "There *is* the well, and the water is sweet" [Ex. 15:25].

❉
THE SOURCE OF THE TRUE
KNOWLEDGE OF GOD

Now we believe, not because of thy (the woman of Samaria) saying; for we have heard him ourselves, and know that this is indeed the Christ, the Savior of the world—John 4:42

All inward knowledge of God, which is the prerogative of every Christian man, is made possible and actual for any of us only by and through the mission, and especially the death, of Jesus Christ our Lord. For therein does He set forth God to be known as nothing else but that supreme suffering and supreme self-surrender upon the Cross ever can do or had done. We know God as He would have us know Him, only when we see Jesus suffering and dying for us; and then adoringly, as one in the presence of a mystery into which he can but look a little way, say that even there and then "he that hath seen *me* hath seen the Father" [John 14:9].

Jesus Christ's blood, the seal of the Covenant, is the great means by which this promise is fulfilled, inasmuch as in that death He sweeps away all the hindrances which bar us out from the knowledge of God. The great dark wall of my sin rises between me and my Father. Christ's blood, like some magic drops upon a fortification, causes all the black barrier to melt away like a cloud; and the access to the throne of God is patent, even for sinful creatures like us. The veil is rent, and by that blood we have access unto the holiest of all.

Christ is the Source of this knowledge of God; inasmuch, further, as by His mission and death there is given to the whole world, if it will receive it, and to all who exercise faith in His name, the gift of that Divine Spirit who teaches in the inmost spirit the true knowledge of His Son. To "delight in the law of the Lord" [Ps. 1:2] is the sure way to know more of the Lord. One act of obedience from the heart will teach us more of God than all the sages can. It is more illuminating simply to do as He willed than to read and think and speculate and study. "If any man wills to do His will, he shall know of the teaching." And mutual possession of God by us, and of us by God, leads to fuller knowledge. To possess God is to love Him; and "he that loveth knoweth God" or, rather is known of God [1 John 4:8].

So, do not be content with traditional religion, with a hearsay Christianity. "Acquaint now thyself with him" [Job 22:21], and be at peace.

A TRIUMPHANT ASSURANCE

Thou hast made the LORD . . . thy habitation; there shall no evil befall thee, neither shall any plague come nigh thy dwelling—Psalm 91:9, 10

We shall understand God's dealings with us, and get to the very throbbing heart of such promises as these in this 91st Psalm, far better if we start from the certainty that whatever it means it does *not* mean that, with regard to external calamities and disasters, we are going to be God's petted children, or to be saved from the things that fall upon other people. No! No! We have to go a great deal deeper than that. If we have felt a difficulty, as I suppose we all have sometimes, and are ready to say with the half-despondent Psalmist, "My feet were almost gone, and my steps had well-nigh slipped" [Ps. 73:2]; when we see what we think the complicated mysteries of the Divine providence in this world, we have to come to this belief, that the evil that is in the evil will never come near the man sheltered beneath God's wing. The physical external event may be entirely the same to him as to another, who is not covered with His feathers. Here are two partners in a business, the one a Christian man, and the other is not. A common disaster overwhelms them. They become bankrupt. Is their insolvency to the one the same as it is to the other? Here are two men on board a ship, the one putting his trust in God, the other thinking it all nonsense to trust anything but himself. They are both drowned. Is drowning the same to the two? As their corpses lie side by side among the ooze, with the weeds over them, and the lobsters at them, you may say of the one, but only of the one, "There shall no evil befall thee, neither any plague come nigh thy dwelling."

For the protection that is granted to faith is only to be understood by faith. It is deliverance from the evil in the evil which indicates, as no exaggeration, nor as merely an experience and a promise peculiar to the old theorizing of Israel, but not now realized—the grand sayings of this psalm. The poison is all wiped off the arrow by that Divine protection. It may still wound, but it does not putrefy the flesh. The sewage water comes down, but it passes into the filtering bed, and is disinfected and cleansed before it is permitted to flow over our fields.

And so, if any of you are finding that the psalm is not outwardly true, and that through the covering wing the storm of hail has come and beaten you down, do not suppose that that in the slightest degree impinges upon the reality and truthfulness of this great promise, "He shall cover thee with his feathers" [Ps. 91:4]. Anything that has come through *them* is manifestly not an "evil." "Who is he that will harm you if ye be followers of that which is good?" [1 Pet. 3:13]. "If God be for us, who can be against us" [Rom. 8:31]? Not what the world calls, and our wrung hearts feel that it rightly calls, "sorrows" and "afflictions." These all work for our good; and protection consists, not in averting their blows, but in changing their character.

July 4

THE COVERING WING

He shall cover thee with his feathers, and under his wings shalt thou trust: his truth is a shield and buckler—Psalm 91:4

The main idea in this image is that of protection and fostering. There seems to me to be a very distinct triad of thoughts. There is the covering wing; there is the flight to its protection; and there is the warrant for that flight. "He shall cover thee with his feathers"; that is the Divine act. "Under his wings shalt thou trust"; that is the human condition. "His truth shall be thy shield and buckler": that is the Divine manifestation which makes the human condition possible. Thus the idea is that of the expanded feather, beneath the shelter of which the callow young lie and are gathered. Whatsoever kites may be in the sky, whatsoever stoats and weasels may be in the hedges, they are safe there. The image suggests not only the thought of protection, but those of fostering, downy warmth, peaceful proximity to a heart that throbs with parental love, and a multitude of other happy privileges realized by those who nestle beneath that wing. But while these subsidiary ideas are not to be lost sight of, the promise of protection is to be kept clear as that chiefly intended by the Psalmist.

This psalm rings throughout with the doctrine that a man who dwells "in the secret place of the Most High" [91:1] has absolute immunity from all sorts of evil, and there are also regions in which that immunity, secured by being under the shadow of the Almighty, is exemplified in the psalm: the one, that of our outward dangers; the other, that of temptation to sin and what we may call spiritual foes. Now, these two regions and departments in which the Christian man does realize, in the measure of his faith, the Divine protection exhibit that protection as administered in two entirely different ways. No man that lies under the shadow of God, and has his heart filled with the continual consciousness of that presence, is likely to fall before the assaults of evil that tempt him away from God; and the defense which He gives against external evils. For, as the New Testament teaches us, we are kept from sin not by any outward breastplate or armor, or even by the Divine wing lying above us to cover us, but by an indwelling Christ in our hearts. His Spirit within us makes us free from the law of sin and death, and conquerors over all temptations.

July 5

A SHELTER FROM THE STORM

A man shall be as a hiding place from the wind, and a covert from the tempest; as rivers of water in a dry place, as the shadow of a great rock in a weary land—Is. 32:2

"Under his wings shalt thou trust" [Ps. 91:4]. Is not that a vivid, intense, picturesque, but most illuminative, way of telling us what is the very essence, and what is the urgency, and what is the worth of what we call faith? The Old Testament is full of the teaching—which is masked to ordinary readers; the same teaching as the New Testament is confessedly full of—of the necessity of faith as the one bond that binds men to God. If only our translators had wisely determined upon a uniform rendering in Old and New Testament of words that are synonymous, the reader would have seen what is often now reserved for the student, that all these sayings in the Old Testament Book about "trusting in God" run on all fours with "believe on the Lord Jesus Christ and thou shalt be saved" [Acts 16:31].

But just mark, the faith which unites with God, and brings a man beneath the shadow of His wings, is nothing more nor less than the flying into the refuge that is provided for us. Does that not speak to us of the urgency of the case? Does that not speak to us eloquently of the perils which environ us? Does it not speak to us of the necessity of flight, swift, with all the powers of our will? Is the faith which is a flying into a refuge fairly described as an intellectual act of believing in a testimony? Surely it is something a great deal more than that! A man out in the plain, with the avenger of blood, hot-breathed and bloody-minded, at his back, might believe, as much as he liked, that there would be safety within the walls of the City of Refuge, but unless he took to his heels without loss of time, the spear would be in his back before he knew where he was. There are plenty of men that know all about the security of the Refuge, and believe it utterly, but never run for it; and so never get into it. Faith is the gathering up of the whole powers of the nature to fling myself into an Asylum, to cast myself into God's arms, to take shelter beneath the shadow of His wings. And unless a man does that, and swiftly, he is exposed to every bird of prey in the sky, and to every beast of prey lurking in wait for him. A man is not saved because he believes that he is saved, but because by believing he lays hold of the salvation. It is not the flight that is impregnable, and makes those behind its strong bulwarks secure. Not my outstretched hand, but a Hand that my hand grasps, is what holds me up. The power of faith is but that it brings me into contact with God, and sets me behind the seven-fold bastions of the Almighty protection.

OUR DIVINE WARRANT

The faithful God, which keepeth covenant and mercy with them that love him and keep his commandments to a thousand generations—Deut. 7:9

You cannot trust a God that has not given you an inkling of His character or disposition, but if He has spoken, then you know where to have Him. How can a man be encouraged to fly into a refuge unless he is absolutely sure that there is an entrance for him into it, and that, entering, he is safe? And that security is provided in the great thought of God's pledge. "Thy righteousness is like the great mountains" [Ps. 36:6]. "Who is like unto Thee, O Lord [Ex. 15:11]; or to Thy faithfulness round about thee" [Ps. 89:8]? That faithfulness shall be our "shield," not a tiny shield that a man could bear upon his left arm, but the word means the large shield, planted in the ground in front of the soldier, covering him, however hot the fight, and circling around him, like a tower of iron.

God is "faithful" to all the obligations under which He has come by making us. That is what one of the New Testament writers tells us when he speaks about Him as "a faithful Creator" [1 Pet. 4:19]. Then, if He has put desires into our hearts, be sure that somewhere there is satisfaction; and if He has given us needs, be sure that in Him there is the supply; and if He had lodged in us aspirations which make us restless, be sure that if we will turn them to Him, they will be satisfied and we shall be at rest. "He never sends mouths but He sends meat to fill them." He remembers our frame, and measures His dealings accordingly. When He made me He bound himself to make it possible that I should be blessed forever. And He has done it.

God is faithful to His word, according to that great saying in the Epistle to the Hebrews, where the writer tells us that by "God's counsel," and "God's oath," "two immutable things," we might have "strong consolation who have fled for refuge to lay hold on the hope set before us" [Heb. 6:17, 18].

God is faithful to His own past. The more He has done the more He will do. "Thou hast been my help; leave me not, neither forsake me" [Ps. 27:9]. Therein we present a plea which God Himself will honor. And He is faithful to His own past in a yet wider sense. For all the revelation of His love and of His grace in times that are gone, though they might be miraculous in their form, are permanent in their essence. So one of the psalmists, hundreds of years after the time that Israel was led through the wilderness, sang, "There did *we*"—of this present generation—"rejoice in Him" [Ps. 66:6]. What has been, is, and will be, for Thou art "the same yesterday, and today, and forever" [Heb. 13:8].

We have no God that lurks in darkness, but one that has come into the light. We have to run, not into a refuge that is built upon a "perhaps," but upon "Verily, verily! I say unto thee." Let us build rock upon rock, and let our faith correspond to the faithfulness of Him that has promised.

July 7

THE ANGEL OF THE LORD

The angel of the Lord encampeth round about them that fear him, and delivereth them—Psalm 34:7

There run throughout the whole of the Old Testament notices of the occasional manifestation of a mysterious person who is named "*the* Angel," "the angel of the Lord." For instance, in the great scene in the wilderness, where the bush burned and was not consumed, He who appeared is named "*the* angel of the Lord" [Ex. 3:2]; and His lips declare *"I Am that I Am"* [3:14]. In like manner, soon after, the Divine voice speaks to Moses of "the Angel in whom is My name." When Balaam had his path blocked among the vineyards [Num. 22:22], it was a *replica* of the figure that stayed his way—a Man with a drawn sword in His hand, who speaks in autocratic and Divine form. When the parents of Samson were notified of the coming birth of the hero [Judg. 13:3], it was the Angel of the Lord that appeared to them, accepted their sacrifice, declared the Divine will, and disappeared in a flame of fire from the altar. A psalm speaks of "the angel of the Lord" as "encamping round about them that fear Him, and delivereth them." Isaiah tells us of the "angel of his presence," who was "afflicted in all Israel's afflictions, and saved them" [see Is. 63:9]. And the last prophetic utterance of the Old Testament is most distinct and remarkable in the strange identification and separation of Jehovah and the Angel, when it says, "the Lord shall suddenly come to his temple, even the messenger of the covenant" [Mal. 3:1]. Now, if we put all these passages—and they are but select instances—if we put all these passages together, I think we cannot help seeing that there runs, as I said, throughout the whole of the Old Testament a singular strain of revelation in regard to a person who, in a remarkable manner, is distinguished from the created hosts of angel beings, and also is distinguished from, and yet in name, attributes, and worship all but identified with, the Lord Himself.

If we turn to the narrative in Joshua 5, we find there similar phenomena marked out. For this mysterious "Man with the sword drawn" in His hand, quotes the very words which were spoken at the bush, when He says "Put off thy shoes from thy feet, for the place whereon thou standest is holy ground" [Ex. 3:5]; and by fair implication, He would have us to identify the persons in these two great theophanies. He ascribes to Himself, in the further conversation in the next chapter, directly Divine attributes, and is named by the sacred name, "The Lord said unto Joshua, see I have given into thine hand Jericho and her king" [Josh. 6:2].

THE WORD OF THE LORD

And the Word was made flesh, and dwelt among us—John 1:14

If we turn to the New Testament we find that there, under another image, the same strain of thought as in the Old Testament is presented. The Word of God, who from everlasting "was with God, and was God" [John 1:1], is represented as being the Agent of Creation, the Source of all human illumination, the Director of Providence, the Lord of the Universe. "By Him were all things created" [Col. 1:16]. So, surely, these two halves make a whole: and the Angel of the Lord, separate and yet so strangely identified with Jehovah, who at the crises of the nation's history, and stages of the development of the process of Revelation, is manifested, and the Eternal Word of God, whom the New Testament reveals to us, are one and the same.

This truth was transiently manifested in the Old Testament. The vision of Joshua (*see* Joshua 5) passed, the ground that was hallowed by His foot is undistinguished now in the sweltering plain around the mound that once was Jericho. But the fact remains: the humanity, that was only in appearance, and for a few minutes assumed then, has now been taken up into everlasting union with the Divine nature, and a Man reigns on the Throne and is Commander of all who battle for the truth and the right. The eternal order of the universe is before us here.

It only remains to say a word in reference to the sweep of the command which Joshua's vision assigns to the Angel of the Lord. "Captain of the Lord's host" [Josh. 5:15] means a great deal more than the true General of Israel's little army. It does mean that, or the words and the vision would cease to have relevance and bearing on the moment's circumstances and need. But it includes also, as the usage of Scripture would sufficiently show, if it were needful to adduce instances of it, all the ordered ranks of loftier intelligent beings, and all the powers and forces of the universe. These are conceived of as an embattled host, comparable to an army in the strictness of their discipline and their obedience to a single will. It is the modern thought that the universe is a Cosmos and not a Chaos, an ordered unit, with the addition of the truth beyond the reach and range of science, that its unity is the expression of a personal will. It is the same thought which the centurion had, to Christ's wonder, when he compared his own power as an officer in a legion, where his will was implicitly obeyed, to the power of Christ over diseases and sorrows and miseries and death, and recognized that all these were His servants, to whom, if His autocratic lips chose to say "Go," they went, and if he said, "Do this," they did it [Matt. 8:5–10]. So the Lord of the universe and its ordered ranks is Jesus Christ. That is the truth which was flashed from the unknown like a vanishing meteor in the midnight before the face of Joshua, and which stands like the noonday sun, unsetting and irradiating for us who live under the gospel.

THE CAPTAIN OF THE LORD'S HOST

And he said, Nay; but as captain of the host of the Lord am I now come—
Josh. 5:14

The army of Israel was just beginning a hard conflict under an untried leader. Behind them Jordan barred their retreat, in front of them Jericho forbade their advance. Most of them had never seen a fortified city, and had no experience nor engines for a siege. So we may well suppose that many doubts and fears shook the courage of the host as it drew around the doomed city. Their chief had his own heavy burden. He seems to have gone apart to meditate on what his next step was to be. Absorbed in thought, he lifts up his eyes mechanically, as brooding men will, not expecting to see anything, and is startled by the silent figure of "a man . . . with his sword drawn" [5:13] in His hand, close beside him. There is nothing supernatural in His appearance; and the immediate thought of the leader is, "Is this one of the enemy that has stolen upon my solitude?" So, promptly and boldly, he strides right up to Him with the quick challenge: "Whose side are you on? Are you one of us, or from the enemy's camp" [see v. 13]? And then the silent lips open: "Upon neither the one nor the other. I am not on your side, you are on Mine, for as *Captain* of the Lord's host am I come up." And then Joshua falls on his face, recognizes his Commander-in-Chief, owns himself a subordinate, and asks for orders. "What saith my Lord unto His servant?" [v. 14].

The Captain of the Lord's host—He Himself takes part in the fight. He is not like a general who, on some safe knoll behind the army, sends his soldiers to death, and keeps his own skin whole; but He *has* fought and He *is* fighting. Do you remember that wonderful picture in two halves, at the end of one of the Gospels, "the Lord was received up into Heaven and sat on the right hand of God . . . they went forth and preached everywhere" [Mark 16:19, 20]? Strange contrasts between the repose of the seated Christ and the toils of His peripatetic servants: Yes: Strange contrast; but the next words harmonize the two halves of it: "The Lord working with them, and confirming the word with signs following" [Mark 16:21]. The Leader does not so rest as that He does not fight; and the servants do not need so to fight as that they cannot rest. Thus the old legends of many a land and tongue have a glorious truth in them to the eye of faith; and at the head of all the armies that are charging against any form of the world's misery and sin there moves the form of the Son of Man, whose aid we have to invoke, even from His crowned repose at the right hand of God. "Gird thy sword upon thy thigh, O most mighty . . . and in thy majesty ride forth prosperously . . . and thy right hand shall teach thee terrible things" [Ps. 45:3, 4].

191

July 10

OUR LEADER IN THE WORLD'S WARFARE

In the world ye shall have tribulation: but be of good cheer; I have overcome the world—John 16:33

If the revelation made to Joshua and his host be for us as truly as for them a revelation of who is our true leader, surely all of us in our various degrees, and especially any of us who have any "Quixotic crusade" for the world's good on our consciences and on our hands, may take the lessons and the encouragements that are here. Own your Leader. That is one plain duty. And recognize this fact, that by no other power than by His, and with no other weapons than those which He puts into our hands, in His Cross and meekness, can a world's evils be overcome, and the victory be won for the right and the truth. I have no faith in crusades which are not under the Captain of our salvation. And I wish that the earnest men, and there are many of them—the laborious and the self-sacrificing men in many departments of philanthropy and benevolence and social reformation—who labor unaware of who is their Leader, and not dependent upon His help, nor trusting in His strength—would see beside them the Man with the drawn sword in His hand [Josh. 5:13], the Christ with the sharp two-edged sword [Heb. 4:12] going out of His mouth, by whom, and by whom alone, the world's evil can be overcome and slain.

Own your General; submit to His authority; pick the weapons that He can bless; trust absolutely in His help. We *may* have, we *shall* have, in all enterprises for God and man that are worth doing, need of patience, just as the army of Israel had to parade for six weary days around Jericho blowing their useless trumpets, while the impregnable walls stood firm, and the defenders flouted and jeered their aimless procession. But the seventh day will come, and at the trumpet blast down will go the loftiest ramparts of the cities that are walled up to heaven, with a rush and a crash, and through the dust and over the ruined rubbish Christ's soldiers will march and take possession. So trust in your Leader, and be sure of the victory, and have patience and keep on at your work.

Do not make Joshua's mistake. "Art Thou for us?"—Nay! "Thou art for *Me.*" That is a very different thing, We have the right to be sure that God is on our side, when we have made sure that we are on God's. So take care of self-will and self-regard, and human passions, and all the other parasitical insects that creep around philanthropic religious work, lest they spoil your service. There is a great deal that calls itself after Jehu's fashion, "My zeal for the Lord" [2 Kgs. 10:16], which is nothing better than zeal for my own notions and their preponderance. Therefore we must strip ourselves of all that, and not fancy that the cause is ours, and then graciously admit Christ to help us, but recognize that it is *His*, and lowly submit ourselves to His direction, and what we do, do, and when we fight, fight, in His name and for His sake.

OUR ALLY IN OUR WARFARE WITH OURSELVES

I can do all things through Christ which strengtheneth me—Phil 4:13

That is the worst fight—our battle with ourselves; far worse than all these Hittites and Hivites, and the other tribes with their barbarous names. Far worse than all external foes are the foes that each man carries about in his own heart. In that slow hand-to-hand and foot-to-foot struggle I do not believe that there is any conquering power available for a man that can for a moment be compared with the power that comes through submission to Christ's command and acceptance of Christ's help. He has fought every foot of the ground before us. We have to "run the race"—to take another metaphor—"that is set before us, looking unto Jesus" [Heb. 12:12], the great Leader, and in His own Self the Perfector of the faith which conquers. In Him, His example, the actual communication of His Divine Spirit, and in the motives for brave and persistent conflict which flow from His Cross and Passion, we shall find that which alone will make us the victors in this destructive warfare. There can be no better directory given to any man than to tread in Christ's footsteps, and learn how to fight from Him, who in the wilderness repelled the triple assault with the single "It is written"; thus recognizing the word and will of God as the only directory and defense. Thus, if we humbly take service in His ranks, and ask Him to show us where our foes within are, and to give us the grace to grapple with them, and cast them out, anything is possible rather than ultimate defeat; and however long and sore the struggle may be, its length and its severity are precious parts of the discipline that makes us strong, and we are at last "more than conquerors through him that loved us" [Rom. 8:37].

Think of Christ, what He is, and what resources He has at His back, of what are His claims for our service, and loyal, militant obedience. Think of the certain victory of all who follow Him among the armies of Heaven, clad in fine linen, clean and white. Think of the crown and the throne for Him that overcomes [Rev. 3:12].

Remember the destructive powers that sleep in Him: the drawn sword in His hand; the two-edged sword out of His mouth; the wrath of the Lamb. Think of the ultimate certain defeat of all antagonisms; of that last campaign when He goes forth with the name written on His vesture and on His thigh, "King of kings and Lord of lords" [Rev. 19:16]. Think of how He strikes through kings in the day of His wrath, and fills the place with the bodies of the dead; and how His enemies become His footstool.

Ponder His own solemn word, "He that is not with me is against me" [Matt. 12:30]. There is no neutrality in this warfare. Either we are for Him or we are for His adversary. "Under which King?—speak or die!" As a sensible man, not indifferent to your highest and lasting well-being, ask yourself, "Can I, with my ten thousand, meet Him with His twenty thousand?" [see Luke 14:31]. Put yourself under His orders, and He will be on your side. "He will teach your hands to war, and your fingers to fight" [Ps. 144:1]; and "will cover your head in the day of battle" [Ps. 140:7], and bring you at last, palm-bearing and laurel-crowned, to that blissful state where there will still be service, and He still be the Captain of the Lord's host, but where swords will be beaten into plowshares and the victors shall need to learn war no more.

July 12

ALL HAVE SINNED

There is no difference; for all have sinned, and come short of the glory of God—
Rom. 3:22, 23

What does the Bible mean by sin? Everything that goes against or neglects God's law. And if you will bring into all the acts of every life the reference, which really is there, to God and His will, you will not need anything more to establish the fact that "all have sinned, and come short of the glory of God." Whatever other differences there are between men, there is this fundamental similarity. Neglect—which is a breach—of the law of God pertains to all mankind. Everything that we do ought to have reference to Him. *Does* everything that we do have such reference? If not, there is a quality of evil in it. For the very definition of sin is living to myself and neglecting Him. He is the Center; and, if I might use a violent figure, every planet that wrenches itself away from gravitation towards, and revolution around, that Center, and prefers to whirl on its own axis, has broken the law of the celestial spheres, and brought discord into the heavenly harmony. All men stand condemned in this respect.

Now, there is no need to exaggerate. I am not saying that all men are on the same level. I know there are great differences in the nobleness, purity, and goodness of lives, and Christianity has never been more unfairly represented than when good men have, as one of them called, with St. Augustine, the virtues of godless men, "splendid vices." But though the differences are not unimportant, the similarity is far more important. The pure, clean-living man, and the gentle, loving woman, though they stand high above the sensuality of the profligate, the criminal, stand in this respect on the same footing that they, too, have to put their hands on their mouths, and their mouths in the dust, and cry, "Unclean!" I do not want to exaggerate, but I am sure that if men will be honest with themselves there is a voice that responds to the indictment when I say sadly, in the solemn language of Scripture, "we all have sinned, and come short of the glory of God. For there is no difference." If you do not believe in a God, you can laugh at the old wife's notion of "sin." If you do believe in a God, you are shut up to believe this other, "Against Thee, Thee only, have I sinned" [Ps. 51:4]. And if this universal fad is indeed a fact, it is the gravest element in human nature. It matters very little, in comparison, whether you and I are wise or foolish, educated or illiterate, rich or poor, happy or miserable. All the superficial distinctions which separate men from one another, and are all right in their own places, dwindle away into nothing before this solemn truth, that in every frame there is a plague spot, and that the leprosy has smitten us all.

"I HAVE SINNED"

Against thee, thee only, have I sinned, and done that which is evil in thy sight—
Psalm 51:4

Do not let us lose ourselves in generalities. All means each, and each means *me*. We all know how hard it is to bring general truths to bear with all their weight upon ourselves. That is an old common phase. "All men think all men mortal but themselves"; and we are quite comfortable when this indictment is kept in the general terms of universality—"all have sinned" [Rom. 3:23]. Suppose I sharpen the point a little—God grant that the point may get to some indurated conscience!—suppose, instead of reading "All have sinned," I encourage each one of my readers to strike out the general word, and put in the individual one, and to say, "*I* have sinned." You have to do with this indictment just as we have to do with the promises and offers of the gospel—wherever there is a "whosoever," put your pen through it, and write your own name over it. The blank check is given to us in regard of the promises and offers, and we have to fill in our own names. The charge is handed to us in regard to this indictment, and if we are wise we shall write our own names there, too. I leave this on your conscience, and I will venture to ask that you would put to yourself the question, "Is it I?" And sure I am that, if you do, you will see a finger pointing out of the darkness, and hear a voice more stern than that of Nathan saying, "Thou art the man" [2 Sam. 12:7].

The people in one crowd that gathered about Christ were not all diseased. Some of them He taught; some of them He cured; but that crowd, where healthy men mingled with cripples, is no type of the condition of humanity. Rather, we are to find it in that Pool of Bethesda, with its five porches [John 5:2], wherein lay a multitude of helpless folk, tortured with varieties of sickness, and none of them sound. Blessed be God! We are in *Bethesda*, which means "house of mercy," and the Fountain that can heal is perpetually springing up beside us all. There is a disease which affects and infects all mankind—Sin is universal, and it is personal. "*I* have sinned."

I ask you to go into the depths of your own heart, and to be honest in recalling your own experience, and to say if, notwithstanding all the gladness of a godless life, there does not lie, grim and silent for the most part, but there, and felt to be there all the same, a great yearning and consciousness of unrest. Every good has in it some fatal flaw and incompleteness. There is always a break in the circle; always a stone missing out of the bracelet. There is always one unlighted window in Aladdin's palace. There is always a Mordecai sitting dark as a thunder-cloud and unparticipant of the common emotion, who makes Haman say, "All this availeth . . . nothing" [Esth. 5:13]. There is always disappointment in earthly fruition. The fish never proves so big when it is lying panting on the grass as it did in the water, when the fisher was struggling with it. The chase is always better than the capture. In all earthly good there is a fatal disproportion between it and the heart that seeks to solace itself with it; so that after all satisfactions, there is the old cry of the heart, "I hunger still." And above all, there is the certainty which pushes itself in—like the skeleton at the feasts of the Egyptian kings, or the mocking slave that walked behind the conqueror in his triumph as he went up the steps of the capitol—the certainty that we have to leave them all behind us. And what is the naked soul going to do when it "flares forth into the dark?"

THE THREE-HEADED EVIL
THING—(PART ONE)

The heart is deceitful above all things, and desperately wicked: who can know it?—Jer. 17:9

I was going to use an inappropriate word, and say, the *superb* ease with which Christ grappled with, and overcame, all types of disease is a revelation on a lower level of the inexhaustible and all-sufficient fullness of His healing power. He can cope with all sin, the world's sin and the individual's. And, as I believe, He alone can do it.

Just look at the problem that lies before any one who attempts to staunch these wounds of humanity. What is needed in order to deliver men from the sickness of sin? Well, that evil thing, like the fabled dog that sits at the gate of the infernal regions, is three-headed. And you have to do something with each of these heads if you are to deliver men from that power.

There is, first, the awful power that evil once done has over us of repeating itself on and on. There is nothing more dreadful, to a reflective mind, than the damning influence of habit. The man that has done some wrong thing once is a *rara avis* indeed. If once, then twice; if twice, then onward and onward through all the numbers. And the intervals between will grow less, and what were isolated points will coalesce into a line; and impulses wax as motives wane, and the less delight a man has in his habitual form of evil the more its dominion over him; and he does it at last, not because the doing of it is any delight, but because the *not* doing of it is a misery. If you are to get rid of sin and to eject the disease from a man, you have to deal with that awful degradation of character and the tremendous chains of custom. That is one of the heads of the monster.

But, as I said, sin has reference to God, and there is another of the heads. For with sin comes guilt. The relation to God is perverted; and the man that has transgressed stands before Him as guilty, with all the dolefulness that that solemn word means; and that is another of the heads.

The third is this—the consequences that follow in the nature of penalty—"Whatsoever a man soweth, that shall he also reap" [Gal. 6:7]. So long as there is a universal rule by God, in which all things are connected by cause and effect, it is impossible but that "Evil shall slay the wicked" [Ps. 34:21]. And that is the third head. These three, habit, guilt, and penalty, have all to be dealt with if you are going to make a thorough job of the surgery.

And here I want not to argue, but to preach. Jesus Christ died on the Cross for you, and your sin was in His heart and mind when He died, and His atoning sacrifice cancels the guilt, and suspends all that is dreadful in the penalty of the sin. Nothing else—nothing else will do that. Who can deal with guilt but the offended Ruler and Judge? Who can trammel up consequences but the Lord of the Universe? The blood of Jesus Christ is the sole and sufficient oblation for, and satisfaction for, the sins of the whole world.

THE THREE-HEADED EVIL THING—(PART TWO)

The sin of Judah is written with a pen of iron, and with the point of a diamond: it is graven upon the table of their heart—Jer. 17:1

Two of the monster's heads are disposed of. What about the third? Who will take the venom out of my nature? What will express the black drop from my heart? How shall the Ethiopian change his skin or the leopard his spots? How can the man that has become habituated to evil "learn to do well"? Superficially there may be much reformation. God forbid that I should forget that, or seem to minimize it. But for the thorough rejection from your nature of the corruption that you have yourself brought into it, I believe—and that is why I am here, for I should have nothing to say if I did not believe it—I believe that there is only one remedy, and that is that into the sinful heart there should come, rejoicing and flashing, and bearing on its broad bosom before it, all the rubbish and filth of that dunghill, the great stream of the new life that is given by Jesus Christ. He was crucified for our offenses, and He lives to bestow upon us the fullness of His own holiness. So the monster's heads are smitten off. Our disease and the tendency to it, and the weakness consequent upon it, are all cast out from us, and He reveals Himself as "the Lord that healeth thee" [Ex. 15:26].

Now, you may say "That is all very fine talking." Yes! But it is something a great deal more than fine talking. For eighteen centuries have established the fact that it is so; and with all their imperfections there have been millions, and there are millions today, who are ready to say, "Behold! It is not a delusion; it is not rhetoric. *I* have trusted in Him, and He has made *me* whole."

Now if these things that I have been saying do fairly represent the gravity of the problem which has to be dealt with in order to heal the sicknesses of the world, then there is no need to dwell upon the thought of how absolutely confined to Jesus Christ is the power of thus dealing. God forbid that I should not give full weight to all other methods for partial reformation and bettering of humanity. I would wish them all God-speed. But there is nothing else that will deal either with my sin in its relation to God, or in its relation to my character, or in its relation to my future, except the message of the gospel. There are plenty of other things, very helpful and good in their places, but I do want to say in one word that there is nothing else that goes deep enough.

HUMAN REMEDIES FOR SIN UNAVAILING

Though thou wash thee with niter, and take thee much soap, yet thine iniquity is marked before me, saith the Lord God—Jer. 2:22

Education? Yes! It will do a great deal, but it will do nothing in regard of sin. It will alter the type of the disease, because the cultured man's transgressions will be very different from those of the illiterate man. But wise or foolish, professor, student, thinker, or savage with narrow forehead and all but dead brain, are alike in this, that they are sinners in God's sight. I would that I could get through the fence that some of you have reared around you, on the ground of your superior enlightenment and education and refinement, and make you feel that there is something deeper than all that, and that you may be a very clever, and a very well educated, a very highly cultured, an extremely thoughtful and philosophical sinner, but you *are* a sinner all the same.

Again, we hear a great deal at present, and I do not desire that we should hear less, about social and economic and political changes, which some eager enthusiasts suppose will bring the millennium. Well, if the land were nationalized, and all the means of production and distribution were nationalized, and everybody got his share, and we were all brought to the communistic condition, what then? That would not make men better, in the deepest sense of the word. The fact is, these people are beginning at the wrong end. You cannot better humanity merely by altering its environment for the better. Christianity reverses the process. It begins with the inmost man, and it works outwards to the circumference; and that is the thorough way. Suppose you took a company of people out of the slums, for instance, and put them into a model lodging-house, how long will it continue a model? They will take their dirty habits with them, and pull down the woodwork to make fires, and make the place where they are as similar as possible to the pigsty where they came from in a very short time. You must change the men, and then you can change their circumstances, or, rather, they will change them for themselves. Now, all this is not to be taken as casting cold water on any such efforts to improve matters, but only as a protest against its being supposed that these *alone* are sufficient to rectify the ills and cure the sorrows of humanity. "They have healed also the hurt of the daughter of my people slightly" [Jer. 6:14]. The patient is dying of cancer, and you are treating him for a skin disease. It is Jesus Christ alone that can cure the sins, and so the sorrows, of humanity.

THE LORD THAT HEALETH THEE

I am the Lord that healeth thee—Ex. 15:26

He . . . healed them that had need of healing—Luke 9:11

All the sick in the crowd around Christ were sent away well; but the gifts He bestowed so broadcast had no relation to their spiritual natures, and gifts that have relation to our spiritual nature cannot be thus given in entire disregard of our actions in the matter.

Christ cannot heal you unless you take His healing power. He did on earth sometimes, though not often, cure physical disease without the requirement of faith on the part of the healed person or his friends, but He cannot do so in regard of the disease of sin. There, unless a man goes to Him and trusts Him, and submits his spirit to the operation of Christ's pardoning and hallowing grace, there cannot be any remedy applied, nor any cure effected. That is no limitation of the universal power of the gospel. It is only saying that if you do not take the medicine you cannot expect that it will do you any good. And surely that is plain, common sense. There are plenty of people who fancy that Christ's healing and saving power will, somehow or other, reach all men, apart from the man's act. It is all a delusion. If salvation could be thus given, independent of the man, it would come down to a mere mechanical thing, and would not be worth the having. So I say, if you will not take the medicine, you cannot get the cure.

I say, further, if you do not feel that you are ill you will not take the medicine. A man crippled with lameness, or tortured with fever, or groping in the daylight and blind, or deaf to all the sounds of this sweet world, could not but know that he was a subject for the healing. But the awful thing about our disease is that the worse you are the less you know it; and that when conscience ought to be speaking loudest it is quieted altogether, and leaves a man often perfectly at peace, so that after he has done evil things he wipes his mouth and says, "I have done no 'harm'" Do not be contented until you have recognized what is true, that you—*you*, stand a sinful man before God.

There is surely no madness comparable to the madness of the man that prefers to keep his sin and die rather than go to Christ and live. Will you look into your own heart? Will you recognize that awful solemn law of God, which ought to regulate all our doings, and has been so often neglected and so often transgressed by each of us? If once you saw yourself as you are, you would turn to Him and say, "Heal me"; and you would be healed, and He would lay His hand upon you. If only you will go, sick and broken, to Him, and trust in His great sacrifice, and open your hearts to the influx of His healing power, He will give you "perfect soundness" [Acts 3:16]; and your song will be, "Bless the Lord O my soul . . . Who forgiveth all thine iniquities; who healeth all thy diseases" [Ps. 103:2, 3].

SEEKING AND FINDING

I will seek that which was lost, and will bring again that which was driven away—Ezek. 34:16

There are two kinds of finding. There is the casual stumbling upon a thing that you were not looking for, and there is the finding as the result of seeking. It is the latter kind that is here. Christ did not casually stumble upon Philip, upon that morning, before they departed from the fords of the Jordan on their short journey to Cana of Galilee. He went to look for another Galilean, one who was connected with Andrew and Peter, a native of the same village. He went and found him; and while Philip was all unexpectant and undesirous, the Master comes to him and lays His hand upon him, and draws him to Himself [see John 1:43].

Now I say that is what Christ often does with people. There are men like "the merchantman that went all over the world seeking goodly pearls," who, with some eager longing to possess light, or truth, or goodness, or rest, search up and down and find it nowhere, because they are looking for it in a hundred different places. They are expecting to find a little here and a little there, and so piece it all together, and make of the fragment one all-sufficing restfulness. Then, when perhaps they are most eager in their search, or, when perhaps it has all died down into despair and apathy, the veil seems to be withdrawn, and they see Him whom they have been seeking all the time and knew not that He was there beside them. All, and more than all, that they sought for in the many pearls is stored for them in the one Pearl of great price [Matt. 13:46]. The ancient covenant stands firm today as forever. "Seek, and ye shall find; knock, and it shall be opened unto you" [Luke 11:9].

But then there are others, like Paul on the road to Damascus; like Matthew, the publican, sitting at the receipt of custom, on whom there is laid a sudden hand, to whom there comes a sudden conviction, on whose eyes, not looking to the east, there dawns the light of Christ's presence. Such cases occur all through the ages, for He is not going to be confined within the narrow limits of answering, seeking, souls, and showing Himself to people that are brought to Him by human instrumentality; but far beyond these bounds He goes, and many a time discloses His beauty and His sweetness to hearts that know not of Him, and who can only say, "Surely the Lord was in this place; and I knew it not" [Gen. 28:16]. "Thou wast found of them that sought thee not" [Rom. 10:20].

THE SEEKING CHRIST

The day following, Jesus would go forth into Galilee, and findeth Philip; and saith
unto him, Follow me—John 1:43

Jesus "findeth Philip," who was not seeking Jesus, and who was brought by nobody. To him Christ reveals Himself as drawing near to many a heart that has not thought of Him, and laying a masterful hand of gracious authority on the springs of life and character in that autocratic word, "Follow Me!" So we have a gradual heightening revelation of the Master's graciousness to all souls, to them that seek and to them that seek Him not. It is a revelation of the seeking Christ.

Everybody that reads this chapter (John 1) with even the slightest attention must observe how "seeking" and "finding" are repeated over and over again. Christ turns to Andrew and John with the question "What *seek* ye?" [v. 38]. Andrew, as the narrative says, "*findeth* his own brother, Simon, and saith unto him, "We have *found* the Messias" [v. 41]. Then, again, Jesus *finds* Philip; and again, Philip, as soon as he has been won to Jesus, goes off to *find* Nathaniel; and his glad word to him is, once more, "We have *found* the Messias." It is a reciprocal play of finding and seeking all through these verses.

As it was in His miracles upon earth, so it has been in the sweet and gracious works of His grace ever since. Sometimes He healed in response to the yearning desire that looked out of sick eyes or that spoke from parched lips. And no man that ever came to Him and said, "Heal me!" was sent away destitute of His blessing. Sometimes He healed in response to the beseeching of those who, with loving hearts, carried their dear ones and laid them at His feet. But, to magnify the spontaneity and the completeness of His own love, and to show us that He is bound and limited by no human cooperation, and that He is His own motive, sometimes He reached out the blessing to a hand that was not extended to grasp it; and by His question, "Wilt thou be made whole?" [John 5:6] kindled desires that else had lain dormant forever.

And so in this story before us: He will welcome and ever answer Andrew and John when they come seeking; He will turn around to them with a smile on His face, that converts the question, "What seek ye?" into an invitation, "Come and see" [John 1:46]. And when Andrew brings his brother to Him, He will go more than halfway to meet him. But when these are won there still remains another way by which He will have disciples brought into His Kingdom, and that is by Himself going out and laying His hand on the man and drawing Him to His heart by the revelation of His own. But He really is seeking us all, whether through human agencies or not; whether our hearts are seeking Him or not, still in deepest truth. There is no heart upon earth which Christ does not desire, and no man nor woman within the sound of His Gospel whom He really is not—in any metaphorical, but in a simple, literal, prosaic sense—seeking that He may draw them to Himself.

CHRIST'S UNSOUGHT LOVE

I am found of them that sought me not—Is. 65:1

Christ's own word is a wonderful one: "The Father *seeketh* such to worship Him" [John 4:23]; as if God went all up and down the world looking for hearts to love Him and to turn to Him with reverent thankfulness. And as the Father, so the Son—for us the revelation of the Father: "The Son of Man is come to *seek* and to save that which was lost" [Luke 19:10]. Nobody on earth wanted Him, or dreamed of His coming. When He bowed the heavens and gathered Himself into the narrow space of the manger in Bethlehem, and took upon Him the limitations and the burdens and the weaknesses of manhood, it was not in response to any petition, it was in reply to no seeking, but He came spontaneously, unmoved, obeying but the impulse of His own heart, and because He would have mercy. He who is the Beginning, and will be first in all things, was first in this. "Before they call I will answer" [Is. 65:24]—and came upon earth unbesought and unexpected, because His own infinite love brought Him hither. Christ's mercy to a world does not come like water in a well that has to be pumped up, by our petitions, by our search, but like water in some fountain, rising sparkling into the sunlight by its own inward impulse. He is His own motive; and came to a forgetful and careless world, like a shepherd who goes after his flock in the wilderness, not because they bleat for him, since they crop the herbage which tempts them even further from the fold and remember him or it no more, but because he cannot have them lost. Men are not conscious of needing Christ till He comes. The supply creates the demand. He is like the "dew . . . that tarrieth not for man, nor waiteth for the sons of men" [Mic. 5:7]. But not only does Christ seek us all inasmuch as the whole conception and execution of His great work are independent of man's desires, but He seeks us each in a thousand ways. He longs to have each of us for His disciples. He seeks each of us for His disciples, by the motion of His Spirit on our spirits, by stirring convictions on our consciences, by pricking us often with a sense of our own evil, by all our restlessness and dissatisfaction, by the disappointments and the losses, as by the brightness and the goodness of earthly providence, and often through such poor agencies as my lips and the lips of other men. The Master Himself, who seeks all mankind, has sought and is seeking you at this moment. Yield to His search! The shepherd goes out on the mountainside, for all the storms and the snow, and wades knee-deep through the drifts until he finds the sheep. And your Shepherd, who is also your Brother, has come looking for you, and at this moment is putting out His hand and laying hold of you through my poor words, and saying to you, as He said to Philip, "Follow Me!"

❀

"FOLLOW ME"

And he saith, Follow me, and I will make you fishers of men—Matt. 4:19

"Jesus findeth Philip, and saith unto him, Follow me" [John 1:43]. No doubt there was a great deal more passed, but no doubt what more passed was less significant and less important for the development of faith in this man than what is recorded. The word of authority, the invitation which was a demand, the demand which was an invitation, and the personal impression which He produced upon Philip's heart, were the things that bound him to Jesus Christ forever. "Follow Me," spoken at the beginning of the journey of Christ and His disciples back to Galilee, so might have meant merely, on the surface, "Come with us on our return." But they have, of course, a much deeper meaning. They mean, Be My disciple. Think what is implied in them, and ask yourself whether the demand that Christ makes in these words is an unreasonable one, and then ask yourself whether you have yielded to it or not. "Follow Me!" We lose the force of the image by much repetition. Think of what it implies. Sheep follow a shepherd; travelers follow a guide. Here is a man upon some dangerous cornice of the Alps, with a bit of limestone as broad as the palm of your hand for him to pick his steps upon, and perhaps a couple of feet of snow above that for him to walk upon, a precipice of two thousand feet on either side. And his guide says, as he ropes himself to him, "Now, look here! You tread where I tread?" Jesus said to Philip, "Follow Me!" Travelers follow their guides, soldiers follow their commanders. There is the hell of the battlefield; here a line of wavering, timid, raw recruits. Their commander rushes to the front, and throws himself upon the advancing enemy with the one word, "Follow!" And the weakest becomes a hero. Soldiers follow their captains.

Your Shepherd comes to you and calls, "Follow Me!" Your Captain and Commander comes to you and calls, "Follow Me!" In all the dreary wilderness, in all the difficult contingencies and conjunctions, in all the conflicts of life, this Man strides in front of us and proposes Himself to us a Guide, Example, Consoler, Friend, Companion, everything; and gathers up all duty, all blessedness, in the majestic and simple words, "Follow Me!"

What business has Jesus Christ to ask me to follow Him? Why should I? Who is He that would set Himself up as being the perfect Example and the Guide for all the world? What has He done to bind me to Him, that I should take Him for my Master, and yield myself up to Him in a subjection that I refuse to the mightiest names in literature and thought and practical benevolence? Who is this that is thus going to dominate over us all? There is only one answer. "This is none other than the Son of God, who has given Himself a ransom for me, and therefore has the right, and therefore He only has the right, to say to me, 'Follow Me!'"

❀

A CALL TO FAITH AND OBEDIENCE

If any man serve me, let him follow me; and where I am, there shall also my
servant be—John 12:26

From the beginning Christ's disciples did not look upon Him as a Rabbi's disciples did, as being simply a teacher, but recognized Him as the Messias, the Son of God, the King of Israel. So that they were called upon by His commands to accept His teaching in a very special way, not merely as Rittel or Gamaliel asked their disciples to accept theirs. Do you do that? Do you take Him as your illumination about all matters of theoretical truth and of practical wisdom? Is His declaration of God your theology? Is His declaration of His own Person your creed? Do you think about His Cross as He did when He elected to be remembered in all the world by the broken body and the shed blood, which were the symbols of His reconciling death? Is His teaching, that the Son of Man comes to give His life a ransom for many, the ground of your hope? Do you follow Him in your belief, and following Him in your belief, do you accept Him as the Savior of your soul, by His death and passion? That is the first step, to follow Him, to trust Him wholly for what He is, the Incarnate Son of God, the Sacrifice for the sins of the whole world, and therefore for yours and for mine. This is a call to faith. It is also a call to obedience. "Follow Me!" certainly means, "Do as I bid you"; but that is harsh. Diligently plant your little feet in His firm footsteps; where you see His track going across the bog, be not afraid to walk after Him, though it may seem to lead you into the deepest and the blackest of it. Follow Him, and you will be right; follow Him, and you will be blessed. Do as Christ did, or as according to the best of your judgment it seems to you that Christ would have done if He had been in your circumstances; and you will not go far wrong. "The Imitation of Christ," which the old anonymous monk wrote his book about, is the sum of all practical Christianity. "Follow Me!" makes discipleship to be something better than intellectual acceptance of His teaching, something more than even reliance for my salvation upon His work. It makes discipleship to be, springing out of these two, the acceptance of his teaching and the consequent reliance, by faith, upon His word—to be a practical reproduction of His character and conduct in mine.

It is a call to communion. If a man follows Christ he will walk close behind Him, and near enough to Him to hear Him speak, to be "guided by His eye." He will be separated from other people and from other things. In these four things, then—Faith, Obedience, Imitation, Communion—lies the essence of discipleship. No man is a Christian who has not in some measure all four. Have you got them?

HESITATING TO FOLLOW CHRIST

And as they followed, they were afraid—Mark 10:32

Quickly a soul may be won or lost! That moment, when Philip's decision was trembling in the balance, was but a moment. It might have gone the other way, for Christ has no pressed men in His army; they are all volunteers. It might have gone the other way. A moment may settle for you whether you will be His disciple or not. People tell us that the belief in instantaneous conversions is unphilosophical; it seems to me that the objections to them are unphilosophical. All decisions are matters of an instant. Hesitation may be long, weighing and balancing may be a protracted process; but the decision is always a moment's work, a knife-edge. And there is no reason whatever why any one may not now, if they will, do as Philip did, on the spot; and when Christ says, "Follow Me," return to Him and answer, "I follow Thee withersoever thou goest" [Luke 9:57].

There is an old Church tradition which says that the disciple who, at a subsequent period, answered Christ, "Lord, suffer me first to go and bury my father" [Luke 9:59], was this same Apostle. I do not think that it is at all likely, but the tradition suggests to us one thought about the reasons why people are kept back from yielding this obedience to Christ's invitation. Many are kept back, as that man in the story was, because there are some other duties, and they are duties, no doubt, which you feel or make to be more important. "I will think about Christianity and about turning religious when this, that, or the other thing is over. I have my position in life to make. I have a great many things to do that must be done at once, and really I have not time to think about it."

There are some that are kept from following Christ because they have never found out yet that they need a guide at all. Then there are some that are kept back because they like very much better to go their own way and to follow their own inclination, and dislike the idea of following the will of another.

There are a host of other reasons, but they are all not worth looking at. They are excuses, they are not reasons. "They all with one consent began to make excuse" [Luke 14:18]. Excuses, not reasons; and manufactured excuses, in order to cover a decision which has been taken before, and on other grounds altogether, which it is not convenient to bring up to the surface!

Follow Him! Trust, obey, imitate, hold fellowship with Him. You will always have a Companion, you will always have a Protector. "He that followeth Me," saith He, "shall not walk in darkness, but shall have the light of life" [John 8:12]. And if you will listen to the Shepherd's voice and follow Him, that sweet old promise will be true, in its deepest and Divinest sense about your life, in time; and your life in the moment of death, the isthmus between two worlds; and about your life in eternity. "They shall not hunger nor thirst, neither shall the sun nor heat smite them; for he that hath mercy on them shall lead them, even by the springs of water shall he guide them" [Is. 49:10]. Follow thou Me!

THE ANTIDOTE TO ALL DESPONDENCY

Hast thou not known? hast thou not heard? the everlasting God, the Lord, the Creator of the ends of the earth, fainteth not, neither is weary?—Is. 40:28

Here is an appeal to the familiar thought of an unchangeable God as the antidote to all despondency and the foundation of all hope. To whom is the prophet speaking? The words of the previous verse tell us, in which he addresses himself to Jacob, or Israel, who is represented as complaining, "My way is hid from the Lord." That is to say, he speaks to the believing, but despondent, part of the exiles in Babylon; and to them He comes with this vehement question, which implies that they were in danger, in their despondency, of practically forgetting the great thought. There is wonder in the question, there is a tinge of rebuke in it, and there is distinctly implied this: that whenever there steals over our spirits despondency or perplexity about our own individual history, or about the peace and the fortunes of the Church or the world, the one sovereign antidote against gloom and low spirits, and the one secret of unbroken cheer and confidence is to lift our eyes to the unwearied God.

The life of men and of creatures is like a river, with its source and its course and its end. The life of God is like the ocean, with joyous movement of tides and currents of life and energy and purpose, but ever the same, and ever returning upon itself. "The Everlasting God" is "the Lord," and Jehovah the Unchanged, Unchangeable, Inexhaustible Being, spends, and is unspent; gives, and is none the poorer; works, and is never wearied; lives, and with no tendency to death in His life; flames, with no tendency to extinction in the blaze. The bush burned and was not consumed: "He fainteth not, neither is weary."

The prophet takes his stand upon the most elementary truths of religion. His appeal to them is: "What do you call God? You call him the Lord, do you not? What do you mean by calling Him that? Do you ever ask yourselves that question? You mean this, if you mean anything: 'He fainteth not, neither is wearied'" [Ex. 3:14]. "Jehovah" is interpreted from the lips of God Himself: "I Am that I Am." That is the expression of what metaphysicians call absolute, underived, eternal Being, limited and shaped and determined by none else, flowing from none else; eternal, lifted up above the fashions of time. Of Him men cannot say "He was" or "He will be," but only "HE IS"—by Himself, of Himself, forever unchanged.

THE COMFORTING GOD

Comfort ye, comfort ye my people, saith your God—Is. 40:1

This magnificent chapter is the prelude or overture to the grand music of the second part of the prophecies of Isaiah. Its first words are its keynote: "Comfort ye, comfort ye my people." That purpose is kept steadily in view throughout; and in this introductory chapter the prophet points to the only foundation of hope and consolation for Babylonian exiles, or for modern Englishmen, to that grand vision of the enthroned God "sitting on the circle of the earth, before whom the inhabitants thereof are as grasshoppers" [Is. 40:22].

"They build too low who build beneath the sky."

For nations and for individuals, in view of political disasters or of private sorrows, the only hold to which cheerful hope may cling is the old conviction, "The Lord God Omnipotent reigneth" [Rev. 19:6].

Notice how, first the prophet points to the unwearied God; and then his eyes drop from Heaven to the clouded, saddened earth, where there are the faint and the weak, and the strong becoming faint, and the youths fading and becoming weak with age. Then he binds together these two opposites—the unwearied God and the fainting man—in the grand thought that He is the Giving God, who bestows all His power on the weary. And see how, finally, he rises to the blessed conception of the unwearied man becoming like the Unwearied God. "*They* shall run, and not be weary; they shall walk, and not faint" [Is. 40:31].

And let me say, here is a lesson for us to learn of meditative reflection upon the truest commonplaces of our religion. There is a tendency among us all to forget the indubitable, and to let our religious though be occupied with the disputable and secondary parts of revelation rather than with the plain deep verities which form its heart and center. The commonplaces of religion are the most important. Everybody needs air, light, bread, and water. Dainties are for the few; but the table which our religion sometimes spreads for them is like that at a rich man's feast—plenty of rare dishes, but never a bit of bread; plenty of wine and wine-glasses, but not a tumblerful of spring water to be had. Every pebble that you kick with your foot, if thought about and treasured, contains the secret of the universe. The common places of our faith are the food upon which our faith will most richly feed.

And so here, in the old, old Word, that we all take for granted as being so true that we do not need to think about it, lies the source of all consolation—the hope for men, for churches, for the world. We all have times, depending on mood or circumstances, when things seem black and we are weary. This great truth will shine into our gloom like a star into a dungeon. Are our hearts to tremble for God's truth today? Are we to share in the pessimist views of some faint-hearted and little-faith Christians? Surely as long as we can remember the name of the Lord, and His unwearied arm, we have nothing to do with fear or sadness for ourselves, or for His Church, or for His world.

POWER FOR THE FAINT

He, giveth power to the faint. . . . Even the youths shall faint and be weary . . . but they that wait upon the Lord shall renew their strength; they shall mount up with wings as eagles; they shall run, and not be weary; and they shall walk, and not faint—Is. 40:29-31

Earth knows no independent strength. All earthly power is limited in range and duration, and by the very law of its being is steadily tending to weakness. But though that has a sad side, it has also a grand and blessed one. Man's needs are the open mouth—if I may say so—into which God puts His gifts. The more sad and pathetic the condition of feeble humanity by contrast with the strength, the immortal strength of God, the more wondrous that grace and power of His, which is not contented with hanging there in the Heavens above us, but bends right down to bless us and to turn us into its own likeness. The low earth stretches, grey and sorrowful, flat and dreary, beneath the blue, arched heaven, but the heaven stoops to encompass and to touch it. "He giveth power to the faint, and to them that have no might He increaseth strength."

All creatural life digs its own grave. "The youths shall faint with the weakness of physical decay, the weakness of burdened hearts, the weakness of consciously distracted natures, the weakness of agonizing conscience. They shall be weary with the weariness of dreary monotony, of uncongenial tasks, of long-continued toil, of hope deferred, of disappointed wishes, of bitter disenchantments, of the learning the lesson that all is vanity, the weariness that creeps over us all as life goes on." All these are the occasions for the inward strength of God to manifest itself even in us; according to the great word that He spoke once and means ever: "My grace is sufficient for thee, for my strength is made perfect in weakness" [2 Cor. 12:9].

Isaiah did not know—or, if he did, he knew it very dimly—what every Christian child knows: that the highest revelation of the power of Him that "fainteth not, neither is weary" [Is. 40:28], is found in Him who, "being weary with His journey, sat thus on the well" [John 4:6], and, being worn out with the long work and excitement of a hard day, slept the sleep of the laboring man on the wooden pillow of the little boat amid the whistle of the tempest and the dash of the waves.

And Isaiah did not know—or, if he did, he knew it very dimly and as from afar—that the highest fulfillment of His own word—"He giveth power to the faint, and to them that have no might He increaseth strength"—would be found when a gentle voice from amid the woes of humanity said: 'Come unto me! All ye that labor and are heavy laden, and I will give you rest. Take my yoke upon you . . . and ye shall find rest unto your souls" [Matt. 11:28, 29].

LIFTED TO THE HIGH LEVEL

*They go from strength to strength; every one of them in Zion appeareth
before God—Psalm 84:7*

The phrase means, of course, the continuous bestowment in unintermitting sequence of fresh gifts of power, as each former gift becomes exhausted, and more is required. Instant by instant, with unbroken flow, as golden shafts of light travel from the central sun, and each beam is linked with the source from which it comes by a line that stretches through millions and millions of miles, so God's gift of strength pours into us as we need. Grace abhors a vacuum, as nature does. And just as the endless procession of the waves rises up on to the beach, or as the restless network of the moonlight irradiation of the billows stretches all across the darkness of the sea, so that unbroken continuity of strength after strength gives grace for grace according to our need; and as each former supply is expended and used up, God pours Himself into our hearts anew. That continuous communication leads to the "perpetual youth" of the Christian soul. For the words of Isaiah, "They shall mount up with wings as eagles" [40:31], might perhaps more accurately be rendered, "They shall put forth their pinions as eagles"—the allusion being to the popular belief that in extreme old age the eagle molted and renewed its feathers—that popular belief which is referred to in Psalm 103, "Who satisfieth thy mouth with good things, so that thy youth is renewed like the eagle's" [v. 5].

The same idea is here that though, according to the law of physical life, decaying strength, and advancing years, that tame and sober and disenchant and often make weary because they are familiar with all things and take the edge off everything—though these tell upon us whether we are Christians or not, and in some important respects tell upon us all alike, yet, if we are waiting upon God, keeping our hearts near Him, living on His love, trying to realize His inward presence and His outstretched hand, then we shall have such a continuous communication of His grace, strength, and beauty as that we shall grow younger as we grow older, and, as the Scotch psalm has it:

"In old age, when others fade,
They fruit still forth shall bring."

Said Swedenborg: "The oldest angels are the youngest," "They that wait upon 'the Lord' [Is. 40:31] have drunk of the fountain of perpetual youth, for the buoyancy and the inextinguishable hope which are the richest possessions of youth may abide with them whose hopes are set on things beyond the sky."

CONTINUOUS STRENGTH

He giveth more grace—James 4:6

God's strength, poured into our hearts, if we wait upon Him, shall fit us for the moments of special hard effort. "They shall run and not be weary," for the crises which require more than an ordinary amount of energy to be put forth; and for the long dreary hours which require nothing but keeping doggedly at monotonous duties, "They shall walk and not faint" [Is. 40:31].

It is a great deal easier to be up to the occasion in some shining moment of a man's life when he knows that a supreme hour has come than it is to keep that high tone when plodding over all the dreary plateaus of uneventful, monotonous travel and dull duties. It is easier to run fast for a minute than to grind along the dusty road for a day.

Many a ship has stood the tempest, and then has gone down in the harbor because its timbers have been gnawed to pieces by white ants. And many a man can do what is wanted in the trying moments, and yet make shipwreck of his faith in uneventful times.

"Like ships that have gone down at sea,
When heaven was all tranquillity."

Soldiers who could stand firm and strike with all their might in the hour of battle will fall asleep or have their courage ooze out at their fingers' ends when they have to keep solitary watch at their posts through a long winter's night. We have all a few moments in life of hard, glorious running; but we have days and years of walking, the uneventful discharge of small duties. We need strength for both; but paradoxical as it may sound, we need it most for the multitude of smaller duties. We know where to get it. Let us keep close to "Christ, the Power of God," and open our hearts to the entering in of His unwearied strength. "Then shall the lame man leap as a hart" [Is. 35:6], and we shall "run with patience the race that is set before us" [Heb. 12:1], if we look to Jesus, and follow in His steps.

A man complains that his path is hidden, his course on earth seems so sad and cloudy and weary as compared with the paths of those great stars that move without friction, effort, confusion, dust, noise, while all these things—friction, effort, confusion, dust, noise—beset our little carts as we tug them along the dreary road of life.

But, says Isaiah, His power does not show itself so nobly up there among the stars as it does down here. It is not so much to keep the strong in their strength as to give strength to the weak. It is much to "preserve the stars from wrong," it is more to restore and to break the power into feeble men; much to uphold all them that are falling so that they may not fall, but it is more to raise up all those that are fallen and are bowed down. So, brother, what God does with a poor, weak creature like me, when He lifts up our weakness and replenishes our weariness; pouring oil and wine into our wounds and a cordial into our lips, and sending us, with the joy of pardon, upon our road again; that is a greater thing than when He rolls Neptune in its mighty orbit around the central sun, or upholds with unwearied arms, from the cycle to cycle, the circle of the heavens with all its stars. "He giveth power to the faint" is His divinest work.

THE PERFECTION OF HOPE

Every man that hath this hope in him purifieth himself, even as he is pure—
1 John 3:3.

What constitutes perfect hope? First, that it shall be certain; and no earthly hope is so. For we all know that there blends with, and shadows the brightness of, every such anticipation an opposite possibility. "It may be; it may not be." And when thus "hopes and fears that kindle hope" are blended as "an indistinguishable throng," and we are tossed from one to the other as a shuttlecock between two battledores, there can be no perfection of hope. If my anticipations are set upon contingent things, they must vary with their objects. You cannot build a solid house on a quagmire; you must have rock for that. So, the only perfect hope is that which grasps a perfect certainty. Christian hope ought to be, if I might so say, tightened up to the level of that on which it is fastened. It is a shame that Christian people should be wavering in their anticipations of that which in itself is certain. A sure and steadfast hope is the only perfect hope.

Again, the perfection of hope lies in its being patient, persistent through discouragement, burning bright in the darkness, like a pillar of fire by night; and most of all in its being operative upon life, and contributing to steadfastness of endurance and to energy of effort. This is exactly what the feeble and fluctuating hopes of earth never do. For the more a man is living in anticipation of an uncertain good, the less is he able, to fling himself with wholeness of purpose and effort into the duties and enjoyments of the present. But a perfect hope will be the ally and not the darkener of the brightness of the present. And if we hope as we should for that we see not, then shall we with patience wait for it. I fancy that the experience of most men is that the more they indulge in the pleasant, but profitless amusement of forecasting to themselves future earthly good, the less are they fit for the strenuous work of today. Tomorrow deceives us when it is an earthly tomorrow. But "every man that hath this hope in Christ," and only the man who has, "purifies himself even as he is pure."

Here, then, is the sort of hope which it is laid upon us Christian people consciously to try to cherish, one which is fixed and certain, one which is the mother of patience and endurance, one which persists through and triumphs over all trouble and sorrow, one which nerves us for effort and opens our eyes to appreciate the blessings of the present, and one which wars against all uncleanness and lifts us up in aspiration and aim toward the purity of Jesus Christ.

Think of the blessedness of living thus, lifted up above all the uncertainties that rack men when they think about tomorrow. Try to realize the blessedness of escaping from the disappointments which come from all earthward-turned expectations, when the radiant bubble bursts, and there is nothing left in our hands but a little dirty soapsuds, as is the case with so many of our fulfilled anticipations of good. Try to realize the blessedness of escaping from that despairing hopelessness that creeps over men as life ebbs away and the years diminish. And remember the buoyant words of the Psalmist, who, because God was his hope, therefore, though he was "old and grey-headed," sang, "I will hope continually" [Ps. 71:14]. The brightest blaze of Christian hope may be on the verge of the darkness of the grave.

THE DISCIPLINE OF HOPE

Wherefore, gird up the loins of your mind, be sober, and hope to the end for the grace that is to be brought unto you at the revelation of Jesus Christ—1 Pet. 1:13

"Gird up the loins of your mind." I suppose I do not need to do more than remind you that this figure, applied to travelers, to soldiers, to any men who have a hard task upon their hands, simply expresses the gathering together of all one's powers, the training one's self for given tasks. It suggests that there is a great deal in this life that makes it very difficult for us to keep firm hold of the facts on which alone a perfect hope can be built. Unless we tighten up our belt, and so put all our strength into the effort, the truths of the resurrection which beget to a lively hope, of the great salvation wrought by Jesus Christ, of the meaning and end of all our trials and sorrows, will slip away from us, and we shall be left at the mercy of the varying anticipations of good or evil which may emerge from the varying circumstances of the fleeting moment. We have, then, to gather ourselves up and set our teeth in the effort to keep hold of Christ, of His work, of its bearing upon ourselves, of the meaning of our sorrows, if we would not have like fluctuations in our heavenly to those which necessarily belong to our earthly hopes.

"Be sober." That means, not only gather yourself together with a consecrated effort, but "keep your heel well down on the necks of lower and earthly desires." The word, of course, points, first, to temperance—not, as we use it, only in respect to one form of sensual indulgence, but to temperance—in regard of all the animal necessities and desires. The fleshly lusts that belong to everybody must be subdued. That goes without saying. But, then, there are others more subtle, more refined, but not less hostile to the perfectness of a heaven-directed hope than are these grosser ones. We must keep down all the desires and appetites of our nature, both of the flesh and of the spirit. For we have only a certain quantity of energy to expend, and if we expend it upon the things of earth there is nothing left for the things above. If you take the river, and lead it all out into the gardens that are irrigated by it, or into the stream that drives your mills, its bed will be left bare, and little of the water will reach the great ocean which is its home. If a gardener wants a tree to grow high, he strips off the side shoots. Our hopes follow our desires. What we deem good is what we hope for; and if our desires all go trailing and groveling along the earth, our hopes will never rise to the heavens. A gorged eagle cannot soar. Christian men whose heads and hearts are stuffed full of the trivialities of earth have little of the perfect hope which fastens on Christ.

THE OBJECT OF CHRISTIAN HOPE

Looking for the blessed hope and the glorious appearing of the great God and Savior Jesus Christ—Titus 2:13

It is interesting to notice the various phases under which the future perfecting of the Christian life and felicity in Heaven is set forth in the New Testament. Sometimes we read of the object of our hope as being the resurrection from the dead; sometimes we read of the "hope of righteousness" [Gal. 5:5]; sometimes we read of the "hope of eternal life" [Titus 1:2]; sometimes of the "hope of the glory of God"; sometimes of the "hope of salvation" [1 Thess. 5:8]. But all these are but the many facets of the one jewel, flashing many-colored and yet harmonious light. Peter adds another general expression when he sums up the felicities and perfectness of that future life in this remarkable and unusual phrase, "the grace that is to be brought" [1 Pet. 1:13].

Now, we generally, in our ordinary, popular, religious speech, draw a broad distinction between "grace" and "glory." But the use of the word here, though unusual, and just because it is unusual, is instructive and significant. It suggests to us the great thought that all the lustrous light that lies beyond, to the furthest distances of eternity, is the free gift of love, undeserved, and bestowing its treasures on those who have no claim to it, at the end of countless millenniums, any more than they had at the beginning. "*Grace* reigns through righteousness unto eternal life" [Rom. 5:21]; and no man of the countless nations of the blessed can say, "Give me the portion for which I have worked" [see Luke 15:12], but all must bow and say, "Give me from Thine own loving heart that which I do not deserve," "the grace that is to be brought at the revelation of Jesus Christ" [1 Pet. 1:13].

Then there is another thought suggested by this remarkable expression, and that is the essential identity of the Christian life here and hereafter. We are accustomed to include all the virtues and blessedness that here belong to faith and love under that one common designation of "grace," while, on the other hand, we name the future heavenly state "glory." But, according to the Apostle, grace and glory are one in essence. The tender green of the springing corn is the prophet of the yellow full ear. What we have here is a spark which shall be fanned yonder into a radiant flame. But the difference is one of degree, and not of kind. "Grace" is "glory" in the bud; "glory" is "grace" in the fruit.

There are many good people who are so unduly conscious of their imperfections and sins that they think it is almost wrong in them to assume the tone of steadfast anticipation which the New Testament sets before us as proper for us, and who scarcely venture to say, "I hope to enter into that rest." Brother! We are neglecting a plain duty and impoverishing ourselves unnecessarily, by the want of a treasure which belongs to us, unless we are making conscious efforts for our increase in hope as in faith and charity.

THE GRACE OF HOPE

Good hope through grace—2 Thess. 2:16

In 1 Peter 1:13 we are exhorted to "hope to the end for the grace that is to be brought unto you at the revelation of Jesus Christ." It is to be "brought unto you." Now, the margins of your Bibles give you a truer notion of the Apostle's meaning. He did not write "that is to be brought," as if the gift was all a future one, but "that is being borne towards you"; or, as one of the old commentators on Peter says, in his archaic and forcible English, "the grace that is a bring to you." The word is the same which is used to describe the audible approach of that mighty wind on the Day of Pentecost—"rushing" [Acts 2:2]. The notion suggested is that this great gift has, as it were, already started on its passage towards us, across the fields of space and the ages of the world. It is in motion towards us, as if some choir of angels were winging their way to this small island in the deep across the abysses, bearing in their hands this holy bestowment. It is bearing down upon us, like a ship at sea, or like some star traveling towards us, first a point of light, then a disc of brightness, then a world of glory which envelops us. That representation is true, because every tick of the pendulum brings "the grace" nearer. Though centuries pass before the light from the far-off shining reaches us, it is traveling, traveling, traveling towards us at every moment. So we *should* hope. Peter further suggests to us that this swiftly moving and approximating grace is all wrapped up in "the appearing of Jesus Christ" [1 Pet. 1:7]. When He comes, it comes; for it is but the impartation of Him, and we know that "when he shall appear we shall be like him, for we shall see him as he is" [1 John 3:2].

Such, then, is the object of Christian hope stated in its most general terms—a grace which includes resurrection, salvation, righteousness, eternal life, the glory of God, and that grace ever tending towards us, and that ever tending grace to be ours in its fullness, when Christ is manifested and "we shall be manifested with him in glory" [Col. 3:4]. How different in its dignity, in its certainty, in its remoteness, which is a blessing—how different from the paltry, shortsighted anticipations of a near future which delude us along the path of earthly effort? Surely, surely, this great and strange prerogative of humanity, the large discourse which looks before and after, was given to us for other purposes than that we should lavish and waste it upon fleeting things! But the most of us behave with that great faculty of anticipating and imagining the future as an astronomer might do, who, having in his possession a telescope fit to pierce the secrets of the skies, should prefer to turn it only upon the trivialities of earth. "Wherefore . . . hope to the end for the grace that is to be brought unto you at the revelation of Jesus Christ" [1 Pet. 1:13].

August 2

FOR HIS SAKE

Thus saith the Lord God: I do not this for your sakes, O House of Israel, but for mine holy name's sake—Ezek. 36:22

The foundation of all God's love to us sinful men lies not in us, nor anything about us, not in anything external to God Himself. He, and He alone, is the cause and reason, the motive and the end, of His own love to our world. And unless we have grasped that magnificent thought as the foundation of all our acceptance in Him, I think we have not yet learned half of the fullness which, even in this world, may belong to our conceptions of the love of God—a love that has no motive but Himself; a love that is not evoked even (if I may so say) by regard to His creatures' wants; a love, therefore, which is eternal, being in that Divine heart before there were creatures upon whom it could rest; a love that is its own guarantee, its own cause—safe and firm, therefore, with all the firmness and serenity of the Divine nature—incapable of being affected by our transgression, deeper than all our sins, more ancient than our very existence, the very essence and being of God Himself. "He frankly forgave them both" [Luke 7:42]. If you seek the source of Divine love, you must go high up into the mountains of God, and learn that it, as all other of His (shall I say?) emotions and feelings and resolutions and purposes owns no reason but Himself, no motive but Himself; lies wrapped in the secret of His nature, who is all-sufficient for His own blessedness, and all whose work and being is caused by, and satisfied, and terminates in His own fullness. "God is love" [1 John 4:16]; therefore, beneath all considerations of what we may want—deeper and more blessed than all thoughts of a compassion that springs from the feeling of human distress and the sight of man's misery—lies this thought of an affection which does not need the presence of sorrow to evoke it, which does not want the touch of our finger to flow out, but by its very nature is everlasting, by its very nature is infinite, by its very nature must be pouring out the flood of its own joyous fullness forever and ever!

GOD'S LOVE DEEPER THAN OUR SINS

I have loved thee with an everlasting love: therefore with lovingkindness have
I drawn thee—Jer. 31:3

"This Man, if He were a prophet, would have known who and what manner of woman this is that toucheth Him" [Luke 7:39], says the unloving and self-right-eous heart, "for she is a sinner." Ah! There is nothing more beautiful than the difference between the thought about sinful creatures which is natural to a *holy* being, and the thought about sinful creatures which is natural to a *self-righteous* being. The one is all contempt; the other, all pity. He knew what she was, and therefore He let her come close to Him with the touch of her polluted hand, and pour out the gains of her lawless life and the adornments of her former corruption upon His most blessed and most holy head. His knowledge of her as a sinner, what did it do to His love for her? It made that love gentle and tender, as knowing that she could not bear the revelation of the blaze of His purity. It smoothed His face and softened His tones, and breathed through all His knowledge and notice of her timid and yet confident approach. "Daughter, I know all about it—all thy wanderings and thy vile transgressions: I know them all, and My love is mightier than all these. *They* may be as the great sea, but My love is like the everlasting mountains, whose roots go down beneath the ocean; and My love is like the everlasting heaven, whose brightness covers it all over." God's love is Christ's love; Christ's love is God's love. And this is the lesson—that this infinite and Divine lovingkindness does not turn away from thee because thou art a sinner, but remains hovering about thee, with wooing invitations and gentle touches, if it may draw thee to repentance, and open a fountain of answering affection in thy seared and dry heart. The love of God is deeper than all our sins.

Sin is but the cloud behind which the everlasting sun lies in all its power and warmth, unaffected by the cloud; and the light will yet strike, the light of His love will yet pierce through, with its merciful shafts bringing healing in their beams, and dispersing all the pitchy darkness of man's transgression. And as the mists gather themselves up and roll away, dissipated by the heat of that sun in the upper sky, and reveal the fair earth below, so the love of Christ shines in, melting the mist and dissipating the fog, thinning it off in its thickest places, and at last piercing its way right through it, down to the heart of the man that has been lying beneath the oppression of this thick darkness, and who thought that the fog was the sky, and that there was no sun there above. Thank God! The everlasting love of God, that comes from the heart of His own being, and *is* there because of Himself, will never be quenched because of man's sin.

THE CHRIST AT THE DOOR

Behold I stand at the door and knock; if any man hear my voice, and open the door, I will come in to him, and will sup with him, and he with me—Rev. 3:20

We have here the exalted Christ asking to be let in to a man's heart. The latter words of the verse suggest the image of a banqueting-hall. The chamber to which Christ desires entrance is full of feasters. There is room for everybody else there but Him. Music and dancing and lights and good cheer and laughter fill the house, and He stands without. There is no room for Him, as there was not at His birth.

Now the plain, sad truth which that sets forth is this, that we are more willing to let anybody and anything come into our thoughts, and find lodgment in our affections, than we are to let Jesus Christ come in. Is it so, or is it not? The doors that swing wide for vanities and selfishness, lusts and passions, whims and fancies, and favorite pursuits, are barred and bolted in His face. We welcome to the chief seats in our hearts His and our worst enemies. They flock in; He stands without, like some exiled and dethroned monarch, who, coming back to his own land and his own palace, stands among the ragged homeless people on the pavement, and sees the upstarts and the rebels passing into the lighted halls; all His own, where He may not enter. Is it so, or is it not?

The reality of Christ's knocking is represented not only as being the touch of an importunate hand, but is accompanied also with the beseeching of a voice. That is not a pretty metaphor only. Jesus Christ is living and working today; He is at your side, present though unseen, working upon you though you know it not; trying to draw you to Himself; pleading with you year by year and moment by moment. It is one of the deepest facts of human existence, a barred heart, and a present Savior suing for entrance.

And how does He sue? Does He not knock at your heart by that Book of which the very spirit in all its parts is the testimony to Him? Is He not knocking at your heart loud blows, by sorrows and gentle touches, waxen touches, soft and warm and sweet as a baby's hand; by the mercies that come to you day by day? When Absalom would not go to Joab, Joab burned his corn, and then Absalom came to him [see 2 Sam. 14:29, 30]. When a man will not come to Christ, sometimes He burns *his* corn, and then, sometimes the man comes. And the further we go from Him, the louder the beckoning impressiveness of the knocks of His hand. Have you never found rising up in your soul a sudden conviction, with which you had nothing to do but to listen to it; telling you what you ought to do and to be? Have you not sometimes had flashing in upon you, like a sudden glare in the dark, the conviction, "I ought to be a Christian and to follow Jesus Christ"? Such voices—

> "Our inward ear
> Catches sometimes from afar.
> Listen, ponder, hold them dear,
> For of God—of God, they are."

Every conviction, every impression, every half inclination towards Him that has risen in your hearts, though you fought against it and smothered it, and did anything with it but obeyed it, has been His knocking there.

CHRIST'S YEARNING COMPASSION

It is the voice of my beloved that knocketh, saying, Open to me . . . for my head is
filled with dew, my locks with the drops of the night—Song 5:2

Men that bear precious gifts for the world do not often need to beg for acceptance, but He comes to it and "prays us with much entreaty that we should receive the gift" [2 Cor. 8:5]. We are mostly too proud to sue for love, especially if once the petition has been repulsed, but He asks to be let into your heart because His nature and His name is Love, and, being such, He yearns to be loved by you, and He yearns to bless you. His asking entrance is, then, a revelation of His tenderness, a revelation of His lowliness, and also a revelation of His patience. Repulsed, He continues to plead; neglected and unanswered, still that uninterrupted craving admission goes on; like Peter at the gate of Mary's house, "He continues knocking." Christ never gives up anybody, Christ never abandons as hopeless the task of drawing *any* to Himself. We are weary of trying to reclaim the "irreclaimable" people, and we talk very glibly—some of us—about the "hopeless classes" that are outside the reach of moral influences, and the patience that accepts as its own the limits which He set for ours, "until seventy times seven" [Matt. 18:22], He will not be put away: but He pleads with you, as He did when you were a little child; as He did in the hot heyday of your early youth, when passions were strong, and novelty was attractive, and bonds were unwelcome, and religion seemed too serious for the brightness that was around you; and as He has done with some of you in the maturity of life, when cares have burdened your hearts, and the deceitfulness of riches and the anxieties of life have made such a din that you could not hear His fingers on the door. He pleads with us all, and after every repulse: "I will *yet* plead with you, saith the Lord" [Jer. 2:9]. At your heart, dear friend, by all your mercies and by all your cares, by the sudden impressions that have been made upon you, by the quick monitions of conscience, by the emotions of the mind within, by the words of human teachers, by His Book and Gospel, by all life and all nature which are in His hands, and by hidden ways which only a Divine foot can tread, He draws nearer to us, pleading with us—all for this, that we will let Him come into our hearts.

So, dear brother, when He stands before you with the old summons and the old promise on His lips, "Lift up your heads! O ye gates! and the King of Glory shall come in" [Ps. 24:7], I encourage you to fling wide your hearts and say to Him: "If ye have judged me to be faithful . . . come into my house" [Acts 16:15]; and He will enter in, and bring with Him His gifts—peace, pardon, purity, and blessedness, and He and you will, even on earth, sit together at His table.

When after tossing and toil on the midnight sea the morning brings us to the shore, we shall find Him waiting with His welcome and a feast spread and prepared by His own hands, to which He will honor us by bidding us bring the results of the long night of labor; and so in highest fashion this great word will be fulfilled, and at His table in His Kingdom the King Himself shall sup with us and we with Him.

August 6

THE RESPONSIBLE POWER OF CHOICE

She obeyed not the voice; she received not correction; she trusted not in the Lord; she drew not near to her God—Zeph. 3:2

"If any man will open the door" [Rev. 3:20]—the door has no handle on the outside. It opens from within. Christ knocks; we open. I do not need to plunge into metaphysics: it is a plain fact that men can, and that men do, reject all this pleading love and meek patience of the beseeching Christ. It is the history of the lives of some of us; hundreds of times we have done it, and have settled ourselves into the attitude and habit of doing it. Do not be sophisticated out of the recognition of the fact that it is your fault if you are not a Christian by any quasi-philosophical theory about responsibility and the like. "If any man open the door," says Christ. The man has to open it; and if the man does not open it, it stops shut.

And how do you open it? If, when He comes to you and says, "Child! thou art sinful; I have died for thee! Trust thyself to Me," thou sayest, "Amen! Lord, I trust"; thou has opened the door. What we call faith—by which we simply mean the yielding of ourselves to Him, and the leaning upon His finished work and His mighty love and His Divine person for our salvation and our purity and our all—is the opening of the door. We open when in faith we yield the will, and say to Him, "Come in, Thou Blessed of the Father!"

Is it not plain that that simple condition is a condition not imposed by any arbitrary action on His part, but a condition indispensable from the very nature of the case? A man cannot get these Divine blessings if He does not want them. You take a hermetically sealed bottle, and put it into the sea; it may float about in mid-ocean for a century, surrounded by a shoreless ocean, and it will be as dry and empty inside at the end as it was at the beginning. So you and I float, live, move, and have our being in that great ocean of the Divine love in Christ; but you can cork up your hearts, and wax them over with an impenetrable cover, through which that grace does not come. And you *do* do it, some of you. If you are doing that, your heart must remain barred to His entrance. There is nothing for it but that if you do not let Christ come in, He must stop outside; and if He stops outside, there stop out with Him all the blessings that He brings. If you do not believe yourself to be a sinner, you will never feel that you need pardon; if you do not feel that you need pardon, you will never take Him for your Savior; if you do not take Him for your Savior, you cannot be saved. God cannot do it, and Christ cannot do it. They have done all they could for you; and He stands before the world and says: "Judge, I pray you, between Me and My vineyard. What could have been done more to it that I have not done in it?" [Is. 5:3, 4]. He has done all He could. Oh, my brother! Open the door, and the great rejoicing tide shall flow in and flood your heart. "Believe on the Lord Jesus Christ, and thou shall be saved" [Acts 16:31].

August 7

HOST AND GUEST IN ONE

He brought me to the banqueting house, and his banner over me was love—
Song 2:4

The entrance of Jesus Christ into the opened heart is no mere metaphor, and it is not weakened down to the presence in the spirit of the influence of His truth, or anything of that sort. There is a deep and substantial reality in the presence within a believing heart of Jesus Christ Himself. It is the central gift and promise of the Gospel, "that Christ may dwell in your hearts by faith" [Eph. 3:17]. The old question that tortured men in early days "Will God in very deed dwell with men upon the earth?" [2 Chr. 6:18] is answered now; and we have not only a Christ that was once incarnated in the son of a virgin to look back upon, but we have a Christ who dwells in our human spirits, if we open them by faith for His entrance. He Himself is the greatest of His gifts, and where He comes there spring, at the touch of His foot, all gracious, noble, and good things in the human heart. He never comes empty-handed, but when He enters in He endows the soul with untold riches.

We have also Christ's presence as a Guest. How wonderful that is! "I will come in and sup with him" [Rev. 3:20]. All sweet and familiar intercourse may be ours. It is even so that He, the glorious Lord, whose majesty, as revealed to John, prostrated even the disciple, who had leaned on His bosom at supper, as one dead, will bring all these splendors into this poor heart! He will come, and that as our Guest. What great and wonderful things are contained in that assurance! Can we present anything to Him that He can partake of? Yes! We may give Him our service, and He will take that; we may give Him our love, and He will regard it as an odor of a sweet smell, and as dainty and delightful food.

Christ comes to us not only as a Guest, but also as Host:—"I will sup with him *and he with Me*" [Rev. 3:20]. As when they invited Him to the rustic wedding at Cana of Galilee, He came as the Guest, but presently He turned the water of earthly felicity into the wine of heavenly gladness, and was Himself the Provider of the feast. As upon that night at Emmaus [Luke 24:13–31], when the two wearied men asked the wearied Companion of their journey to come in and stay with them at their humble meal, and He took His place at the table as an invited Guest, but in a moment assumed the *role* of the Master of the house, and broke the bread and blessed it, so making their gift to Him into His to them. So when He comes into your heart, and you offer Him your poor fare, your loyalty and your love and your faith and your service, He gives you the powers and the resources to love and serve Him; and still more, He gives you Himself, the Bread of God that came down from heaven, that your soul may feed upon that, and be satisfied and glad. As when some great prince offers to honor a poor subject with his presence, and let him provide some insignificant portion of the entertainment, while all the substantial and costly parts of it come in the retinue of the monarch, from the palace.

CHRIST GLORIFIED IN HIS SAINTS

He shall come to be glorified in his saints—2 Thess. 1:10.

The two Epistles to the Thessalonians, which are the Apostle's earliest letters, both give very great prominence to the thought of the second coming of our Lord to judgment. In the immediate context we have that coming described, with circumstances of majesty and of terror. He "shall be revealed . . . with his mighty angels" [v. 7]. "Flaming fire" [v. 8] shall herald His coming; vengeance shall be in His hands; punishment shall follow His sentence; everlasting destruction shall be the issue of evil confronted with "the face of the Lord"—for so the words in the previous verse, rendered "the presence of the Lord" might more accurately be translated.

And all these facts and images are, as it were, piled up in one half of the Apostle's sky, as in thunderous lurid masses; and on the other side there is the pure blue and the peaceful sunshine. For all this terror and destruction, and flashing fire, and punitive vengeance come to pass in the day when "He shall come to be glorified in His saints, and to be wondered at in all them that believe."

Christ is glorified in the men who are glorified in Christ. If you look on a couple of verses you will find that the Apostle returns to this thought, and expresses in the clearest fashion the reciprocal character of that "glorifying" of which he has been speaking. "The name of our Lord Jesus Christ," says he, "may be glorified in you, and ye in him" [v. 12].

So, then, glorifying has a double meaning. There is a double process involved. It means either "to make glorious" or "to manifest as being glorious." And men are glorified, in the former sense, in Christ, that Christ in them may, in the latter sense, be glorified. He makes them glorious by imparting to them of the lustrous light and flashing beauty of His own perfect character, in order that that light, received into their natures, and streaming out at last conspicuously manifest from their redeemed perfectness, may redound to the praise and the honor, before a whole universe, of Him who has thus provided their weakness with His own strength, and transmitted their corruptibility into His own immortality. We are glorified in Christ in some partial, and sinfully fragmentary manner here; we shall be so perfectly in that day. And when we are thus glorified in Him, then—wondrous thought!—even we shall be able to manifest Him as glorious before some gazing eyes, which without us would have seen Him as less fair. Dim, and therefore great and blessed, thoughts about what men may become are involved in such words. The highest end, the great purpose of the Gospel and of all God's dealings with us in Christ Jesus is to make us like our Lord. As we have borne the image of the earthly we shall also bear the image of the heavenly. "We, beholding the glory, are changed into the glory" [see 1 Cor. 3:18].

"YE ARE MY WITNESSES"

And for their sakes I sanctify myself, that they also may be sanctified in truth—
John 17:19

The glorifying of men in Christ, which is the goal and highest end of Christ's Cross and Passion and of all God's dealings, is accomplished only because Christ dwells in the men whom He glorifies. And as is the Son with the Father, participant of mutual and reciprocal glorification, so is the Christian with Christ, glorified in Him and therefore glorifying Him.

What may be involved therein of perfect moral purity, of enlarged faculties and powers, of a bodily frame capable of manifesting all the finest issues of a perfect spirit, it is not for us to say. These things are great, being hidden; and are hidden because they are great. But whatever may be the lofty heights of Christlikeness to which we shall attain, all shall come from the indwelling Lord who fills us with His own Spirit.

And then, according to this great teaching, this glorified humanity perfected and separated from all imperfection, and helped into all symmetrical unfolding of dormant possibilities, shall be the highest glory of Christ even in that day when He comes in His glory and sits upon the throne of His glory with His holy angels with Him. One would have thought that if the Apostle wanted to speak of the glorifying of Jesus Christ, he would have pointed to the Great White throne, His majestic Divinity, the solemnities of His judicial office; but he passes by all these, and says, "Nay! The highest glory of the Christ lies here, in the men whom He has made to share His own nature."

The artist is known by his work. You stand in front of some great picture, or you listen to some great symphony, or you read some great book, and you say, "This is the glory of Raphael, Beethoven, Shakespeare." Christ points to His saints, and He says, "Behold My handiwork! Ye are My witnesses. This is what I can do."

But the relation between Christ and His saints is far deeper and more intimate than simply the relation between the artist and his work; for all the flashing light of moral beauty, of intellectual perfectness which the Christian man can hope to receive in the future is but the light of the Christ that dwells in them, "and of whose fullness have all we received" [John 1:16]. Like some poor vapor, in itself white and colorless, which lies in the eastern sky there, and as the sun rises is flushed up into a miracle of rosy beauty, because it has caught the light among its flaming threads and vaporous substance, so we, in ourselves pale, ghostly, colorless as the mountains when the Alpine snow passes off them, being recipient of an indwelling Christ, shall blush and flame in beauty. "Then shall the righteous shine forth as the sun in the kingdom of their Father" [Matt. 13:43]. Or, rather, they are not suns shining by their own light, but moons reflecting the light of Christ, who is their Light.

And perchance some eyes, incapable of beholding the sun, may be able to look undazzled upon the sunshine in the cloud, and some eyes that could not discern the glory of Christ as it shines in His face, as the sun shines in its strength, may not be too weak to behold and delight in the light as it is reflected from the face of His servants. At all events, He shall come to be glorified in the saints whom He has made glorious [see 2 Thess. 1:10].

MIRACLES OF GRACE

It shall be to them a renown the day that I shall be glorified—Ezek. 39:13

The transformation of men is the great miracle and marvel of Christ's power. "He shall come . . . to be admired"—which word is employed in its old English significance, "to be wondered at"—"in all them that believe" [2 Thess 1:10]. So fair and lovely is He that He needs but to be recognized for what He is in order to be glorified. So great and stupendous are His operations in redeeming love that they need but to be beheld to be the object of wonder. "His name shall be called Wonderful" [Is. 9:6]. And wonderfully the energy of His redeeming and sanctifying grace shall then have wrought itself out to its legitimate end. There you get the crowning marvel of marvels, and the highest of miracles. He did wonderful works upon earth which we rightly call miraculous—things to be wondered at; but the highest of all His wonders is the wonder that takes such material as you and me, and by such a process and on such conditions simply because we trust Him, evolves such marvelous forms of beauty and perfectness from us. "He is to be wondered at in all them that believe."

Such results from such material! Chemists tell us that the black bit of coal in your grate and the diamond on your finger are varying forms of the one substance. What about a power that shall take all the black coals in the world and transmute them into flashing diamonds, prismatic with the reflected light that comes from His face and made gems on His strong right hand? The universe shall wonder at such results from such material, at the process by which they were accomplished, wondering at the depth of the process by which they were accomplished, wondering at the depth of His pity, revealed all the more pathetically now from the Great White Throne, which casts such a light on the Cross of Calvary; wondering at the long, weary path which He who is now declared to be the Judge humbled Himself to travel in the quest of these poor sinful souls whom He has thus redeemed and glorified. The miracle of miracles is redeeming love; and the high-water mark of Christ's wonders is touched in this fact, that out of men He makes saints, and out of saints He makes perfect likenesses of Himself.

There will be spectators of this glory. To whomsoever in the whole universe Christ at that Great Day shall be manifested, to them, whoever they be, will His glory, in His glorified saints, be a revelation beyond what they have known before. "Every eye shall see Him" [Rev. 1:7]. And whatsoever eyes look upon Him, then on His throne, they shall behold the attendant courtiers and the assessors of His judgment, and see in them the manifestation of His own lustrous light.

We need not speculate; it is better not to enter into details. But this at least, is clear, that the solemn winding up of the long, mysterious, sad, blood-and-tear-stained history of man upon the earth is to be an object of interest and a higher revelation of God to other creatures than those that dwell upon the earth; and we may well believe that for that moment, at all events, the center of the universe, which draws the thoughts of all thinking, and the eyes of all seeing, creatures to it shall be that valley of judgment wherein sits the Man Christ and judges men, and around Him the flashing reflectors of His glory in the person of His saints.

FAITH THE PATH TO GLORY

He shall come . . . to be admired in all them that believed—2 Thess. 1:10

That is to say, they who on earth were His, consecrated and devoted to Him, and in some humble measure partaking even here of His reflected beauty and imparted righteousness—these are they in whom He shall be glorified. They who "believed": poor, trembling, struggling, fainting souls, that here on earth, in the midst of many doubts and temptations, clasped His hand; and howsoever tremulously, yet truly put their trust in Him, these are they in whom He shall "be admired."

The simple act of faith knits us to the Lord. If we trust Him, He comes into our hearts here, and begins to purify us and to make us like Himself; and, if that be so, and we keep hold of Him, we shall finally share in His glory.

What a hope, what an encouragement, what a stimulus and exhortation to humble and timorous souls there is in that great word, "In *all* them that believed"! Howsoever imperfect, still they shall be kept by the power of God unto that final salvation. And when He comes in His glory, not one shall be wanting that put their trust in Him. It will take them all, each in his unique way reflecting it, to set forth adequately the glory. As many diamonds around a central light, which from each facet give off a particular ray and a definite color, so all that circle around Christ, and partaking of His glory, will each receive it, transmit it, and so manifest it in a different fashion. And it needs the innumerable company of the redeemed, each a unique perfectness, to set forth all the fullness of the Christ that dwells in us.

So, beginning with simple faith in Him, partially receiving the beauty of His transforming Spirit, seeking here on earth by assimilation to the Master in some humble measure to adorn the doctrine and to glorify the Christ, we may hope that each blackness shall be all changed into brightness, our limitations done away with, our weakness lifted into rejoicing strength; and that we shall be like Him, seeing Him as He is, and, glorified in Him, shall glorify Him before the universe.

You and I will be there. Choose whether He shall be revealed and the light of His face be to you like a sword whose flashing edge means destruction, or whether the light of His face shall fall upon your heart, because you love Him and trust Him, like the sunshine on the Alpine snow, lifting it to a more lustrous whiteness, and tinging it with an ethereal hue of more than earthly beauty, which no other power but an indwelling Christ can give. He shall come with "everlasting destruction from the presence" [2 Thess. 1:9]; and "He shall come to be glorified in His saints, and to be wondered at in all them that believed." Choose which of the two shall be your portion in that day.

CITIZENSHIP IN THE HEAVENS

Our conversation is in heaven; from whence also we look for the Savior, the Lord Jesus Christ—Phil. 3:20

The figure of citizenship is, of course, originally drawn from the registers of the tribes of Israel. In that use, though not without a glance at some higher meaning, it appears in the Old Testament, where we read of "those who are written among them living in Jerusalem"; or "are written in the writing of the house of Israel" [Ezek. 13:9]. And the thought that comes out of this great metaphor is that all of us, if we are Christian people belong to another polity, another order of things than that in which our outward lives are spent. And the plain, practical conclusion that comes from it is, cultivate the sense of belonging to another order. Just as it swelled the heart of a Macedonian Philippian with pride, when he thought that he did not belong to the semi-barbarous people around him, but that his name was written in the books that lay in the Capitol of Rome, so should we cultivate that sense of belonging to another order. It will make our work here none the worse, but it will fill our lives with the sense of nobler affinities, and point our efforts to grander work than any that belongs to the things that are seen and temporal [see 2 Cor. 4:18]. Just as the little groups of Englishmen in treaty-ports own no allegiance to the laws of the country in which they live, but are governed by English statutes, so we have to take our orders from headquarters to which we have to report. Men in our Colonies get their instructions from Downing Street. The officials there, appointed by the Home Government, think more of what they will say about them at Westminster than of what they say about them at Melbourne. So we are citizens of another country, and have to obey the laws of our own kingdom, and not those of the soil on which we dwell. Never mind about the opinions of men, the battlements of the people in the land you live in. To us, the main thing is that we be acceptable, well-pleasing unto Him. Are you solitary? Cultivate the sense of, in your solitude, being a member of a great community that stretches through all the ages, and binds into one the inhabitants of eternity and of time.

Remember that this citizenship in the heavens is the highest honor that can be conferred upon a man. The patricians of Venice used to have their names inscribed upon what was called the "golden book" that was kept in the Doge's palace. If our names are written in the book of gold in the heavens, then we have higher dignities than any that belong to the fleeting chronicles of this passing, vain world. So we can accept with equanimity evil report or good report, and can acquiesce in a wholesome obscurity, and be careless though our names appear on no human records and fill no trumpet of fame blown by earthly cheeks. Intellectual power, wealth, gratified ambition, and all the other things that men set before them are small indeed compared with the honor, with the blessedness, with the repose and satisfaction that attend the conscious possession of citizenship in the heavens. Let us lay to heart the great words of the Master, which put a cooling hand on all the feverish ambitions of earth: "In this rejoice, not that the spirits are subject unto you, but rather rejoice that your names are written in Heaven" [Luke 10:20].

NAMES IN THE BOOK OF LIFE

And with other of my fellow laborers, whose names are in the book of life—
Phil. 4:3

Paul was as gentle as he was strong. Winsome courtesy and delicate considerateness lay in his character, in beautiful union with fiery impetuosity and undaunted tenacity of conviction. We have here a remarkable instance of his quick apprehension of the possible effects of his words, and of his nervous anxiety not to wound even unreasonable susceptibilities.

He had had occasion to mention three of his fellow workers, and he wishes to associate with them others whom he does not purpose to name. Lest any of these should be offended by the omission, he soothes them with this graceful, half-apologetic reminder that their names are inscribed on a better page than his. It is as if he had said, "Do not mind though I do not mention you individually. You can well afford to be anonymous in my letter since your names are inscribed in the Book of Life."

There is a consolation for obscure good people, who need not expect to live except in two or three loving hearts; and whose names will only be preserved on moldering tombstones, that will convey no idea to the reader. We may well dispense with other commemoration if we have this.

It is hard to realize the essentially individualizing and isolating character of our relation to Jesus Christ. But we shall never come to the heart of the blessedness and the power of His Gospel unless we translate all "us"–es and "everyones" and "worlds" in Scripture into "I" and "Me," and can say not only He gives Himself to be "the propitiation for the sins of the whole world" [1 John 2:2], but "He loved *me* and gave Himself for *me*" [see Gal. 2:20]. The same individualizing love which is manifested in that mighty universal Atonement, if we rightly understand it, is manifested in all His dealings with us. One by one we come under His notice; the Shepherd tells His sheep singly as they pass out through the gate or into the fold. He knows them all by name. "I have called thee by thy name; thou art mine" [Is. 43:1].

Lift up your eyes and behold who made all these—the countless host of the nightly stars. The nebulae to our eyes are blazing suns and planets to His. "He telleth the number of the stars; He calleth them all *by name* by the greatness of His power, for that He is strong in might; not one faileth" [Is. 40:26]. So we may nestle in the protection of His hand, sure of a separate place in His knowledge and His heart.

DIVINE INDIVIDUALIZING KNOWLEDGE AND CARE

Fear not . . . I have redeemed thee; I have called thee by thy name; thou art mine—Is. 43:1

In the Old Testament the Book of Life is called "Thy Book," in the New it is called "the Lamb's Book." That is of a piece with the whole relation of the New to the Old, and of Jesus Christ, the Incarnate Word and Manifester of God, to the Jehovah revealed in former ages. For, unconditionally, and without thought of irreverence or idolatry, the New Testament lifts over bodily, and confers upon Jesus Christ the attributes which the Old jealously preserved as belonging only to Jehovah. And thus Christ, the Manifester of God, and the Mediator to us of all Divine powers and blessings, takes the book and makes the entries in it. Each man of us, as in your ledgers, has a page to himself. His account is opened, and is not confused with other entries. There is individualizing love and care, and, as the basis of both, individualizing knowledge. My name, the expression of my individual being, stands there. Christ does not deal with me as one of a crowd, nor fling out blessings broadcast, that I may grasp them in the midst of a multitude if I choose to put out a hand, but He deals with each of us singly, as if there were not any beings in the world but He and I, our two selves, all alone.

Deliverance and security are the results of that individualizing care. In one of the Old Testament instances of the use of this metaphor, we read that, in the great day of calamity and sorrow, "thy people shall be delivered, every one that shall be found written in thy book" [Dan. 12:1]. So we need not dread anything if our names are there. The sleepless King will read the Book, and will never forget, nor forget to help and succor, His poor servants.

But there are two other variations of this thought in the Old Testament even more tenderly suggestive of that individualizing care and strong sufficient love than the emblem of "the Book." We read that when, in the exercise of his official functions, the high priest passed into the tabernacle, he wore upon his *breast*, near the seat of personality and the home of love, the name of the tribes graven, and that the same names were written on his shoulders, as if guiding the exercise of his power. So we may think of ourselves as lying near the beatings of His heart, and as individually the objects of the work of His almighty arm. Nor is this all. For there is yet another and still tenderer application of the figure, when we read of the Divine voice as saying to Israel, "I have graven thee on the palms of my hands" [Is. 49:16]. The name of each who loves and trusts and serves is written there—printed deep in the flesh of the Sovereign Christ. We bear in our bodies the marks, the *stigmata*, that tell whose slaves we are—"the marks of the Lord Jesus" [Gal. 6:7]. And He bears in His body the marks that tell who His servants are.

THE BOOK OF LIFE

A book of remembrance was written before him for them that feared the Lord,
and that thought upon his name—Mal. 3:16.

The "Book of Life," it is called in the New Testament. Its designation in the Old might as well be translated "the book of living" as "the book of life." It is a register of the men who are truly alive.

Now, that is but an imaginative way of putting the commonplace of the New Testament, that anything which is worth calling life comes to us, not by creation or physical generation, but by being born again through faith in Jesus Christ, and by receiving into our else dead spirits the life which He bestows upon all them that trust Him. In the New Testament "life" is far more than "being"; far more than physical existence; removed by a whole world from these lower conceptions, and finding its complete explanation only in the fact that the soul which is knit to God by conscious surrender, love, aspiration, and obedience, is the only soul that really lives. All else is death—death! He "that liveth in pleasure is dead while he liveth" [1 Tim. 5:6]. The ghastly imagination of one of our poets, of the dead man standing on the deck pulling at the ropes by the side of the living, is true in a very deep sense. In spite of all the feverish activities, the manifold vitalities, of practical and intellectual life in the world, the deepest, truest life of every man who is parted from God by alienation of will, by indifference, and neglect of love, lies sheeted and sepulchered in the depths of his own heart. Brother, there is no life worth calling life, none to which that august name can without degradation be applied, except the complete life of body, soul, and spirit, in lowly obedience to God in Christ. The deepest meaning of the work of the Savior is that He comes into a dead world, and breathes into the bones—very many and very dry—the breath of His own life. Christ has died for us; Christ will live in us if we will; and, unless He does, we are twice dead.

Do not put away that thought as if it were a mere pulpit metaphor. It is a metaphor, but yet in the metaphor there lies this deepest truth, which concerns us all, that only he is truly himself, and lives the highest, best, and noblest life that is possible for him, who is united to Jesus Christ, and drawing from Christ his own life. "He that hath the Son hath life: he that hath not the Son hath not life" [1 John 5:12]. Either my name and yours are written in the Book of Life, or they are written in the register of a cemetery. We have to make our choice which.

August 16

"IS MY NAME WRITTEN THERE?"

Another book was opened, which is the book of life—Rev. 20:12

We read, in the highly imaginative picture of the final judgment, that when the thrones are set, two books are opened, one the Book of Life, the other the book in which are written the deeds of men, and that by these two books men are judged. There is a judgment by conduct. There is also a judgment by the Book of Life. That is to say, the question at last comes to be, "Is this man's name written in that book?" Is he a citizen of the kingdom, and therefore capable of entering into it? Has he the life from Christ in his heart? Or, in other words, the question is, first, Has the man who stands at the bar faith in Jesus Christ? And, second, Has he proved that his faith is genuine and real by the course of his earthly conduct? These are the books from which the judgment is made. We read further in that blessed vision—the vision of the City of God "coming down out of heaven as a bride adorned for her husband" [Rev. 21:2]—that only they enter in there who are "written in the Lamb's book of life" [Rev. 21:27]. Only citizens are capable of entrance into the city; aliens are necessarily shut out. The Lord, when He writeth up His people, shall count that this man was born there, though he never trod its streets while on earth, and therefore can enter into his native home. What need we care what other people may think about us, or whether the "hollow wraith of dying fame" that comes like a nimbus around some men may fade wholly or not, so long as we may be sure of acknowledgment and praise from Him whom acknowledgment and praise are precious indeed.

Remember that names can be blotted out of the book. The metaphor has often been pressed into the service of a doctrine of unconditional and irreversible predestination. But, rightly looked at, it points in the opposite direction. Remember Moses's agonized cry, "Blot me . . . out of thy book" [Ex. 33:32], and the Divine answer, "him that sinneth against me, his name will I blot out of my book" And remember that it is only to "him that overcometh" that the promise is made, "I will not blot him out" [Rev. 3:5, 12] We are made partakers of Christ if we "hold fast the beginning of our confidence firm unto the end."

Remember that it depends upon ourselves whether our names are there or not. John Bunyan describes the armed man who came up to the table where the man with the book and the inkhorn was seated, and said, "Set down my name." And you and I may do that. If we cast ourselves on Jesus Christ, and yield our wills to be guided by Him, and give our lives for His service, then He will write our names in His book. If we trust Him we shall be citizens of the City of God, shall be filled with the life of Christ, shall be objects of an individualizing love and care, shall be accepted in that day, and shall enter in through the gates into the city. "They that forsake me . . . shall be written on the earth" [Jer. 17:13], and there wiped out as are the children's scribbles on the sand when the ocean comes up. They that trust in Jesus Christ shall have their names written in the Book of Life, graven on the High Priest's breastplate, and inscribed on His mighty hand and His faithful heart.

PERSECUTION FOR CHRIST'S SAKE

If they have persecuted me, they will also persecute you; if they have kept my saying, they will keep yours also—John 15:20

We may fairly infer that in the reception a disciple of Christ may expect from the world, we have one of the points in which, very specially, the likeness of a true disciple to the Master will be brought out. If they have called Him Beelzebub, they will not grace us with the fine names of approbation and flattery. "If they have not received My sayings," they will turn a deaf ear to yours. "If ye were of the world, the world would love his own" [John 15:19]. Now, let me say a plain word about this matter. That law is in a fashion abrogated now. Nineteen centuries have not passed in vain. The "world"— meaning thereby the aggregate of godless men, "society," to use a modern phrase—has been largely leavened by Christian principles and sentiment. An atmosphere has been created, else all these centuries would have passed in vain. But while that is quite true, and I suppose in lands like ours we do not need to be afraid of the rougher forms of the world's enmity, it does not seem to me that in substance this law has ceased to operate, nor will it, until either the Church has become wholly worldly—which it never will do—or until the world has become wholly Christ's. There are plenty of evidences around us that it still remains true that an out-and-out consistency of Christian conduct shall be unwelcome to the mass of society. You have only to look at the bitter antagonism to aggressive Christianity which is manifested in much of our popular literature to see that. They used to burn us; they only sneer at us nowadays; but the sentiment is pretty much the same. In your Christian activity, touch the social sins of this generation and you will see the claws come out fast enough, and scratch deep enough, for all the velvet skin and the purring that sometimes is heard. Let a man live the life, and shape himself after Christ's pattern, and he will not miss having to bear his share of the treatment given to his Master. If we take Him for our pattern, and try to be like Him, we have to make up our minds to "go forth unto Him without the camp, bearing His reproach" [Heb. 13:13], and to live a godly life amid ungodly people; and that will never be done without some experience of the deep-seated antagonism between the true disciple and the world.

THE DISCIPLE AS HIS LORD

The Lord will perfect that which concerneth me—Psalm 138:8

It is enough for the disciple that he be as his master, and the servant as his lord—
Matt. 10:25

The disciple's schooling is not ended until he has learned all that the master can teach; and the duty of the servant is not performed until he has done all that the Lord commands. There is no adequate end to the experiences of the imperfect Christian life on earth, except that of being wholly assimilated to the character of Jesus Christ. So much accomplished, and so much unaccomplished—the contradiction between the two halves cannot continue forever. The likeness of Jesus Christ, which is imperfectly realized in a man here, has in it "the promise and the potency" of a perfect conformity hereafter. Michaelangelo left several of his works with a part finished and polished to the last point of statuesque perfection, and the rest rough marble, with the marks of a tool upon it here and there. The face or the form was half-extricated from, and half still embedded in, the rude and formless block. You can see in Baalbec a pillar partially rounded and hewn out of the rock, and the rest of it still undelivered from its environment. So the Christian life here, in its incompleteness, prophesies of that which is to come. For if Christ is the Worker, then His work must correspond to His own perfection. If He is our Master, then He will not cease His teaching until we have learned all His "treasures of wisdom and knowledge" [Col. 2:3]. If He is our Lord, then we shall be perfectly like Himself. Never shall it be said of this man that "he be perfectly like Himself." Never shall it be said of this man that "he began to build, and was not able to finish" [Luke 14:30]. "The Lord will perfect that which concerneth me."

"It is enough for the disciple that he be as his master." Is it *not* enough for the heart, enough to know for the mind, amid all the dimness and the darkness of that future? We know not what lies beyond the pass: the fair lands on the other side the mountains are all unseen; but, as Richard Baxter says in his hymn—"It is enough that Christ knows all, And I shall be *like* Him." If that likeness is to be completed hereafter, it must be begun here. Whatever speculations men may indulge in about the effect of passing beyond the vale, there is nothing either in what we know of the phenomenon of death, nor in what Scripture plainly teaches, to warrant the belief that the accident of dying shall revolutionize a man's attitude to Jesus Christ. And it is a desperate risk to run, that we should trust to begin beyond the grave a life dead against the life that was lived here. We do know that, if imperfectly, we try to follow Christ on earth, there we shall follow the Lamb wherever He goes. We do know that if here we enter ourselves in Christ's school, there we shall get our remove to a higher form. We do know that if here the likeness begins, there it shall be perfected. As some poor bit of glass, smitten by a sunbeam, blazes with the light which it reflects, so when we behold His countenance "as the sun shineth in his strength" [Rev. 1:16], we, too, "shine forth as the sun in the Heavenly Father's Kingdom" [Matt. 13:43].

So the question comes to be, "Am I Christ's scholar? Have I begun to be like Him?" Then I have the beginnings of peace and of heart-satisfaction. To be like Christ is enough for a man; nothing *less* is.

"IT IS THE LORD"

That disciple whom Jesus loved saith unto Peter, It is the Lord—John 21:7

Now and always, as in that morning twilight on the Galilean lake, Christ comes to men. Everywhere He is present, everywhere revealing Himself. Now, as then, our eyes are holden by our own fault, so that we recognize not the merciful Presence which is all around us. Now, as then, it is they who are nearest to Christ by love who see Him first. Now, as then, they who are nearest to Him by love are so because He loves them, and because they know and believe the love which He has to them. Only they who love see Christ. John, the Apostle of Love, knew Him first. In religious matters love is the foundation of knowledge. There is no way of knowing a person except love. A man cannot argue his way into knowing Christ. No skill in drawing inferences will avail him there. The treasures of wisdom—earthly wisdom—are all powerless in that region. Man's understanding and natural capacity—let it keep itself within its own limits and region, and it is strong and good, but in the region of acquaintance with God and Christ, the wisdom of this world is foolishness, and man's understanding is not the organ by which he can know Christ. Oh no! There is a better way than that: "He that loveth not knoweth not God, for God is love" [1 John 4:8]. As it is, in more feeble measure, with regard to our personal acquaintance with one another, where it is not so much the power of the understanding, or the quickness of the perception, or the talent and genius of a man, that make the foundation of his knowledge of his friend, as the force of his sympathy and the depth of his affection; so—with the necessary modification arising from the transference from earthly acquaintance to the great Friend and Lover of our souls in heaven—so is it with regard to our knowledge of Christ. Love will trace Him everywhere. Love's quick eye pierces through disguises impenetrable to a colder scrutiny. Love has in it a longing for His presence which makes us eager and quick to mark the lightest sign that He for whom it longs is near, as the footstep of some dear one is heard by the sharp ear of affection long before any sound breaks the silence to those around. Love to Him strips from our eyes the film that self and sin, sense and custom, have drawn over them. It is these which hide Him from us. It is because men are so indifferent to, so forgetful of, their best Friend that they fail to behold Him. "It is the Lord" is written large and plain on all things, but, like the great letters on a map, they are so obvious, and fill so wide a space, that they are not seen. They who love Him know Him, and they who know Him love Him. The true eye-salve for our blinded eyes is applied when we have turned with our hearts to Christ. The simple might of faithful love opens them to behold a more glorious vision than the mountain full of chariots of fire, which once flamed before the prophet's servant of old—even the august and ever-present form of the Lord of life, the Lord of history, the Lord of providence. When they who love Jesus turn to see the voice that speaks with them, they ever behold the Son of man in His glory; and where others see but the dim beach and a mysterious stranger, it is to their lips that the glad cry first comes, "It is the Lord!"

A NEW NAME AND A NEW NATURE

If any man be in Christ . . . behold, all things are become new—2 Cor. 5:17

Jesus Christ gave the Apostle, whom He called to Himself in the early days, a new name, in order to prophesy the change which, by the discipline of sorrow and the communication of the grace of God, should pass over Simon Barjona, making him into a Peter, the Man of Rock. With characteristic independence, Saul chooses for himself a new name, which shall express the change that he feels has passed over his inmost being. True, he does not assume it at his conversion, but that is no reason why we should not believe that he assumes it because he is beginning to understand what it is that has happened to him at his conversion.

The central heart of Christianity is the possession of a new life, communicated to us through faith in that Son of God who is the Lord of the Spirit. Wheresoever there is a true faith, there is a new nature.

Opinions may play upon the surface of a man's soul, like the moonbeams on the silver sea, without raising its temperature one degree or sending a single beam into its dark caverns. And that is the sort of Christianity that satisfies a great many of you—a Christianity of opinion, a Christianity of surface creed, a Christianity which at the best slightly modifies some of your outward actions, but leaves the whole inner man unchanged.

Paul's Christianity meant a radical change in his whole nature. He went out of Jerusalem a persecutor; he came into Damascus a Christian. He rode out of Jerusalem hating, loathing, despising Jesus Christ; he groped his way into Damascus broken, bruised, clinging contrite to His feet, and clasping His Cross as his only hope. He went out proud, self-reliant, pluming himself upon his many prerogatives, his blue blood, his pure descent, his Rabbinical knowledge, his pharasaical training, his externally religious earnestness, his pure morality; he rode into Damascus blind in the eyes, but seeing in the soul, and discerning that all these things were, as he says in his strong vehement way, "but dung" [Phil. 3:8] in comparison with his winning Christ. And his theory of conversion, which he preaches in all his epistles, is but the generalization of his own personal experience, which suddenly, and in a moment, smote his old self to shivers, and raised up a new life, with new tastes, views, tendencies, aspirations, with new allegiance to a new King. Such changes, so sudden, so revolutionary, cannot be expected often to take place among people who, like us, have been listening to Christian teaching all our lives. But unless there be this infusion of a new life into men's spirits which shall make them love and long and aspire after new things that once they did not care for, I know not why we should speak of them as being Christians at all. The transition is described by Paul as "passing from death unto life" [1 John 3:14]. That cannot be a surface thing. A change which needs a new name must be a profound change. Has our Christianity revolutionized our nature in any such fashion? It is easy to be a Christian after the superficial fashion which passes muster with so many of us. A verbal acknowledgment of belief in truths which we never think about, a purely external performance of acts of worship, a subscription or two winged by no sympathy, and a fairly respectable life between the cloak of which all evil may burrow undetected—make the Christianity of thousands. Paul's Christianity transformed him; does yours transform you? If it does not, are you quite sure that it is Christianity at all?

SAUL AND PAUL

Saul, who also is called Paul, filled with the Holy Ghost—Acts 13:9

Paul is a Roman name. He strips himself of his Jewish connections and relationships. His fellow countrymen who lived among the Gentiles were in the habit of doing the same thing; but they carried *both* their names—their Jewish for use among their own people, their Gentile one for use among Gentiles. Paul seems to have altogether abandoned his old name of Saul. It was almost equivalent to seceding from Judaism. It is like the acts of the renegades one sometimes hears of, who are found by some travelers dressed in turban and flowing robes, and bearing some Turkish name; or like some English sailor, lost to home and kindred, who deserts his ship in some island of the Pacific, and drops his English name for some barbarous title, in token that he has given up his faith and his nationality.

The spirit which led the Apostle to change the name of Saul, with its memories of the royal dignity which, in the person of its great wearer, had honored his tribe, for a Roman name is the same which he formally announces as a deliberately adopted law of his life: "To them that are without law I became as without law . . . that I might gain them that are without law. . . . I am made all things to all men, that I might by all means save some" [1 Cor. 9:20–22].

It is the very inmost principle of the gospel. The principle that influenced the servant in this comparatively little matter is the principle that influenced the Master in the mightiest of all events. "Who, being in the form of God, thought it not robbery to be equal with God: But made himself of no reputation, and took upon him the form of a servant, and was made in the likeness of men: And being found in fashion as a man, he humbled himself, and became obedient unto death" [Phil. 2:6–8]. "Forasmuch as the children were partakers of flesh and blood, he himself likewise took part of the same" [Heb. 2:14]; and the mystery of incarnation was transacted, because when the Divine would help men, the only way by which the infinite love could reach this end was that the Divine should become man; identifying Himself with those whom He would help, and stooping to the level of the humanity that He would lift.

Sympathy is the parent of all wise counsel, because it is the parent of all true understanding of our brethren's wants; sympathy is the only thing to which people will listen; sympathy is the only disposition correspondent to the message that we Christians are entrusted with. For a Christian man to carry the gospel of infinite condescension to his fellows in a spirit other than that of the Master, and the gospel which He speaks, is an anomaly and a contradiction.

You remember the old story of some heroic missionary that wanted to carry the gospel of Jesus Christ among captives, and as there was no other way of reaching them, he let himself be sold for a slave, and put out his hands to have the manacles fastened upon them. It is the law for all Christian service: become like them if you will help them. "To the weak as weak, all things to all men, that we might by all means save some" [1 Cor. 9:22]. And, my brother, there was no obligation on Paul's part to do Christian work which does not lie on you.

MEMORIALS OF VICTORY

Ye are our glory and joy—1 Thess. 2:20

Paul's name was that of his first convert. He takes it, as I suppose, because it seemed to him such a blessed thing that of the very moment when he began to sow, God helped him to reap. He had gone out to his work, no doubt, with much trembling, with weakness and fear. And here, at once, the fields were white already to the harvest.

Great conquerors have been named from their victories: Africanus, Germanicus, Nelson of the Nile, Napier of Magdala, and the like. Paul names himself from the first victory that God gave him to win; and so, as it were, carries ever at his breast a memorial of the wonder that through him it had been given to preach, and that not without success, among the Gentiles "the unsearchable riches of Christ" [Eph. 3:8].

That is to say, this man Paul thought of it as his highest honor, and the thing best worthy to be remembered about his life, that God had helped him to help his brethren to know the common Master. Is that your idea of the best thing about a life? What would you like to have for an epitaph on your grave, professing Christian? "He was rich; he made a big business." "He was famous, he wrote books." "He was happy and fortunate." Or, "He turned many to righteousness"? "This man flung away his literary tastes, his home joys, and his personal ambition, and chose as that for which he would live, and by which he would wish to be remembered, that he should bring dark hearts to the light in which he and they together walked"?

His name, in its commemoration of his first success, would act as a stimulus to service and to hope. No doubt the Apostle, like the rest of us, had his times of indolence and languor, and his times of despondency when he seemed to have labored in vain and spent his strength for naught. He had but to name himself to find the antidote to both the one and the other, and in the remembrance of the past to find a stimulus for service for the future, and a stimulus for hope for the time to come. His first convert was to him the first drop that predicts the shower, the first primrose that prophesies the wealth of yellow blossoms and downy green leaves that will fill the woods in a day or two. The first convert "bears in his hand a glass which showed many more." Look at the workmen in the streets trying to get up a piece of the roadway. How difficult it is to lever out the first paving-stone from the compacted mass! But when once it has been withdrawn, the rest is comparatively easy. We can understand Paul's triumph and joy over this first stone which he had worked out of the strongly cemented wall and barrier of heathenism; and his conviction that having thus made a breach, if it were but big enough to get the end of his lever in, the fall of the whole was only a question of time. I suppose that if the old alchemists had only turned one grain of base metal into gold they might have turned tons, if only they had had the retorts and the appliances with which to do it. And so, what has brought one man's soul into harmony with God, and given one man the true life, can do the same for all men. In the first fruits we may see the fields whitening to the harvest. Let us rejoice, then, in any little work that God helps us to do, and be sure that if so great be the joy of the first fruits, great beyond speech will be the joy of the ingathering.

THE SPIRIT OF PAUL'S LIFE'S WORK

Neither count I my life dear unto myself, so that I might finish my course . . . and the ministry which I have received of the Lord Jesus—Acts 20:24

Paul, contemplating for his life's work preaching among the Gentiles, determines at the beginning, "I lay down all of which I used to be proud. If my Jewish descent and privileges stand in my way, I cast them aside. I wrap them together in one bundle, and toss them behind me, that I may be the better able to help some to whom they would have hindered my access." A man with a heart will throw off his silken robes that his arm may be bared to rescue and his feet free to run to succor. The only way to help people is to go down to their level. If you want to bless them you must identify yourself with them. It is no use standing on an eminence above them, and patronizingly talking down to them. You cannot scold, or hector, or lecture men into the possession and acceptance of religious truth if you take a position of superiority. As our Master has taught us, if we want to make blind beggars see, we must take the blind beggars by the hand.

"Paul" means "little"; "Saul" means "desired." he abandons the name that prophesied of favor and honor, to adopt a name that bears upon its very front a profession of humility. His very name is the condensation into a word of his abiding conviction. "I am less than the least of all saints" [Eph. 3:8]. Perhaps even there may be an allusion to his low stature, which may be pointed at in the sarcasm of his enemies that his letters were strong, though his bodily presence was "weak." If he was, as Monsieur Renan calls him, "an ugly little Jew," the name has a double appropriateness. But, at all events, it is an expression of the spirit in which he sought to do his work. The more lofty the consciousness of his vocation, the more lowly will a true man's estimate of himself be. The higher my thought of what God has given me grace to do, the more shall I feel weighed down by the consciousness of my unfitness to do it.

So, for all hope, for all success in our work, for all growth in Christian grace and character, this disposition of lowly self-abasement and recognized unworthiness and infirmity is absolutely indispensable. The mountaintops that lift themselves to the stars are barren, and few springs find their rise there. It is in the lowly valleys that the flowers grow and the rivers run. And it is they who are humble and lowly in heart to whom God gives strength to serve Him, and the joy of accepted service. Learn your true life's task by identifying yourself with the humbler brethren whom you would help. Learn the spirit of lowly self-abasement. And, above all, learn this, that unless you have the life of God in your heart, you have no life at all. If you have that faith by which we receive into our spirits Christ's own spirit to be our life, then you are a new creature, with a new name, perhaps dimly visible, and faintly audible, amid the imperfections of earth, but sure to shine in the Lamb's Book of Life; and to be read, "with tumults of acclaim," before the angels of Heaven. "I will give him a white stone, and in the stone . . . a new name written, which no man knoweth saving he that receiveth it" [Rev. 2:17].

PROGRESSIVE BRIGHTNESS

The path of the just is as the shining light that shineth more unto the
perfect day—Prov. 4:18

This is what a Christian life ought to be. The light of the Christian life, like its type in the heavens, may be analyzed into three beams: purity, knowledge, blessedness; and these three, blended together, make the pure whiteness of a Christian soul. Every Christian life should be a life of increasing luster, uninterrupted, and the natural result of increasing communion with, and conformity to, the very fountain itself of heavenly radiance. Progress is laid down emphatically in Scripture as the mark of a religious life. In many ways Scripture lays it down as a rule that life in the highest region, like life in the lowest, is marked by continual growth. It is so in regard of all other things. Continuity in any kind of practice gives increasing power in the art. The artisan, the blacksmith with his hammer, the skilled artificer at his trade, the student at his subject, the good man in his course of life, and the bad man in his, do equally show that use becomes second nature. And so let me say what incalculable importance there is in our getting habit, with all its mystical power to mold life, on to the side of righteousness, and of becoming accustomed to do good, and so being unfamiliar with evil.

This intention of continuous growth is marked by the gifts that are bestowed upon us in Jesus Christ. He gives us—and it is by no means the least of the gifts that He bestows—an absolutely unattainable aim as the object of our efforts. For He bids us not only be perfect, as our Father in Heaven is perfect, but He bids us be entirely conformed to His own Self. The misery of men is that they pursue aims so narrow and so shabby that they can be attained, and are therefore left behind, to sink hull down on the backward horizon. But to have before us an aim which is absolutely unreachable, instead of being, as ignorant people say, an occasion of despair and of idleness, is, on the contrary, the very salt of life. It keeps us young, it makes hope immortal, it emancipates from lower pursuits, it diminishes the weight of sorrows, it administers an anesthetic to every pain. If you want to keep life fresh, seek for that which you can never fully find.

Christ gives us infinite powers to reach that unattainable aim, for He gives us access to all His own fullness, and there is more in His storehouses than we can ever take, not to say more than we can ever hope to exhaust. And therefore, because of the aim that is set before us, and because of the powers that are bestowed upon us to reach it, there is stamped upon every Christian life unmistakably, as God's purpose and ideal concerning it, that it should forever and ever be growing nearer and nearer, as some ascending spiral that circles ever closer and closer, and yet never absolutely unites with the great central Perfection which is Himself. So for every one of us, if we are Christian people at all, "this is the will of God, even your sanctification" [1 Thess. 4:3].

INTERRUPTED LIVES, ARRESTED DEVELOPMENT

For when for the time ye ought to be teachers, ye have need that one teach you again which be the first principles of the oracles of God—Heb. 5:12

Consider the sad contrast of too many Christian lives. There are many so-called and, in a fashion, really Christian people, to whom Christ and His work are mainly, if not exclusively, the means of escaping the consequences of sin—a kind of "fire-escape." And to very many it comes as a new thought, in so far as their practical lives are concerned, that these ought to be lives of steadily increasing deliverance from the love and power of sin, and steadily increasing appropriation and manifestation of Christ's granted righteousness. There are, I think, many of us from whom the very notion of progress has faded away. I am sure there are some of us who were a great deal further on, on the path of the Christian life, years ago, when we first felt that Christ was anything to us, than we are today.

There is an old saying of one of the prophets that a child would die a hundred years old, which in a very sad sense is true about very many folk within the pale of the Christian church who are seventy-year-old babes still, and will die so. Suns "growing brighter and brighter until the noonday!" There are many of us who are a great deal more like those strange variable stars that sometimes burst out in the heavens into a great blaze, that bring them up to the brightness of stars of the first magnitude, for a day or two, and then they dwindle until they become little specks of light that the telescope can hardly see.

And there are hosts of us who are instances, if not of arrested, at any rate of unsymmetrical, development. The head, perhaps, is cultivated; the intellectual apprehension of Christianity increases, while the emotional and the moral and the practical part of it are all neglected. Or, the converse may be the case; and we may be full of gush and of good emotion, and of fervor when we come to worship or to pray, and our lives may not be a hair the better for it all. Or, there may be a disproportion because of an exclusive attention to conduct and the practical side of Christianity, while the rational side of it, which should be the basis of all, and the emotional side of it, which should be the driving power of all, are comparatively neglected.

So, what with interruptions, what with growing by fits and starts, and long, dreary winters like the Arctic winters, coming in between the two or three days of rapid, and therefore brief and unwholesome, development, we must all, I think, take to heart the condemnation, when we compare the reality of our lives with the Divine intention concerning them. Let us ask ourselves, "Have I more command over myself than I had twenty years ago? Do I live nearer Jesus Christ today than I did yesterday? Have I more of His Spirit in me? Am I growing? Would the people that know me best say that I am growing in the grace and knowledge of my Lord and Savior?" Astronomers tell us that there are dark suns, that have burned themselves out, and are wandering unseen through the skies. I wonder if there are any extinguished suns among my readers.

FROM DAWN TO NOON

They that be wise shall shine as the brightness of the firmament, and they that turn many to righteousness as the stars forever and ever—Dan. 12:3

The most radiant thing on earth is the character of a good man. The world calls men of genius and intellectual force its lights. The Divine estimate, which is the true one, confers the name on righteousness. This Divine purpose concerning us may be realized by us, the *Alpha* and the *Omega* of which, the one means which includes all other, is laid down by Jesus Christ Himself when He said, "Abide in me, and I in you" [John 15:4], so shall ye bring forth much fruit. Our path will brighten, not because of any radiance in ourselves, but in proportion as we draw nearer and nearer to the fountain of heavenly radiance. The planets that move around the sun, further away than we are on the earth, get less of its light and heat; and those that circle around it within the limits of our orbit, get proportionately more. The nearer we are to Him, the more shall we shine. The sun shines by its own light, drawn indeed from the shrinkage of its mass, so that it gives away its very life in warming and illuminating its subject-worlds. But we shine only by reflected light, and therefore, the nearer we keep to Him the more shall we be radiant.

That keeping in touch with Jesus Christ is mainly to be secured by the direction of thought and love and trust to Him. If we follow close upon Him, we shall not walk in darkness. It is to be secured and maintained very largely by what I am afraid is much neglected by Christian people of all sorts nowadays, and that is the devotional use of their Bibles. That is the food by which we grow. It is to be secured and maintained still more largely by that which I, again, am afraid is but very imperfectly attained to by Christian people now, and that is, the habit of prayer. It is to be secured and maintained, again, by the honest conforming of our lives, day by day, to the present amount of our knowledge of Him and of His will. Whosoever will make all his life the manifestation of his belief, and turn all his creed into principles of action, will grow both in the comprehensiveness and in the depths of his Christian character. "Ye are light in the Lord" [Eph. 5:8]. Keep in Him, and you will become brighter and brighter. So shall we "go from strength to strength, till we appear before God in Zion" [Ps. 84:7].

THE EARTHLY SETTING, THE BRIGHTER RISING

Then shall the righteous shine forth as the sun in the kingdom of their Father—
Matt. 13:43

Beauty, intellect, power, goodness, all go down into the dark. The sun sets, and there is left a sad and fading glow in the darkening pensive sky, which may recall the vanished light for a little while to a few faithful hearts, but steadily passes into the ashen gray of forgetfulness. The momentary setting is but apparent; and, ere it is well accomplished, a new sun swims into the "ampler ether, the diviner air" of that future life, "and, with new spangled beams, flames in the forehead of the morning sky."

The reason for the inherent brightness is that the soul of the righteous man passes from earth into a region out of which we "gather all things that offend, and them which do iniquity" [Matt. 13:40]. There are other reasons for it, but that is the one which our Lord dwells on. Or, to put it into modern scientific language, environment corresponds to character. So, when the clouds have rolled away, and no more mists from the undrained swamps of selfishness and sin and animal nature rise up to hide the radiance, there shall be a fuller flood of light poured from the re-created sun.

That brightness thus promised has for its highest and most blessed character that it is conformity to the Lord Himself. For, as you may remember, the last use of this emblem that we find in Scripture refers not to the servant, but to the Master, whom His beloved disciple in Apocalyptic vision saw, with His "countenance as the sun shining in his strength" [Rev. 1:16]. Thus, "we shall be like him, for we shall see him as he is" [1 John 3:2]. And, therefore, that radiance of the sainted dead is progressive, too. For it has an infinite fullness to draw upon; and the soul that is joined to Jesus Christ, and derives its luster from Him, cannot die until it has outgrown Jesus and emptied God. The sun will one day be a dark, cold ball. We shall outlast it.

But remember that it is only those who here on earth have progressively appropriated the brightness that Christ bestows who have a right to reckon on that better rising. It is contrary to all probability to believe that the passage from life can change the ingrained direction and set of a man's nature. We know nothing that warrants us in affirming that death can revolutionize character. Do not trust your future to such a slim chance. Here is a plain truth. They who on earth are as the shining light that shines more and more until the "perfect day," shall, beyond the shadow of eclipse, shine on as the sun does, behind the opaque, intervening body, all unconscious of what looks to mortal eyes on earth an eclipse, and "shall shine forth as the sun in the kingdom of their Father." For all that we know, and are taught by experience, religious and moral distinctions are eternal. "He that is righteous, let him be righteous still; and he that is filthy, let him be filthy still" [Rev. 22:11].

THE FRIEND OF GOD

He was called the Friend of God—James 2:23

When and by whom was he so called? There are two passages in the Old Testament in which an analogous designation is applied to the patriarch, but probably the name was one in current use among the people, and expressed in a summary fashion the impression that had been made by the history of Abraham's life. A sweet fate to have that as the brief record of a character, and to be known throughout the ages by such an epitaph! As many of us are aware, this name, "the Friend," has displaced the proper name, Abraham, on the lips of all Muslim people to this day; and the city of Hebron, where his corpse lies, is commonly known simply as "the Friend." How beautiful and blessed a thought it is which underlies this and similar representations of Scripture—namely, that the bond which unites us to God is the very same as that which most sweetly and strongly ties men to one another; and that, after all, religion is nothing more nor else than the transference to Him of the emotions which make all the sweetness of human life and society.

But while this belief in God was the very nerve and center of Abraham's whole character, and was the reason why he was called the friend of God, we must also remember that, as James insists upon it here, it was no mere idle assent, no mere intellectual conviction that God could not tell lies, which was dignified by the name of belief, but that it was, as James insists upon in the context, a trust which proved itself to be valid, because it was continually operative in the life. "Faith without works is dead" [James 2:20; 2:26]. "And Abraham, our father, was he not justified by works?" [James 2:21].

And so the Epistle to the Hebrews, if you will remember, traces up to his faith all the chief points in his life. "By faith . . . he went out; by faith he dwelt in tabernacles," in the promised land, believing that it should be his and his seed's. "By faith" he offered up his son on the altar [Heb. 11:8–17].

And then, in the future life, with new modes of manifestation and new capacities of apprehension, we shall draw nearer and nearer to the sun that we beheld here shining through the mists and the clouds; and it will be to us as it would be to an inhabitant of the furthest planet that wheels his course away out in what seems to us darkness and cold, if he were brought and set down in that one which circles around the sun in the narrowest orbit, and receives most of his fervid beams and dazzling light. If we, amid the shows and gauds of time and the crowds of thronging men and the distractions of our daily occupations, steadfastly seek and see the Lord, and have beams coming from Him, as a light shining in a dark place, He will lift us yonder, and turn the whole benediction of the sunlight of His face upon us, and, saturated with the brightness, we shall walk in the light of His countenance and be among the people of the blessed.

GOD'S FAMILIARITY WITH HIS FRIENDS

And the Lord said, Shall I hide from Abraham that thing which I do?—Gen. 18:17

"I call you not servants . . . but I have called you friends; for all things that I have heard of my Father I have made known unto you" [John 15:15]. So much for God's frankness. What about Abraham's frankness with God? Remember how he remonstrated with Him; how he complained to Him of His dealings; but for the friendship which underlay it, and which is expressed in words. And let us take the simple lesson that if we are friends and lovers of God, we shall delight in His company. It is a stranger kind of religion that does not care to be with God, that would rather think about anything else than about Him, that is all unused to quiet, solitary conversation and communion with Him, but it is the religion of I wonder how many of us? He would be a strange friend that never crossed your threshold if he could help it; that was evidently uncomfortable in your presence, and ill at ease till he got away from you; and that when he came was struck dumb, and had not a word to say for himself, and did not know or feel that he and you had any interests or subjects in common. Is that not a good deal like the religion of hosts of professing Christians?

If we are friends of God we shall have no secrets from Him. There are very few of those that are dearest to us to whom we could venture to lay bare all the depths of our hearts. There are black things down in the cellars that we do not like to take our friends down into. We keep them upstairs, in the rooms for company. But you can take God all through the house. And if there is the trust and the love that I have been speaking about, we shall not be afraid to spread all our foulness and our meanness and our unworthy thoughts of, and acts towards, Him before His "pure eyes and perfect judgment."

Tell God all, if you mean to be a friend of His. And do not be afraid to tell Him your harsh thoughts of Him, and your complaints of Him. He never resents anything that a man that loves Him says *about* Him, if he says it *to* Him. What He resents—if I might use the word—is our huddling up grudges and murmurings and doubts in our own hearts, and saying never a word to the Friend against whom they offend. Out with it all. Complaints, regrets, questionings, petitions, hot wishes—take them all to Him; and be sure that, instead of breaking, they will, if spoken, cement the friendship, which is disturbed by secrecy on our parts.

If we are God's lovers He will have no secrets from us. "The secret of the Lord is with them that fear him; and he will show them his covenant" [Ps. 25:14]. There is a strange wisdom and insight, sometimes amounting even to prophetic anticipation, which creeps into a simple heart that is knit closely to God. But whether the result of our friendship with Him be such communication of such kinds of insight or no, we may be sure of this, that if we trust Him, and love Him, and are frank with Him, He will in so far be frank with us, that He will impart unto us Himself, and in the knowledge of His love we shall find all the knowledge that we need.

A MUTUAL FRIENDSHIP

And the Lord spake unto Moses face to face, as a man speaketh unto his friend—
Ex. 33:11

Abraham, the humble earthly friend of God, did as God bade him, substantially, all his life, from the day when he made the "Great Refusal," and left behind him home and kindred and all, until the day when he went up the sides of Moriah to offer there his son. Abraham met God's wishes because Abraham trusted and loved God.

And what about the Divine Friend? Did He not meet Abraham's wishes? You remember that wonderful scene, which presents, in such vivid and dramatic form, the everlasting truth that the man who bows his will to God bows God's will to his, when he pleaded for Sodom, and won his case by persistence and importunity of lowly prayer. And these historical notices on both sides are for us the vehicles of the permanent truth, that, if we are God's lovers and friends, we shall find nothing sweeter than bowing to His will and executing His commandments. The very mark and signature of love is that it delights to divine and fulfill the desires of the beloved, and that it molds the will of each of the parties into conformity with the will of the other.

What a commentary our religion is upon such thoughts! To how many of us is the very notion of religion that of a prohibition of things that we would much like to do, and of commands to do things that we would much rather not do? All the slavery of abject submission, of reluctant service, is swept away when we understand that friendship and love find their supreme delight in discovering and in executing the will of the beloved. And surely if you and I are the friends of God, the cold words, "duty," "Must," "should," will be struck out of our vocabulary, and will be replaced by "delight," "cannot but," "will"! For friends find the very life—I was going to say the voice—of their friendship in mutual obedience.

And God, the heavenly Friend, will do what we wish. In that very connection did Jesus Christ put the two thoughts of friendship with Him and His executing His disciples' behests; in one breath saying, "Ye are my friends if ye do whatsoever I command you" [John 15:14], and in the next, "Ye shall ask what ye will, and it shall be done unto you" [John 15:7]. This conformity of will, so that there is but one will in the two hearts, which is the very consummation and superlative degree of human friendship and love, applies as truly to the friendship between man and God.

GOD'S METHOD OF GIVING

He that spared not his own Son, but delivered him for us all, how shall he not with him also freely give us all things?—Rom. 8:32

Abraham's gift of his son to God was but a feeble shadow of God's gift of His Son to men. And if the surrender on the part of the human friend was the infallible token of his love, surely the surrender on the part of the heavenly Friend is not less the infallible sign of His love to all the world. If we are God's friends and lovers we shall give Him, in glad surrender, our whole selves. And if you feel that you have separate interests from Him; if you keep things and do not let Him say, "These are Mine"; if you grudge sacrifice, and will not hear of self-surrender, and are living lives centered in, ruled by, devoted to, self, you have little reason to call yourself a Christian. "Ye are my friends if ye," not only "do whatsoever I command you," but "if you give yourself to me" [John 15:14]. Yield yourself to God, and in the giving of yourself to Him you will get back yourself glorified and blessed by the gift. There is no friendship where self shuts out the friend from the participation in what is the other's. As long as "mine" lives on this side of a high wall, and "thine" on the other, there is but little friendship. Down with the wall, and say about everything, "Ours"; and then you have a right to say, "I am the friend of God."

"I am thy shield; fear not, Abram" [Gen. 15:1], said God, when His friend was in danger from the vengeance of the Eastern kings whom he had defeated. And all through life the same strong arm was cast around him. And Abraham had to stand up for God amid this heathen people. If we are God's friends and lovers He will take up our cause. Be sure that if God be for us it matters not who is against us [see Rom. 8:31]. What would you think of a man who, in going away to a far-off country, said to some friend, "I wish you would look after so-and-so for me as long as I am gone"; and the friend would say, "Yes!" and never give a thought nor lift a finger to discharge the obligation? God trusts His reputation to you. He has interests in this world that you have to look after. You have to defend Him as much as He has to defend you. And it is the dreadful contradiction of religious people's profession of religion that they often care so little, and do so little, to promote the cause, to defend the name, to adorn the reputation, and to further what I may venture to call the interests of their heavenly Friend in the world.

Can you venture to say that you are a friend of God? If you cannot, what are you? Our relations to men admit of our dividing them into three—friends, enemies, nothings. We may love, we may hate, we may be absolutely indifferent and ignorant. I am afraid the three states cannot be transferred exactly to our relations to God. If not His friend, what are you? Have you only a far-off bowing acquaintance with Him? Well, then, that is because you have neglected, if you have not spurned, His offered friendship. And oh, how much you have lost! No human heart is a millionth part so sweet, and so capable of satisfying you, as God's. All friendship here has its limits, its changes, its end; God's is boundless, immutable, eternal.

GOD MANIFEST IN THE FLESH

Who is the image of the invisible God, the firstborn of every creature—Col. 1:15

Why does our Lord on one occasion (John 14:9) charge Philip with not knowing Him? Because Philip had said, "Lord! Show us the Father and it sufficeth us." And why was that question a betrayal of Philip's ignorance of Christ? Because it showed that he had not discerned Him as being "the Only Begotten of the Father, full of grace and truth" [John 1:14], and had not understood that "He that hath seen me hath seen the Father" [John 14:9]. "You do not know, and not knowing that, all your knowledge of Me, howsoever tender and sweet it may have been, howsoever full of love and reverence and blind admiration—all your knowledge of Me is but twilight knowledge, which may well be called ignorance." Not to know Christ as the manifest God is practically to be ignorant of Him altogether. Philip asked for some visible manifestation, such as their old books told them had been granted to Moses on the mountain, to Isaiah in the temple, and to many another one besides.

But if such a revelation had been given—and Christ could have given it if He wanted to—what a poor thing it would have been, put side by side with that mild and lambent light that was ever streaming from Him, making God visible to every sensitive and responsive nature! For these external manifestations for which Philip is here hungering, what could they show? They could show certain majestic, splendid, pompous, outside characteristics of God, but they could never show *God*, much less could they show "the Father." Righteousness and love, the revelation of these two, could be entrusted to no flashing brightness, and to no thunder and lightning. There can be no revelation of these things to the outward eye, but only to the inward heart through the medium of a human life. For not the power which knows no weariness, not the eye which never closes, not the omniscience which holds all things, great and small, in its grasp, make God. These are but the fringe, the outermost parts, of the circumference; the living Center is a Righteous Love. And you cannot reveal that any means but by showing it in action; nor show it in action by any means so sure as in a human life. Therefore, above all other forms of manifestation of God, stands the Person of Jesus Christ—God manifest in the flesh.

Jesus is Lord. My brother, a Man, is King of the universe. The new thing in Christ's return to "the glory which I had with thee before the world was" [John 17:5] is that He took the Manhood with Him in indissoluble union with the Divinity, and that a Man is Lord. So you and I can cherish that wonderful hope. "To him that overcometh will I grant to sit with me in my throne" [Rev. 3:21]. Nor need we ever fear but that all things concerning ourselves and our dear ones, and the church and the world, will be ordered aright, for the hand that sways the universe is the hand that was many a time laid in blessing upon the sick and the maimed, and that gathered little children to His bosom.

September 2

CHRIST'S OWN CLAIM

*No man knoweth the Son, but the Father; neither knoweth any the Father, save
the Son, and he to whomsoever the Son willeth to reveal him—Matt. 11:27*

It seems to me that if there is anything certain at all, it is certain that Jesus Christ,
while upon earth, claimed habitually to be the visible manifestation of God, in a degree, in a manner wholly unlike that in which a pure, good, wise, righteous man may
claim to shine with some reflected beams of Divine brightness. And we have to reckon
and make our account with that, and shape our theology accordingly.

I come to some of you who admire and revere this great Teacher, this pure Humanity, who know much of Him, who seek to follow in His footsteps in some measure,
but who stand outside that innermost circle wherein He manifests Himself as the God
Incarnate, the Sacrifice, and the Savior of the sins of the world; and while I thankfully
admit that a man's relation to Christ may be a great deal deeper and more vital and
blessed than his articulate creed, I am bound to say that not to know Him in this His
very deepest and most essential character is little different from being ignorant of Him
altogether.

Here is a great thinker or teacher, perhaps, whose fame has filled the world, whose
books are upon every student's shelf; he lives in a little remote country hamlet: the cot-
tagers beside him know him as a kind neighbor and a sympathetic friend. They never
hear of his books, they never heard of his thoughts, they do not know anything of what
he has done all over the world. Do you call that knowing him? You do not know a man
if you only know the surface and not the secrets of his being. You do not know a man if
you only know the subordinate characteristics of his nature, but not the essential ones.
The very heart of Christ is this: the Incarnate God, the sacrifice for the sins of the whole
world.

You may be disciples, in the imperfect sense in which the apostles were disciples
before the Cross and the Resurrection and the Ascension, imperfect disciples like them,
but without their excuse for it. You will never know Him until you know Him as the
Eternal Word, and until you can say, "We beheld His glory, the glory as of the Only
Begotten of the Father, full of grace and truth" [John 1:14]. Not seeing that, you see but
as a dim speck, or a star a little brighter than its brethren that hang in the heavens of
history, Him who really is the Central Sun, from whom all light comes, to whom the
whole creation moves. If you know Him for the Incarnate Word and Lamb who bears
the world's sin, you know Him for what He is. All the rest is most precious, most fair;
but without that central truth, you have but a fragmentary Christ, and nothing less than
the whole Christ is enough for you.

THE PATIENT TEACHER AND THE SLOW SCHOLARS

Jesus saith unto him, Have I been so long time with you, and yet hast thou not known me, Philip? He that hath seen me hath seen the Father—John 14:9

In these words we have a glimpse into the pained and loving heart of our Lord. We very seldom hear Him speak about His own feelings or experience; and when He does, it is always in some such incidental way as this. So that these glimpses, like little windows opening out upon some great prospect, are the more precious to us.

I think we shall not misunderstand the tone of this question to Philip if we see in it wonder, pained love, and tender, chiding remonstrance. "Have I been so long with you, and yet hast thou not known me?" In another place we read: "He marveled because of their unbelief." And here there is almost a surprise that He should have been shining so long and so near, and yet the purblind eyes should have seen so little.

But there is more than that, there is a complaint and pain in the question—the pain of vainly endeavoring to teach, vainly endeavoring to help, vainly endeavoring to love. And there are few pains like that. All men that have tried to help and bless their fellows have known what it is to have their compassion and their efforts thrown back upon themselves. And there are few sorrows heavier to carry than this: the burden of a heart that would desire to pour its love into another heart if that heart would only let it, but is repelled and obliged to bear its treasures unimparted. The slowness of the pupil is the sorrow of the honest teacher; the ingratitude and non-receptiveness of some churlish nature that you tried to lavish good upon, have they not often brought a bitterness to your hearts? If ever you have had the bitter experience of a child or a friend or a dear one that you have tried to get by all means to love you, and to take your love, and who has thrown it all back in your face, you may know in some faint measure what was at least one of the elements which made Him the "Man of Sorrows and acquainted with grief" [Is. 53:3]. But there is not only the pain caused by slow apprehension and unrequited love, but also the depth and patience of a clinging love that is not turned away by the pain. How tenderly the name "Philip" comes in at the end! It recalls that other instance when a whole world of feeling and appeal was compressed into the one word to the weeping woman, "Mary," and when another world of unutterable rapture and surprise was in her one answering word, "Rabboni." We may think of that patient love of His that will not be soured by any slowness or scantiness of response. Dammed back by our sullen rejection, it still flows on, seeking to conquer by long-suffering. Refused, it still lingers around the closed door of the heart and knocks for entrance. Misunderstood, it still meekly manifests itself. The same feelings of pain and patient love are in the heart of the enthroned Christ today. Mystery and paradox as it may be, I suppose that there passes over even His victorious and serene repose in the heavens some shadow of pain and sorrow still, when you and I turn away from Him. We cannot understand it; but if it be true that He has still a "fellow-feeling of our pains," it is not less true that His love is still wounded by our lovelessness, and His manifestation of Himself made sad by the slowness of our reception of Him.

OUR NARROW VISION OF CHRIST

Having eyes, see ye not? and having ears, hear ye not?—Mark 8:18

In Christ there are infinite depths to be experienced and to become acquainted with; and if we know Him at all as we ought to do, our knowledge of Him will be growing day by day. But how many of us stand at the same spot that we did when we first said that we were Christians?

We are like the Indians that live in rich gold countries, that could only gather the ore that happened to lie upon the surface or could be washed out of the sands of the river; but in this great Christ there are depths of gold, great reefs and veins of it, that will enrich us all if we dig—and we shall not get it unless we do.

He is the boundless ocean. We have contented ourselves with coasting along the shore and making timid excursions from one headland to another; let us strike out into the middle deep and see all the wonders that are there. This great Christ is like the infinite sky with its unresolved nebulae. We have but looked with our poor dim eyes; let us take the telescope that will reveal to us suns blazing where now we only see darkness.

If we have any true knowledge of Jesus Christ at all, it ought to be growing every day. And why does it not? Why does it not? You know a man because you are much with him. As the old proverb says, "If you want to know anybody, you must summer and winter with them"; and if you want to know Jesus Christ, there must be a great deal more meditative thoughtfulness and honest study of His life and work than any of us have ever put forth. We know people, too, by sympathy and by love and by keeping near them. Keep near your Master, Christian men! Oh, it is a wonder and a shame and a sin for us professing Christians that, having tasted the sweetness of His love, we should come down so low as to long for the garbage of earth. Who is fool enough to prefer vinegar to wine, bitter herbs to grapes, dross to gold? Who is there that, having consorted with the King, would gladly herd with ragged rebels? And yet that is what we do. We love one another, the world, people around us. We labor in the effort to make acquaintances, to surround ourselves with friends, and to fill our hearts from these many fountains. All right and well! But let us seek to know Christ more, and to know Him most chiefly in this, that He is for us the manifest God and the Savior of the world.

Some of us may have seen a weighty acknowledgment from a distinguished biologist, lately deceased, which strikes me as relevant to this thought. Listen to his confession: "I know from experience the intellectual distractions of scientific research, philosophical speculation, and artistic pleasures, but am also well aware that even when all are taken together, and well sweetened to taste, in respect of consequent reputation, means, social position, etc., the whole concoction is but as high confectionery to a starving man. . . . It has been my lot to know not a few of the foremost men of our generation, and I have always observed that this is profoundly true." That is the testimony of a man that had tried the highest, least material forms of such a trust. And I know that there is an "amen!" to it in every heart, and I lift up opposite to all such experiences the grand summary of Christian experience: "We which have believed do enter into rest" [Heb. 4:3].

DO YOU KNOW JESUS?

This is life eternal, that they should know thee, the only true God, and Jesus Christ, whom thou hast sent—John 17:3

It is the great wonder of human history that after eighteen hundred years the world knows so little of Jesus Christ. The leaders of opinion, the leaders of the literature of England, the men that profess to guide the thoughts of this generation, how little they know, really, about this Master! What profound misconceptions of the whole genius of Christianity, and of Him who is Christianity, we see among the teachers who pay Him high homage and conventional respect, as well as among those who profess to reject Him and His mission! Some people take a great deal more trouble to understand Buddha than they do to understand Christ. How little, too, the mass of men know about Him! It is enough to break one's heart to look around one, and think that He has been so long time with the world, and that this is all which has come of it.

Light has been shining for all these eighteen hundred years, and yet the mist is so little cleared away, and the ice is so little melted. The great proof that the world is bad is that it does not believe in Jesus Christ the Son of God, and that He has stood before it for nearly nineteen centuries now, and so few have been led to turn to Him with the adoring cry, "My Lord and my God" [John 20:28]. But let us narrow our thoughts to ourselves. This question comes to many of you who shall read these lines in a very pointed way. You have known about Jesus Christ all your lives, and yet in a real, deep sense you do not know Him at this moment. For the knowledge of which I speak is the knowledge of acquaintance with a person rather than the knowledge that a man may have of a book. And it is the knowledge of experience. Have you that? Do you know Christ as a man knows about his neighbor across the street there, that has lived beside him for twenty-five years and never spoken to him once all the time? Is that your knowledge of Christ? If so, it is no knowledge at all. "I have heard of thee by the hearing of the ear" [Job 42:5], describes all the acquaintance which a great many of us have with Him.

Oh, my brother! The very fact that He has been so long with you is the reason why you know so little about Him. People that live close by something that men come from the ends of the earth to see have often never seen it. A man may have lived all his life within sound of the Niagara, and perhaps never have gone to look at the rush of the waters.

Is that what you do with Jesus Christ? Are you so accustomed to hear about Him that you do not know Him; having so long heard of Him that you never came to see Him?

ALL STRENGTH IN CHRIST

I can do all things through Christ which strengtheneth me—Phil. 4:13

"I can do all things." That rendering of Paul's words does not exactly represent what he really meant. In one aspect they say more than Paul says, and in another less. For he is not only speaking about what he can do, but also of what he can endure. Action is but half—and often the lesser half—of life; so we have to widen the expression to include both doing and bearing. But, on the other hand, "all things" must be subject to some limitations. Common sense dictates these. The Apostle is making no preposterous claim to a kind of quasi-omnipotence. He felt himself ready for anything that might come. "I am instructed both to be full and to be hungry, both to abound and to suffer need. . . . I have learned in whatsoever state I am, therewith to be content" [Phil. 4:11, 12] But "content" is not Paul's meaning. The plain rendering is "self-sufficient." Take away from that word all the arrogance that is in it, and understand it to mean *independent of circumstances* or *lord of externals*. What Paul says is that he is ready for everything, equipped for any fortune, able to do whatever is commanded, able to bear whatever is imposed.

We have here just the true attitude for a Christian soul: to be so far self-sufficing as that externals do not gain the mastery. We should be able always to keep the bilge-water down by working the pumps, and to have our hands on the tiller and follow the course which the Master-Navigator has chartered out for us, whatever winds blow or waves roll. So shall we have strength for all things, and be equal to any variety of fortune. In some great cathedral the temperature will vary little between midsummer and midwinter. The walls are thick; and it matters not whether the sunshine be blazing on the piazza outside or whether icicles be hanging from the cornices of the building, there is the same atmosphere within. We should carry our atmospheres with us. Our spiritual heat, like the temperature of our bodies, should keep pretty nearly the same at the poles and at the equator.

"I have strength for everything." Now, that may be said in a great many different keys and moods, and may be the expression of almost opposite feelings. It may be the proud boast of an unnatural and over-strained stoicism which tries to crush down the sensibilities of human nature, and thereby destroys the nature that it is trying to steady. Or the boast may come from an under-estimate of the difficulties and vicissitudes that fall to be encountered in every life, and an over-estimate of our poor powers to face them. Many a young man flings himself into the battle of life with an unbounded confidence that he is equipped for all its events, and by the time that gray hairs begin to show upon the black head, instead of saying, "I can do all things," he is ready to wail, "I can do nothing; I am an utter failure." But "I can do all things" may be said, and ought to be said, by us, as the result of our simply leaning on an Almighty strength. Then levity, ignorance of one's own weakness, ignorance of the saw-toothed ranks of enemies that beset every attempt at noble life, disappear, and what on other lips sounds like the most arrogant and insane presumption, which is sure to be punished, comes to be an utterance fitted for the lips of the humblest and the most self-distrustful. "I have strength for anything," and yet not, I, "but Christ liveth in me" [Gal. 2:20].

TRIUMPHANT CONFIDENCE

*I rejoiced in the Lord greatly, that now at the last your care of me hath flourished
again. . . . Not that I speak in respect of want: for I have learned, in whatsoever
state I am, therewith to be content—Phil. 4:10, 11*

I believe that one of the great secrets of the weakness of modern Christianity is that practically that doctrine—no, do not let us call it a doctrine—that fact of the dwelling of the Christian soul in Christ, and the reciprocal indwelling of Christ, in every believing heart, has, to a large extent, faded out of popular conceptions of Christianity. We talk a great deal, and we cannot talk too much, but we may talk too exclusively, about Christ *for* us. We must regard that as the basis of all Christ's work. But then the New Testament builds upon it this other truth—Christ in us and we in Christ. I would that Christian people realized more as a simple fact—mystical, if you like, and none the worse for that—that there is a union between the believing spirit and the Christ whom it trusts, so close and intimate as that local metaphors of mutual indwelling do but partially express it. As the branch is in the vine so are we in Christ. As the soul is in the body so is Christ in us; the Life of our lives, the Soul of our souls. And it is by union with Jesus Christ, and by this most deep and real dwelling in Him as the atmosphere, in which we "live and move and have our being" [Acts 17:28], that the word ceases to be presumption and becomes humility; self-distrust and confidence in Him.

I wish sometimes that I could get Christian people to take the epistles, and read them through once, for one purpose, that is, to note the variety of applications in which that phrase *"in* Christ Jesus" occurs. If anybody would do that, he would get a new impression of the reality and of the prominence in the whole scheme of Christianity, of the thought—*"in* Him."

How is that indwelling to be realized? You perhaps say, "Oh! Such a union with Christ is mystical; it is far away from our ordinary experience." Yes! I believe it is far away from ordinary experience. But there is no reason why it should be so. For, however profound the thought, the way of making it a fact in our lives is as plain as the thought is profound. You are in Him when you trust Him. You are not in Him if your confidence is in self, or in creatures. You are not in Him if all the day long your mind is busy with other thoughts, and your heart with other affections. But you are in Him if you are occupied, heart and mind, with Him and with His truth. You are in Him if, trusting Him, and having Him present by the direction of mind and heart towards Him, as the motive and power of your lives, you serve Him with lowly obedience. And you are not in Him if you assert your own independence, and perk yourself up in His face and say, "Not as Thou wilt, but as I will." Trust, meditation, practical obedience—these are the three angels that guide us into the very presence of the Most High.

September 8

SPIRITUAL DECLENSION AND CHANGE

Be astonished, O ye heavens, at this! And be ye very desolate, saith the Lord; for my people have committed two evils: they have forsaken me, the fountain of living waters, and hewed them out cisterns, broken cisterns, that can hold no water—Jer. 2:12, 13

It does seem inexplicable that if a man has once got a glimpse of the beauty, precious-ness, and sweetness of Christ, His love and His power, his eyes should ever turn away or his heart ever become unfaithful. And yet it is the history of the Church as a whole, and of the individual members of it. As to the Church as a whole, how early it needed to be said, "Ye have left your first love"! and how constantly it has had to be repeated ever since! The apostles were not cold in their graves when grievous wolves began to enter in and spoil the flock. The law seems to work almost inevitably that close on the heels of every period of earnestness and quickened life there shall follow a period of re-action and torpor. However high the arrow is shot, the impulse that sped it on its way heavenward soon seems to die, and gravitation begins, and down it comes again.

Look at Germany after the Reformation. Look at the England of the eighteenth century after the outburst of Puritanism. Look at the deadness that fell upon the first periods of this century after the strong new life of Whitefield and the Wesleys. Look all over the history of the Church, and you find the same thing. Then ask the question: Is there any more convincing proof of a living Christ than the fact that the Church has not been dead and buried long ago? And is there any better sign that Christianity is not of man than the fact that it has always been so hard for men to keep themselves for any length of time upon its level?

I am sure there is not a man or a woman reading this that has not had moments of illumination, when the conscience was quickened, and things that they thought they believed all their days flared out upon them with altogether strange and startling force and reality. And what has become of the moments, what has become of the impres-sions that were made upon us then? Where have they all disappeared to? And what is left behind when the heavens have closed again? Use and wont have gathered about us once more; the old opium sedatives that have lulled us to sleep so often have been quaffed again; and after the momentary illumination and expansion, we have fallen back into the miserable old ruts of half belief and whole indifference, and yet call ourselves Christians. I was reading in a book of African travel the other day that the great moun-tain peak of Kilimanjaro will lie for weeks and weeks hidden behind the mists, except now and then in the morning, when, like an apparition, its wedge forces itself through the rolling vapor, and for half-an-hour it gleams there, the lord of the landscape; and then it is blotted out. How many of our lives in their *morning* hours had a vision, when the rolling lies, unsubstantial but opaque, which veiled the realities have been swept away, and for an instant you saw what is always there, whether you see it or not, the re-ality of God in Christ, His love and His work for you?

THE FASCINATING INFLUENCES
OF THE WORLD

O foolish Galatians, who hath bewitched you, before whose eyes Jesus Christ hath been evidently set forth crucified among you?—Gal. 3:1

What glittering eye is it, envious and covetous, that has "overlooked" you, as they say about infants unaccountably wasting, and so made you to wither away?

Let us understand clearly about this matter, that whatever blame may be laid at the door of external causes, and of what we may call fascinations, what gives them all their power is our own weakness and folly. It is all very well to analyze the causes of religious declension, and to try and guard ourselves against them, but that is leading men upon a false quest, unless we remind ourselves at the beginning that the real cause lies within. No outward temptation, nothing in earth, hell, or heaven, has any power to turn away my eyes from Jesus Christ unless I choose to give it the power. I am not to put the blame of my feeble Christian life, or of my utter irreligion upon anything or anybody, but only myself. If I had not combustibles in my heart, it would do me no harm to put ever so fierce a light to it. But if I carry about a keg of gunpowder within me, I am not to blame the match if there comes an explosion. It is because our hearts do not find in Jesus Christ all that they crave that we are unfaithful and turn away from Him; and it is because our hearts are foolish and bad that they do not find in Jesus Christ all that they crave. If you and I were as we should be, there would not be a desire in us that would not be met in our loving Lord, in His sweetness and grace. And if there were not a desire in us that was not met in our loving Lord's sweetness and grace, then all these temptations might play upon us innocuously, and we should walk through the fire and not be harmed. So let us take it all to ourselves, and remember that whatever temptations may be brought to bear upon us, we, we alone, are responsible for the effects that they produce.

Who, then, are the fascinators? I am not going to deal at all with the immediate occasion of these words, which referred to the Galatians falling away from the doctrinal Christianity preached by Paul; but I will just remind you in passing that the thing which caused all this vehemence of argument and expostulation on the part of the Apostle was that the Galatian Christians had listened to teachers who did not deny salvation by faith in Jesus Christ, but who sought to make an outward rite necessary, side by side with faith. It makes no difference to the principle involved that the rite which the Judaising teachers tried to force on the Gentiles who believed was circumcision, and that the rites which the modern Judaisers make essential are Baptism and Lord's Supper. The principle is identical; and wherever you get an attempt to mix up these two things, salvation through faith in Jesus Christ and salvation through sacraments, the sledge-hammer blows of this Epistle to the Galatians come down upon the unnatural amalgam and smite it to pieces. It is hard for men to keep up on the level of the New Testament and of its spiritual conceptions of worship. It is hard to use ordinances and rites as merely material aids to spiritual apprehension and affection. It is hard to keep them in their due place of subordination.

THE POWER OF THE FLESH

Thus saith the Lord, Cursed be the man that trusteth in man, and maketh flesh his arm—Jer. 17:5.

The "flesh" is ever apt to make "sacraments" out of "ordinances," and to blend in disastrous union a faith in Jesus Christ and a faith in them. It cannot be done. It must be the one thing or the other. The reliance on the sacraments will in the long run kill the faith in Christ, or the faith in Christ drive out the reliance on the sacraments. Little as it may seem so at first, all experience has proved that Paul spoke with unerring instinct when he declared to the Galatians that if they yielded to the teaching of the Judaisers, and submitted to circumcision as necessary, they would get no good from Christ. He must be all or nothing. This was the earliest corruption of Christianity. It subsists perennially through the generations; it crops up ever and anon when we thought it was cut down. It is all about us in England today, devastating the churches; and its roots are in each of us. Nothing but Christ's Cross, and nothing as bringing the power of that Cross into my life but my simple faith—that is what Paul preached; and if he could have stood today, and seen men running after sacraments and ritual and outward forms and the aesthetics of worship, and turning the preacher of a gospel into the priest of a sacrament, his voice would have rung out in as earnest and as surprised remonstrance: "Oh, foolish! Who hath bewitched you?" [Gal. 3:1].

But we are all in danger from other fascinations and seducers, such as worldly cares, occupations, and treasures. "As thy servant was busy here and there, he was gone" [1 Kgs. 20:40], said the negligent soldier, to account for the escape of the prisoner in his charge. That is exactly the history of the way in which a great many men's Christianity trickles out of them without their knowing it. They are too busy to look after it, or even to notice its escape, and so drop, drop, drop, slow and unnoticed through the leak it slips, until there is none left; and the man fancies the vessel is full, till he comes to need to draw on it, and then! How many of us, I wonder, are like the elm trees that have sent their top roots down to a layer of innutritious earth, and are standing magnificent stems, but hollow inside, ready to be blown over in the first gale of wind?

Oh! How much Christian life is murdered every year! How much devotion dies in the air of the business street! How hard it is for you that have to go away every Monday morning, and keep at it all the week long, to keep up the fervor of your faith and the simplicity of your piety! Brother, there is only one way to do it, and that is to keep near to the Master, whose strength will hold you up. The attrition of worldly cares eats away the impression upon our hearts. As the soft south wind gradually eats away the inscriptions off the temples that may front it, so the writing upon our hearts is blurred by the constant, soft, moist breath of earth's business and cares impinging upon it.

And the fascinations that slay most of us are all summed up in the solemn old words: "The lust of the flesh, and the lust of the eye, and the pride of life" [1 John 2:16]. These bewitch you, before whose eyes Christ was set forth.

THE EVIL EYE

If thine eye be evil, thy whole body shall be full of darkness—Matt. 6:23

The reference to the evil eye gives special emphasis to the words in Galatians 3:1, *"Before whose eyes* Jesus Christ hath been evidently set forth." For the evil eye, according to the old superstition, operated most powerfully on the people who allowed their eyes to dwell upon it. If the Galatians had kept their gaze fixed on Jesus Christ, the tempter's fatal glance would have had no power over them. The Galatian Christians, with characteristic Celtic fickleness, had fallen away from the apostolic doctrine, and had cooled in the fervor of their love to Himself. It looks, thinks Paul, as if some malignant sorcerer had affected them.

If we would escape the power of these evil eyes, we must so order our religious lives as to keep the facts of Christ's work and death for us ever before our minds. We shall not be able to keep that vision of Christ crucified before our eyes in the midst of daily distractions unless it is stamped deep on mind and heart by the habit of quiet meditation. The absence of that habit is one chief reason for the weakness of so much of our modern Christianity. Meditation is almost a lost art among us. I wonder how many of us there are who, from one week's end to another, ever spend ten minutes' quiet thought upon the Cross, not so much for the purpose of investigation or confirmation or proof, but simply for the purpose of getting the sweetness of the thought more and more into our hearts, and the power of it more and more into our lives?

How often do you realize that great truth of Christ crucified for you? Do you ever think of it? Does the memory of Him and of His death for you come to you in your daily work and struggles?

I beseech you, fix your thoughts and your love on Him, and look away from all else. Make Him and His love and His death the theme of your thankful meditation in many a quiet hour of high communion. Try to have that vision as your companion everywhere, and on every common thing to see "placarded" the Crucified Christ. That sight will take the brightness out of many a false glitter, as a poor candle pales before the electric light, or as the sun puts even *it* to shame. It will make many a tempting fiend, who squats at your ear to drop his poison in, start up in his own shape. If you look to Jesus crucified for you, He will give you "power to tread upon the serpent and the scorpion, and nothing shall by any means hurt you." You may be as powerless of yourself before temptations as a humming-bird before a snake; but if you look fixedly to Him, neither the glittering eye of the serpent nor the forked tongue with its hiss will harm or frighten you. And the question of Paul, instead of being one of indignant rebuke and wonder, will become to each of us the expression of our triumphant confidence that we shall "tread upon the serpent and the adder," and conquer our tempters: "Who is he that will bewitch us, if before our eyes there ever shines Christ crucified?"

THE AMULET

But God forbid that I should glory, save in the cross of our Lord Jesus Christ, by whom the world is crucified unto me, and I unto the world—Gal. 6:14

The counter-charm that keeps a man safe from the enchantments of the world lies in these words: "Before whose eyes Jesus Christ was evidently set forth crucified" [Gal. 3:1]. The secret of security is, do not look at the glittering eye that would fascinate you. And the way to do that is to fix your eye on something else. A man that has to walk across a foaming torrent upon some narrow plank knows that the only way to keep himself steady is to fix his eye upon something on the farther side. If he looks to his feet, or the bridge, or the water as it boils among the rocks below, down he will go. The one safety is, fix your eye upon the point to which you go, and keep steadfastly looking at that; and your feet will take care of themselves.

And so it is in this matter. If we are to have the power of turning away from these things that tempt us, and are thus to deprive the sorcerer of his influence, because we will not look at him, we must look at Jesus Christ. Hearts and minds that are occupied with Him will not be at leisure for lower and grosser tastes. An empty vessel let down into the ocean will have its sides bulged in far more quickly than one that is filled. Fill your hearts, and keep them full, with Jesus Christ, and they will be able to resist the pressure of temptation.

The true way to conquer temptations is not to fight them in detail, but to go up into a loftier region, where they cease to be temptations. How is it that grown men do not like the candy that used to tempt them when they were children? They have outgrown them. Then outgrow the temptations of the world! How is it that there are no mosquitoes nor malaria on the mountain tops! They cannot rise above the level of the swamps by the river. Go up to the mountain top, and neither malaria nor mosquitoes will follow you—which being interpreted is, live near Jesus Christ, and keep your hearts and minds occupied with Him, and you will dwell in a region high above the temptations which buzz and sing, which infest and slay, on the lower levels.

But remember that it is the contemplation of Christ crucified which has this power to elevate and act as a charm against the spells of evil. There is not substance or transforming power enough in a Christianity without a Cross to overcome the world. It has always been the case that when Christ's death has ceased to be the center of the Church's faith and testimony, the church has become worldly. When men have not had a crucified Christ to gaze upon, they have turned to look at the fascinators, and their very life has been sucked out of them. It is only by His Cross that the world becomes dead to me, and I unto the world. The victorious power of Christianity lies in the continual contemplation of Christ's death for me.

THE ATTACHMENTS OF FAITH

These all died in faith, not having received the promises, but having seen them from afar off, . . . and confessed that they were strangers and pilgrims on the earth—Heb. 11:13

The great roll call of heroes of faith in this chapter (Heb. 11) goes upon the supposition that the living spirit of religion was the same in Old and in New Testament times. In both it was faith which knit men to God. It has often been alleged that that great word *faith* has a different significance in this Epistle from that which it has in the other New Testament writings. The allegation is largely true; in so far as the things believed are concerned they are extremely different, but it is not true in so far as the person trusted or in so far as the act of trusting are concerned—these are identical. It was no mere temporal and earthly promise on which the faith of these patriarchs was builded. They looked indeed for the land, but in looking for the land they looked "for the City which hath foundations"; and their future hopes had the same dim haze of ignorance, and the same questions unresolved about perspective and relative distances which our future hopes have; and their faith, whatever were its contents, was fundamentally the same out of a soul casting itself upon God which is the essence of our faith in the Divine Son in whom God is made manifest. So with surface difference there is a deep-lying, absolute oneness in the faith of the Old Testament and ours, in their essential nature, in the Object which they grasp, and in their practical effects upon life. Therefore these words, describing what faith did for the world's gray forefathers, have a more immediate bearing upon us than at first sight may appear, and may suggest for us some thoughts about the proper, practical issues of Christian faith in our daily lives.

Observe that the words, "And were persuaded of them" [v. 13], in our King James Version are a gloss—no part of the original text. Observe, further, that the adverb "afar off" is intended to apply to both the clauses: "Having seen them" and "embraced them." And that, consequently, "embraced" must necessarily be an inadequate representation of the writer's idea; for you cannot *embrace* a thing that is "afar off"; and to "embrace for the promises" was the very thing that these men did *not* do. The meaning of the word is, here, not *embraced,* but *saluted,* or *greeted:* and the figure that lies in it is a very beautiful one. As some traveler topping the watershed may see far off the white porch of his home, and wave a greeting to it, though it be distant, while his heart goes out over all the intervening, weary leagues; or as some homeward-bound crew catch, away yonder on the horizon, the tremulous low line that is home, and welcome it with a shout of joy, though many a billow dash and break between them and it, these men looked across the weary waste, and saw far away; and as they saw, their hearts went out toward the things that were promised, because they "judged him faithful who had promised" [v. 11]. And that is the attitude and the act which all true faith in God ought to operate in us.

FAITH'S VISION

Faith is the substance of things hoped for, the evidence of things not seen—
Heb. 11:1

People say, "Seeing is believing." I should be disposed to turn the adage right around and to say, "Believing is seeing." For there is a clearer insight, and a more immediate, direct contact with the thing beheld, and a deeper certitude in the vision of faith than in the poor purblind sight of sense, all full of illusions, and which has no real possession in it of the things which it beholds. The sight that faith gives is solid, substantial, clear, certain. If I might so say, the true exercise of faith is to stereoscope the dim, ghostlike realities of the future, and to make them stand out solid in relief there before us. And he who, clasping the hand, and if I might so say, looking through the eyes of God, sees the future, in humble acceptance of His great words of promise, in some measure as God sees it—he has a source of knowledge, clear, immediate, certain, which sense, with its lies and imperfections, is altogether inadequate even to symbolize. The vision of faith is far deeper, far more real, far more correspondent to the realities, and far more satisfying to the eye that gazes, than is any of the sight of sense. Do not be deceived or seduced, by talk that assumes to be profound and philosophical, into believing that when you venture your all upon God's Word, and doing so say, "I know, and behold mine inheritance," you are saying more than calm reason and common sense teaches us. We have the thing, and we see it, if we believe Him that in His Word shows it to us.

This vision of faith, with all its blessed clearness and certitude and sufficiency, is not a direct perception of the things promised, but only a sight of them in the promise. And does that make it less blessed? Does the astronomer that sits in his chamber, and when he would most carefully observe the heavens, looks downward onto the mirror of the *reflecting* telescope that he uses, feel that he sees the starry lights less clearly and less really than when he gazes up into the abyss itself and sees *them* there? Is not the reflection a better and a more accurate source of knowledge for him than even the observation direct of the sky would be? And so, if we look down into the promise, we shall see, gleaming and glittering there, the starry points which are the true images adapted to our present sense and power of reception of the great invisible lights above. Thank God that faith looks to the promises and not to the realities, else it were no more faith, and would lose some of its blessedness.

Let me remind you that this vision of Faith varies in the measure of our faith. It is not always the same. Refraction brings up sometimes, above the surface of the sea, a spectral likeness of the opposite shore; and men stand now and then upon our Southern coasts, and for an hour or two, in some conditions of the atmosphere, they see the low sandhills of the French or the Belgian coast, as if they were in arm's length. So Faith, refracting the rays of light that strike from the Throne of God, brings up the image, and when it is strong the image is clear, and when it flags the image "fades away into the light of common day"; and where there glowed the fair outlines of the far-off land, there is nothing but a weary wash of waters and a solitary stretch of sea.

THE DETACHMENTS OF FAITH

Ye are no more strangers and foreigners, but ye are fellow citizens with the saints,
and of the household of God—Eph. 2:19

Faith produces a sense of detachment from the present. "They confessed that they were strangers and pilgrims on the earth" [Heb. 11:13]. Now, there are two different kinds of consciousness that we are strangers and foreigners here. There is one that merely comes from the consideration of the natural transiency of all earthly things and the shortness of human life; there is another that comes from the consciousness that we belong to another kingdom and another order. A "stranger" is a man who, in a given constitution of things, in some country with a settled government, owes allegiance to another king and belongs to another polity. A "pilgrim" or a "foreigner" is a man who is only in the place where he now is for a little while. So the one of the two words expresses the idea of belonging to another state of things, and the other expresses the idea of transiency in the present condition.

But the true Christian consciousness of being "a stranger and a foreigner" comes, not from any thought that life is fleeting and ebbing away, but from the better and more blessed operation of the faith which reveals the things promised, and knits me so closely to them that I cannot but feel separated from the things that are around me. Men that live in mountainous countries, when they come down into the plains, be it Switzerland or the Highlands or anywhere else, pine and fade away, sometimes with the intensity of the "Heimweh," the homesickness which seizes them. And we, if we are Christians, and belong to the other order of things, shall feel that this is not the native soil, nor here the home in which we would dwell. Abraham could not go to live in Sodom, though Lot went; and he and his son and grandson kept themselves outside of the organization of the society in the midst of which they dwelt, because they were so sure that they belonged to another. They "dwelt in *tents* because they looked for the *City.*"

My brother! Does your faith lessen the bonds that bind you to earth? Does it detach you from the things that are seen and temporal? Or is your life ordered upon the same maxims, and devoted to the pursuit of the same objects, and gladdened by the same transitory and partial successes, and embittered by the same fleeting and light afflictions which rule and sway as the tempest sways the grass on the sandbanks, as the lives that are rooted only in earth? If so, what business have we to call ourselves Christians? If so, how can we say that we live by faith when we are so blind, and so incapable of seeing afar off, that the smallest trifle beside us blots out from our vision, as a fourpenny-piece held up against your eyeball might do the sun itself in the heavens there. True faith detaches a man from this present. If your faith does not do that, look into it, and see where the falsity of it is.

FAITH TRIUMPHANT IN DEATH

He looked for a city which hath the foundations, whose builder and
maker is God—Heb. 11:10

Faith triumphs in the article of death. "These all died in faith" [Heb. 11:13]. That is a very grand thought as applied to those old patriarchs, that just *because* all their lives long God had done nothing for them of what He had promised, *therefore* they died believing he was going to do it. All the disappointments fed their faith. Because the words on which they had been leaning all their lives had not come to a fulfillment, therefore they must be true. That is a strange paradox, and yet it is the one which filled these men's hearts with peace, and which made the dying Jacob break in upon his prophetic swan song, at the close, with the verse which stands in no relation to what goes before it or what comes after it, "I have waited for Thy salvation, O Lord" [Gen. 49:18]. "These all died in faith" just because they had "not received the promises" [Heb. 11:13]. So, for us, the end of life may have a faith nurtured by disappointments, and made more sure of everything because it has nothing; certain that he calls into existence another world to redress the balance of the old, because here there has been so much of bitterness and weariness and woe.

And our end, like theirs, may be an end beautified by a clear vision of the things that "no man hath seen, nor can see" [1 Tim. 6:16]; and into the darkness there may come for us, as there came of old to another, an open heaven and a beam of God's glory smiting us on the face and changing it into the face of an angel. And so there may come for us all in that article and act of death a tranquil and cheerful abandonment of the life which has been futile and frail, except when thought of as the vestibule of Heaven. Some men cling to the vanishing skirts of this earthly life, and say, "I will not let thee go." And others are able to say, "Lord! I have waited for thy salvation" [Gen. 49:18]. "Now lettest thou thy servant depart in peace" [Luke 2:29].

"These all died in faith"; and the sorrows and disappointments of the past made the very background on which the bow of promise spanned the sky, beneath which they passed into the Promised Land. "These all died in faith"; with a vision gleaming upon the inward sense which made the solitude of death bliss, and with a calm willingness "to depart, and to be with Christ, which is far better" [Phil. 1:23].

Choose whether you will live by sense and die in sorrow, or whether you will live by the faith of the Son of God, and die to enter "the city which hath foundations" [Heb. 11:10], which He has built for them that love Him, and which even now, "in seasons of calm weather," we can see shining on the hilltop far away.

THE SILENCE OF SCRIPTURE

Many other signs therefore did Jesus in the presence of his disciples, which are not written in this book: but these are written that ye might believe that Jesus is the Christ, the Son of God; and that believing ye might have life in his name—
John 20:30, 31

The silence of Scripture is quite as eloquent as its speech. Think, for instance, of how many things in the Bible are taken for granted that you would not expect to be taken for granted in a book of religious instruction. It takes for granted the Being of a God. It takes for granted our relations to Him. It takes for granted our moral nature. In its later portions, at all events, it takes for granted the future life. Look at how the Bible, as a whole, passes by, without one word of explanation or alleviation, a great many of the difficulties which gather around some of its teaching. For instance, we find no attempt to explain the Divine nature of our Lord, or the existence of the three Persons in the Godhead. It has not a word to say in explanation of the mystery of prayer, or of the difficulty of reconciling the omnipotent will of God on the one hand with my own free will on the other. It has not a word to explain, though many a word to proclaim and enforce, the fact of Christ's death as the atonement for the sins of the whole world. Observe, too, how scanty the information on points on which the heart craves for more light. How closely, for instance, the veil is kept over the future life! How many questions which are not prompted by mere curiosity our sorrow and our love ask in vain!

Nor is the incompleteness of Scripture as a historical book less marked. Nations and men appear on its pages abruptly, rending the curtain of oblivion, and striding to the front of the stage for a moment, and then they disappear, swallowed up of night. It has no care to tell the stories of any of its heroes, except for so long as they were the organs of that Divine breath, which, breathed through the weakest reed, makes music. The self-revelation of God, not the acts and fortunes of even His noblest servants, is the theme of the Book. It is full of gaps about matters that any showy scholar or philosopher or theologian would have filled up for it. There it stands, a Book unique in the world's history, unique in what it says, and no less unique in what it does not say.

Why was it that in the Church, after the completion of the Scriptural canon, there sprang up a whole host of apocryphal gospels, full of childish stories of events which they felt had been passed over with strange silence in the teachings of the four evangelists? Put the four Gospels down by the side of the two thick octavo volumes which it is the regulation thing to write nowadays about any man that has a name at all, and you will feel their incompleteness as biographies. They are but a pen-and-ink drawing of the sun! And yet, although they be so tiny that you might sit down and read them all in an evening over the fire, is it not strange that they have stamped on the whole world an image so deep and so sharp, of such a character as the world never saw besides? They are fragments, but they have left a symmetrical and a unique impression on the consciousness of the whole world.

THE INCOMPLETENESS OF SCRIPTURE

There are also many other things which Jesus did, the which, if they should be written every one, I suppose that even the world itself could not contain the books that should be written—John 21:25

Christ, the Son of God, is the Center of Scripture; and the Book—whatever be the historical facts about its origin, its authorship, and the date of the several portions of which it is composed—the Book is a unity, because there is driven right through it, like a core of gold, either in the way of prophecy and onward-looking anticipation, or in the way of history and grateful retrospect, the reference to the one "Name that is above every name," the name of the Christ, the Son of God.

"They that went before, and they that followed cried, Hosanna; Blessed is he that cometh in the name of the Lord" [Mark 11:9]. That Christ towers up above the history of the world and the process of revelation, like Mount Everest among the Himalayas. To that great peak all the country on the one side runs upwards, and from it all the valleys on the other descend; and the springs are born there which carry verdure and life over the world.

And all the imcompleteness of Scripture, its fragmentariness, its carelessness about persons, are intended, as are the slight parts in a skillful painter's handiwork, to emphasize the beauty and the sovereignty of that one central Figure on which all the lights are concentrated, and on which he has lavished all the resources of his art. So God—for *God* is the Author of the Bible—on this great canvas has painted much in sketching outline, and left much unfilled in, that every eye may be fixed on the central Figure, the Christ of God, on whose head comes down the dove, and around whom echoes the Divine declaration: "This is My beloved Son, in whom I am well pleased" [Matt. 17:5].

But it is not merely in order to represent Jesus as the Christ of God that these are written, but it is that this representation may become the object of our faith. If the intention of Scripture had been simply to establish the fact that Jesus was the Christ and the Son of God, it might have been done in a very different fashion. A theological treatise would have been enough to do that. But, if the object be that men should not only accept with their understandings the truth concerning Christ's office and nature, but that their hearts should go out to Him, and that they should rest their sinful souls upon Him *as* the Son of God and the Christ, then there is no other way to accomplish that but by the history of His life and the manifestation of His heart. If the object were simply to make us know about Christ, we do not need a Book like this; but if the object is to lead us to put our faith in Him, then we must have what we have here, the infinitely touching and tender figure of Jesus Christ Himself set forth before us in all its sweetness and beauty, as He lived and moved and died for us.

Do you believe that Jesus is the Christ, the Son of God? Do you trust your soul to Him in these characters? If you do, I think we can shake hands. If you do not, you have failed to allow Scripture to do its work on you, and you have not reached the point which all God's lavish revelation has been expended on the world that you and all men might attain.

THE ULTIMATE PURPOSE OF GOD'S WORD

They are they which testify of me; and ye will not come to me, that ye might have life—John 5:39, 40

Scripture is not given to us merely to make us know something about God in Christ, not only in order that we may have faith in the Christ thus revealed to us, but for a further end—great, glorious, but not distant—namely, that we may "have life in His Name." "Life" is deep, mystical, inexplicable by any other words than itself. It includes pardon, holiness, well-being, immortality, Heaven; but it is more than they all.

This life comes into our dead hearts, and quickens them by union with God. That which is joined to God lives. Union with Christ in His Sonship will bring life into dead hearts. He is the true Prometheus that has come from Heaven with fire, the fire of the Divine Life in the reed of His humanity; and He imparts it to us all if we will. He lays Himself upon us, as the prophet laid himself on the little child in the upper chamber; and lip to lip, and beating heart to dead heart, He touches our death, and it is quickened into life. And the condition on which that great Name will bring to us life is simply our faith. If you trust Him as the Son of God who comes down to earth that we in Him might have the immortal life He is ready to give, the end that God has in view in all His revelation, that Christ had in view in His bitter Passion, has been accomplished for you. If you do not, it has not. You may admire Him, you may think loftily of Him, you may be ready to call Him by many great and appreciative names, but unless you have learned to see in Him the Divine Savior of your souls, you have not seen what God means you to see. But if you have, then all other questions about this Book, important as they are in their places, may settle themselves as they will; you have got the kernel, the thing that it was meant to bring you. Many an erudite scholar that has studied the Bible all his life has missed the purpose for which it was given; and many a poor old woman in her garret has found it. It is not meant to be wrangled over, it is not meant to be read as an interesting product of the religious consciousness, it is not to be admired as a specimen of the literature of a nation that had a genius for religion, but it is to be taken as being God's great Word to the world, the record of the revelation that He has given us in His Son. The Eternal Word is the theme of all the written Word. Have you made the jewel which is brought us in that casket your own? Is Jesus to you the Son of the living God, believing on whom you share His life, and become sons of God by Him? Can you take on to your thankful lips that triumphant and rapturous confession of the doubting Thomas—the flag flying on the completed roof-tree of this Gospel—"My Lord and my God" [John 20:28]? If you can, you will receive the blessing which Christ then promised to all of us standing beyond the limits of that little group, "that have not seen and yet have believed" [John 20:29]—even that eternal life which flows into our dead spirits from the Christ, the Son of God, who is the Light of the world and the Life of men.

September 20

YOU NEED A REFUGE

I looked on my right hand, and beheld; but there was no man that would know
me: refuge failed me; no man cared for my soul—Psalm 142:4

There is nothing sadder than the strange power which men have of blinking the great facts of their own condition and of human life. I know few things that seem to me more tragic, and certainly none that are more contemptible, than the easy-going, superficial optimism, or the easy-going, superficial negligence, with which hosts of people altogether slur over, even if they do not deny, the plain fact that every man and woman of us stands here in this world, though compassed by many blessings, and in the enjoyment of much good, and having many delights flowing into our lives, and being warranted in laughter and mirth, still stands like an unsheltered fugitive in the open, with a ring of enemies round about that may close in upon him. Self-interest seems often to be blind, and in many, I am sure, it is blind to the plainest and largest truths with reference to themselves, their necessities, and their conditions. After all that we say about the beauty and the brightness and the joyfulness of life and the beneficence of God, we live in a very stern world. There are evils that may come, and there are some that certainly will come. Young people—thank God for it, but do not abuse it—are buoyant in hope, and take short views, and are glad, where older folk, that have learned what life is generally, have sober estimates of its possibilities, and their radiant vision has toned down into a very subdued gray. Sorrow, disappointments, broken hopes, hopes fulfilled *and* disappointed—and that is worst of all—losses, inevitable partings when the giant shrouded figure of Death forces its way in at the rose-covered portal in spite of the puny efforts of Love to keep it out, sicknesses, failures in business, grief of such a kind that I cannot touch—the slings and arrows of outrageous fortune, and all the ills that flesh is heir to—these lie waiting somewhere on the road for every one of us. Are you going to stand in the unsheltered plain, a mark for all these? Do you think you can front them in your own strength? Are you able, calmly and soberly, remembering the possibilities that lie in the black clouds over your head, to say, "Pour on! I will endure?" Nay! Verily; you need a refuge.

You carry your own worst danger buttoned up in your own waistcoats and gowns; you bear about with you in your hearts, in your passions, in your desires, a vase of combustibles amid the sparks of a volcano, so to speak. And any one of these that fill the air may drop into it, and bring about a conflagration. No man that has measured himself, the irritability of his nerves, the excitability of his passions, the weakness of his will, and its ugly trick of going over to the enemy at the very critical moment of the fight, but, if he is a wise man, will say, "I need something stronger than myself to fall back upon, I need some damp cloth or other to be laid over the magazine of combustibles in my heart: I need a refuge from myself.

THE VOICE OF CONSCIENCE

I remember God, and was troubled: I complained, and my spirit was over-
whelmed—Psalm 77:3

You carry—no matter whence it came, or how it was developed; that is of no consequence, you have got it you carry a conscience, that is not altogether silent in any
man, I suppose and that certainly is not altogether dead in you. Its awful voice speaks
many a time in the silence of the night, and in the depths of your own heart, and tells
you that there are evil things in your past and a page black in your biography which you
can do nothing to cancel or to erase the stains from or to tear out. "What I have written
I have written" [John 19:22]. And so long as memory holds her place, and conscience is
not shattered altogether, there needs no other hell to make the punishment of the evildoer. You need a refuge from the stings of the true indictments of your own consciences.

Your conscience is a prophet. It is not, nowadays, fashionable to preach about the
Day of Judgment—more's the pity, I think. We say that every one of us shall give an
account of ourselves to God. Have you ever tried to believe that about yourself, and to
realize what it means? Think that all, down to the oozy depths that we are ashamed
to look at ourselves, shall be spread out before the "pure eyes and perfect judgment of the
all-judging" God. Oh! Brother, you will need a refuge, "that we may have boldness in the
Day of Judgment" [1 John 4:17]. These things that I have been speaking about, external
ills, ungoverned self, the accusations of conscience, which is the voice of God, and that
future to which we are all driving as fast as we can—these things are *truths;* and, being
truths, they should enter in, as operative facts, into your lives. My question is, Have
they done so?

You need a refuge—have you ever calmly contemplated the necessity? Oh! Do not
let that dogged ignorance of the facts bewitch you any longer. Do not let the inconse-
quent levity that cannot see an inch beyond its nose hide from you the realities of our
own condition. People in the prisons, during the September massacres of the French
Revolution, although the wagons were coming for some of them the next morning, and
the guillotine was waiting for them—used to amuse themselves as if they were free, and
entertained themselves with a ghastly mockery of joy. That is something like what some
of us do. One has seen a mule going down in Alpine pass, ambling quite comfortably
along, with one foot over a precipice, and a thousand feet to fall if it slips. That is how
some of us travel along the road. Sheep will nibble the grass, stretching their stupid
necks a little bit further to get an especially succulent tuft on the edge of the cliffs, with
eight hundred feet and a crawling sea at the bottom of it to receive them if they stumble. Do not be like that. "Be ye not as the horses or the mules that have no understanding," but look the facts in the face, and do not be content till you have acted as they
prescribe.

THE REFUGE THAT YOU NEED

Thou hast been a strength to the poor, a strength to the needy in his distress, a refuge from the storm, a shadow from the heat—Is. 25:4

The writer of the Epistle to the Hebrews describes the Christian's Refuge as "the hope set before us" [6:18]. Now! By "hope" there, he obviously means, not the emotion, but the Object upon which it is fixed. For it is something "set before" him—that is to say, external to him, and on which, when it *is* set before him, he can lay an appropriating hand, so that by the hope here is meant the thing hoped for. That, of course, is a very common usage, in which we transfer the name of a feeling to the thing that excites it. So here it is the thing that Christians have laid hold of which is called "the hope set before us."

That thing set before men as the object of hope is the great and faithful promise of God, confirmed by His oath long ago to the ancient patriarchs, the promise of Divine blessings and of a future inheritance. And, says the solid substance to grasp and cling to that Abraham of old had. For God said to him, "Blessing, I will bless thee" [Heb. 6:14], and He says it to us; and that is a "refuge." God said to him, "Thou shalt have a land for an inheritance" [Num. 26:54], and He says it to us; and that is a Refuge. The presence of God, and the promise of a blessed inheritance, are the elements of the hope of which the writer is speaking. Then, in his rapid way, he crowds figure upon figure, and not content with two, the asylum and the strong stay, he adds a third, and likens this hope to the anchor of the soul, giving steadfastness and fixity to the man who clings, being in itself "sure" so that it will not break, and "steadfast" so that it will not drag. He goes on to say that this object of hope enters "into that within the veil" [Heb. 6:19]. But notice that in the very next verse he speaks of some one else that entered within the veil—namely, Jesus Christ. So, as in a dissolving view, you have, first, the figure of Hope, as the poets have painted her, calm and radiant and smiling; and then that form melts away, and there stands instead of the abstraction Hope, the Person Jesus Christ. Which, being translated into plain words, is just this, the Refuge is Christ. Jesus Christ is our Hope—and Refuge, because He is our Priest. Ah, dear brother, all other enemies and ills are tolerable, and a man may make shift to bear them all without God, though he will bear them very imperfectly; but the deepest need of all, the most threatening enemy of all, can only be dealt with and overcome by the gospel which proclaims the Priest whose death is the abolition of Death, whose sacrifice is the removal of sin.

How utterly different all the inevitable ills and sorrows of this mortal life become when we lay hold on Him, and find shelter there! "A man shall be as a hiding place from the wind and a covert from the tempest, as rivers of water in a dry place, as the shadow of a great rock in a weary land" [Is. 32:2]. We can bear sickness and sorrows and disappointments and failures and partings and all griefs, and the arrow-heads are blunted, or, at all events, the poison is wiped off the barbs when we have Christ for our Refuge and our Friend.

FLEEING AND CLINGING

We . . . who have fled for refuge to lay hold of the hope set before us—Heb. 6:8

The writer blends two vivid metaphors here, the one of a fugitive unsheltered in the open, surrounded by foes; the other of a man grasping some strong stay. Look at the two pictures. "Fled for refuge." The scene brought before us is that of a man flying for his life, with the pursuer clattering at his heels, and his lance-point within a yard of the fugitive's back. Grass will not grow under that man's feet; he will not stop to look at the flower by the road. The wealth of South Africa, if it were spread before him, would not check his headlong flight. It is a race for life. If he gets to the open gate he is safe. If he is overtaken before he reaches it, he is a dead man. The moment he gets within the portal the majesty of law compasses him about, and delivers him from the wild justice of revenge. "By-and-bye" kills its tens of thousands. For one man that says, "I am not a Christian, and, what is more, I never intend to be," there are a dozen that say, "Tomorrow! Tomorrow!" "Let me sow my wild oats as a young man; let me alone for a little while. I am busy at present; when I have a convenient season I will send for thee." What would have become of the man-slayer if he had curled himself up in his cloak, and laid down beside his victim, and said, "I am too tired to run for it"? He would have been dead before morning. A rabbi's scholar, as the Jewish traditions tells us, once said to him, "Master! When shall I repent?" "The day before you die," said the Rabbi. The scholar said, "I may die today." Then said the Rabbi, "Repent today." "Choose you this day" [Josh. 24:15] whether you will stand unsheltered out there, exposed to the pelting hustling of the pitiless storm, or will flee to the Refuge and be saved.

Look at the other picture: "to lay hold of the hope." Perhaps the allusion is to the old institution of Sanctuary, which perhaps existed in Israel, and at any rate was well known in ancient times. When a man grasped the horns of the altar he was safe. If so, the two metaphors may really blend into one: the flight first, and then the clutching to that which, so long as the twining fingers could encompass it, would permit no foe to strike the fugitive. This metaphor speaks of the fixity of the hold with which we should grasp Jesus Christ by our faith. The shipwrecked sailor up in the rigging, with the wild sea around him, and the vessel thumping upon the sand, will hold on, with frozen fingers, for hours, to the shrouds, knowing that if he slips his grasp the next hungry wave will sweep him away and devour him. And so you should cling to Jesus Christ with the consciousness of danger and helplessness, with the tight grasp of despair, with the tight grasp of certain hope.

I remember reading of an inundation in India, when a dam, away up in a mountain gorge, burst at midnight. Mounted messengers were sent down the glen to gallop as hard as they could and rouse the sleeping villagers. Those who rose and fled in an instant were in time to reach the high ground, as they saw the tawny flood coming swirling down the gorge, laden with the wrecks of happy homes and many a corpse. Those who hesitated and dawdled were swept away by it.

CHRIST'S COMING TO THE WORLD—(PART ONE)

And the Spirit and the bride say, Come. And let him that heareth, say, Come—
Rev. 22:17

The two halves of this verse do not refer to the same persons of the same "coming." The first portion is an invocation or a prayer; the second portion is an invitation or an offer. The one is addressed to Christ, the other to men. The commentary upon the former is the last words of the Book, where we find the seer answering the promise of his master: "Surely, I come quickly!" with the sigh of longing: "Even so, Come, Lord Jesus" [Rev. 22:20]. And in precisely a similar fashion the bride here, longing for the presence of the bridegroom, answers His promise: "Surely, I come quickly!" which occurs a verse or two before, with the petition which all who hear it are bidden to swell till it rolls in a great wave of supplication to His feet.

And then with that coming, another "coming" is connected. The one is the coming of Christ to the world at last; the other is the coming of men to Christ now. The double office of the Church is represented here, the voice that rose in petition to Heaven has to sound upon earth in proclamation. And the double relation of Christ to His Church is implied here. He is absent, therefore He is prayed to come; but He is in such a fashion present as that any who will can come to Him. He will come again; but ere He does, and because He will, men are invited to approach Him now, and if we do, to our hearts, too, His appearing will be a joy and not a terror. And the sweetness of His presence with us amid the shows of time will be perfected by the glories of our presence with Him when He comes at last.

Christ has come, Christ will come. These are the two great facts from which, as from two golden hooks, the whole chain of human history hangs in a mighty curve. The one fills all the past, the other should brighten all the future. Memory should feed upon the one, hope should leap up to grasp the other. And so closely are these two connected as that the former is incomplete and ineffectual without the latter. He *has* come, therefore He *will* come.

And that coming is to be in bodily form, even as the angels said: "This same Jesus . . . shall so come *in like manner* as ye have seen him go" [Acts 1:11]. What was the likeness? The differences are enormous: He came in weakness; He will come in power. He came in humiliation; He will come in glory. He came to redeem; He will come to judge. But the similarity is this, that as in true bodily form He truly entered into human conditions, and walked among men upon earth, having a local habitation and a name among us, so He comes again in no metaphor, in no ideal fashion, but in simple corporeal reality, once more manifest the visible among the children of earth.

He came in obscurity, stealing into the world with but a handful of poor shepherds for the witnesses. He will come, "and every eye shall see him" [Rev. 1:7]. He will come in a body no less truly human, no less really corporeal, but in a body of glory, which shall fitly manifest and ray out the indwelling of Divinity. And He comes for judgment, and He comes to perfect the union between Himself and all humble hearts that love Him and trust Him.

CHRIST'S COMING TO THE WORLD—(PART TWO)

He that shall come will come, and will not tarry—Heb. 10:37

In anticipation of that ultimate coming, in bodily form, the close of earth's sorrows and the consummation of earth's history, there are many comings of Christ through the ages; and like in principle, though lesser in degree, destructions of Jerusalem, and falls of the Roman Empire by Gothic invasions, and Reformations of the Popish corrupt Church, and French Revolutions, and American Wars of Slavery, and many another secular change by which the old order changeth, yielding place to new, are what the old prophets called "Days of the Lord," the same in principle as that last great day. Christ "comes," though He is always present in human history—comes to our apprehensions in eras of rapid change, in revolutionary times when some ancient iniquity is smitten down, and some new fair form emerges from the chaos. The electricity is long in gathering during the fervid summer heat, in the slow moving and changing clouds; but when it is gathered, there comes the flash. The snow is long in collecting on the precipitous face of the Alp; but when the weight has become sufficient, down it rushes, the white death of the avalanche. For fifty-nine (silent) minutes and fifty-nine (silent) seconds the hand moves around the dial, and at the sixtieth it strikes. So, at long intervals in history of nations, a crash comes, and men say: "Behold the Lord! He cometh to judge the world" [see Ps. 98:9].

Surely, surely, it needs no words to enforce the thought that all who love Him and all who love truth and righteousness, which are His, and all who desire that the world's sorrows should be alleviated and the world's evils should be chastised and smitten, must lift up the old, old cry: "Even so, Come, Lord Jesus" [Rev. 2:20]. The bride must long for the coming of the bridegroom. Burdened hearts that writhe and are afflicted with the sorrows of humanity, and hearts that plod wearily along some lonely path in darkness and in pain—these all lift up their cry to Him, the Avenger, the Lover, the Judge, the Purifier, that He would come with that rod of His mouth which slays the wicked, and that fiery indignation which burns up only the evil that is killing mankind.

The earnest belief in, and the longing for the coming of, Jesus Christ has been too much surrendered to one school of interpreters in unfulfilled prophecy, who have no greater claim to possess it than the rest of us. It belongs, or ought to belong, to us all. All the signs of the times, intellectual and social; the rottenness of much of our life; the abounding luxury; the hideous vice that flaunts unblamed and unabashed before us all; the unsettlement of option in which it is unbelief that seems to be "removing the mountains" that all men thought stood fast and firm forever—all these things cry out to Him whose ear is not deaf even if our voice does not join in the cry, and invite Him to come.

Let you heart be so near to Him, your soul so full of His love and the longing for some of His presence, that you, too, may join in that universal prayer which the genius of the great Puritan has put into the music of these words: "Come forth out of Thy royal pavilion, oh, Thou Prince of all the kings of the earth. Put on the visible robes of Thine imperial majesty; take unto Thee the unlimited scepter which Thy heavenly Father hath bequeathed Thee; for now the voice of Thy Bride calls Thee, and all creatures sigh to be renewed."

THE WONDERFUL INVITATION

And let him that is athirst, come: And whosoever will, let him take the water of
life freely—Rev. 22:17

In these words there are echoes of precious older words, "Ho, every one that thirsteth, come ye to the waters; and he that hath no money, come, let him buy . . . yea, come, buy wine and milk without money and without price" [Is. 55:1]. And again, "if any man thirst, let him come unto me, and drink" [John 7:37]. On both of these more ancient sayings, the saying of the evangelical prophet and the saying of our Lord Himself, these great words seem to be founded.

What is it to come? Christ said, standing in the Temple courts, "If any man thirst, let him come unto Me, and drink." Christ is now absent, but still His bodily presence did not make coming to Him any the easier when He was here. Many of those that touched His garments, and clasped His hands, and looked into His eyes were an infinite distance from Him.

What is it to come? Listen to His own explanation: "He that cometh unto me shall never hunger, and he that believeth on me shall never thirst" [John 6:35]. Then "coming" and "taking" and "drinking" are all but various forms of representing the one act of believing in Him. We come to Him when we trust Him. We are separated from Him by all the distance between earth and heaven, corporeally. He is near every one of us in spirit, and He is ready to come so much nearer that He will dwell in our hearts and break down all the barriers between us, if we will only draw near to Him. My friend, let no vague metaphor blind you to the simple requirement which is here. To "come to Christ" is nothing more than to trust Him. Lean your weight upon Him, and your soul leaps over the gulfs in which stars and systems move, and touches the Son of man at the right hand of God. Faith has a long arm; it can grasp "the High Priest that is passed *into* the heavens" [Heb. 4:14], and is exalted far above them all. To come to Christ is only as a sinful man laden with infirmities and stooping beneath many a burden of sin and sorrow and sore weakness; to lean my sinful self upon Him, and so to be joined to the Lord. To come to Christ is faith.

Who is it that are asked to come? "He that thirsteth" and "he that willeth." The one phrase expresses the universal condition, the other only the limitation necessary in the very nature of things. "He that thirsteth." Who does not? The desires of every soul are deep and ravenous and fierce. Your heart is parched for love; your mind, whether you know it or not, is restless and thirsty for truth that you can cleave to in all circumstances. Your will longs for a loving authority that shall subdue and tame it. Your conscience is calling out for cleaning, for pacifying, for purity. Your whole being is one great want and emptiness. "My soul thirsteth for God, for the living God" [Ps. 42:2]; it is only He that can slake the thirst, that can satisfy the hunger. You have tried other things, plenty of them; and has not your experience been that all other sources of satisfaction or delight have done for you what the sea water does to the half-mad shipwrecked sailor that will drink it? They make men thirstier and drive them madder. Every man may come; for we are all perishing by the side of muddy and waterless springs, from which we have madly sought to slake an immortal thirst.

September 27

"WHOSOEVER WILL"

Ho, every one that thirsteth, come ye to the waters, and he that hath no money;
come ye, buy, and eat; yea, come, buy wine and milk without money and
without price—Is. 55:1

"Whosoever will." A wish is enough, but a wish is indispensable. How strange, and yet how common, it is that the thirsty man is not the willing man! There are people miserable for want of Christ, and half believing that this is what makes them miserable, and who yet have not the will to take Him for their own. There is no barrier but the barrier that you yourself build in an averted will or in indifference.

These two words gather the whole of humanity, and beneath their ample folds everyone of us may shelter him or herself. "Let him that is athirst come" [Rev. 22:17]. Lord! My lips are cracking and black with the parched misery. "Whosoever will." My friend, do you say, "Whosoever will not, *I* will, and do, now."

Further, what is offered? "The water of life" [Rev. 21:6]. Something that shall satisfy all the immortal thirst of the soul. And what is that? Not a thing, but a Person. The water of life, in its deepest interpretation, is Christ Himself; even as He said, "If any man thirst, let him come to *me*, and drink" [John 7:37]. And if only you will go and trust yourself to Him, His Spirit shall pass into your spirit, and with the communication of His Spirit there will be given an inward fountain that will spring up into life everlasting. It were a poor thing if the offer that Christ makes were only of some external gift that should satisfy our aspirations and still our desires. What He promises and gives is an inward spring that shall well up within us, and shall go with us wherever we go. "He that believeth on me, out of his belly shall flow rivers of living water" [John 7:38, 39]. This spake "He of the Spirit." The promise to us all is of the gift of His own precious Self, to dwell in our hearts; to make us blessed, peaceful, calm; to fill our desires, to gladden our whole nature, to dominate our wills, to cleanse our consciences, to inform our understandings, and flood our hearts with the peaceful deluge of His own love and perfect life. "If any man thirst, let him come to Me, and drink."

And what are the conditions? "Let him take the water of life for nothing," as the word might have been rendered, "For nothing." He says to us, "I will not sell it to you, I will give it to you." And too many of us say to Him, "We had rather buy it, or at any rate pay something towards it." No effort, no righteousness, no sacrifice, no anything is wanted: "Without money and without price." You have only got to give up yourself. "Sell all that thou hast" [Luke 18:22]. Self is "all that thou hast." Sell. Part with it. Buy—by the surrender of all confidence in anything that you can do or are. Come, not too proud to owe your salvation wholly to undeserved, unpurchased mercy.

> Nothing in my hand I bring
> Simply to Thy cross I cling.

Take the water of life "freely."

CHRIST'S COMING AND MEN'S COMING

I came that they might have life, and that they might have it more abundantly—
John 10:10

If any man thirst, let him come unto me, and drink—John 7:37

There is a twofold connection between the two comings that I would point out to you, and leave to your thoughts. Christ does not yet come in order that men may come to Him. There are many reasons beyond our reach and ken why for so long a time the Lord of the servants is absent from His household: but among these reasons certainly not the least is, that all the world may hear that great pleading voice of invitation, and may come to Him, their Savior and their Judge. Even as He Himself said, in words the whole sweep and meaning of which we do not yet understand, "This gospel of the kingdom must first be preached in all the world . . . and then shall the end come" [Matt. 24:14]. So that He delays His drawing near, in His glad news may flash, and to every spirit the invitation may come. Christ tarries that *you* may hear, and repent, and come to Him. That is the first phase of the connection between these two things.

The other is—because Christ will come to the world, therefore let us come to Him now. Joyful as the spring after the winter, and as the sunshine after the darkness, so that coming of His ought to be to all; and though it be the object of desire to all hearts that love Him, and the healing for the miseries and sorrows of the world, do not forget it has a very solemn and very terrible side. He comes, when He does come, to judge you and me and the rest of our brethren. He comes, not as of old, in lowliness, to heal and to succor and to save, but He comes to heal and to succor and to save all them that love His appearing, and them only, and He comes to judge all men whether they love His appearing or no. "Every eye shall see him." [Rev. 1:7]. "To what end," said one of the old prophets, "is the day of the Lord unto you? The day of the Lord is darkness and not light" [Amos 5:18]. Let that certain coming of the Lord be to you what it ought to be—a mighty motive for your coming to Him. Make your choice whether your heart shall leap up with gladness when the joyful cry is heard: "Behold! the bridegroom cometh" [Matt. 25:6]; or whether you will call upon the rocks and the hills to fall upon you and cover you from His face [Rev. 6:16]. Come to Him now, trust Him, "take the water of life freely" [Rev. 22:17], and thus "ye shall have a song as in the night, when a holy solemnity is kept" [Is. 30:29], and boldness of heart, and not be ashamed before Him at His coming.

THE SOUL LONGING FOR GOD

O God, thou art my God; early will I seek thee: my soul thirsteth for thee, my flesh longeth for thee in a dry and thirsty land, where no water is—Psalm 63:1

In that arid tract which stretches along the western shore of the Dead Sea, and thence northward, David was twice during his adventurous life: once during the Sauline persecution, once during Absalom's revolt. It cannot be the former of these which is referred to here, because the Psalmist was not then a king; it must therefore be the latter.

That was the darkest hour of his life. His favorite and good-for-nothing son was seeking to grasp his scepter; his familiar friends in whom he trusted had lifted up the heel against him. He knew that his own sin had come back to roost with him; and so, with bleeding heart, with agonized conscience, with crushed spirit, he bowed himself, and meekly and penitently accepted the chastisement. Therefore it was sweetened to him; and this psalm, with its passion of love and mystic rapture, is a monument for us of how his sorrows had brought him to a closer union with God, as our sorrow may do for us; like some treasure washed to our feet by a stormy sea.

This longing is not that of a man who has no possession; rather is it the desire of a heart which is already in union for a closer union; rather is it the tightening of the grasp with which the man already holds his Father in Heaven. All begins with the utterance of a personal appropriating faith. "O God, Thou art my God!" That is the beginning of all personal religion—when I am conscious of a personal relation with God; when I feel that He and I possess each other by a mutual love; when I put out my hand, and humbly, but confidently, claim my individual portion in the world-wide power and love. A Christian is he who says, "He loved *me*, and gave Himself for *me*." We must individualize, and appropriate as our very own, the promises and the grace that belong to the whole world. "O God, Thou art *my* God?"

Notice the picturesque, poetic beauty of taking his surroundings as the emblem of his feelings. Nature seems to reflect his mood. He looks out on the stony, monotonous, burned-up, barren country about him; at the cracks in the soil gaping for the rain which comes not; and he sees the emblem of a heart yearning after God and not possessing Him. He and his men have been toiling, wearied, across the "burning sand," looking in all the torrent-beds for some drop of water to cool their parched throats, and finding none. And that seems to him like the search of a soul after a far-off God: "My soul thirsteth for Thee . . . in a dry and thirsty land, where no water is."

Notice, also, the intensity of the desire. Think of the picture that rises from these graphic words. Here is the caravan toiling through the desert: men's lips black with thirst; their parched tongues lolling from their mouths; a film comes over their glazing eyes, their steps totter, their heads throb, and far away yonder there is a stunted tree which tells of water near it. How they plunge their lips into the black mud when they come to it, and with what a fierce passion they satisfy their cravings!

Can anybody say that this is an honest description of the ordinary experience of ordinary Christians! Is that, or anything like it, true about you! What sort of Christians are we if it is not?

THE HABITUAL DESIRE OF THE SOUL

To see thy power and thy glory, so as I have seen thee in the sanctuary.—
Psalm 63:2

When was it that David thus longed for God? In the midst of his sorrow. Even then the thing that he wanted most was not restoration to Jerusalem, or the defeat of his enemies, but union with God. Oh! That is a test of faith, one which very little of our faith could stand, that even when we are ringed about by calamities that seem to crush us, what we long for most is not the removal of the sorrow, but the presence of our Father. Good men are generally driven away from Him. What does your sorrow do for you, friend? Does it make you writhe in impatience? Does it make you murmur sullenly against His imposition of it? Or does it make you feel that now in the stress and agony there is nothing that you can grasp and hold to but Him, and Him alone? And so in the hour of darkness and need is my prayer, in its deepest meaning, not, "Take away Thy heavy hand from me," but, "Give me more of Thyself, that Thy hand may thereby be lightened?"

I notice that this longing, though it be stuck out by sorrow, is not forced upon him for the first time by sorrow. The second verse of the psalm might be more accurately rendered: "So have I gazed upon Thee in the sanctuary, to see Thy power and Thy glory." That is to say, as in the sorrows and in the wilderness he is conscious of this desire after God, so amid the sanctities of the Tabernacle and the joyful services and sacrifices of its ritual worship, does he remember that he looked through the forms to Him that shone in them, and in them beheld His power and His glory. So the longing that springs in his heart is an old longing. He remembers that his days of sorrow are not the first days in which He has been driven to say, "Come Thou and help me." He can remember glad, peaceful moments of communion, and these are homogeneous and of a piece with his religious contemplations in his hours of sorrow.

That life is but a poor, fragmentary one which seeks God by fits and starts; and that seeking after God is but a half-hearted and partial one which is only experienced in the moments of pain and grief. It is well to cry for Him in the wilderness, but it is not well that it should only be in the wilderness in which we cry for Him. It is well when darkness and disaster teach us our need of Him; but is not well when we require the darkness and the disaster to teach us our need.

And, on the other hand, that is but a poor, fragmentary life, and that religion is but a very incomplete and insincere one, which is more productive of raptures in the sanctuary than of seeking after God in the wilderness. There are plenty of Christian people who have a great deal more consciousness of God's presence in the idle emotions of a church or a chapel than in the strenuous efforts of daily life. Both things separately are maimed and miserable; and both must be put together—the communion in the sanctuary and the communion in the wilderness, seeking after Him in the sanctities of worship, and seeking after Him in the prose of daily life—if ever the worship of the sanctuary or the prose of daily life are to be brightened with His presence.

THE LONGING SOUL SATISFIED

Because thy lovingkindness is better than life, my lips shall praise thee.
Thus will I bless thee while I live: I will lift up my hands in thy name.
My soul shall be satisfied as with marrow and fatness—Psalm 63:3-5

Life is good mainly as the field upon which God's lovingkindness may be manifested and grasped. It is like the white sheet on which the beam of light is thrown, worth everything as the medium for the manifestation of that lustrous light. It is like a stained-glass window, only a poor bit of glass till the sunshine gleams behind it, and then it flashes up into ruby and purple and gold. Life is best when through life there filters or flashes on us the brightness of the lovingkindness of the Lord.

And all real religion includes in it a calm, deliberate fixed preference of God to life itself. Does your religion do that? Can you say, "It were wise and it were blessed to die, to get more of God into my soul"? If not, our longing, which is the very language of the Spirit in our hearts, has to be intensified much before it reaches its fitting height.

And then, still further, this longing is accompanied with a firm resolve of continuance: "Thus will I bless Thee while I live." "Thus"—as I am doing now in the midst of my longing—"I will lift up my hands in Thy name." "My soul shall be satisfied as with marrow and fatness."

Notice how very beautiful that immediate turn in the Psalmist's feelings is. The fruition of God is contemporaneous with the desire after God. The one moment, "my soul thirsteth"; the next moment, "My soul is satisfied." As in the wilderness when the rain comes down, and in a couple of days what was baked earth is flowery meadow, and all the torrent-beds where the white stones glistened ghastly in the heat are foaming with rushing water and fringed with budding willows—so in the instant in which a heart turns with true desire to God, in that instant does God draw near to it. The Arctic spring comes with one stride; today snow, tomorrow flowers. There is no time needed to work this telegraph; while we speak He hears; before we call He answers. We have to wait for many of His gifts, never for Himself. We have to wait sometimes when by our own faults we postpone the coming of the blessings that we have asked. If we are thinking more about Absalom and Ahithophel than about God, more about our sorrows and our troubles than about Himself; if we are busy with other things; if having asked we do not look up and expect; if we shut the doors of our hearts as soon as our prayer is offered, or languidly stroll away from the place of prayer before the blessing has fluttered down upon our souls—of course we do not get it. But God is always waiting to bestow; and all that we need to do is to open the sluices, and the great ocean flows in, or as much of it as our hearts can hold. "My soul thirsteth" is the experience of the one moment, and ere the clock has ticked again "my soul shall be satisfied."

THE FULLNESS OF GOD'S SUPPLY

They shall be abundantly satisfied with the fatness of thy house; and thou shalt make them drink of the river of thy pleasures—Psalm 36:8

The soul that possesses God is fed full. The emblem here, of course, is of a joyful feast, possibly of a sacrificial one; but the fact is that whoever has a living hold of God, and a little bit of God lovingly embedded in his heart, has got as much as he wants; absolute and all-sufficient good. If I may say so, every hollow in my nature answers to a protuberance in His; and when you put the two together, the little heart is filled by the great heart that has come to it. We are at rest when we have God, and to long for Him is to insure the possession of an absolute and all-sufficient good.

The satisfied soul breaks into the music of praise. "My mouth shall praise thee with joyful lips when I remember thee upon my bed, and meditate on thee in the night watches" [Ps. 63:5, 6]. There is a reference, no doubt, there, to the little camp in the wilderness, where David and his men, protected by no one except God, laid themselves down to sleep beneath the Syrian sky with all its stars, and where the leader, no doubt, often awoke in the night, with pricked-up ears listening for the sound of the approaching enemy. And even then into his heart there steals the thought of his great Protector; and as he says in another of the Psalms dating from this period, "I will lay me down in peace and sleep, for thou makest me to dwell, in safety." The heart that feeds upon God is secure, and breaks into songs in the night, and music of praise. That feast always has minstrels at it. The spontaneous utterance of a heart feeding on God is thankfulness and music of praise, which is as natural as smiles when we are glad, or as tears when we mourn.

And then, this satisfaction leads on to an absolute security. "Because thou hast been my help, therefore in the shadow of thy wings will I rejoice" [Ps. 63:7]. Such a past and such a present can only have one kind of future as their consequence—a future in which the seeking soul nestling itself beneath the great wings outstretched shall crowd close to the Father's heart, and be guarded by His love. If we hold fellowship with Him, He protects us. As another psalm says, using a similar metaphor: "He that dwelleth in the secret place of the most High shall abide under the shadow of the Almighty" [Ps. 91:1]. Communion with God means protection by God.

The part of the seeking soul is the certain pledge of its future. The uncertainties of the dim tomorrow, in so far as earth is concerned, are so many that we can never say, "Tomorrow shall be as this day." And in regard of all other sources of blessing, the dearest and the purest, we have all to feel, with sinking, sickening hearts, that the longer we have had them the nearer comes the day of their certain loss. But about Him we can say, "Because thou *hast* been my help, therefore in the shadow of thy wings *will* I rejoice." And in union with Him we can look out over all the dim sea that stretches before us; and though we know not what storms may vex its surface, or wither its currents may carry us, we can say, "Thou wilt be with Me, and in Thee I shall have peace."

THE SATISFIED SOUL
STILL SEEKING

My soul followeth hard after thee: thy right hand upholdeth me—Psalm 63:8

The word translated *followeth* here literally means *to cleave* or *to cling*. And there is a beautiful double idea of a twofold relationship expressed in that somewhat incongruous form of speech "cleave after Thee," the former word giving the idea of union and possession, the latter suggesting the other idea of search and pursuit: so that the two main currents of thought in the psalm are repeated in that little phrase; and we are back again—though with a wonderful difference—to the ground tone of the first section. There the soul "thirsteth"; here "the soul cleaveth after"—both expressive of pursuit, but the latter, as consequent upon the satisfaction which followed upon the thirst, speaks of a more profound possession and of a less sense of want.

"My soul cleaveth after God." That is to say, inasmuch as He is infinite, and this nature of mine is incapable of indefinite expansion, each new possession of Him which follows upon an enlarged desire will open the elastic walls of my heart so that they shall enclose a wider space and be capable of holding more of God, and therefore I shall possess more. Desire expands the heart; possession expands the heart. More of God comes when we can hold more of Him, and the end of all fruition is the renewed desire after further fruition.

This world's gifts cloy and never satisfy; God satisfies and never cloys. And we have, and we shall have, if we are His children, the double delight of a continual fruition and a continued desire. So we shall ascend, if I may say so, in ever higher and higher spirals, which will rise further and draw in more closely towards the unreached and unattainable Throne of the Blessed Himself: "My soul thirsteth"; "my soul is satisfied"; "my satisfied soul still longs and follows."

And then there is also very beautifully here the cooperation and reciprocal action of the seeking soul and of the sustaining God. "My soul followeth hard after thee; thy right hand upholdeth me." We hold and we are held. We hold because we are held, and we are held while we hold. We follow, and yet He is with us; we long, and yet we possess; we pursue, and yet in the very act of pursuit we are upheld by His hand. We shall not follow unless He holds us up. He will not hold us up unless we follow. All controversies of grace and freewill are reconciled and lulled to sleep in these great words: "My soul followeth hard after thee; thy right hand upholdeth me."

THE CERTAINTY OF VICTORY

But those that seek my soul, to destroy it, shall go into the lower parts of the earth.
They shall fall by the sword: they shall be a portion for foxes. But the king shall
rejoice in God; every one that sweareth by him shall glory: but the mouth of them
that speak lies shall be stopped—Psalm 63:9-11

This last portion of the psalm describes one consequence of pressing after God. The soul thus cleaving and following is gifted with prophetic certainty. "Those that seek my soul to destroy it are destined for destruction" (so is the probable rendering); they "shall go into the lower parts of the earth"—swallowed up like Korah and his rebellious company. "They shall each be given up to the power of the sword" (as the words might be rendered); "they shall be a portion for foxes" (or *jackals*, as the word means). Their unburied bodies shall lie in the wilderness, and the jackals shall tear and devour. David regarded his enemies as God's enemies. David's point of view permitted him to exult with a stern but not unrighteous joy in their destruction. But these words are not prayer nor imprecation, but prophecy and the insight of a soul conscious of union with God, and therefore assured that everything which stands in the way of its possession of the God whom it loves is destined for annihilation.

And, disengaging the words from the mere husk and shell of Old Testament experience, all of us, if we cleave to God, may have this confidence, that nothing can hinder our fellowship with God, and that whatsoever stands in the way of our closer union with Him shall be swept out of the way. David's certainty of the destruction of his foes is the same triumphant assurance, on a lower spiritual level, as Paul's trumpet blast of victory: "Who shall separate us from the love of God? Shall tribulation, or distress, or persecution, or famine, or nakedness, or peril, or sword?" "Nay, in all these things"—and over all these things—"we are more than conquerors through Him that loved us" [Rom. 8:35, 37].

There is the other side of this prophetic certainty here. "The King shall rejoice in God; every one that sweareth by him shall glory" [Ps. 63:11]. He and his faithful followers shall realize a Divine deliverance, which shall be the subject of their praise; and the adversary's lips shall be sealed with silence, their vindication shall stick in their throat, and they shall be dumb before the judgment of Almighty God. That confidence, too, may stand as a symbol of the certainty of hope which refreshes the soul which seeks sorrow and fear. We, too, may find in our present union with God a prophecy, fixed and firm as the pillars of His throne, of our future kingly dignity, and rapturous joy in Him. It is reserved not for us only, but for all whose lips confessed Him on earth and shall therefore be opened to lift up before Him triumphant praise, which shall drown the discords of opposing voices, and no more be broken by sobs or weeping.

We are all thirsty! Do you know what it is that makes you restless? Do you know who it is that you need? Listen to Him that says, "If any man thirst, let him come to me, and drink" [John 7:37]. Choose whether you will thirst with mad and aimless cravings, and perish in a dry land; or whether you will come to the Fountain of Life in Christ your Savior, and slake your thirst at God Himself.

THE PARADOX OF LOVE'S MEASURE

Of his fullness have we all received, and grace for grace—John 1:16

It is the immeasurable measure, the boundless bounds and dimensions of the love of Christ, which fires the Apostle's thoughts when writing to the Ephesian Church (Eph. 3:17–19). Of course he had no separate idea in his mind attaching to each of these measures of magnitude, but he gathered them all together simply to express the one thought of the greatness of Christ's love.

Depth and height are the same dimension measured from opposite ends. The one begins at the top and goes down, the other begins at the bottom and goes up, but the surface is the same in either case. So we have the three dimensions of a solid here—breadth, length, and depth.

And I suppose that I may venture to use these expressions with a somewhat different purpose from that for which the Apostle employs them; and to see in each of them a separate and blessed aspect of the love of God in Jesus Christ our Lord.

And that love which thus towers above us, and gleams the summit and the apex of the universe, like the shining cross on the top of some lofty cathedral spire, does not gleam there above us inaccessible, nor lie before us like some pathless precipice, up which nothing that has not wings can ever hope to rise; but the height of the love of Christ is a hospitable height, which can be scaled by us. Nay, rather, that heaven of love, which is higher than our thoughts, bends down, as by a kind of optical delusion the physical heaven seems to do, towards each of us, only with this blessed difference, that in the natural world the place where heaven touches earth is always the furthest point of distance from us; and in the spiritual world, the place where heaven stoops to me is always right over my head, and the nearest possible point to me. He has come to lift us to Himself. And this is the height of His love, that it bears us up, if we will, up and up to sit upon that throne where He Himself is enthroned.

So around us all, as some sunny tropical sea may embosom in its violent waves a multitude of luxuriant and happy islets, so all of us, islanded on our little individual lives, lie in that great ocean of love, all the dimensions of which are immeasurable, and which stretches above, beneath, around, shoreless, tideless, bottomless, endless.

But remember! This ocean of love you can shut out of your lives. It is possible to plunge a jar into the mid-Atlantic, further than soundings have ever descended, and to bring it up on deck as dry inside as if it had been lying on an oven. It is possible for us to live and move and have our being in that sea of love, and never to have got one drop of its richest gifts into our hearts or our lives. Open your heart for Him to come in by humble faith in His great sacrifice for you. For if Christ dwell in your heart by faith, then, and only then, will experience be your guide; and you will be able to comprehend the boundless greatness, the endless duration, the absolute perfection, and to know the love of Christ which passeth knowledge.

THE BREADTH OF THE LOVE OF CHRIST

There the glorious Lord will be unto us a place of broad rivers and streams—
Isaiah 33:21

The love of God in Christ Jesus is as broad as humanity. As all the stars lie in the firmament, so all creatures rest in the heaven of His love. Mankind has many common characteristics. We all suffer, we all sin, we all hunger, we all aspire; and, we all occupy precisely the same relation to the love, the Divine love, which lies in Jesus Christ. There are no stepchildren in His great family, and none of them receive a more grudging or less ample share of His love and goodness than any other. Broad as the race, and curtaining it over as some great tent may enclose on a festal day a whole tribe, the breadth of Christ's love is the breadth of humanity. And it is universal because it is Divine. No human heart can be stretched so as to comprehend the whole of the members of mankind, and no human heart can be so emptied of self as to be capable of this absolute universality and impartiality of affection. But the intellectual difficulties which stand in the way of the width of our human affection, and the moral difficulties which stand still more frowningly and forbiddingly in the way, all disappear before that love of Christ's which is close and tender, and clinging with all the tenderness and closeness and clingingness of a human and lofty and universal and passionless and perpetual, with all the height and breadth and calmness and eternity of a Divine, heart.

And this broad love, broad as humanity, is not shallow because it is broad. Our human affections are too often like the estuary of some great stream which runs deep and mighty as long as it is held within narrow banks, but as soon as it widens becomes slow and powerless and shallow. The intensity of human affection varies inversely as its extension. A universal philanthropy is a passionless sentiment. But Christ's love is deep, though it be wide, and suffers no diminution because it is shared among a multitude. It is like the great feast that He Himself spread, five thousand men, women, and children, all seated at a table, "and they did all eat and were filled" [Matt. 14:20].

The whole love is the property of each recipient of it. It is not as it is with us, who give a part of our heart to this one and to that one, and share the treasure of our affections among a multitude. All this gift belongs to every one, just as all the sunshine comes to every eye, and as every beholder sees the moon path across the dark waters, stretching from the place where he stands to the center of light.

There are two ways of arguing about the love of Christ, both of them valid, and both of them needing to be employed by us. We have a right to say, "He loves all, therefore He loves me." And we have a right to say, "He loves me, therefore He loves all." For surely the love that has stooped to me can never pass by any human soul. What is the breadth of the love of Christ? It is broad as mankind, it is narrow as myself.

THE LENGTH OF CHRIST'S LOVE

The mercy of the Lord is from everlasting to everlasting upon them that fear him—Psalm 103:17

What is the length of the love of Christ? If we are to think of Him only as a man, however exalted and however perfect, you and I have nothing in the world to do with His love. When He was here on earth it may have been sent down the generations in some vague, pale way, as the shadowy ghost of love may rise in the heart of a great statesman or philanthropist for generations yet unborn, which he dimly sees will be affected by his sacrifice and service. But we do not call that love. Such a poor, pale, shadowy thing has no right to the warm, throbbing name; has no right to demand from us any answering thrill of affection; and unless you think of Jesus Christ as something more and other than the purest and the loftiest benevolence that ever dwelt in human form, I know of no intelligible sense in which the length of His love can be stretched to touch you. And if we content ourselves with that altogether inadequate and lame conception of Him and of His nature, of course there is no present bond between any man upon earth and Him, and it is absurd to talk about His present love as extending in any way to me. But we have to believe, rising to the full height of the Christian conception of the nature and person of Christ, that when He was here on earth the Divine that dwelt in Him so informed and inspired the human as that the love of His man's heart was able to grasp the whole, and to separate the individuals that should make up the race till the end of time; so as that you and I, looking back over all the centuries, and asking ourselves what is the length of the love of Christ, can say, "It stretches over all the years, and it reached then as it reaches now to touch me, upon whom the ends of the earth have come."

That thought of eternal beings, when we refer it to God, towers above us and repels us; and when we turn it to ourselves, and think of our own life as unending, there comes a strangeness and an awe that is almost shrinking over the thoughtful spirit. But when we transmute it into the thought of a love whose length is unending, then, over all the shoreless, misty, melancholy sea of eternity, there gleams a light, and every wavelet flashes up into glory. There is another measure of the length of the love of Christ. "Lord! How oft shall my brother sin against me, and I forgive him?" "I say not unto thee Until seven times, but Until seventy times seven" [Matt. 18:21, 22]. So said the Christ, multiplying perfection into itself twice—two sevens and a ten—in order to express the idea of boundlessness. And the law that He laid down for His servant is the law that binds Himself. The pitying Christ, the eternal Lover of all wandering souls, looks down from Heaven upon every one of us; goes with us in all our wanderings; bears with us in all our sins. His pleadings sound on, like some stop in an organ continuously persistent through all the other notes. And around His throne are written the Divine words which have been spoken about our human love modeled after His. "Charity suffereth long, and is kind. . . . is not easily provoked, . . . beareth all things" [1 Cor. 13:4–7]. The length of the love of Christ is the length of eternity, and out-measures all human sin.

THE HEIGHT AND DEPTH OF THE LOVE OF CHRIST

O the depth of the riches both of the wisdom and the knowledge of God!—
Rom. 11:33

Depth and height are but two ways of expressing the same dimension; the one we begin at the top and measure down, the other we begin at the bottom and measure up. The top is the Throne; and the downward measure—how is it to be stated? In what terms of distance are we to express it? How far is it from the Throne of the Universe to the manger at Bethlehem and the Cross at Calvary and the sepulchre in the garden! That is the depth of the love of Christ. Howsoever far may be the distance from that loftiness of co-equal Divinity in the bosom of the Father, and radiant with glory, to the lowliness of the form of a servant, and the sorrows, limitations, rejections, pains, and final death—that is the measure of the depth of Christ's love. As if some planet were to burst from its track and plunge downward in among the mists and the narrowness of our earthly atmosphere, so we can estimate the depth of the love of Christ by saying, "he came from above, He tabernacled with us." The way to measure the depth is to begin at the Throne, and go down to the Cross and to the foul abysses of evil. The way to measure the height is to begin at the Cross and the foul abysses of evil, and to go up to the Throne. That is to say, the topmost thing in the Universe, the shining apex and summit, glittering way up there in the radiant unsetting light, is the love of God in Jesus Christ.

A well-known modern scientist has hazarded the speculation that the origin of life on this planet has been the falling upon it of the fragment of a meteor from some other system, with a speck of organic life upon it, from which all has developed. Whatever may be the case in regard of the physical life, that is absolutely true in the case of spiritual life. It all comes because this Heaven-descended Christ has come down the long staircase of Incarnation, and has brought with Him into the clouds and oppressions of our terrestrial atmosphere a germ of life which He has planted in the heart of the race, there to spread forever. That is the measure of the depth of the love of Christ. And there is another way to measure it. My sins, my helpless miseries, are deep: but they are shallow as compared with the love that goes down beneath all sin; that is deeper than all sorrow, deeper than all necessity; that shrinks from no degradation; that turns away from no squalor; that abhors no wickedness so as to avert its face from it. When a coal-pit gets blocked up by some explosion, no brave rescuing party will venture to descend into the lowest depths of the poisonous darkness until some ventilation has come there. But this loving Christ goes down, down, down into the thickest, most pestilential hand to the most abject and undermost of all the victims. How deep is the love of Christ? The deep mines of sin and of alienation are all undermined and countermined by His love. Sin is an abyss, a mystery, how deep only they know who have fought against it; but

"O Love! thou bottomless abyss,
My sins are swallowed up in Thee."

October 9

DEATH AND GROWTH

And Joseph died, and all his brethren, and all that generation. And the children of Israel were fruitful, and increased abundantly, and multiplied, and waxed exceeding mighty—Ex. 1:6, 7

Here we have an illustration of a two fold process which is always at work—silent dropping away and silent growth. It seems to me that the writer of these words in Exodus, probably unconsciously, being profoundly impressed with certain features of that dropping away, reproduces them most strikingly in the very structure of his sentence: "Joseph died, and all his brethren, and all that generation." The uniformity of the fate, and the separate times at which it befell individuals, are strongly set forth in the clauses, which sound like the three-fold falls of earth on a coffin. They all died, but not all at the same time; they went one by one, one by one, till, at the end, they were all gone.

If you were ever out at sea, and looked over a somewhat stormy water, you will have noticed, I dare say, how strangely the white crests of the breakers disappear, as if some force, acting from beneath, had plucked them under, and over the spot where they gleamed for a moment runs the blue sea. So the waves break over the great ocean of time, I might say, like swimmers pulled under by sharks—man after man, man after man, gets twitched down, till at the end—"And Joseph died, and all his brethren, and all that generation."

There is another process going on side by side with this. In the vegetable world, spring and autumn are two different seasons; May rejoices in green leaves and opening buds, and nests with their young broods; but winter days are coming when the greenery drops and the nests are dry, and the birds flown. But the singular and impressive thing (which we should see if we were not so foolish and blind) is that at the same time the two opposite processes of death and renewal are going on; so that if you look at the facts from the one side, it seems nothing but a charnel-house and a *Golgotha* that we live in, while, seen from the other side, it is a scene of rejoicing, budding young life and growth. You get these two processes in the closest juxtaposition in ordinary life. There is many a house where there is a coffin upstairs and a cradle downstairs. The churchyard is often the children's playground. The web is being run down at the one end and woven at the other. Wherever we look—

"Every moment dies a man,
Every moment one is born."

"Joseph died, and all his brethren, and all that generation. And the children of Israel . . . multiplied . . . exceedingly."

But there is another thought here than that of the contemporaneousness of the two processes, and that is, as it is written on John Wesley's monument in Westminster Abbey, "God buries the workmen and carries on the work." The great Vizier who seemed to be the only protection of Israel is lying in "a coffin in Egypt." And all these truculent brothers of his that had tormented him, they are gone, and the whole generation is swept away. What of that? They were the depositories of God's purposes for a little while. Are God's purposes dead because the instruments that wrought them in part are gone? By no means. If I might use a very vulgar proverb, "There are as good fish in the sea as ever came out of it," especially if God casts the net. So when the one generation has passed away, there is the other to take up the work.

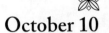

"GOD BURIES HIS WORKMEN, AND CARRIES ON HIS WORK"

Then I said, I have labored in vain, I have spent my strength for nought and in vain: yet surely my judgment is with the Lord, and my work with my God—
Is. 49:4

The twofold process always at work—the silent dropping away and silent growth—suggests lessons which should be enforced. Let us be quite sure that we give them their due weight in our thoughts and lives, that we never give an undue weight to the one half of the whole truth. There are plenty of people who are far too much, constitutionally and (perhaps by reason of a mistaken notion of religion) religiously, inclined to the contemplation of the more melancholy side of these truths; and there are a great many people who are far too exclusively disposed to the contemplation of the other. But the bulk of us never trouble our heads about either the one or the other, but go on, forgetting altogether that swift, sudden, stealthy, skinny hand that is put out to lay hold of the swimmer and then pull him underneath the water; and which will clasp us by the ankles one day, and draw us down. Do you ever think about it? If not, surely, surely you are leaving out of sight one of what ought to be the formative elements in our lives. And then, on the other hand, when our hearts are faint, or when the pressure of human mortality—our own, that of our dear ones, or that of others—seems to weight us down, or when it looks to us as if God's work was failing for lack of people to do it, let us remember the other side. So we shall keep the middle path, which is the path of safety, and so avoid the folly of extremes. This double contemplation of the two processes under which we live ought to stimulate us to service. It ought to say to us, "Cast in your lot with that work which is going to be carried on through the ages. See to it that your little task is in the same line of direction as the great purpose which God is working out—the increasing purpose which runs through the ages." An individual life is a mere little backwater, as it were, in the great ocean. But the minuteness does not matter, if only the great tidal wave which rolls away out there, in the depths and the distance among the fathomless abysses, tells also on the tiny pool far inland and yet connected with the sea, with some narrow long fiord.

If my little life is part of that great ocean, then the ebb and flow will alike act on it and make it wholesome. If my work is done for God, I shall never have to look back and say, as we certainly shall say one day, either here or yonder, unless our lives be thus part of the Divine plan, "What a fool I was! Seventy years of toiling and moiling and effort and sweat, and it has all come to nothing; like a long algebraic sum that covers pages of intricate calculations, and the *pluses* and *minuses* just balance each other: and the net result is a big round zero." So let us remember the twofold process, and let it stir us to make sure that "in our embers" shall be "something that doth live," and that, not "Nature," but something better—God—remembers what was so fugitive. It is not fugitive if it is a part of the mighty whole.

OUR INSIGNIFICANT AND UNFINISHED WORK

And he died in a good old age, full of days, riches, and honor; and Solomon his son reigned in his stead—1 Chr. 29:28

Joseph might have said when he lay dying: "Well! Perhaps I made a mistake after all. I should not have brought this people down here, even if I have been led hither. I do not see that I have helped them one step towards the possession of the land." Do you remember the old proverb about certain people who should not see half-finished work? All our work in this world has to be only what the physiologists call functional. God has a great scheme running on through ages. Joseph gives it a helping hand for a bit, and then somebody else takes up the running, and carries the purpose forward a little further. A great many hands are placed on the ropes that draw the car of the Ruler of the world—and one after another they get stiffened in death; but the car goes on. We should be contented to do our little bit of the work: never mind whether it is complete and smooth and rounded or not; never mind whether it can be isolated from the rest and held up, and people can say "He did that entire thing unaided." That is not the way for most of us. A great many threads go to make the piece of cloth, and a great many throws of the shuttle to weave the web. A great many bits of glass make up the mosaic pattern; and there is no reason for the red bit to pride itself on its fiery glow, or the gray bit to boast of its silvery coolness. They are all parts of the pattern, and as long as they keep their right places they complete the artist's design. Thus, if we think of how one soweth our fathers, and to hand on unfinished tasks to them that come after us. It is not a great trial of a man's modesty, if he lives near Jesus Christ, to be content to do but a very small bit of the Master's work.

Moses dies; Joshua catches the torch from his hand. And the reason why he catches the torch from his hand is because God said, "As I was with Moses, so I will be with thee" [Josh. 1:5]. Therefore we have to turn away in our contemplations from the mortality that has swallowed up so much wisdom and strength, eloquence and power, which the Church or our own hearts seem so sorely to want; and, while we do, we have to look up to Jesus Christ, and say, "He lives! He lives! No man is indispensable for public work, or for private affection and solace, so long as there is a living Christ for us to hold by." We often need that conviction for ourselves. When life seems empty and hope dead, and nothing is able to fill the void or still the pain, we have to look to the vision of the Lord sitting on the empty throne, high and lifted up, and yet very near the aching and void heart. Christ lives, and that is enough. So the separated workers in all the generations, who did their little bit of service, like the many generations of builders who labored through centuries upon the completion of some great cathedral, will be united at the last; "and he that soweth, and he that reapeth, shall rejoice together" in the harvest which neither the sower nor the reaper had produced, but He who blessed the toils of both.

COSTLY AND FATAL HELP

He sacrificed unto the gods of Damascus, which smote him; and he said, Because the gods of the kings of Syria help them, therefore will I sacrifice to them, that they may help me. But they were the ruin of him, and of all Israel—2 Chr. 28:23

Ahaz came to the throne when a youth of twenty. From the beginning he reversed the policy of his father, and threw himself into the arms of the heathen party. In a comparatively short reign of sixteen years he stamped out the worship of God, and nearly ruined the kingdom. He did not plunge into idolatry for lack of good advice. The greatest of the prophets stood beside him. Isaiah addressed to him remonstrances which might have made the most reckless pause, and promises which might have kindled hope and courage in the bosom of despair. Hosea in the northern kingdom, Micah in Judah, and other less brilliant names were among the stars which shone even in that dark night. But their light was all in vain. The foolish lad had the bit between his teeth, and like many other young men, thought to show his "breadth" and his "spirit" by neglecting his father's counselors and abandoning his father's faith. He was ready to worship anything that called itself a God, always excepting Jehovah. The more he multiplied his gods the more he multiplied his sorrows, and the more he multiplied his sorrows the more he multiplied his gods. From all sides the invaders came; from north, northeast, east, southeast, south, they swarmed in upon him. They tore away the fringes of his kingdom; and hostile armies flaunted their banners beneath the very walls of Jerusalem. And then, in his despair, like a scorpion in a circle of fire, he inflicted a deadly wound on himself by calling in the fatal help of Assyria. Loathing nothing, that warlike power responded, scattered his less formidable foes, and then swallowed the prey which it had dragged from between the teeth of the Israelites and Syrians. The result of Ahaz's frantic appeals to false gods and faithless men may still be read on the Cuneiform inscriptions, where amid a long list of unknown tributary kings, stands, with a Philistine on one side of him and an Ammonite on the other, the shameful record, "Ahaz of Judah."

Is the breed extinct, think you? Is there anybody who, if he cannot get what he wants by fair ways, *will* try to get it by foul? Do none of you ever bow down to Satan for a slice of the kingdoms of this world? Ahaz has got plenty of brothers and sisters.

This story illustrates what, is only too true. Look at the so-called cultured classes of Europe today; turning away, as so many of them are, from the Lord God of their fathers—what sort of things are they worshiping instead? Scraps from Buddhism, the Vedas, any sacred books but the Bible; quackeries and charlatanism, and dreams and fragmentary philosophies all pieced together, to try and make up a whole, instead of the old-fashioned whole that they have left behind them. "The garment is narrower than that a man can wrap himself in it." And a creed patched together so will never make a seamless whole which can be trusted not to rend. Ahaz had, as he thought, two strings to his bow. He had the gods of Damascus, and of other lands up there; he had the King of Assyria down here. They both of them exacted onerous terms before they would stir a foot to his aid. Do *you* buy this world's help any cheaper? You get nothing for nothing in that market. It is a big price.

WHOLE-HEARTED RELIGION

They . . . sought him with their whole desire; and he was found of them: and the Lord gave them rest round about—2 Chr. 15:15

One reason why the great mass of professing Christians make so little of their religion is because they are only half-hearted in it. If you divide a river into two streams the force of each is less than half the power of the original current; and the chances are that you will make a stagnant marsh where there used to be a flowing stream. "All in all, or not at all," is the rule for life in all departments. It is a rule in daily business. A man that has only half himself in his profession or trade, while the other half is dreaming, is predestined to fail. The same is true about our religion. If you and I attend to it as a kind of by-occupation; if we give the balance of our time and the superfluity of our energy, after we have done a hard day's work—say, an hour upon a Sunday—to seeking God, and devote all the rest of the week to seeking worldly prosperity, it is no wonder if our religion languishes, and is mainly a matter of forms, as it is with such hosts of people that call themselves Christians. There is more unconscious unreality in the average Christian man's endeavor to be a better Christian than there is in almost anything else in the world:

> "One foot on the sea, and one on land,
> To one thing constant never."

That is why so many of us know nothing of a progressive strengthening of our faith, and an increasing conquest of ourselves, and a firmer grasp of God, and a fuller realization of the blessedness of walking in His ways. This whole-heartedness does not mean that there are to be no other desires, for it is a great mistake to pit religion against other things which are meant to be its instruments and its helps. We are not required to seek nothing else in order to seek God wholly. He demands no impossible and fantastic detachment of ourselves from the ordinary and legitimate occupations, affections, and duties of human life; but He does ask that the dominant desire after Him should be powerful enough to express itself through all our actions, and that we should seek for God in them and for them in God. There must be detachment if there is to be attachment. If some climbing plant, for instance, has twisted itself around the unprofitable thorns in the hedge, the gardener, before he can get it to go up the support that it is meant to encircle, has to carefully detach it from the stays to which it has wantonly clung, taking care that in the process he does not break its tendrils and destroy its power of growth, So, to train our souls to cleave to God, and to grow on around the great stay that is provided for us, there is needed, as an essential part of the process, the voluntary, conscious, conscientious, and constant guarding of ourselves from the vagrancies of our desires, which send out their shoots away from Him.

It is when God comes into the Temple that Dagon falls on the threshold. It is when a new affection begins to spring in the heart that old loves are thrust out of it. To seek Him with the whole heart is to engage the whole self in the quest, and that is the only kind of seeking which has the certainty of success.

THE SEARCH THAT ALWAYS FINDS

And ye shall seek me, and find me, when ye shall search for me with all your heart—Jer. 29:13

Anything is possible rather than that a whole-hearted search after God should be a vain search. For there are, in that case, *two* seekers—God is seeking for us more truly than we are seeking for Him. And if the mother is seeking her child, and the child its mother, it will be a very wide desert where they will not meet. "The Father seeketh such to worship him" [John 4:23]. That is—the Divine activity is going about the world, searching for the heart that turns to Him, and it cannot but be that they that seek Him shall find Him. Open the windows, and you cannot keep out the sunshine; open your lungs, and you cannot keep out the air. "In him we live and move and have our being" [Acts 17:28]; and if our desires turn, however blindly, to Him and are accompanied with the appropriate action, heaven and earth are more likely to rush to ruin than such a searching to be frustrated of its aim.

Is there anything else in the world of which you can say, "Seek, and ye shall find" [Luke 11:9]? We, with white hairs on our heads, have we found anything else in which the chase was sure to result in the capture; in which capture was sure to yield all that the hunter had wished? There is only one direction for a man's desires and aims in which disappointment is an impossibility. In all other regions the most that can be promised is, "Seek, and *perhaps* you will find"; and when you have found, perhaps you will find that the prize was not worth the finding. Or it is, "Seek, and *possibly* you may find; and after you have found and kept for a little while, you may lose." Though it may be

"Better to have loved and lost
Than never to have loved at all,"

a treasure that slips out of our fingers is not the best treasure that we can search for. But here the assurance is, "Seek, and ye *shall* find; and shall never lose. Find, and you shall always possess."

What would you think of a company of gold seekers, hunting about in some exhausted claim for hypothetical grains—ragged, starving—and all the while in the next gulley were lying lumps of gold for the picking up? And that figure fairly represents what people do and suffer who seek for good and do not seek for God. That turning of mind, will, and affection towards God must be ours if we are to be among those wise and happy seekers who are sure to find that which—or rather Him whom—they seek, and to rest in Him whom they find. The famous saying which prefers the search after to the possession of truth is more proud than wise; but the comparison which it institutes is so far true that there is a joy in the aspiration after and the efforts towards truth only less joyous than that which attends it attainment. But truth divorced from God is finite and may pall, become familiar and lose its radiance, like a gathered flower; and hence the preference for the search is intelligible, though one-sided. But God does not pall, and the more we find Him the more we delight in Him. The highest bliss is to find Him, the next highest is to seek Him; and, since seeking and finding Him are never wholly separate, these kindred joys blend their lights in the experience of all His children.

THE REST OF FINDING CHRIST

There I will meet with thee, and I will commune with thee from above the mercy seat—Ex. 25:22

Seeking God does not cover our heads from the storm of external calamities, nor arm our hearts against the darts and daggers of many a pain, anxiety, and care; but disturbance around is a very small matter if there be a better thing—rest within. Do you remember who it was that said, "In the world ye shall have tribulation . . . but in me ye shall have peace" [see John 16:33]? Then we have, as it were, two abodes—one, as far as regards the life of sense, in the world of sense—another, as far as regards the inmost self, which may, if we will, be in Christ. A vessel with an outer casing and a layer of air between may be kept at a temperature above that of the external atmosphere. So we may have around us—and, if God so wills, let us not kick against His will—the very opposite of repose; we may have conflict and stir and strife, and yet a better rest than that of King Asa and his people (*see* 2 Chr. 15:15) may be ours. "Rest round about" is sometimes good and sometimes bad. It is often bad, for it is the people that "have no changes" who most usually "do not fear God." But rest within, that is sure to come when a man has sought with all his desire for God, whom he has found in all His fullness, is good only and best of all.

We all know, thank God! In worldly matters and in inferior degree, how blessed and restful it is when some strong affection is gratified, some cherished desire fulfilled! Though these satisfactions are not perpetual, nor perfect, they may teach us what a depth of blessed and calm repose, incapable of being broken by any storms or by any tasks, will come to and abide with the man whose deepest love is satisfied in God, and whose most ardent desires have found more than they sought for in Him! Be sure of this, dear friend, that if we do thus seek, and thus find, it is not in the power of anything "that is at enmity with joy" utterly to "abolish or destroy" the quietness of our hearts. "Rest in the Lord, and wait patiently for him" [Ps. 37:7]. They who thus repose will have peace in their hearts, even while tasks and temptations, changes and sorrows, disturb their outward lives.

Thus we may have the peace of God, rest in and from Him, entering into us, and in due time, by His gracious guidance and help, we shall enter into eternal rest. While to seek is to find Him, in a very deep and blessed sense, even in this life; in another aspect all our earthly life may be regarded as seeking after Him, and the future as the true finding of Him. That future shall bring to those whose hearts have turned from the shows and vanities of time to God a possession of Him so much fuller than was experienced here that the lesser discoveries and enjoyments of Him which are experienced here, scarcely deserve in comparison to be called by the same name. "He was found of them, and the Lord gave them rest round about" [2 Chr. 15:15], as well as within, in the land of peace, where sorrow and sighing, and toil and care, shall pass from memory; and they that warred against us shall be far away.

THE SHEPHERD-KING

The Lord is my shepherd: I shall not want—Psalm 23:1

The king who had been the shepherd-boy, and had been taken from the quiet flock of sheep to rule over Israel, sings this little psalm of Him who is the true Shepherd and King of men. We do not know at what period of David's life it was written, but it sounds as if it were the work of his later years. There is a fullness of experience about it, and a tone of subdued, quiet confidence, which speak of a heart mellowed by years and of a faith made sober by many a trial. A young man would not write so calmly, and a life which was just opening would not afford material for such a record of God's guardianship in all changing circumstances. If, then, we think of the psalm as the work of David's later years, is it not very beautiful to see the old king looking back with such vivid and loving remembrance to his childhood's occupation, and bringing up again to memory in his palace the green valleys, the gentle streams, the dark glens where he had led his flock in the old days; very beautiful to see him traversing all the stormy years of warfare and rebellion, of crime and sorrow, which lay between, and finding in all God's guardian presence and gracious guidance? The faith which looks back and says, "It is all very good," is not less than that which looks forward and says, "Surely goodness and mercy shall follow me all the days of my life" [Ps. 23:6]. There is nothing difficult to understand in the psalm. The train of thought is clear and obvious. The experiences which it details are common, the emotions it expresses simple and familiar. The tears that have been dried, the fears that have been dissipated, by this old song; the love and thankfulness which have found in them their best expression, prove the worth of its simple words. It lives in most of our memories. There is a double progress of thought in it. It rises, from memories of the past and experiences of the present care of God, to hope for the future. *"The Lord is my Shepherd"—"I will fear no evil."* Then, besides this progress from what was and is to what will be, there is another string, so to speak, on which the gems are threaded. The various methods of God's leading of His flock, or, rather, we should say, the various regions into which He leads them, are described in order. These are: Rest, Work, Sorrow; and this series is so combined with the order of time already adverted to, as that the past and the present are considered as the regions of rest and of work, while the future is anticipated as having in it the valley of the shadow of death [Ps. 23:4].

GOD LEADS HIS SHEEP INTO REST

He maketh me to lie down in green pastures; he leadeth me beside
the still waters—Psalm 23:2

It is the hot noontide, and the desert lies baking in the awful glare, and every stone on the hills of Judea burns the foot that touches it. But in that panting, breathless hour, here is a little green glen, with a quiet brook, and a moist lush herbage all along its course, and great stones that fling a black shadow over the dewy grass at their base; and there would the shepherd lead his flock, while the sunbeams, like swords, are piercing everything beyond that hidden covert. Sweet silence broods there. The sheep feed and drink, and couch in cool lairs till he calls them forth again. So God leads His children. Rest and refreshment are put *first,* as being the most marked characteristic of God's dealings. After all, it is so. The years are years of unbroken continuity of outward blessings. The reign of afflictions is ordinarily measured by days. Weeping endures for a night. It is a rainy climate where half the days have rain in them; and that is an unusually troubled life of which it can with any truth be affirmed that there has been as much darkness as sunshine in it.

But it is not mainly of outward blessings that the Psalmist is thinking; they are precious chiefly as emblems of the better spiritual gifts. And it is not an accommodation of his words, but is the appreciation of their truest spirit, when we look upon them, as the instinct of devout hearts has ever done, as expressing both God's gift of temporal mercies and His gift of spiritual good, of which higher gift all the lower are meant to be significant and symbolic. Thus regarded, the image describes the sweet rest of the soul in communion with God, in whom alone the hungry heart finds food that satisfies, and from whom alone the thirsty soul drinks draughts deep and limpid enough. This rest and refreshment has for its consequence the restoration of the soul, which includes in it both the invigoration of the natural life by the outward sort of these blessings, and the quickening and restoration of the spiritual life by the inward feeding upon God and repose in Him.

The Divine rest is not only a pattern of what our earthly life may become, but is a prophecy of what our heavenly life shall surely be. There is a basis of likeness between the Christian life on earth and the Christian life in heaven, so great as that the blessings that are predicted of the one belong to the other. Only here they are in blossom, sickly often, putting out very feeble shoots and tendrils; and yonder, transplanted into their right soil, and in their native air, with heaven's sun upon them, they burst into richer beauty, and bring forth fruits of immortal life. Heaven is the earthly life of a believer glorified and perfected. If here by faith we enter into the beginning of rest, yonder, through death with faith, we shall enter into the perfection of it. Heaven will be for us in work, and work that is full of rest. Our Lord's heaven is not an idle heaven, and the heaven of all spiritual natures is not idleness. Man's delight is activity. The loving heart's delight is obedience. The saved heart's delight is grateful service. The joys of heaven are not the joys of passive contemplation, of dreamy remembrance, of perfect repose; but they are described thus: "They rest not day nor night" [see Rev. 4:8]. His servants serve Him and see His face. Heaven is perfect *"rest."*

October 18

GOD GUIDES HIS PEOPLE INTO WORK

He leadeth me in the paths of righteousness for his name's sake—Psalm 23:3

The quiet mercies of the preceding verse are not in themselves the end of our Shepherd's guidance; they are means to an end, and that is—work. Life is not a fold for the sheep to lie down in, but a road for them to walk on. All our blessings of every sort are indeed given to us for our delight. They will never fit us for the duties for which they are intended to prepare us, unless they first be thoroughly enjoyed. The highest good they yield is only reached through the lower one. But, then, when joy fills the heart, and life is bounding in the veins, we have to learn that these are granted, not for pleasure only, but for pleasure in order to power. We get them, not to let them pass away like waste steam puffed into empty air, but that we may use them to drive the wheels of life. The waters of happiness are not for a luxurious bath where a man may lie, till, like flax steeped too long, the very fiber be rotted out of him; a quick plunge will brace him, and he will come out refreshed for work. Rest is to fit for work; work is to sweeten rest. All this is emphatically true of the spiritual life; its seasons of communion, its hours on the mount, are to prepare for the sore sad work in the plain. And he is not the wisest disciple who tries to make the Mount of Transfiguration the abiding place for himself and his Lord.

It is not well that our chief object should be to enjoy the consolations of religion; it is better to seek first to do the duties enjoined by religion. Our first question should be, not "How may I enjoy God?" but "How may I glorify Him?" "A single eye to His glory" means that even our comfort and joy in religious exercises shall be subordinated, and, if need were, postponed, to the doing of His will. While, on the one hand, there is no more certain means of enjoying Him than that of humbly seeking to walk in the ways of His commandments, on the other hand, there is nothing more evanescent in its nature than a mere emotion, even though it be that of joy in God, unless it be turned into a spring of action for God. Such emotions, like photographs, vanish from the heart unless they be fixed. Work for God is the way to fix them. Joy in God is the strength of work for God, but work for God is the perpetuation of joy in God. Here is the figurative expression of the great evangelical principle, that works of righteousness must follow, not precede, the restoration of the soul. We are justified, not by works, but for works; or, as the Apostle puts it, which sounds like an echo of this psalm, we are "created in Christ Jesus unto good works, which God hath before ordained *that we should walk in them*" [Eph. 2:10]. The basis of obedience is the sense of salvation. We work, not *for* the assurance of acceptance and forgiveness, but *from* it. First the restored soul; then the paths of righteousness for *His* Name's sake who has restored me, and restored me that I may be like Him.

THE PATH OF SORROW

Yea, though I walk through the valley of the shadow of death, I will fear no evil;
for thou art with me: thy rod and thy staff, they comfort me—Psalm 23:4

The "valley of the shadow of death" does not only mean the dark approach to the dark dissolution of soul and body, but any and every gloomy valley of weeping through which we have to pass. Such sunless gorges we have all to pass at some time or other. It is striking that the Psalmist puts the sorrow, which is as certainly characteristic of our lot as the rest or the work, into the future. Looking back, he sees none. Memory has softened down all the past into one uniform tone, as the mellowing distance wraps in one solemn purple the mountains which, when close to them, have many a barren rock and gloomy rift. All behind is good. And, building on this hope, he looks forward with calmness, and feels that no evil shall befall. But it is never given to human heart to meditate of the future without some foreboding. And when "Hope enchanted smiles," with the light of the future in her blue eyes, there is ever something awful in their depths, as if they saw some dark visions behind the beauty. Some evils may come; some will probably come; one, at least, is sure to come. However bright may be the path, somewhere on it, perhaps just around that turning, sits the "shadow feared of man." So there is never pure hope in any heart that wisely considers the future. But to the Christian heart there may be this—the conviction that sorrow, when it comes, will not be evil, because God will be with us; and the conviction that the Hand which guides us into the dark valley will guide us through it and up out of it. Yes, strange as it may sound, the presence of Him who sends the sorrow is the best help to bear it. The assurance that the Hand which strikes is the Hand which binds up, makes the stroke a blessing, sucks the poison out of the wound of sorrow, and turns the rod which smites into the staff to lean on.

The sheep are led by many a way, sometimes through sweet meadows, sometimes limping along sharp-flinted dusty highways, sometimes high up over rough rock mountain-passes, sometimes down through deep gorges, with no sunshine in their gloom; but they are ever being led to one place; and when the hot day is over, they are gathered into one fold, and the sinking sun sees them safe, where no wolf can come, nor any robber climb up any more, but all shall rest forever under the Shepherd's eye.

October 20

THE BLIND WATCHERS AT THE CROSS

And sitting down they watched him there—Matt. 27:36

How possible it is to look at Christ on the Cross and see nothing! For half a day there they sat. It was but a dying Jew that they saw—One of three. A touch of pity came into their hearts once or twice, alternating with mockery which was not savage because it was simply brutal; but when it was all over, and they had pierced His side, and gone away back to their barracks, they had not the least notion that they, with their dim purblind eyes, had been looking at the most stupendous miracle in the whole world's history; and had been gazing at the thing into which angels desired to look; and had seen that to which the hearts and the gratitude of unconverted millions would turn for all eternity. They laid their heads down on their pillows that night and did not know what had passed before their eyes; and they shut the eyes that had served them so ill, and went to sleep, altogether unconscious that they had seen the pivot on which the whole history of humanity had turned; and been the unmoved witnesses of God manifest in the flesh, dying on the Cross for the whole world, and for them. And if we thus look, and look with calm, unmoved hearts; if we look without personal appropriation of that Cross and dying love to ourselves and if we look without our hearts going out in thankfulness and laying themselves at His feet in a calm rapture of life-long devotion, then we need not wonder that four ignorant heathen men sat and looked at Him for four long hours and saw nothing, for we are as blind as they ever were.

You say, "We see." Do you see? Do you look? Does the look touch your hearts? Have you fathomed the meaning of the fact? Is it to you the incarnation of the loving God for your salvation? Is it to you the death on which all your hopes rest? You say you see. Do you see that in it? Do you see your only ground of confidence and peace? And do you so see that, like a man that has looked at the sun for a moment or two, when you turn away your head you carry the image of what you beheld still stamped on your eyeball, and have it both as a memory and a present impression? So, is the Cross photographed on your heart? And is it true about us that every day and all days we behold our Savior, and, beholding Him, are being changed into His likeness? Is it true about us that we look to Him with faith and love, and make His Cross our own, and keep it ever in our memory, ever before us as an inspiration and a hope and a joy and a pattern, then we see. If not, "for judgment am I come into this world, that they which see not might see, and that they which see might be made blind" [John 9:39]. For no men are so blind to the infinite pathos and tenderness, power, mystery, and miracle of the Cross, as those who all their lives have heard a gospel which has been held up before their lackluster eyes, and have looked at it so long that they cannot see it any more. Let us pray that our eyes may be purged; that we may see, and, seeing, may copy, that dying love of the ever-loving Lord.

"BE CAREFUL FOR NOTHING"

Take therefore no thought for the morrow: for the morrow shall take thought for the things of itself. Sufficient unto the day is the evil thereof—Matt. 6:34

An apparently impossible advice. That word "careful," in a great many places in the New Testament, does not mean what it has come to mean today; but it means what it *should* still mean, "full of care." And "care" meant, not prudent provision, forethought, the occupation of a man's common sense with his duty and his work and his circumstances, but it meant the thing which of all others unfits a man most for such prudent provision, and that is, the nervous irritation of a gnawing anxiety which, as the word in the original means, tears the heart apart and makes a man quite incapable of doing the wise thing, or seeing the wise thing to do, in the circumstances. "Careful" here means neither more nor less than "anxious."

But even with that explanation, is it not like an unreachable ideal that Paul puts forward? "Be anxious about nothing" [see Phil. 4:6]. How can a man who has to face the possibilities that we all have to face, and who knows himself to be as weak to deal with them as we all are—how can he help being anxious? There is no more complete waste of breath than those sage and reverend words of advice which people give us, not to do the things nor to feel the emotions which our position make absolutely inevitable and almost involuntary. Here, for instance, is a man surrounded by all manner of calamity and misfortune; and some well-meaning, but foolish, friend comes to him, and, without giving him a single reason for the advice, says, "Cheer up, my friend!" Why should he cheer up? What is there in his circumstances to induce him to fall into any other mood? Or some unquestionable peril is staring him full in the face, coming nearer and nearer to him, and some well-meaning, loose-tongued friend, says to him, "Do not be afraid!" But he *ought* to be afraid. That is about all the worldly wisdom and morality have to say to us when we are in trouble and anxiety. "Shut your eyes very hard, and make believe very much, and you will not fear." An impossible exhortation! It is just as easy to bid a ship in the Bay of Biscay not to rise and fall upon the wave, but to keep an even keel—just as easy to tell the willows in the riverbed that they are not to bend when the wind blows—as it is to come to me, and say to me, "Be careful about nothing," unless you have a great deal more than that to say. I must be, and I ought to be, anxious about a great many things. Instead of anxiety being folly, it will be wisdom; and the folly will consist in not opening our eyes to facts, and in not feeling emotions that are appropriate to the facts which force themselves against our eyeballs. Threadbare maxims, stale, musty old commonplaces of unavailing consolation and impotent encouragement say to us, "Do not be anxious." We try to stiffen our nerves and muscles in order to bear the blow; or some of us, more basely still, get into a habit of feather-headed levity, making no forecasts, nor seeing even what is plainest before our eyes. But all that is of no use when once the hot pincers of real trouble, impending or arrived, lay hold of our hearts. Then, of all idle expenditures of breath in the world, there is none to the wrung heart more idle and more painful than the one that says, Be anxious about nothing.

HOW TO OBEY AN APPARENTLY IMPOSSIBLE INJUNCTION

Be careful for nothing; but in everything by prayer and supplication with thanksgiving let your requests be made known unto God—Phil. 4:6

Paul here directs to the mode of feeling and action which will give exemption from the else inevitable gnawing of anxious forethought. He introduces his positive counsel with an eloquent "But," which implies that what follows is the sure preservative against the temper which he deprecates. "But in everything by prayer and supplication with thanksgiving let your request be made known unto God."

There are, then, these alternatives. If you do not like to take the one, you are sure to have to take the other. There is only one way out of the wood, and it is this which Paul expands in these last words. If a man does not pray about everything, he will be worried and anxious about most things. If he does pray about everything, he will not be troubled, beyond what is good for him, about anything. So there are these alternatives; and we have to make up our minds which of the two we are going to take. The heart is never empty. If not full of God, it will be full of the world and of worldly care. Luther says somewhere that a man's heart is like a couple of millstones; if you do not put something between them to grind, they will grind each other. It is because God is not in our hearts that the two stones rub the surface off one another. So the victorious antagonists of anxiety is trust, and the only way to turn gnawing care out of my heart and life is to usher God into it, and to keep Him resolutely in it.

"In everything." If a thing is great enough to threaten to make me anxious, it is great enough for me to talk to God about. If He and I are on a friendly footing, the instinct of friendship will make me speak. If so, how irrelevant and superficial seem to be discussions whether we ought to pray about worldly things or confine our prayers entirely to spiritual and religious matters! If God and I are on terms of friendship and intimacy of communication, there will be no question as to what I am to talk about to Him; I shall not be able to keep silent as to anything that interests me. And we are not right with God unless we have come to that point. That entire openness of speech marks our communications with Him; and that as naturally as men, when they come from business, like to tell their wives and children what has happened to them since they left home in the morning, so naturally we talk to our Friend about everything that concerns us. "In *everything* let your requests be made known unto God." That is the wise course, because a multitude of little pimples may be quite as painful and dangerous as a large ulcer. A cloud of gnats may put as much poison into a man with their many stings as will a snake with its one bite. And if we are not to get help from God by telling Him about little things, there will be very little of our lives that we shall tell Him about at all. For life is a mountain made up of minute flakes. The years are only a collection of seconds. Every man's life is an aggregate of trifles. "In *everything* make your requests known."

THE CURE FOR ANXIETY

Casting all your care upon him, for he careth for you—1 Pet. 5:7

"By prayer" [Phil. 4:6]: that does not mean, as a superficial experience of religion is apt to suppose it to mean, actual petition that follows. For a great many of us the only notion that we have of prayer is asking God to give us something that we want. But there is a far higher region of communion than that, in which the soul seeks and finds, and sits and gazes, and aspiring possesses, and possessing aspires. Where there is no spoken petition for anything affecting outward life, there may be the prayer of contemplation such as the burning seraphs before the Throne do ever glow with. The prayer of silent submission, in which the will bows itself before God; the prayer of quiet trust, in which we do not so much seek as cleave; the prayer of still fruition—these, in Paul's conception of the true order, precede "supplication." And if we have such union with God, by realizing His presence, by aspiration after Himself, by trusting Him and submission to Him, then we have the victorious antagonist of all our anxieties, and the "cares that infest the day shall fold their tents" and "silently steal away." For if a man has that union with God which is effected by such prayer as I have been describing, it gives him a fixed point on which to rest amid all perturbations. It is like bringing a light into a chamber when thunder is growling outside, which prevents the flashing of the lightning from being seen.

Years ago an ingenious inventor tried to build a vessel in such a fashion as that the saloon for passengers should remain upon one level, however the hull might be tossed by waves. It was a failure, if I remember rightly. But if we are thus joined to God, He will do for our inmost hearts what the inventor tried to do with the chamber within his ship. The hull may be buffeted, but the inmost chamber where the true self sits will be kept leveled and unmoved. Prayer in the highest sense, by which I mean the exercise of aspiration, trust, submission—prayer will fight against and overcome all anxieties.

"By prayer and supplication" [Phil. 4:6]. Actual petition for the supply of present wants is meant by "supplication." To ask for that supply will very often be to get it. To tell God what I think I need goes a long way always to bringing me the gift that I do need. If I have an anxiety of which I am ashamed to speak to Him, that silence is a sign that I ought not to have it; and if I have a desire that I do not feel I can put into a prayer, that feeling is a warning to me not to cherish such a desire.

THANKSGIVING AN ANTIDOTE OF CARE

I will sacrifice unto thee with the voice of thanksgiving—Jon. 2:9

There are many vague and oppressive anxieties that come and cast a shadow over our hearts, that, if we could once define and put into plain words, we should find that we vaguely fancied them a great deal larger than they were, and that the shadow they flung was immensely longer than the thing that flung it. Put your anxieties into definite speech. It will reduce their proportions to your own apprehension very often. Speaking them, even to a man who may be able to do little to help, eases them wonderfully. Put them into definite speech to God, and there are very few of them that will survive.

"By prayer and supplication with thanksgiving" [Phil. 4:6]. That thanksgiving is always in place. If one only considers what he has from God, and realizes that whatever he has he has received from the hands of Divine love, thanksgiving is appropriate in any circumstances. Do you remember when Paul was in jail at the very city to which this letter (Philippians) went, with his back bloody with the rod and his feet fast in the stocks, how then he and Silas "prayed and sang praises to God" [Acts 16:25]? Therefore the obedient earthquake came and set them loose. Perhaps it was some reminiscence of that night which moved him to say to the church that knew the story—of which perhaps the jailer was still a member—"By prayer and supplication with thanksgiving make your requests known unto God."

One aching nerve can monopolize our attention and make us unconscious of the health of all the rest of the body; so, a single sorrow or loss obscures many mercies. We are like men that live in a narrow alley in some city, with great buildings on either side towering high above their heads, and only a strip of sky visible. If we see up in that strip a cloud, we complain and behave as if the whole heavens, right away around the three hundred and sixty degrees of the horizon, were black with tempest. But we see only a little strip, and there is a great deal of blue in the sky; however, there may be a cloud in the patch that we see above our heads, from the alley where we live. Everything, rightly understood, that God sends to men is a cause of thanksgiving; therefore, "in everything by prayer and supplication with thanksgiving let your requests be made known unto God."

"Casting all your *anxieties* upon Him," says Peter, "for He"—not *is anxious;* that dark cloud does not rise much above the earth—but, "He careth for you" [see 1 Pet. 5:7]. And that loving guardianship and tender care is the one shield, armed with which we can smile at the poisoned darts of anxiety which would else fester in our hearts and, perhaps, kill. "Be careful for nothing"—an impossibility unless "in everything" we make "our requests known unto God."

A FATHER'S DISCIPLINE

For they verily for a few days chastened us after their own pleasure; but he for our profit, that we might be partakers of his holiness—Heb. 12:10

Few words of Scripture have been more often than these laid as a healing balm on wounded hearts. They may be long unnoticed on the page, like a lighthouse in calm sunshine; but sooner or later the stormy night falls, and then the bright beam flashes out and is welcome. They go very deep into the meaning of life as discipline. They tell us how much better God's discipline is than that of the most loving and wise parents; and they give that superiority as a reason for our yielding more entire and cheerful obedience to Him than we do to such.

Now, to grasp the full meaning of these words, we have to notice that the earthly and the heavenly disciplines are described in four contrasted clauses, which are arranged in what students call inverted parallelism—that is to say, the first clause corresponds to the fourth, and the second to the third. "For a few days" pairs off with "that we might be partakers of His holiness." Now, that does not seem a contrast at first sight; but notice that the "for" in the former clause is not the "for" of duration, but of direction. It does not tell us the space during which the chastisement or discipline lasts, but the end towards which it is pointed. The earthly parent's discipline trains boy or girl for circumstances, pursuits, occupations, professions, all of which terminate with the brief span of life. God's training is for an eternal day. It would be quite irrelevant to bring in here any reference to the length of time during which an earthly father's discipline lasts, but it is in full consonance with the writer's intention to dwell upon the limited scope of the one and the wide and eternal purpose of the other. Then, as for the other contrast—"for their own pleasure," or, as the Revised Version reads it, "as seemed good to them"—"but He for our profit." Elements of personal peculiarity, whim, passion, limited and possibly erroneous conceptions of what is the right thing to do for the child, enter into the training of the wisest and most loving among us; and we often make a mistake and do harm when we think we are doing good. But God's training is all from a simple and unerring regard to the benefit of His child. God corrects, chastens, trains, educates. That is the deepest word about everything that befalls us. All which befalls us has a will behind it, and is co-operant to an end. Life is not a heap of unconnected incidents, like a number of links flung down on the ground, but the links are a chain, and the chain has a staple. It is not a law without a law-giver that shapes men's lives. It is not a blind impersonal chance that presides over it. These very meteors that astronomers expect tonight to be flying and flashing through the sky in apparent wild disorder, all obey law. Our lives, in like manner, are embodied thoughts of God's, in as far as the incidents which occur in them are concerned. We may mar, may fight against, may contradict the presiding Divine purpose; but yet, behind the wild dance of flashing and transitory lights that go careening all over the sky, there guides, not an impersonal Power, but a living, loving Will. *He*, not *it*; *He*, not *they*—men, circumstances, what people call second causes—*He* corrects, and He does it for a great purpose.

THE SAINTS' PUPILAGE

Give instruction to a wise man, and he will be yet wiser; teach a just man, and he will increase in learning—Prov. 9:9

The world is God's nursery. There are many mansions in the Father's house [see John 14:2]; and this is where He keeps the little ones. That is the true meaning of everything that happens to us. It is education. It would not be worth doing at all if it were not. Life is given to us to teach us how to live, to exercise our powers, to give us habits and facilities of working. We are like boys in a training ship that lies for most of the time in harbor, and now and then goes out upon some short and easy cruise, not for the sake of getting anywhere in particular, but for the sake of exercising the lads in seamanship. There is no meaning worthy of *us*—to say nothing of God—in anything that we do, unless it is looked upon as schooling. We all say we believe that. I am afraid very many of us forget it.

But that conception of the meaning of each event that happens to us carries with it the conception of the whole of this life as being an education towards another. I do not understand how any man can bear to live here, and to do all his painful work, unless he thinks that by it he is getting ready for the life beyond; and that "nothing can bereave him of the force that he made his own, being here." The rough ore is turned into steel by being

> "Plunged into baths of hissing tears
> And heated all with hopes and fears.
> And battered with the shocks of doom."

And then—what then? Is an instrument thus fashioned and tempered and polished destined to be broken and thrown as rubbish into the void? Certainly not! If this life is education, as is obvious upon its very face, then there *is* a place where we shall exercise the facilities that we have acquired here, and manifest in loftier forms the characters which we have made our own.

If we carry these thoughts with us habitually, what a difference it will make upon everything that faces us! You hear men often murmuring about the mysteries of the pain and sorrow and suffering of this world, wondering if there is any loving will behind it all. That perplexed questioning goes on the hypothesis that life is meant mainly for enjoyment or for material good. If we once apprehended in its all-applicable ranges this simple truth, that life is a discipline, we should have less difficulty in understanding what people call the mysteries of Providence. I do not say it would interpret everything, but it would interpret an immense deal. It would make us eager, as each event came, to find out its special mission, and what it was meant to do for us. It would dignify trifles, and bring down the overwhelming magnitude of the so-called great events, and would make us lords of ourselves, and lords of circumstances, and ready to wring the last drop of possible advantage out of each thing that happened to us. Life is a Father's discipline.

THE GUIDING PRINCIPLE OF CHRISTIAN DISCIPLINE

Now no chastening for the present seemeth to be joyous, but grievous: neverthe-
less afterward it yieldeth the peaceable fruit of righteousness unto them which are
exercised thereby—Heb. 12:11

I have already said that, even in the most wise and unselfish training by an earthly parent, there will mingle subjective elements, peculiarities of view and thought, and
sometimes of passion and whim and other ingredients, which detract from the value of
all such training. The guiding principle for each earthly parent can only be the parent's
conception of what is for the good of the child, even at the best; and oftentimes that is
not purely the guide by which the parent's disciple is directed. So the words (Heb.
12:10) turn us away from all these incompletenesses, and tell us, "He for our profit"—
with no sidelong look to anything else, and with an entirely wise knowledge of what is
for our good, so that the result will be always and only for our good. This is the point of
view from which every Christian man ought to look upon all that comes upon him.

What follows? This, plainly:—there is no such thing as evil except the evil of sin.
All that comes is good, of various sorts and various complexions, but all generically the
same. The flood comes up over the fields, and men are in despair. It goes down; and
then, like the slime left from the Nile in flood, there is better soil for the cultivation of
our fields. Storms keep sea and air from stagnating. All that men call evil, in the material world, has in it a soul of good. If it be that all my life is paternal discipline, and that
God makes no mistakes, then I can embrace whatever comes to me, and be sure that in
it I shall find that which will be for my good.

It is easy to say so when things go well; but, surely, when the night falls is the time
for the stars to shine. The gracious word should shine upon some of us in today's perplexities and pains and disappointments and sorrows—"He for our profit." That great
thought does not in the least deny the fact that pain and sorrow and so-called evil are
very real. There is no false stoicism in Christianity. The mission of our troubles would
not be effected unless they did trouble us. The good that we get from a sorrow would
not be realized unless we did sorrow. "Weep for yourselves," said the Master, "and for
your children" [Luke 23:28]. It is right that we should writhe in pain. It is right that
we should yield to the impressions that are made upon us by calamities; but it is not
right that we should be so affected as that we should fail to discern in them this gracious
thought—"for our profit." God sends us many love-tokens, and among them are the
great and the little annoyances and pains that occur in our lives; and on each of them, if
we would look, we should see, written in His own hand, this inscription: "For your
good." Do not let us have our eyes so full of tears that we cannot see, or our hearts so full
of regrets that we cannot accept, that sweet, strong message. The guiding principle of all
that happens to us is God's unerring knowledge of what will do us good. That will not
prevent, and is not meant to prevent, the arrow from wounding, but it does wipe the
poison off the arrow, and diminish the pain, and should diminish the tears.

THE AIM OF ALL GOD'S CORRECTION

Whom the Lord loveth he chasteneth, and scourgeth every son whom he receiveth—Heb. 12:6

The earthly parent trains his son, or her daughter, for earthly occupations. These last a little while. God trains us for an eternal end. Holiness, likeness to God, is the only end which it is worthy of a man, being what he is, to propose to himself as the issue of his earthly experience. If I fail in that, whatever else I have accomplished, I fail in everything. I may have made myself rich, cultured, learned, famous, refined, prosperous; but if I have not at least begun to be like God in purity, in will, in heart, then my whole career has missed the purpose for which I was made, and for which all the discipline of life has been lavished upon me. Fail there, and wherever you succeed you are a failure. Succeed there, and wherever you fail you are a success.

That great and only worthy end may be reached by the ministration of circumstances and the discipline through which God passes us. These are not the only ways by which He makes us partakers of His holiness, as we well know. There is the work of that Divine Spirit who is granted to every believer to breathe into him the holy breath of an immortal and incorruptible life. To work along with these there is the influence that is brought to bear upon us by the circumstances in which we are placed and the duties which we have to perform. These may all help us to be nearer and more like God.

That is the intention of our sorrows. They will wean us; they will refine us; they will blow us to His breast, as a strong wind might sweep a man into some refuge from itself. I am sure there are some who can thankfully attest that they were brought nearer to God by some short, sharp sorrow than by many long days of prosperity.

But the sorrow that is meant to bring us nearer to Him may be in vain. The same circumstances may produce opposite effects. I daresay there are people who will read these words who have been made torn and sullen and bitter and paralyzed for good work because they have some heavy burden to carry, or some wound or ache that life can never heal. We are often like shipwrecked crews, of whom some are driven by the danger to their knees, and some are driven to the wine casks. Take care that you do not waste your sorrows; that you do not let the precious gifts of disappointment, pain, loss, loneliness, ill-health, or similar afflictions that come in your daily life, mar you instead of mending you. See that they send you nearer to God, and not that they drive you further from Him. See that they make you more anxious to have the durable riches and righteousness which no man can take from you, than to grasp at what may yet remain of fleeting earthly joys. So let us try to school ourselves into the habitual and operative conviction that life is discipline. Let us beware of getting no good from what is charged to the brim with good. May it never have to be said of any of us that we wasted the mercies which were judgments, too, and found no good in the things that our tortured hearts felt to be also evils, lest God should have to wail over any of us, "In vain have I smitten your children; they received no correction" [Jer. 2:30].

October 29

THE CHARGE TO THE TEMPLE WATCHERS

Behold, bless ye the Lord, all ye servants of the Lord, which by night stand in the house of the Lord! Lift up your hands in the sanctuary, and bless ye the Lord. The Lord that made heaven and earth bless thee out of Zion—Psalm 134:1-3

Figure to yourself the band of white-robed priests gathered in the court of the Temple, their flashing torches touching pillar and angle with strange light, the city sunk in silence and sleep—and before they part to their posts the chant rung in their ears;

"Behold! bless ye the Lord,
All ye servants of the Lord,
Who by night stand in the House of the Lord,
Lift up your hands in the sanctuary,
And bless the Lord."

The *priests'* duty is to praise. It is because they are the servants of the Lord that, therefore, it is their business to bless the Lord. It is because they stand in the House of the Lord that it is theirs to bless the Lord. They who are gathered into His House, they who hold communion with Him, they who can feel that the gate of the Father's dwelling, like the gate of the Father's heart, is always open to them, they who have been called in from their wanderings in a homeless wilderness, and given a place and a name in His House better than that of sons and daughters, have been so blessed in order that, filled with thanksgiving for such an entrance into God's dwelling and of such an adoption into His family, their silent lips may be filled with thanksgiving and their redeemed hands be uplifted in praise. So for us Christians. We are servants of the Lord—His priests. That we "stand in the House of the Lord" expresses not only the fact of our great privilege of confiding approach to Him and communion with Him, whereby we may ever abide in the very Holy of Holies, and be in the secret place of the Most High, even while we are busy in the world; but it also points to our duty of ministering—for the word "stand" is employed to designate the attendance of the priests in their office, and is almost equivalent to "serve." The purpose of that full horn of plenty, charged with blessings which God has emptied upon our heads, is that our dumb lips may be touched into thankfulness, because our selfish hearts have been wooed and charmed into love and life.

The rabbis had a saying that there were two sorts of angels: the angels that served, and the angels that praised; of which, according to their teaching, the latter were the higher in degree. It was only a half-truth, for true service is praise. But whatever the form in which praise may come, whether it be in the form of vocal thanksgiving, or whether it be the glad surrender of the heart, manifested in the conscious discharge of the most trivial duties; whether we lift up our hands in the sanctuary, and "bless the Lord" with them, or whether we turn our hands to the tools of our daily occupation and handle them for His sake—alike we may be praising Him. And the thing for us to remember is that the place where we, if we are Christians, stand, and the character which we, if we are Christians, sustain, bind us to live blessing and praising Him while we live.

SERVICE AND COMMUNION

Whoso offereth praise glorifieth me; and to him that ordereth his conversation aright will I show the salvation of God—Psalm 50:23

It is not enough to patrol the temple courts unless we "lift up our hands in the sanctuary" [Ps. 134:2], and with our hearts "bless the Lord." And all we who in any degree and any department are officially or semi-officially connected with the work of the Christian Church have very earnestly and especially to lay this to heart. We ministers, deacons, Sunday-school teachers, tract distributors, have much need to take care that we do not confound watching in the courts of the temple with lifting up our own hands and hearts to our Father that is in Heaven, and remember that the more outward work we do the more inward life we ought to have. The higher the stem of the tree grows, and the broader its branches spread, the deeper must strike and the wider must extend its underground roots, if it is not to be blown over and become a withered ruin.

And so will you take the plain lesson that is here: all ye that stand ready for service, and doing service, all "ye that stand in the House of the Lord, behold"—your peril and your duty—and "bless ye the Lord. And remember that the more work the more prayer to keep it from rotting; the more effort the more communion; and that at the end we shall discover with alarm, and with shame confess, "I kept others' vineyards, and my own vineyards have I not kept"; unless, like our Master, we prepare for a day of work and toil in the temple by a night of quiet communion with our Father on the mountainside.

And then there is another lesson, and that is that all times are times for blessing God. "Ye who by night stand in the House of the Lord, bless the Lord" [see Ps. 134:1–3]. So, though no sacrifice was smoking on the altar, and no choral songs went up from the company of praising priests in the ritual service, and although the nightfall had silenced the worship and scattered the worshipers, yet some low murmur of praise would be echoing through the empty halls all the night long, and the voice of thanksgiving and of blessing would blend with the clank of the priests' feet on the marble pavements as they went their patrolling rounds; and their torches would send up a smoke not less acceptable than the wreathing columns of the incense that had filled the day. And so, as in some convents you will find a monk kneeling on the steps of the altar at each hour of the four-and-twenty, adoring the Sacrament exposed upon it, so (but in inmost Christian heart there should be a perpetual adoration and a continual praise—a prayer without ceasing. What is it that comes first of all into your minds when you wake in the middle of the night? Yesterday's business, tomorrow's vanities, or God's present love and your dependence upon Him?

In the night of sorrow, too, do our songs go up, and do we hear and obey the charge which commands not only perpetual adoration, but bids us fill the night with music and with praise? Well for us if it be, anticipating the time when "they rest not day and night saying, Holy, holy, holy" [Rev. 4:8]!

RECIPROCAL BLESSING

I will bless thee . . . and thou shalt be a blessing—Gen. 12:2

There are two kinds of blessing which answer to one another—God's blessing of man and man's blessing of God. The one is communicative, the other receptive and responsive. The one is the great stream which pours itself over the precipice, the other is the basin into which it falls, and the showers of spray which rise from its surface, rainbowed in the sunshine, as the cataract of Divine mercies comes down upon it. God blesses us when He gives. We bless God when we thankfully take, and praise the Giver. God's blessing, then, must ever come first. We love Him because He first love us. Ours is but the echo of His; but the acknowledgment of the Divine act, which must precede our recognition of it, as the dawn must come in order that the birds may wake to sing.

Our highest service is to take the gifts of God, and with glad hearts to praise the Giver. Our blessings are but words. God's blessings are realities. We wish good to one another when we bless each other. But He does good to men when He blesses them. Our wishes may be deep and warm, but how ineffectual; they flutter around the heads of those whom we would bless, but how seldom do they actually rest upon their brows! But God's blessings are powers; they never miss their mark. Whom He blesses are blessed indeed. The channel through which God's blessings come is—"out of Zion" [Ps. 128:5]. For the Jew, the fullness of the Divine glory dwelt between the Cherubim, and the richest of the Divine blessings were bestowed on the waiting worshipers there. And no doubt it is still true that God dwells in Zion, and blesses men from thence. The correspondence in Christianity to the temple where God dwelt and from which He scattered His blessings is twofold—one proper and original, the other secondary and derived. In the true sense, Jesus Christ is the Temple. In Him God dwelt: in Him man meets God; in Him was the place of Revelation; in Him the place of Sacrifice. "In this place is one greater than the temple"; and the abiding of Jehovah above the mercy-seat was but a material symbol, shadowing and foretelling the true indwelling of all the fullness of the Godhead bodily in that true tabernacle which the Lord hath pitched and not man. So the great Fountain of all possible good and benediction, which was opened for the believing Jew in "Zion," is open for us in Jesus Christ, who stood in the very court of the temple, and called in tones of clear, loud invitation: "If any man thirst, let him come unto me and drink" [John 7:37]. We may each pass through the rent veil into the holiest of all, and there, laying our hand on Jesus, touch God, and opening our empty palm extended to Him, can receive from Him all the blessing that we need. There is another application of the temple symbol in the New Testament—a derivative and secondary one—to the Church, that is, to the aggregate of believers. In that Zion all God's best blessings are possessed and stored, that the Church may, by faithful service, impart them to the world. Whosoever desires to possess these blessings must enter thither, not by any ceremonial act or outward profession, but by becoming one of those who put their whole heart's confidence in Jesus Christ. If we are knit to Christ by our faith, we share, in proportion to our faith, in all the wealth of blessing with which God has blessed Him. We possess Christ and in Him all.

CHRISTIAN SELF-POSSESSION

This is the will of God, even your sanctification. . . . that every one of you should know how to possess his vessel in sanctification and honor—1 Thess. 4:3, 4

Self-control is self-possession, as the popular use of that word "self-possessed" hints at. A man that has the mastery of his inclinations, dispositions, emotions, and passions, and can keep them all down where they ought to be, is the man whom we call "self-possessed"—which is just to say, that only he who governs himself by temperate reason and firm will and pure conscience, only he is, in truth, his own owner and master. Why, to take one of the most plain and obvious instances: suppose a drunkard who resolves, with all the power left to his enfeebled will, that he will never touch drink again. He goes out into the street full of his resolution, and before he has gone a couple of hundred yards, and passed a tavern or two, it all oozes out at his fingertips, and in he goes. Is he master of himself? Does he own himself, in any true sense of the expression? No! That tyrannous lust dominates; to it he belongs; he has no power of governing his own nature. His reason, his will, his conscience are all drowned out of sight by the flood of ungoverned passion that comes rushing from his indulged animal appetite like winter torrents from the recesses of the hills, that cover fertile lands with hideous slime and sterile gravel. You cannot call such a man as that his own master. To use a common phrase, *he,* at any rate, cannot call his soul his own. It belongs to the tempter whom he cannot resist. That, of course, is an illustration of an extreme kind, drawn from a vulgar appetite, but the principle involved in it can be applied to other much more refined and subtle desires. Wherever there is a passion, an inclination that masters a man, and brushes aside the sovereign faculties of reason and will and conscience, and says to them, "You may all lay your heads together as you like, but I am going to take the reins into my hands," *there* is a man who does not belong to himself, but to the dominant inclination and to the object which excites it.

Self-sacrifice is self-possession. From a selfish point of view, it is an outright mistake to make myself my own aim and center. "Who pleasure follows, pleasure slays," says the poet. The surest way to gratify and satisfy all that is good in myself is to put the satisfaction of self out of sight, and to yield myself up to something higher and nobler. They tell us that if a man gazes full-front at the Pleiades they do not appear so bright, and he cannot count so many of them as if he looks a little on one side of them. Whoever makes self the aim of his vision and of his effort thereby defeats his own end, and ceases to possess himself. There are far sweeter delights in the love of others, to which a man yields up himself, than are ever found in loving self. The poignant joys that spring in a heart that is inflamed by high enthusiasm for any great cause, be it what it may, are nobler, rarer, more thrilling by far, than any which are to be found on the low levels of self-indulgence. The secret of happiness is self-oblivion. "He that loveth his life shall lose it" [John 12:25] is true all around the circumference of a man's nature.

A BETTER AND AN ENDURING SUBSTANCE

Knowing in yourselves that ye have in heaven a better and an enduring substance—Heb. 10:34

The writer has just spoken in the previous clause about taking "joyfully the spoiling of your *goods*," and for "substance" he employs a word closely related to that, which is translated "goods." So that he is pointing back, and suggesting that the wealth that had been taken was trivial and poor in comparison with the wealth which the believing Hebrews retained. They had lost farthings; they had kept pounds.

That possession is better, just because it is within and not without. The wealth that a man *has* is only apparently his possession. There is many a man in Manchester about whom we say, "He *has* mills or capital amounting to so many thousands, or millions," when it would be a great deal truer to say, "The mills and the capital and the millions have him." He is not their owner; he is their slave. But even when outward possessions do not become tyrants, it is still true that whatever lies outside of us is less precious than what we have within. Love is more than money; peace is more than plenty. It is better to have a quiet heart than a full cupboard [see Prov. 15:16; 1 Pet. 3:4]. It is better to have a clear record of conscience than a bank note with a heavy balance on the credit side. What we *have,* or what has us, is small in comparison with what we *are.* The wealth within is the true wealth; and there is nothing that will satisfy a man except having himself remade after the image of Jesus Christ, and so being "lord of himself if not of lands." The difference between these two kinds of possession is the difference between having to go a weary way to a well with a pitcher, and bringing back a scanty and not very pure or cool supply, and having a fountain in your courtyard. "A good man shall be satisfied from himself," says the Book of Proverbs [14:14]; and that is better than being a pauper dependent on the contingent satisfactions that come from anything outside of us.

"A better and an enduring substance"—or, perhaps, we should rather say, better *because* enduring. Nothing can deprive me of myself but myself. Only its own hands can break the sweet bonds that knit a believing soul to Jesus Christ. The world may blow its fiercest hurricanes of losses, and sorrows may come storming upon us, but they will only blow the dead leaves off the tree, while the living ones remain, and the strong trunk and sturdy branches are unharmed. The branches may toss; the stem and the roots are unmoved. So it is better to have wealth which the world cannot give and cannot take away than to be enriched with all the fast-fading sweets that it offers [Matt. 6:19–21].

This wealth is better because it is altogether unaffected by and persistent through that change which takes away everything besides. As the grim psalm has it, "his glory shall not descend after him" [Ps. 49:17]. As the grim saying has it, "Shrouds have no pockets." The corpse laid out upon a board to be buried has the hands that clutched straightened out, open and empty forevermore. But we take *ourselves* with us when we go—what we have made of ourselves, and what Christ in us has made of us. "Blessed are the dead which die in the Lord, for . . . their works do follow them" [Rev. 14:13], and their wealth goes with them.

THE MISSION OF PERSECUTION

For ye had compassion of me in my bonds, and took joyfully the spoiling of your goods—Heb. 10:34

The possession of the enduring substance of Christ lifts us above all loss or change. "Ye took *joyfully* the spoiling of your goods," says the writer of the Epistle to the Hebrews, speaking to his hearers of some afflictions and persecutions which have long faded out of memory. We know not what the circumstances were to which he refers. Evidently there had been some pretty stringent and severe persecution of Christians, which had led to large financial losses. "Ye took *joyfully* the spoiling of your goods." How came it that they were so turned about from man's usual attitude as to welcome what most people resist, or at least regret? How came it? Why—"knowing that ye have in heaven a better and an enduring substance" [Heb. 10:34]. It does not matter much to the man that has vaults on vaults full of sacks of bullion whether a few shillings may be lost in the course of a day's work. It does not matter much to the merchant who has his warehouse piled with goods though one or two day's transactions may be unprofitable. And if we have the durable riches in the possession of our own selves, we can afford to look—and we shall look—with comparatively quiet hearts on the going of all that can go, and be able to bear losses and sorrows, and "all the ills that flesh is heir to," in an altogether different fashion from what we should do if we could not fall back upon the wealth within, and feel that nothing can touch that.

If we rightly understood the mission of loss, pain, or sorrow, and that each was intended to make us possess more fully the only true riches—that each was meant to make us better, more masters of ourselves, and enriched by such possession—we should not so often murmur or faint when the blows come, nor be so ready to exclaim, "Oh! The mysteries of Providence!" but rather be quick to say, "All things work together for good to them that love God" [Rom. 8:28]. For, if my "loss" of outward things makes me "gain" in patience, in refinement, in fixed faith in Jesus Christ, in quiet submission to Him, then I enter the item on the wrong page if I put it upon the "losses" side of the book. I should put it on the "profits" side; for it profits a man more to gain himself than to gain or keep the whole world [Mark 8:36].

So the right understanding of what our wealth is, and the right understanding of the relation of sorrow and pain and loss to the true wealth in ourselves, would make us not only take patiently, but "joyfully," all possible disaster and loss. And we may come to reproduce that heroism of glad faith which the old prophet showed when he sang, "Although the fig tree shall not blossom, neither shall fruit be in the vines; the labour of the olive shall fail, and the fields shall yield no meat; the flock shall be cut off from the fold, and there shall be no herd in the stalls: Yet I will rejoice in the LORD, I will joy in the God of my salvation" [Hab. 3:17, 18].

THE DIVINE HOST AND THE HUMAN GUESTS

Thou preparest a table before me in the presence of mine enemies; thou anointest my head with oil; my cup runneth over—Ps. 23:5

Life is a sore fight; but to the Christian man, in spite of all the tumult, life is a festal banquet. There stand the enemies, ringing him around with cruel eyes, waiting to be let slip upon him like eager dogs around the poor beast of the chase. But, for all that, here is spread a table in the wilderness, made ready by invisible hands, and the grim-eyed foe is held back in the leash till the servant of God has fed and been strengthened. This is our condition—always the foe, always the table. What sort of a meal should that be? The soldiers who eat and drink, and are drunken in the presence of the enemy, like the Saxons before Hastings, what will become of them? Drink the cup of gladness, as men do when their foe is at their side, looking askance over the rim, and with one hand on the sword, ready! Ready, against treachery and surprise. But the presence of the danger should make the feat more enjoyable, too, by the moderation it enforces and by the contrast it affords—as to sailors on the shore, or soldiers in a truce. Joy may grow on the very face of danger, as a slender rosebush flings its bright sprays and fragrant blossoms over the lip of a cataract; and that not the wild mirth of men in a pestilence, with their "Let us eat and drink; for tomorrow we die" [1 Cor. 15:32], but the simple-hearted gladness of those who have preserved the invaluable childhood gift of living in the present moment, because they know that tomorrow will bring God, whatever it brings, and not take away His care and love, whatever it takes away.

This, then is the form under which the experience of the past is presented in the second portion of this Shepherd psalm—joy in conflict, rest and food even in the strife. Upon that there is built a hope which transcends that in the previous portion of the psalm. As to this life, *"Goodness and mercy shall follow me"* [v. 6]. This is more than *"I will fear no evil"* [v. 5]. That said, Sorrow is not evil if God be with us. This says, Sorrow is mercy. The one is hope looking mainly at outward circumstances; the other is hope learning the spirit and meaning of them all. These two angels of God—Goodness and Mercy—shall follow and encamp around the pilgrim. The enemies whom God held back while he feasted may pursue, but will not overtake him. They will be distanced sooner or later; but the white wings of these messengers of the covenant shall never be far away from the journeying child, and the air shall often be filled with the music of their coming, and their celestial weapons shall glance around him in all the fight, and their soft arms shall bear him up over all the rough ways, and up higher at last to the throne.

THE LONELINESS OF CHRIST

Behold, the hour cometh, yea, is now come, that ye shall be scattered, every man to his own, and shall leave me alone; and yet I am not alone, because the Father is with me—John 16:32

That is not the aspect of our Lord's sorrows, the element of our Lord's Passion, which is most often dealt with and thought about; but it is a very real one, and one that I think deserves to be far more considered than we are in the habit of doing. Attention has been too exclusively directed to the physical sufferings of our Lord's Passion, and to the mysterious element in His mental passion which made it unique and atoning. We have too much forgotten the sorrows which pressed upon Him as upon us, the same in kind, only infinitely deeper in degree, and hence we have lost some of the sense of reality of our Lord's sufferings of these sorrows. I do not know that any is more sharp than the solitude in which He lived and yet more awful solitude in which He died. Jesus Christ was the loneliest man that ever lived. A little ignorant love and a little outward companionship He had; and soothing and strengthening it was to be surrounded by the affection even of such ignorant friends as the disciples. But there was not a single human being who fully understood or believed Him. There were none who sympathized with His aims, none who could receive His confidences. His thoughts were unshared, His words unintelligible, His life's purpose shrouded in mystery. "He came to His own and His own received Him not" [John 1:11]. "His soul was as a star, and dwelt apart." And so He traveled on, bearing a great burden of love which none would accept; the loneliest soul that ever wore human flesh.

All great spirits are solitary; the men that lead the world have to go before the world, and to go by themselves. Starlings fly in flocks, the eagle soars singly. And so the pages of the biographies, teachers and religious reformers, and thinkers and pathbreakers generally, tell us of the pains of uncomprehended aims, of the misery of living apart from one's kind, of the agony of hungering for sympathy, for comprehension, for acceptance of a truth which dooms it possessors to isolation. But all that men have experienced in that kind is as nothing as compared with the blackness of darkness which the loneliness of Jesus Christ assumed as it settled down upon Him.

Let me remind you what it was that condemned Him to this absolute loneliness. It was the very purity and sinlessness of His nature which necessarily made Him separate from sinners. He saw eternal things as no other eye saw them, and His vision of land, where others saw only cloud, parted Him from them.

He read men as no other eye read them: He saw not only the clock-face, but the springs. He looked upon the flesh and behind the spirit, its inmost essence, its destiny and end. Before His human eye there stood plainly manifested the pale kingdoms of the dead, and all that vision separated Him from men. The children on the street used to point at Dante as he passed, saying, "There goes the man that has seen hell," and to shrink from him as if he carried his own atmosphere in which others could not breathe. But the equal vision which Christ had of all things, of all men, of all worlds, made His life an absolute solitude; and when He spake that He knew, and testified what He had seen, no man received His testimony. Hence came a deeper loneliness.

LIFE'S ISOLATIONS

I have trodden the winepress alone—Is. 63:3

The very things that made the solitude of Christ made its agony. The same characteristics in Jesus Christ which separated Him from men made Him feel, as no other man ever felt, the pain and bitterness of being so separated. Other men wear an armor of selfishness and, alas! of proclivity to evil which makes it less of a torture to be brought close to it. But He stood with bared breast, and every blow struck full home. Christ was lonely in the midst of crowds. It would have been so much easier for Him to have come neither eating nor drinking; or like John the Baptist, to have gone into the desert and lived an ascetic life of outward solitude there. But that could not be. He must be kindly with His kind. He had to live the life which was to be every man's pattern and inspiration. So He must enter into all common relationships, and hallow ordinary duties and scenes by Himself passing through them. Therefore He came eating and drinking, and sat at feasts where there was no love and scant courtesy, and kept company with men, the very association with whom was a deeper solitude than He would have found in the dreariest wilderness.

Christ's loneliness deepened as the end drew near. The disciples understood Him even less when He spoke about His death than in the rest of His teaching. He had, in a very special sense, to go down into the valley alone. Death is ever a solitude, and, perhaps, is most terrible because it is. The fondest love can only go with us to the gate. We must part outside the barrier, and all alone pass in and take our journey. But His death, compassed by treachery, and preceded by the flight of His friends and the denial of His chief apostle, was, in a very special sense, a solitary death. The little faith which had feebly been building itself up in some hearts was shattered. The love seemed to have gone. No man in all the world believed in Him now. "We trusted" [Luke 24:21] was the most they would say. And so, wrapped in darkness, He dies, as He had lived, alone! How profoundly must our Lord have felt the pain of His solitude! The thought of His loneliness is made more bitter to Him by its contrast with the companionship which His faithless followers so easily secured. "Ye shall be scattered, every man to his own" [John 16:32]. They had all congenial surroundings and friends to return to, and fleeing to that shelter, they leave Him solitary, like a traveler, on a waste unsheltered heath, to meet the whole fury of the storm. "*His* own" [John 1:11], to whom He had come with hands outstretched craving a welcome, had turned from Him, and the isolation aggravated even the solemn pains of His test passion.

The piteous petition that came from His lips in Gethsemane reveals this: "My soul is exceeding sorrowful, even unto death. Tarry ye here and watch with me" [Matt. 26:38]. Even the company of these three, who understood so little, and the imperfection of whose love He saw so plainly, was a kind of solace. And when even that poor staff broke as he leaned upon it, pain as well as wonder spoke in the gentle remonstrance, "Could ye not watch with me one hour?" [Matt. 26:40]. Lonely and hungering for human companionship, He entered into the agony and fought His last fight for us all that we might not fight it alone.

CHRIST'S VOLUNTARY SUFFERINGS

*Therefore doth my Father love me, because I lay down my life, that I may take it
again. No man taketh it away from me, but I lay it down of myself—*
John 10:17, 18

All the suffering and solitude of Christ were voluntarily endured, and that for
us. All man's sorrow He experienced. Every ingredient that adds bitterness to our
cup was familiar to His taste, and He tasted them, as He tasted death, "for every man"
[Heb. 2:9], that His experience of them might make them less hard for us to bear, and
that the touch of His lips lingering on the cup might sweeten the draught for us.

His endurance of this, as of all the sorrows of human life, was at every moment a
fresh act of willing surrender of Himself for us. He wore our manhood and He bore
manhoods' griefs, not because He must, but because He would. He willed to be born.
He willed to abide in the flesh. He willed, pang by pang, to bear our sorrows. He could
have ended it all. But His love held Him here. That was the cord which bound Him to
the stake. His enemies were wiser than they knew, when they mocked at Him, and said
He saved others—and precisely, therefore—Himself He cannot save. So all that dreary
solitude in which He groped for a hand to grasp and found none was voluntarily borne
and was as truly a part of His bearing the consequences of man's sin, as when He bowed
His head to death, and, therefore, to be gazed on by us with thankfulness as an element
in the suffering wherewith He has redeemed us.

These thoughts may encourage us all to bear the necessary isolation of life, and in a
special manner may strengthen some of us whom God in His providence has called
upon to live outwardly lonely lives. But after all companionship, we have to live alone.
Each man has to live his own life. We come singly into the world; and though God
setteth the solitary in families, and there are manifold blessings of love and companionship for the most of us, yet the awful burden of personality weighs upon us all. Alone
we live in the depths of our hearts; alone we have to front joy and sorrow. If you are
wise, you will be wise for thyself, and, if you scorn, you alone shall bear it. The heart
knoweth its own bitterness. All human love feels its own limitations in presence of the
impossibility of sharing the bodily sicknesses of those nearest to us. Two hearts shall be
bound in closest love, and the one shall beat languidly in a wasted frame and the other
throb in ruddy health. Two hearts shall be knit in tender sympathy, and the one shall
have a sense of guilt from some dark passage in its past history, of which no shadow
falls on the other. For some of us solitary days are appointed. We may think of Christ
and see the prints of His footsteps before us on the loneliest road. If any of us are called
to know the pain of unsatisfied longings for earthly companions, let us stretch out our
hands to lay hold on the hand of that solitary Man who knew this, as He knows all,
sorrow. He felt all the bitterness of having to stand alone, with no arm to lean upon
and no heart to trust. If we are left alone, let us make Christ our companion. We shall
not be utterly solitary if He is with us. Perhaps God takes away earthly props that our
love and desires may reach higher, and entwined around the throne where Christ sits.

THE COMPANION OF THE LONELY CHRIST

I am not alone, but I and the Father that sent me—John 8:16

One cannot but feel the sudden change in the words from plain time to exulting notes, from the pathetic minors of an Aeolian harp to the joyous clang of the trumpet. "Yet I am not alone, for the Father is with Me." Here is the reality of the perpetual Divine presence with Christ and through Him with us. That is the first point: "the Father is with Me." Now, we are not concerned here with that mysterious and Divine union between the Divine Father and the Divine Son, which, as I believe, is a distinct revelation of Scripture, taught in such words as, "The only begotten Son which is in the bosom of the Father" [John 1:18]; or, "I and my Father are one" [John 10:30]; or, by His Name, "the Son of man which is in Heaven" [John 3:13]. All that belongs to another region, where thought and language can safely go no farther than as His own declarations lead them. But here it is the presence of God with Christ's perfect manhood which is spoken of—a presence the same in kind, however different in degree, which is granted to all loving and pure hearts.

Take the words, then, as a wonderful utterance of our Lord's own consciousness. That nature, perfect in mind, in will, in heart, was always conscious of an unbroken union with God. The mind was filled with His truth, the will ever consciously bowing to His supreme law; the heart ever at rest in His perfect love and goodness. Like some pure mirror of steel, on which there is no dint nor scratch nor stain, but every portion of it capable, and equally capable, of receiving and flashing back in brightness the rays of the sun, the whole Man, Christ Jesus, spread Himself out, if I may so say, beneath the luster of God, and was shone upon with the unvarying radiance of His unclouded presence.

And that is possible for us through Him. "I do always," said He, "those things that please Him." and, therefore, "the Father hath not left me alone" [John 8:29]. We can come to Him, though our natures, as compared with His, be like the same shield—all battered and bruised, and stained with evil, and eaten into with rust, and incapable of catching the light or of throwing it back. We can go to that Christ in whom we come near to God, and in whom God comes near to us; and, holding by Him, we can enter into the fellowship, the wondrous fellowship, of the Father God, who will draw near to our minds and hearts and wills, and make all the fitful and fleeting days of our earthly existence stately and noble, and happy with the benediction and the elevation of His felt presence. "The Father is with me" [John 16:32]. My brother, is He with you, or has He ever been with you in such a fashion as this? It is possible that He should be. Christ has brought the Father near to us; He will bring us near to the Father. He is near us in His own gracious presence, and in Him God is near. His Name is Immanuel—God with us [Matt. 1:23]. "He that hath the Son hath the Father also" [1 John 2:23]. He lived alone, and went down into death alone, that no soul need ever be solitary any more.

A SUFFICIENCY FOR ALL NEED

I am poor and needy, yet the Lord thinketh upon me—Psalm 40:17

The joy and triumph which ring through the words of Christ, "I am not alone," suggest the sufficiency of that Divine presence for all the needs of the heart. Christ felt that He was not alone, that the dreariness of the solitude had passed away, because the Father's presence was enough. He was the loneliest of men, and He was also the most rich in sufficient companionship—the most sad and the most happy. So the surface and the depth of His life present the sharpest contrasts. Opposites meet in Him: He was the Man of Sorrows, and acquainted with grief [Is. 53:3], "and yet God anointed Him with the oil of gladness above His fellows" [see Ps. 45:7; Heb. 1:9]. He was "sorrowful, yet always rejoicing; as poor, yet making many rich; as having nothing, and yet possessing all things" [2 Cor. 6:10]. For Him the Father's presence was sunshine in the darkness; summer in the depth of winter; life in the very jaws of death.

And for you and me the Father's presence will be enough, too. It will not be exactly the same thing as the society and communion of dear ones, and there may be a sense of loss and pain with us, as there was with Him, but yet the blessed consciousness of God's presence will satisfy our hearts. So, whether we have to walk a lonely road, or are compassed by lovers and friends, and yet feel often much apart, let us lift our hearts to God in Christ, and He will come to be our companion. God and you will make society enough for you. "Thou hast made him exceeding glad with thy countenance" [Ps. 21:6].

We never know the blessedness of God's presence till we have felt the loneliness of life. "I was left alone and I saw this great vision" [Dan. 10:8]. We must detach ourselves from earth, and shut our doors about us before we can have the vision of God. Solitude is the mother of all great and holy thoughts. To enter into thyself, said one of the mystics, is to ascend to Heaven. He who is at all times alone, said another, is worthy of God who is then present. Prayer is the flight of the lonely soul to the alone God.

The blessed communion between Christ and God, the Man Christ Jesus and His Divine Father, was broken once, My God! My God! Why hast thou forsaken me?" [Matt. 27:46; Mark 15:34]. Broken once—wherefore? How? Because He, in the depth of His love, in the might of His sympathy, in the reality of His union with mankind, so identified Himself with us, in our sins and in their punishment, that the last issue of sin fell upon Him, and He tasted the most extreme bitterness of the cup, in the separation from God, which is eternal death. That was for us and for all men. "I could wish myself accursed," said the servant. The Master did more than wish; He made Himself a curse for us. He bore that last, most awful, consequence of sin, and was left alone, bereft of God, in the darkness, that we might never lose the light of God's face, nor the strength and joy of our Father's presence.

Let us bow with hushed and grateful spirits before that miracle and mystery of love, and yield ourselves to Him. Trusting to Him, we shall never be solitary anymore, for He hath said, "Lo! I am with you always" [Matt. 28:20].

"FEAR NOT: ONLY BELIEVE"

But when Jesus heard it, he answered him, saying, Fear not: believe only, and she shall be made whole—Luke 8:50

This is the word of cheer which sustains a staggering faith. How preposterous this rekindling of hope must have seemed to Jairus when the storm had blown out the last flickering spark! How irrelevant, if it were not cruel, the "Fear not" must have sounded when the last possible blow had fallen. And yet, because of the word in the middle, embedded between the obligation to hope and the prohibition to fear, neither the one nor the other is preposterous. "Only believe." That is in the center; and on the one side, "Fear not!"—a command ridiculous without it; and on the other side, hope!—an injunction impossible apart from faith.

Jesus Christ is saying the very same things to us. His fundamental commandment is, "Only believe"; and there effloresce from it the two things, courage that never trembles, and hope that never despairs. "Only believe." Usually He made the outflow of His miraculous power contingent upon the faith either of the sufferer himself or of some others. There was no necessity for the connection. We have instances in His life of miracles wrought without faith, without asking; simply at the bidding of His own irrepressible pity. But the rule in regard to His miracles is, that faith was the condition which drew out the miraculous energy. The connection between our faith and our experience of His supernatural sustaining, cleansing, gladdening, enlightening power is closer than that. For, without our trust in Him, He can do no mighty works upon us; and there must be confidence on our part before there is in our experience the reception into our lives of His highest blessings; just because they are greater and deeper, and belong to a more inward sphere than these outward and inferior miracles of bodily healing. Therefore the connection between our faith and His gifts to us is inevitable and constant, and the commandment, "Only believe," assumes a more imperative stringency in regard to our spiritual experience, than it ever did in regard to those who felt the power of His miracle-working hand. So it stands for us as the one central appeal and exhortation which Christ, by His life, by the record of His love, by His Cross and Passion, by His dealings and pleadings with us, through His Spirit, and His providence today, is making to us all. "Only believe"—the one act that vitally knits the soul to Christ, and makes it capable of receiving unto itself the fullness of His loftiest blessings.

HOPE AND FEAR

Fear not, for I am with thee, and will bless thee—Gen. 26:24

Faith is the one counterpoise of fear. There is none other for the deepest dreads that lie cold and paralyzing, though often dormant, in every human spirit; and that ought to lie there. If a man has not faith in God, in Christ, he *ought* to have fear. For there rise before him—solitary, helpless, inextricably caught into the meshes of this mysterious and awful system of things—a whole host of possible, or probable, or certain calamities; and what is he to do? Stand there in the open, with the pelting of the pitiless storm coming down upon him? The man is an idiot if he is not afraid. And what is to calm those rational fears—the fear of wrath, of life, of death, of what lies beyond death? You cannot whistle them away. You cannot ignore them always. You cannot grapple with them in your own strength. "Only believe," says the Comforter and the Courage-Bringer. The attitude of trust banishes dread, and nothing else will effectually and reasonably do it. I will forewarn you whom ye shall fear—Him who can slay and who judges. You have, and you cannot break, a connection with God. He ought to be one of two things: your ghastliest dread or your absolute trust. "Only believe." "Fear not." Believe not, *then* be afraid; for you have reason to be.

Men say, "Oh! Keep your courage up," and they contribute no means to keep it up. Christ says, "Fear not, only believe," and gives to faith the courage which He enjoins. Like a child that never dreams of any mischief being able to reach it when the mother's breast is beneath its head and the mother's arms are around its little body, each of us may rest on Christ's breast, and feel His arm around us. Then we may smile at all that men call evils; and whether they are possible, or probable, or certain, we can look at them all and say, "I have circumvented you." "All things work together for good to them that" [Rom. 8:28] trust Christ. "Fear not: only believe."

But, on the other hand, from that simple faith will spring up also hope that cannot despair. "She shall be made whole" [Luke 8:50], said the Master to Jairus. Irreversible disasters have no place in Christian experience. There are no irrevocable losses to him who trusts. There are no wounds that cannot be staunched, when we go to Him who has the balm and the bandage. Although it is true that dead faces do not smile again upon us until we get beyond earth's darkness, it is also true that bonds broken may be knit in a finer fashion, if faith instead of sense weaves them together; and that in the great future we shall find that the true healing of those that went away was not by deliverance from, but by passing through the death that emancipates from, the long disease of earthly life.

If we trust Christ, we may "hope perfectly." If we do not trust Him, our firmest hopes are as spiders' webs that are swept away by a broom, and our deepest desires remain unfulfilled. "Only believe." Then, on the one side, "Fear not," and on the other side, "Hope ever."

THE VOICE WHICH SOFTENS THE GRIMNESS OF DEATH

But he said, Weep not: she is not dead, but sleepeth—Luke 8:52

Our Lord reaches the house of affliction, and finds it a house of hubbub and noise. The hired mourners, with their shrill shrieks, were there already, bewailing her. The tumult jarred upon His calmness, and He says, "Weep not; she is not dead, but sleepeth." One wonders that some people have read those words as if they declared that the apparent physical death was only a swoon or a faint, or some kind of coma, and that so there was no miracle at all in the case. "They laughed Him to scorn, knowing that she was dead" [v. 53]. You can measure the hollowness of their greed by its change into scornful laughter when a promise of consolation began to open before them. And you can measure their worth as witnesses to the child's resurrection by their absolute certainty of her death. But notice that our Lord never forbids weeping unless He takes away its cause. "Weep not" is another of the futile forms of words with which men try to encourage and comfort one another. There is nothing more cruel than to forbid tears to the sad heart. Jesus Christ never did that except when He was able to bring that which took away occasion for weeping. He lets grief have its way. He means us to run rivers of waters down our cheeks when He sends us sorrows. We shall never get the blessing of them till we have felt the bitterness of them. We shall never profit by them if we stoically choke back the manifestations of our grief, and think that it is submissive to be restrained. Let sorrow have its way. Tears purge the heart from which their streams come. But Jesus Christ says to us all, "Weep not," because He comes to us all with that which, if I may so say, puts a rainbow into the teardrops, and makes it possible that the great paradox should be fulfilled in our hearts, "as sorrowful, yet always rejoicing" [2 Cor. 6:10]. Weep not; or, if you weep, let the tears have thankfulness as well as grief in them. It is a difficult commandment, but it is possible when His lips tells us not to weep, and we have obeyed the central exhortation, "Only believe." How He smoothes away the grimness of death! I do not claim for Him anything like a monopoly of that most obvious and natural symbolism which regards death as a sleep. It must have occurred to all who ever looked upon a corpse. But I do claim that when He used the metaphor, and by His use of it modified the whole conception of death in the thoughts of His disciples, He put altogether different ideas into it from that which it contained on the lips of others. He meant to suggest the idea of repose:

"Sleep, full of rest from head to foot."

The calm immobility of the body, so lately racked with pain, or restless in feverish tossings, is but a symbol of the deeper stillness of truer repose which remaineth for the people of God. He meant to suggest the idea of separation from this material world. He did not mean to suggest the idea of unconsciousness. A man is not unconscious when he is asleep, as dreams testify. He meant, above all, if a sleep, then waking. So the grim fact is smoothed down, not by blinking any of its aspects, but by looking deeper into them. They who, only believing, have lived a life of courage and of hope, and have fronted sorrows, and felt the benediction of tears, pass into the great darkness, and know that they there are rocked to sleep on a loving breast, and, sleeping in Jesus, shall wake with the earliest morning light.

A LIFE-GIVING WORD OF POWER

And he put them all out, and took her by the hand, and called, saying, Maid, arise. And her spirit came again, and she arose straightway—Luke 8:54, 55

"Maid, arise!" All the circumstances of the miracle are marked by the most lovely consideration, on Christ's part, of the timidity of the little girl of twelve years of age. It is because of this that He seeks to raise her in privacy, whereas the son of the widow of Nain, and Lazarus, were raised amid a crowd. It is because of this that He selects as His companions in the room only the three chief apostles as witnesses, and the father and mother of the child. It is because of that He puts forth His hand and grasps hers, in order that the child's eyes when they open should see only the loving faces of parents, and the not less loving face of the Master; and that her hand, when it began to move again, should clasp, first, His own tender hand. It is for the same reason that the remarkable appendix to the miracle is given—"He commanded that they should give her meat" [v. 55]. Surely that is an inimitable note of truth. No legend-manufacturer would have dared to drop down to such a homely word as that, after such a word as "Maiden, arise!" An economy of miraculous power is shown here, such as was shown when, after Lazarus came forth, other hands had to untie the grave-clothes which tripped him as he stumbled along. Christ will do by miracle what is needful and not one hair's breadth more. In His calm majesty He thinks of the hungry child, and leaves to others the task of giving her food. That homely touch is, to me, indicative of the simple veracity of the historian.

But the life-giving word itself—what can we say about it? Only this one thing: here Jesus Christ exercises a manifest Divine prerogative. It was no more the syllables that He spoke than it was the touch of His hand that raised that child. What was it? The putting-forth of His will, which went away straight into the darkness; and if the dis-embodied spirit was in a locality, went straight there, and somehow or other, laid hold of the spirit, and, somehow or other, reinstated it in its home. Christ's will, like the king's writ, runs through all the universe. "He spake, and it was done" [Ps. 33:9]—whose pre-rogative is that? God's; and God manifest in the flesh exercised it. The words of the Incarnate Word have power over physical things.

Here, too, is the prelude and firstfruits of our resurrection. Not that there are not wide differences between the raising of this child and that future resurrection to which Christian hope looks forward, but that in this little one incident—little compared with the majestic scale of the latter—there come out these two things: the demonstration that conscious life runs on, irrespective of the accident of its being united with or sepa-rated from a bodily organization; and the other, that Jesus Christ has power over men's spirits, and can fit them at His will to bodies appropriate to their condition. Time is no element in the case. What befalls the particles of the human frame is no element in the case. "Thou sowest not the body that shall be" [1 Cor. 15:37]. But if that Lord had the power, which He showed in that one chamber, with that one child, then, as a little win-dow may show us great matters, so we see through this single incident the time when "all that are in the graves shall hear his voice, and shall come forth" [John 5:28, 29].

THE GREAT ALTERNATIVE

Elijah came unto all the people and said, How long halt ye between two opinions?
If the Lord be God, follow him; but if Baal, then follow him—1 Kgs. 18:21

The vehement question of Elijah is, perhaps, still more picturesque in the original, for one rendering gives, "How long limp ye on two knees?" A vulgar, but expressive, figure by which indecision is likened to a cripple hobbling along first on one knee and then on the other. But whether that be so or no, there is no mistaking the ring of contempt and impatience with which the prophet, so convinced himself, rebukes the pitiable weakness that sought to unite two such discrepancies as the worship of God and the worship of Baal. Unite, I say; for it is to be observed that, in accordance with the tone of the question and the facts of the case, the worship of idols was not proposed as a substitute for, but as an accompaniment and a form of, worship of Jehovah. The only person that objected was Jehovah. Polytheism is always hospitable; for when "there are gods many and lords many" [1 Cor. 8:5], one or two more make very little difference, and Baal had no objection to Jehovah's altar standing behind his. But Jehovah is intolerant, for He is alone. "Thou shalt have no other gods before me" [Ex. 20:3], and to enthrone another is to dethrone Him.

What do I mean by choice? I mean, first, an honest fronting of all the facts of the case, so far as these are ascertainable. Have you ever sat down and taken stock of your position? Have you ever looked at the claims of God revealed in Christ—at your own natures, and what they tell you you ought to be to Him, and He, and He only, may be to you. Have you fronted eternity, and given that its due weight as a factor in the decision of your conduct? Unless you have, you may say, "I *choose* not to be a Christian," but the word choice is as much misapplied to that instinctive decision as it would be to the child's act when it puts out its hand to lay hold of the moon. First and foremost, the state of the case should be looked at all around; and until you have done that you have no business to make a choice; for God gave you the power of choice that it should be ruled by your reason, and your reason directed by your conscience, and your conscience illuminated by His revelation.

And then I mean that a deliberate decision should be made in accordance with the evidence, and that you should not, first of all, contemplate the facts of the case, and then shut your eyes, and, to use a vulgar expression, "go it blind," and decide as you like and not as reason and conscience tell you. And I mean, further, that on the back of intelligent weighing of the facts and deliberate decision, molded by these, there should come appropriate action. "If the Lord be God, follow Him."

Now, I believe that these three things are deplorably lacking, as in regard to the lives of all of us, so most eminently in regard of the lives of the great majority of people who have not committed the keeping of their souls to Jesus Christ, and taken service in His army.

"NOW IS THE ACCEPTED TIME"

Remember now thy Creator in the days of thy youth, while the evil days come not,
nor the years draw nigh, when thou shalt say, I have no pleasure in them—
Eccl. 12:1

Would it not have been a very sensible thing of the Israelites on Carmel if, after they saw the miracle of the fire falling from heaven, they had said to the prophet, "We will hear thee again on this matter?" They were wiser. Conviction followed immediately. Resolution and action came close on the heels of conviction. "All the people fell on their faces and they said, The Lord, He is God. The Lord, He is God" [1 Kgs. 18:39]. That is a wise course always. Tomorrow is the fool's plea, by which he cheats himself, but cheats neither this inexorable universe for the God that made it. Many a man dies a drunkard who for half a lifetime has been saying, "Tomorrow I will begin to reform." and when the last of the tomorrows has sunk into yesterday, it leaves him as it found him. Procrastination in doing right is continuance in doing wrong. We live in too uncertain and too strenuous a world to allow any grass to grow under our feet in putting into exercise our deliberate decisions. That is true all around, but most eminently in regard of our submission to Jesus Christ.

Consider how much youth needs the guidance and the grace of Jesus Christ. Your experience is little, your hopes are bright, your passions are strong, your temptations are many. Everything is fresh and radiant around you. With the unreflectiveness and the buoyant hopefulness which are your beautiful privileges, and are so soon knocked out of us, you are eager to cast yourself into the fray. You sometimes think that religion is very good for old people like me, but not necessary for you. "Wilt thou not from this time cry unto me, My Father, thou art the guide of my youth?" [Jer. 3:4]. That will keep you from many a sore heart and from many a sad hour.

Consider how favorable youth is to decision. We older men are like flies in a spider's web, with a hundred filaments, poisonous and dirty, spun around us, and making movement difficult. You have but little of that yet. You are not yet tied and bound by the cords of your sins. You have not many deep-rooted evil habits to break. There are not many black pages on your diary which you would wish to erase, and which make you feel that the tragedy of life is "What I have written I have written" [John 19:22]. This is your time to plant. Your lives are before you, your characters as yet are plastic. The lava is molten; it is hardening very fast. Do you not put off this deliberate decision about which I am speaking till it is hardened into rock.

Consider how much you gain by youthful decision for Jesus Christ. So much the longer blessedness, so many more hours of peaceful growth; no cleft in your lives between a past that your cheek burns to think about, and a poor present in which you try to redeem it, the mystic influence of habit on the side of godliness. Oh, it is beautiful! When we have "first the blade, then the ear, then the full corn in the ear." And the men that have done most work for God and man in the world are, in nine cases out of ten, the men who in their early days were kept innocent and ignorant of much transgression because they were the servants of the Lord from their youth.

BLESSED UNCONSCIOUSNESS

Moses wist not that the skin of his face shone while he talked with Him—
Ex. 34:29

The experience of Moses teaches us that the loftiest beauty of character comes from communion with God. That is the use that the Apostle makes of this remarkable incident in 2 Corinthians 3, where he takes the light that shone from Moses' face as being the symbol of the better luster that gleams from all those who behold (or reflect) the glory of the Lord with unveiled faces, and, by beholding, are changed into the likeness of that on which they gaze with adoration and longing. The great law to which, almost exclusively, Christianity commits the perfecting of individual character is this: Look at Him till you are like Him, and in beholding, be changed. There have been in the past, and there are today, thousands of simple souls shut out by lowliness of position and other circumstances from all the refining and ennobling influences of which the world makes so much, who yet in character and bearing, and sometimes in the very look of their meek faces, are living witnesses how true and mighty to transform a nature is the power of loving gaze upon Jesus Christ. There is no influence to refine and beautify men like that of living near Jesus Christ, and walking in the light of that beauty which is the radiance of the Divine glory and the express image of His Person.

But, then, the bearer of the radiance is unconscious of it. In all regions of life the consummate apex and crowning charm of excellence is unconsciousness of excellence. Whenever a man begins to suspect that he is good he begins to be bad; and you rob every virtue and beauty of character of some portion of its attractive fairness when the man who bears it knows, or fancies that he knows, it. The more a man is like Christ, the less he knows it; and the better he is the less he suspects it. Let us try to lose ourselves in Jesus Christ. It is safe for us to leave all thoughts of our miserable selves behind us, if instead of them we have the thought of that great, sweet, dear Lord filling mind and heart.

Think constantly and longingly of the unattained. "Brethren, I count not myself to have apprehended" [Phil. 3:13]. Endless aspiration and a stinging consciousness of present imperfection are the loftiest states of man here below. The people down in the valley, when they look up, may see our figures against the skyline, and fancy us at the summit; but our loftier elevation reveals untrodden heights beyond, and we have only risen so high in order to discern more clearly how much higher we have to rise. The best way to keep unconscious of present attainments is to set our faces forward, and to make "all experience" as an arch where through gleams that untraveled world to which we move. Let us cultivate a clear sense of our own imperfections. We do not need to try to learn our goodness that will suggest itself to us only too clearly; but what we do need is to have a very clear sense of our shortcomings and failures, our faults of temper, our faults of desire, our faults in our relations to our fellows. A true man will never be so much ashamed of himself as when he is praised, for it will always send him to look into the deep places of his heart, and there will be plenty of ugly creeping things under the stones there if he will only turn them up and look beneath.

November 17

TRAGIC UNCONSCIOUSNESS

He wist not that the Lord was departed from him—Judg. 16:20

Samson, fresh from his coarse debauch, and shorn of the locks which he had vowed to keep, strides out into the air, and tries his former feats. But his strength has left him because the Lord has left him; and the Lord has left him because, in his fleshly animalism, he has left the Lord. The strong man made weak is unconscious of his weakness. All evil, by its very nature, tends to make us insensitive to its presence. Conscience becomes dull by practice of sin and by neglect of conscience, until that which at first was as sensitive as the palm of a little child's hand becomes as if it were "seared with a hot iron" [1 Tim. 4:2]. The foulness of the atmosphere of a crowded hall is not perceived by the people in it. It needs a man to come in from the outer air to detect it. We can accustom ourselves to any stinking and poisonous atmosphere, and many of us live in one all our days, and do not know that there is any need of ventilation or that the air is not perfectly sweet. The deceitfulness of sin is its great weapon. Christian people may lose their strength because they let go of their hold upon God, and know nothing about it. Spiritual declension, all unconscious of its own existence, is the very history of hundreds of nominal Christians. When the life-blood is pouring out of a man, he faints before he dies. The swoon of unconsciousness is the condition of some professing Christians. Frost-bitten limbs are quite comfortable, and only tingle when circulation is coming back. I remember a great elm tree, the pride of an avenue in the south, that had spread its branches for more years than the oldest man could count, and stood, leafy and green. Not until a winter storm came one night and laid it low with a crash did anybody suspect what everybody saw in the morning—that the heart was eaten out of it, and nothing left but a shell of bark. Some Christian people are like that: they manage leaves, and even some fruit; but when the storm comes, they will go down, because the heart has been out of their religion for years. And so, because there are so many things that mask the ebbing away of a Christian life, and because our own self-love and habits come in to hide declension, let us watch ourselves very narrowly. Unconsciousness does not mean ignorant presumption or presumptuous ignorance. It is difficult to make an estimate of ourselves by poking into our own sentiments and supposed feelings and convictions, and the estimate is likely to be wrong. There is a better way than that. Two things tell what a man is—one, what he wants, and the other, what he does. As the will is, the man is. Where do the currents of your desires set? If you watch their flow, you may be pretty sure whether your religious life is an ebbing or a rising tide. The other way to ascertain what we are is rigidly to examine and judge what we do. "Let us search and try our *ways*, and turn again to the Lord" [Lam. 3:40]. Actions are the true test of a man. Conduct is the best illumination of character, especially in regard to ourselves. So watch, and be sober—sober in our estimate of ourselves, and determined to find every lurking evil, and to drag it forth into the light.

A COMPANIONSHIP THAT CHEERS

Can two walk together, except they be agreed?—Amos 3:3

There are three phrases in the Old Testament very like each other and yet presenting different facets or aspects of the same great truth. Sometimes we read about "walking before God," as Abraham was bid to do. That means ordering the daily life under the continual sense that we are ever in the great Taskmaster's eye. Then there is "walking after God," and that means conforming the will and active efforts to the rule that He has laid down; setting our steps firm on the paths that He has prepared, that we should walk in them; and accepting His providential plans. But also, then, high above both these conceptions of a devout life, is the one which was realized in the case of the patriarch Enoch—walking "with God." For to walk before Him may have with it some tremor, and may be undertaken in the spirit of the slave, who would be glad to get away from the jealous eye that rebukes his slothfulness; and "walking after Him" may be a painful and partial effort to keep His distant figure in sight; but to "walk with Him" implies a constant, quiet sense of His Divine presence which forbids that I should ever be lonely, which guides and defends, which floods my soul and fills my life, and in which, as the companions pace along side by side, words may be spoken by either, or blessed silence may be eloquent of perfect trust and rest.

But far above us as such experience seems to sound, such a life is a possibility for every one of us. We *may* be able to say, as truly as our Lord said it, "I am not alone, because the Father is with me." It is possible that the dreariest solitude of a soul, such as is not realized when the body is removed from men, but is felt most in the crowded city, where there is none that loves or fathoms and sympathizes, may be turned into blessed fellowship with Him. Yes! But that solitude will not be so turned unless it is first painfully felt. As Daniel said, "I was left alone, and I saw this great vision" [Dan. 10:8]. We need to feel in our deepest heart that loneliness on earth before we walk with God.

If we are so walking, it is no piece of fanaticism to say that there will be mutual communications. As really as it was ever true that the Lord said unto Abraham, or Isaiah, or Paul, it is true that He now speaks to the man that walks with Him. Frank speech on both sides beguiles many a weary mile when lovers or friends foot it side by side. And this pair of friends, of whom I have spoken, have mutual fellowship. God speaks with His servant now, as of old, "as a man speaketh unto his friend" [Ex. 33:11]. And we, on our parts, if we are truly walking with Him, shall feel it natural to speak frankly to God. As two friends on the road will interchange remarks about trifles, and, if they love each other, the remarks about the trifles will be weighted with love, so we can tell our smallest affairs to God; and, if we have Him for our Pilgrim-Companion, we do not need to lock up any troubles or concerns of any sort, big or little, in our hearts, but may speak them all to our Friend that goes with us.

COMMUNION WITH GOD

If we walk in the light, as He is in the light, we have fellowship one with another,
and the blood of Jesus Christ his Son cleanseth us from all sin—1 John 1:7

The "two" whom the prophet Amos (3:3) would desire to see walking together are God and Israel; and his question suggests not only the companionship and communion with God which are the highest form of religion, and the aim of all forms and ceremonies of worship, but also the inexorable condition on which alone that height of communion can be secured and sustained. Two *may* walk together, though the one be God in Heaven and I be the other in Manchester. But they have to be agreed thus far, at any rate, that both shall wish to be together, and both be going the same road.

The two *may* walk together. That is the end of all religion. What are creeds for? What are services and sacraments for? What is theology for? What is Christ's redeeming act for? All culminate in this true, constant fellowship between men and God. And unless, in some measure, that result is arrived at in our cases, our religion, let it be as orthodox as you like; our faith in the redemption of Jesus Christ, let it be as real as you will; our attendance at services and sacraments, let them be as punctilious and regular as may be—are all "sounding brass and tinkling cymbal" [see 1 Cor. 13:1]. Get side by side with God. That is the meaning of the whole, and fellowship with Him is the climax of all religion.

It is also the secret of all blessedness, the only thing that will make a life absolutely sovereign over sorrow, and fixedly unperturbed by all tempests, and invulnerable to all the slings and arrows of outrageous fortune. Hold fast by God, and you have an amulet against every evil, and a shield against every foe, and a mighty power that will calm and satisfy your whole being. Nothing else, nothing else will do so. As Augustine said, "O God! Thou hast made us for Thyself, and in Thyself only are we at rest." If the Shepherd is with us, we will fear no evil.

There may be, and therefore there should be, running unbroken through a Christian life, one long, bright line of communion with God and happy inspiration from the sense of His presence with us. Is it a line in *my* life, or is there but a dot here, and a dot there, and long breaks between? The long embarrassed pauses in a conversation between two who do not know much of, or care much for, each other are only too like what occurs in many professing Christians' fellowship with God. Their communion is like those time-worn inscriptions that archaeologists dig up, with a word clearly cut and then a great gap, and then a letter or two, and then another gap, and then a little bit more reading, and then the stone broken, and all the rest gone. Did you ever read the meteorological reports in the newspapers and observe a record like this: "Twenty minutes sunshine out of a possible eight hours?" Do you not think that such a state of affairs is a little like the experience of a great many Christian people in regard to their communion with God? It is broken at best, and imperfect at the most complete, and shallow at the deepest. Rise to the height of your possibilities, and live as close to God as He lets you live, and nothing will much trouble you.

FOLLOWING AFAR OFF

But Peter followed Him afar off—Matt. 26:58
Many women were there beholding afar off—Matt. 27:55

The consciousness of God's presence with us is a very delicate thing. It is like a very sensitive thermometer, which will drop when an iceberg is a league off over the sea, and scarcely visible. We do not want His company, or we are not in harmony with His thoughts, or we are not going His road, and therefore, of course, we part. At bottom there is only one thing that separates a soul from God, and that is sin—sin of some sort, like tiny grains of dust that get between two polished plates in an engine, that ought to move smoothly and closely against each other. The obstruction may be invisible, and yet be powerful enough to cause friction which hinders the working of the engine and throws everything out of gear. A light cloud, that we cannot see, may come between us and a star, and we shall only know it is there because the star is *not* visibly there. Similarly, many a Christian, quite ignorantly, has something or other in his habits or in his conduct or in his affections which would reveal itself to him, if he would look, as being wrong because it blots out God.

Let us remember that very little divergence will, if the two paths are prolonged far enough, part their other ends by a world. Our way may go off from the ways of the Lord at a very acute angle. There may be scarcely any consciousness of parting company at the beginning. Let the man travel on upon it far enough, and the two will be so far apart that he cannot see God or hear Him speak. Take care of the little divergences which are *habitual*, for their accumulate results will be complete separation. There must be absolute surrender if there is to be uninterrupted fellowship.

Such, then, is the direction in which we are to look for the reasons for our low and broken experiences of communion with God. Oh, dear friend, when we do as we sometimes do, wake with a start, like a child that all at once starts from sleep and finds that its mother is gone—when we wake with a start to feel that we are alone, then do not let us be afraid to go straight back. Only be sure that we leave behind us the thing that parted us.

You remember how Peter signalized himself on the lake, on the occasion of the second miraculous draught of fishes, when he floundered through the water, and clasped Christ's feet. He did not say then, "Depart from me, for I am a sinful man, O Lord" [Luke 5:8]. He had said that before on a similar occasion, when he felt his sin less; but knew that the best place for the denier was with his head on Christ's bosom.

So, if we have parted from our Friend, there should be no time lost ere we go back. May it be with us all that we walk with God, so that at last the great promise may be fulfilled about us, that we shall walk with Him in white, being, by His love, accounted "worthy," and so "follow," and keep company with, "the Lamb whithersoever He goeth" [see Luke 9:57].

THE REFUGE OF THE DEVOUT SOUL

Because thou hast made the Lord, which is my refuge, even the most High, thy habitation—Psalm 91:9

This cry of the devout soul, recognizing God as its Asylum and Home, comes in response to a revelation of God's blessing and to large words of promise. Let us be sure that we *are* hearkening to the voice with which He speaks through our daily circumstances as well as by the unmistakable revelation of His will and heart in Jesus Christ. And then let us be sure that no word of His that comes fluttering down from the heavens, meaning a benediction and enclosing a promise, shall fall at our feet ungathered and unregarded, or shall be trodden into the dust by our careless heels. The manna lies all about us; let us see that we gather it. Turn His promises into your creed, and whatever He has declared in the sweet thunder of His voice, loud as the voice of many waters, and melodious as harpers harping with their harps, do you take for your profession of faith in the faithful promises of your God.

This cry of the devout soul suggests to me that our response ought to be the establishment of a close personal relation between us and God. "Thou, O Lord, art *my* Refuge." We must isolate ourselves and stand, God and we, alone together—at heart-grips, we grasping His hands, and He giving Himself to us—if the promises which are sent down into the world for all who will make them theirs can become ours. They are made payable to your order, you must write your name on the back before you get the proceeds. There must be what our good old Puritan forefathers used to call, in somewhat hard language, "the appropriating act of faith," your hand to grasp them, and say "mine," not "ours." The thought of others as sharing in them will come afterwards, for he who has once realized the absolute isolation of the soul and has been alone with God, and in solitude has taken God's gifts as his very own, is he who will feel faith and blessings. The "ours" will come; but you must begin with the "mine"—"*my* Lord and *my* God" [John 20:28]. "Who loved *me*, and gave himself for *me*" [Gal. 2:20]. Just as when the Israelites gathered on the banks of the Red Sea, and Miriam and the maidens came out with songs and timbrels, though their hearts throbbed with joy, and music rang from their lips for national deliverance, their hymn made the whole deliverance the property of each, and each of the chorus sang, "The Lord is my Strength and my Song, He also is become my Salvation," so we must individualize the common blessing. Every poor soul has a right to the whole of God; and unless a man claims all the Divine nature as his, he has little chance of possessing the promised blessings.

This cry of the devout soul recognizes God as He to whom we must go because we need a refuge. Only he who knows himself to be in danger thinks himself a refuge. It is only when we know our danger and defenselessness that God, as the Refuge of our souls, becomes precious to us. So, underlying, and an essential part of, all our confidence in God is the clear recognition of our own necessity. The sense of our own emptiness must precede our grasp of His fullness.

November 22

GOD'S ANSWER TO THE SOUL'S CRY

Who is he that will harm you, if ye be followers of that which is good—
1 Pet. 3:13

Did you ever notice that there are two dwelling-places spoken of in the 91st Psalm? "Thou hast made . . . the most High thy habitation" [v. 9]; "There shall no plague . . . come nigh thy dwelling" [v. 10] ; or, literally translated, as in the Revised Version, "a tent"—a particular kind of abode. The same word, "habitation," is employed in the 90th Psalm—"dwelling place" [v. 1]. Beside that venerable and ancient abode that has stood fresh, strong, incorruptible, and unaffected by the lapse of millenniums, there stands the little transitory canvas tent in which our earthly lives are spent. We have two dwelling places. By the body we are brought into connection with this frail, evanescent, illusory outer world, and we try to make our homes out of shifting rubble, and dream that we can compel mutability to become immutable, that we may dwell secure. We need a better dwelling place than earth and that which holds to earth. We have God Himself for our true Home. Never mind what becomes of the tent as long as the mansion stands firm. Do not let us be saddened, though we know that it is canvas, and that the walls will soon rot and must some day be folded up and borne away, if we have the Rock of Ages for our dwelling place.

But the wide scope and the paradoxical completeness of the promise itself, instead of being a difficulty, point the way to its true interpretation. "There shall no plague come nigh thy dwelling"—and yet we are smitten down by all the woes that afflict humanity. "No evil shall befall thee"—and yet "all the ills that flesh is heir to" are dealt out sometimes with a more liberal hand to them who abide in God than to them who dwell only in the tent upon earth. What then? Is God true, or is He not? Did this Psalmist mean to promise the very questionable blessing of escape from all the good of the discipline of sorrow? Is it true, in the unconditional sense in which it is often asserted, that "prosperity is the blessing of the Old Testament, and adversity of the New?" I think not; and I am sure that this Psalmist, when he said "there shall no evil befall thee, nor any plague come nigh thy dwelling," was thinking exactly the same thing which Paul had in his mind when he said, "All things work together for good to them that love God, to them that are called according to his purpose" [Rom. 8:28]. If I make God my Refuge, I shall get something a great deal better than escape from outward sorrow—namely, an amulet which will turn the outward sorrow into joy. The bitter water will still be given me to drink, but it will be filtered water, out of which God will strain all the poison, though He still leaves plenty of the bitterness in it; for bitterness is a tonic. The evil that is in the evil will be taken out of it, in the measure in which we make God our Refuge, and "all will be right that seems most wrong" when we recognize it to be "His sweet will." Nothing can be "evil" which knits me more closely to God; and whatever tempest drives me to His breast, though all the four winds of the heavens strove on the surface of the sea, it will be better for me than calm weather that entices me to stray farther away from Him.

THE EXALTED CHRIST

So then after the Lord had spoken unto them, he was received up into heaven,
and sat on the right hand of God—Mark 16:19

How strangely calm and brief this record of so stupendous an event? Do these spar-
ing and reverent words sound to you like the product of a devout imagination, embell-
ishing with legend the facts of history? To me their very restrainedness, calmness,
matter-of-factness, if I may so call it, is a strong guarantee that they are the utterance of
an eyewitness, who verily saw what he tells so simply. There is something sublime in the
contrast between the magnificence and almost inconceivable grandeur of the thing communicated, and the quiet words, so few, so sober, so wanting in all detail, in which it
is told.

That stupendous fact of Christ sitting at the right hand of God is the one that
should fill the preset for us all, even as the Cross should fill the past, and the coming for
Judgment should fill the future. So for us the one central thought about the present, in
its loftiest relations, should be the enthroned Christ at God's right hand.

We are taught to believe, according to His own words, that in His ascension Christ
was but returning whence He came, and entering into the "glory which He had with the
Father before the world was" [see John 17:5]. And that impression of a return to His
native and proper abode is strongly conveyed to us by the narrative of His ascension.
Contrast it for instance with the narrative of Elijah's rapture, or with the brief reference to Enoch's translation. The one was taken by God up into a region and a state
which he had not formerly traversed; the other was borne by a fiery chariot to the heavens; but Christ slowly sailed upwards, as it were, by His own inherent power, returning
to His abode, and ascending up where He was before.

But while this is one side of the profound fact, there is another side. What was new
in Christ's return to His Father's bosom? This, that He took His manhood with Him.
It was the Everlasting Son of the Father, the Eternal Word, which from the beginning
"was with God and was God" [see John 1:1], that came down from heaven to earth to
declare the Father; but it was the Incarnate Word, the Man Christ Jesus, that went back
again. This most blessed and wonderful truth is taught with emphasis in His own words
before the council, "Ye shall see the Son of *man* sitting on the right hand of power"
[Matt. 26:24]. Christ, then, today bears a human body; not, indeed, the body of His
humiliation, but the body of His glory, which is none the less a true corporeal frame,
and necessarily requires a locality. His ascension, wherever He may have gone, was the
true carrying of a real humanity, complete in all its parts, Body, Soul, and Spirit, up to
the very Throne of God.

Where that locality is it is worthless to speculate. Scripture says that He ascended
up "far above all heavens" [Eph. 4:10]; or, as the Epistle to the Hebrews has it, in the
proper translation, the High Priest "is passed *through* the heavens" [see 4:14], as if all
this visible material creation was rent asunder in order that He might soar yet higher beyond its limits, wherein reign mutation and decay. But wheresoever that place may be,
there *is* a place in which now, with a human body as well as a human spirit, Christ is sitting at the right hand of God.

November 24

OUR BROTHER IN HEAVEN

In my Father's house are many mansions; if it were not so, I would have told you.
I go to prepare a place for you—John 14:2

L et us thankfully think how, in the profound language of Scripture, "the Forerunner is for us entered" [Heb. 6:20]; how, in some mysterious manner, of which we can but dimly conceive, that entrance of Christ in His complete humanity into the highest heavens is the preparation of a place for us. As if, without His presence there, there were no entrance for human nature within that state, and no power in a human foot to tread upon the crystal pavements of the Celestial City, but as if, where He is, there the path is permeable, and the place native to all that love and trust Him.

Stand, therefore, with these disciples, as they gazed upon their ascended Savior, and looking upwards as the cloud receives Him out of our sight, our faith follows Him, still our Brother, still clothed with humanity, still wearing a bodily frame; and we say, as we lose Him from our vision, "What is man?" [Heb. 2:6]. Capable of being lifted to the most intimate participation in the glories of Divinity, and though he be poor and weak and sinful here, yet capable of union and assimilation with the Majesty that is on high. For what Christ's body is, the bodies of them that love and serve Him shall surely be, and He, the Forerunner, is entered there for us, that we, too, in our turn, may pass into the light, and walk in the full blaze of the Divine glory, as of old the children in the furnace, unconsumed, because companioned by "One like unto the Son of man" [Rev. 1:3].

The exalted Christ, sitting at the right hand of God, is the pattern of what is possible for humanity, and the prophecy and pledge of what will be actual for all that love Him and bear the image of Him upon earth that they may be conformed to the image of His glory, and be with Him where He is. What firmness, what reality, what solidity this thought of the bodily exalted Christ gives to the else dim and vague conceptions of a heaven beyond the stars and beyond our present experience! I believe that no doctrine of a future life has strength and substance enough to survive the agonies of our hearts when we part from our dear ones, the fears of our spirits when we look into the unknown, inane future for ourselves, except only this which says Heaven is Christ and Christ is Heaven, and points to Him and says, "Where He is, there, and that, also shall His servants be."

November 25

THE RESTING SAVIOR

Looking unto Jesus, the author and finisher of our faith, who for the joy that was set before him endured the cross, despising the shame, and is set down at the right hand of the throne of God—Heb. 12:2

It is finished—John 19:30

The disciples' vision of their ascended Lord expresses absolute repose after sore conflict. It is the same thought which is expressed in those solemn Egyptian colossal statues of deified conquerors, elevated to mysterious union with the God, and yet men still, sitting before their temples in perfect stillness, with the mighty hands lying quiet on the restful limbs; with calm faces out of which toil and passion and change seem to have melted, gazing out with open eyes as over a silent prostrate world. So, with the Cross behind, with all the agony and weariness of the arena, the dust and the blood of the struggle left beneath, He "sitteth at the right hand of God, the Father Almighty." The rest of the Christ after His Cross is parallel with and carries the same meaning as, the rest of God after the Creation. Why do we read "He rested on the seventh day from all His works" [Gen. 2:2]? Did the Creative Arm grow weary? Was there toil for the Divine nature in the making of a universe? Does He not speak and it is done? Is not the calm, effortless putting-forth of His will the cause and the means of Creation? Does any shadow of weariness steal over that life which lives and is not exhausted? Does the bush consume in burning? Surely not. He rested from His works, not because He needed to recuperate strength after action by repose, but because the works were perfect; and in sign and token that His ideal was accomplished, and that no more was needed to be done. And, in like manner, the Christ rests after His Cross, not because He needed repose even after that terrible effort, and was panting after His race, and so had to sit there to recover, but in token that His work was finished and perfected; that all which He had come to do was done; and in token, likewise, that the Father, also, beheld and accepted the finished work. Therefore, the session of Christ at the right hand of God is the proclamation from the Heaven of what He shouted with His last dying breath upon the Cross: "It is finished!" It is the declaration that the world has had all done for it that Heaven can do for it. It is the declaration that all which is needed for the regeneration of humanity has been lodged in the very heart of the race, and that henceforward all that is required is the evolving and the development of the consequences of that perfect work which Christ offered upon the Cross. So, the writer of the Epistle to the Hebrews contrasts the priests who stood "daily ministering and offering oftentimes the same sacrifices" which "can never take away sins" [Heb. 10:11], with the fact that "this Man, after He had offered one sacrifice for sins forever, sat down at the right hand of God" [Heb. 10:12]; testifying thereby that His Cross is the complete, sufficient, perpetual atonement and satisfaction for the sins of the whole world. So we have to look back to that past as interpreted by this present, to that Cross as commented upon by this Throne, and to see in it the perfect work which any human soul may grasp, and which all human souls need, for their acceptance and forgiveness.

OUR INTERCEDING PRIEST

Wherefore he is able also to save them to the uttermost that come unto God by him, seeing he ever liveth to make intercession for them. For such an high priest became us, who is holy, harmless, undefiled, separate from sinners, and made higher than the heavens, Who needeth not daily, as those high priests, to offer up sacrifice, first for his own sins, and then for the people's: for this he did once, when he offered up himself—Heb. 7:25-27

So the Scripture declares. The Epistle to the Hebrews over and over again reiterates that thought that we have a Priest that has passed into the heavens, there to appear in the presence of God for us. And the Apostle Paul, in that great linked climax in the eighth chapter of the Epistle to the Romans, has it, "Christ that died, yea! rather, that is risen again, who is even at the right hand of God, who also maketh intercession for us" [v. 34]. There are deep mysteries connected with that thought of the intercession of Christ. It does not mean that the Divine heart needs to be won to love and pity. It does not mean that in any mere outward and formal fashion He pleads with God, and softens and placates the Infinite and Eternal love of the Father in the heavens. It, at least, plainly means this, that He, our Savior and Sacrifice, is forever in the presence of God, presenting His own blood as an element in the Divine dealing with us, modifying the incidence of the Divine law, and securing, through His own merits and intercession, the outflow of blessings upon our heads and hearts. It is not a complete statement of Christ's work for us that He died for us. He died that He might have somewhat to offer. He lives that He may be our Advocate as well as our Propitiation with the Father. And just as the high priest once a year passed within the curtain, and there in the solemn silence and solitude of the holy place, sprinkled the blood that he had there, not without trembling, and but for a moment permitted to stay in the awful Presence, thus, but in reality and forever, with the joyful gladness of a Son in His own calm home, His habitation from eternity, Christ *abides* in the Holy Place; and, at the right hand of the Majesty of the Heavens, lifts up that prayer, so strangely compact of authority and submission: "Father, I *will* that these whom Thou hast given Me be with Me where I am" [see John 17:24]. The Son of Man at the right hand of God is our Intercessor with the Father. "Seeing, then, that we have a great High Priest that is passed into the Heavens . . . let us hold fast our profession" [Heb. 4:14].

THE EVER-ACTIVE HELPER
OF THE SAINTS

Thou hast ascended on high, thou hast led thy captivity captive; thou hast received gifts for men, yea, for the rebellious also, that the Lord God might dwell among them—Psalm 68:18

The "right hand of God" is the Omnipotent energy of God; and howsoever certainly the language of Scripture requires for its full interpretation that we should firmly hold that Christ's glorified body dwells in a place, we are not to omit the other thought, that to sit at the right hand also means to wield the immortal energy of that Divine nature over all the field of the Creation and in every province of His dominion. So that the ascended Christ is the ubiquitous Christ; and He who is "at the right hand of God" is wherever the power of God reaches throughout His whole universe.

Remember that it was once given to a man to look through the opened heavens (through which Christ had "passed") and to "see the Son of man standing (not sitting) at the right hand of God" [Acts. 7:56]. Why to the dying first martyr was there granted that vision thus varied? Wherefore was the attitude changed but to express the swiftness, the certainty of His help, and the eager readiness of the Lord, who starts to His feet, as it were, to succor and to sustain His dying servant?

And so we may take that great joyful truth that, both as receiving gifts for man and bestowing gifts upon them, and as working by His providence in the world, and on the wider scale for the well-being of His children and of the Church, the Christ that sits at the right hand of God wields, ever with eager cheerfulness, all the powers of omnipotence for our well-being, if we love and trust him. We may look quietly upon all perplexities and complications, because the hands that were pierced for us hold the helm and the reins, because the Christ who is our Brother is the King, and sits supreme at the center of the universe. Joseph's brethren that came up in their hunger and their rags to the land, and found their brother next the throne, were startled with a great joy of surprise, and fears were calmed and confidence sprang in their hearts. Shall not we be restful and confident when our Brother, the Son of man, sits ruling all things? "We see not yet all things put under" us; "but we see Jesus" [Heb. 2:8, 9], and that is enough. Therefore, set your affections on things above. Our hearts travel where our dear ones are. Oh, how strange and sad it is that professing Christians, whose lives, if they are Christians at all, have their roots and are hid with Christ in God, should turn so few, so cold thoughts and loves thither! Surely, "where your treasure is, there will your heart be also" [Matt. 6:21; Luke 12:34]. Surely, if Christ is your treasure, you will feel that with Him is home, and that this is a foreign land! "Set your affection," then, "on things above" [Col. 3:2], while life lasts; and when it is ebbing away, perhaps to our eyes, too, Heaven may be opened, and the vision of the Son of man standing to receive and to welcome us may be granted, and when it has ebbed away, His will be the first voice to welcome us, and He will lift us to share in His glorious rest, according to His own wondrous promise, "To him that overcometh will I grant to sit with me in My throne, even as I also overcame, and am set down with my Father in his throne" [Rev. 3:21].

WHAT LASTS!

Whether there be prophecies, they shall fail; whether there be tongues, they shall cease; whether there be knowledge, it shall vanish away. . . . And now abideth faith, hope, charity, these three—1 Cor. 13:8, 13

We discern the run of the Apostle's thought best by thus omitting the intervening verses and connecting these two. The part omitted is but a buttress of what has been stated in the former of our two verses; and when we thus unite them, there is disclosed plainly the Apostle's intention of contrasting two sets of things, three in each. The one is prophecies, tongues, knowledge; the other, faith, hope, charity. There also comes out distinctly that the point mainly intended by the contrast is the transiency of the one and the permanence of the other. I ask this question: What will drop away? Paul answers, "Prophecies, tongues, knowledge." Now these three were all extraordinary gifts belonging to the present phase of the Christian life. But inasmuch as these gifts were the heightening of natural capacities and faculties, it is perfectly legitimate to enlarge the declarations and to use these three words in their widest significance. So understand they come to this, that all our present modes of apprehension and of utterance are transient, and will be left behind.

"Knowledge, it shall be done away," and it shall be done away with because the perfect absorbs into itself the imperfect, as the inrushing tide will obliterate the little pools in the rocks on the seashore. "We shall know face to face," which is what philosophers call by intention. Here our knowledge creeps from point to point, painfully amassing facts, and thence, with many hesitations and errors, groping its way towards principles and laws. Here it is imperfect, with many a gap in its circumference; or like the thin red line which shows the traveler's route across a boundless prairie, or like the spider's thread in the telescope, stretched across the blazing disc of the sun—"but then face to face" [1 Cor. 13:12]. Incomplete knowledge shall be done away; and so many of its objects will drop, so much of what makes the science of earth will be antiquated and obsolete. What would the handloom weaver's knowledge of how to throw his shuttle be worth in a weaving-shed with a thousand looms? Just so much will the knowledge of earth be when we get yonder.

Modes of utterance will cease. With new experiences will come new methods of communication; as a man can speak and beasts can only growl or bark, so a man in heaven, with new experiences, will have a new method of communication. The comparison between that mode of utterance which we now have and that which we then possess will be like the difference between the old-fashioned semaphore, that used to wave about clumsy wooden arms, in order to convey intelligence, and the telegraph. Think, then, of a man going into that future life, and saying, "*I* knew more about Sanscrit than anybody that ever lived in Europe"; "*I* sang sweet song"; "*I* was a past master in philology, grammars, and lexicons"; "*I* was a great orator." "Tongues shall cease," and the modes of utterance that belonged to earth will drop away and be of no more use.

If these things are true with regard even to the highest form of these high and noble things, how much more and more solemnly true are they with regard to the aims and objects which most of us have in view! They will all drop away, and we shall be left, stripped of what, for most of us, has made the whole interest and activity of our lives.

THE LOVE OF THE DEPARTING CHRIST

When Jesus knew that his hour was come that he should depart out of this world unto the Father, having loved his own which were in the world, he loved them unto the end—John 13:1

The latter half of St. John's Gospel, which begins with these words, is the Holy of Holies of the New Testament. Nowhere else do the blended lights of our Lord's superhuman dignity and human tenderness shine with such lucid brightness. Nowhere else is His speech at once so simple and so deep. Nowhere else have we the heart of God so unveiled to us. On no other page, even of the Bible, have so many eyes, glistening with tears, looked and had the tears dried. The immortal words which Christ spoke in that upper chamber are his highest self-revelation in speech, even as the Cross to which they led up is His most perfect self-revelation in act.

Many good commentators prefer to read, "He loved them unto the *uttermost,*" rather than "unto the *end*"—so taking them to express the depth and degree rather than the permanence and perpetuity of our Lord's love. And that seems to me to be by far the worthier and the nobler meaning, as well as the one which is borne out by the usual signification of the expression in other Greek authors. It is much to know that the emotions of these last moments did not interrupt Christ's love. It is even more to know that in some sense they perfected it, giving even a greater vitality to its tenderness and a more precious sweetness to its manifestations. So understood, the words explain for us why it was that in the sanctity of the upper chamber there ensued the marvelous act of the foot-washing, the marvelous discourses which follow, and, the climax of all, that High-Priestly prayer. They give utterance to a love which Christ's consciousness at that solemn hour tended to shapen and to deepen. "He knew that His hour was come." All His life was passed under the consciousness of a Divine necessity laid upon Him, to which He lovingly and cheerfully yielded Himself. On His lips there are no words more significant, and few more frequent, than that Divine "I must!" "It behooves the Son of man to do" this, that, and the other—yielding to the necessity imposed by the Father's will, and sealed by His own loving resolve to be the Savior of the world. And, in like manner, all through His life He declares Himself conscious of the hours which mark the several crises and stages of His mission. They come to Him and He discerns them. No external power can coerce Him to any act till the hour comes. No external power can hinder Him from the act when it comes. When the hour strikes, He hears the phantom sound of the bell, and hearing, He obeys. And thus, at the last and supreme moment, to Him it dawned unquestionable and irrevocable. How did He meet it? While, on the one hand, there was the shrinking of which we have such pathetic testimony in the broken prayer that He Himself amended: "Father, Save me from this hour . . . but for this cause came I unto his hour" [John 12:27]. There is a strange, triumphant joy that blends with the shrinking that the decisive hour is at last come—not that now the hour had come for suffering or death or bearing the sins of the world—all which aspects of it were, nevertheless, present to Him, as we know, but that now He was soon to leave all the world beneath Him and to return to the Father.

THE DIVINE-HUMAN SAVIOR

This man receiveth sinners, and eateth with them—Luke 15:2

Does not the love of Jesus help us to realize how truly bone of our bone and flesh of our flesh, and bearing a heart thrilling with all innocent human emotions, that Divine Savior was? We, like Him, have known what it is to feel, because of approaching separation from dear ones, the need for a tenderer tenderness. At such moments the masks of use and wont drop away, and we are eager to find some word, to put our whole souls into some look, our whole strength into one clinging embrace that may express all our love, and may be a joy to two hearts forever after to remember. The Master knew that longing, and felt the pain of separation: and He, too, yielded to the human impulse which makes the thought of parting the key to unlock the hidden chambers of the most jealously-guarded heart, and let the shyest of its emotions come out for once into the daylight. But there is not only in this a wonderful expression of the true humanity of the Christ, but along with that a suggestion of something more sacred and deeper still. For surely, amid all the parting scenes that the world's literature has enshrined, amid all the examples of self-oblivion at the last moment, when a martyr has been the comforter of his weeping friends, there are none that without degradation to this can be set by the side of this supreme and unique instance of self-oblivion. Did not Christ, for the sake of that handful of poor people, first and directly, and for the rest of us afterwards, of course, secondarily and indirectly, so suppress all the natural emotions of these last moments as that their absolute absence is unique and singular, and points onward to something more—namely, that this Man, who was susceptible of all human affections, and loved us with a love which is not merely high above our grasp, absolute, perfect, changeless, and Divine, but with a love like our own human affection, had also more than a man's heart to give us, and gave us more, when, that He might comfort and sustain, He crushed down Himself and went to the Cross with words of tenderness and consolation and encouragement for others upon His lips. And if the prospect only sharpened and perfected, nor interrupted for one instant the flow of His love, the reality has no power to do aught else. In the glory, when He reached it, He poured out the same loving heart; and today He looks down upon us with the same face that bent over the table in the upper room, and the same tenderness flows to us. When John saw his Master next, after His ascension, amid the glories of vision in his rocky Patmos, though His face was as the sun shines in his strength, it was the old face. Though His hands bare the stars in a cluster, it was the hands that had been pierced with the nails. Though the breast was girded with the golden girdle of sovereignty and of priesthood, it was the breast on which John's happy head had lain; and though the "Voice was as the sound of many waters" [see Rev. 1:15], it soothed itself to a murmur, gentle as that with which the tideless sea about Him rippled upon the silvery sand when He said, "Fear not . . . I am the First and the Last." "Knowing that He goes to the Father He loves to the uttermost," and, being with the Father, He still so loves.

December 1

THE FAITHFUL LOVE
OF THE CHRIST

Hereby perceive we the love of God, because he laid down his life for us—
1 John 3:16

The love of Jesus Christ is a love which is faithful to the obligations of its own past. Having loved, He loves. Because He had been a certain thing, therefore He is and He shall be that same. That is an argument that implies Divinity. About nothing human can we say, Because it has been, therefore it shall be. About much that is human we have to say the converse, Because it has been, therefore it will cease to be. And though, they are few and they are poor who have had no experience in their lives of human hearts whose love in the past has been such that it manifestly is forever, yet we cannot with the same absolute confidence say about one another, even about the dearest, "Having loved, he loves." But we can about this Christ. There is no exhaustion in that great stream that pours out from His heart; no diminution in its flow.

The terror, the agony, the shame, the mysterious burden of a world's sins were to be laid upon Him. All these elements are submerged, as it were, and become less conspicuous than the one thought of leaving behind all the limitations and the humiliations and the compelled association with evil which, like a burning brand laid upon a tender skin, was an hourly and momentary agony to Him, and soaring above them all, unto His own calm home, His habitation from eternity with the Father, as He had been before the world was. How strange this blending of shrinking and of eagerness, of sorrow and of joy, of human trembling consciousness of impending death and of triumphant consciousness of the approach of the hour when the Son of man, even in His bitterest agony and deepest humiliation, should, paradoxically, be glorified, and should leave the world to go unto the Father!

They tell us that the central light of our system, that great sun itself, pouring out its rays exhausts its warmth; and were it not continually replenished must gradually, and even though continually replenished, will one day cease to flame, and be a dead, cold mass of ashes. But this central Light, this heart of Christ, which is the Sun of the World, shall endure like the sun; and after the sun is cold, His love shall last forever.

He pours it out, and there is none the less to give. There is no bankruptcy in His expenditure, no exhaustion in His effort, no diminution in His stores. "Thy mercy . . . endureth forever" [Ps. 138:8]; "Thou hast loved, therefore Thou wilt love," is a syllogism for time and for eternity on which we may build and rest secure.

TO THE UTTERMOST

In his love and in his pity he redeemed them—Is. 63:9

The love of Christ is a love which has special tenderness towards its own. "Having loved His own, He loved them unto the end" [John 13:1]. These poor men who, with all their errors, did cleave to Him; who, in some dim way, understood somewhat of His greatness and His sweetness—and do you and I do more?—who, with all their sins, yet were true to Him in the main; who had surrendered very much to follow him, and had identified themselves with Him—were they to have no special place in His heart because in that heart the whole world lay? Is there any reason why we should be afraid of saying that the universal love of Jesus Christ, which gathers into His bosom all mankind, does fall with special tenderness and sweetness upon those who have made Him theirs and have surrendered themselves to be His? Surely it must be that He has special nearness to those that love Him; surely it is reasonable that He should have special delight in those who try to remember Him; surely it is only what one might expect of Him that He should in a special manner honor the drafts, so to speak, of those that have confidence in Him, and have pinned their whole lives upon Him! Surely, because the sun shines down upon dunghills and all impurities, that is no reason why it should not lie with special brightness on the polished mirror that reflects its luster! Surely, because Jesus Christ loves the publicans and the harlots, and the outcasts and the sinners, that is no reason why He should not bend with special tenderness over those who, loving Him, try to serve Him, and have set their whole hopes upon Him. The rainbow strides across the sky, but there is a rainbow in every little dewdrop that hangs glistening on the blades of grass. And there is nothing limited, nothing sectional, nothing narrow in the proclamation of a special tenderness of Christ towards His own, when you accompany with that truth this other, that all men are asked by Him to come into that circle of "His own," and that only they themselves shut any men out therefrom. The whole world dwells in His love. But there is an inner chamber in which He discovers all His heart to those who find in that heart their Heaven and their all. "He came to his own," in the wider sense of the word, and "his own received him not" [John 1:11]: but also, "having loved His own, He loved them unto the end" [John 13:1]. There are textures and lines which can only absorb some of the rays of light in the spectrum; some that are only capable of taking, so to speak, the violet rays of judgment and of wrath, and some who open their hearts for the ruddy brightness at the other end of the line. Do you see to it, brother, that you be of that inner circle who receive the whole Christ into their hearts, and to whom He can unfold the fullness of His love.

THE SHEPHERD'S LOVE FOR THE SCATTERED FLOCK

I pray not that thou shouldest take them out of the world, but that thou shouldest keep them from the evil—John 17:15

The necessities and dangers of the friends of Christ made His love specially tender. "He loved His own which were in the world." And so loving them, "loved them unto the end."

We have, running through these precious discourses recorded by John, many allusions to the separation which was to ensue, and to His leaving His followers in circumstances of peculiar peril, defenseless and solitary. "I come unto Thee, and am no more in the world" [17:11], says He in the final high-priestly prayer, "but these are in the world . . . Holy Father, keep through thine own name." The same contrast between the certain security of the Shepherd and the troubled perils of the scattered flock seems to be in the words just quoted (John 13:1), and suggests a sweet and blessed reason for the special tenderness with which He looked upon them. As a dying father on his deathbed may yearn over orphans that he is leaving defenseless, so Christ here is represented as conscious of an accession even to the tender longings of His heart when He thought of the loneliness and the dangers to which His followers were to be exposed.

It seems a strange contrast between the emperor sitting on the throne there between the purple curtains and the poor athletes wrestling in the arena below; it seems strange to think that a loving Master has gone up into the mountain, and has left His disciples to toil in rowing on the stormy sea of life; but the contrast is only apparent—for you and I, if we love and trust Him, are with Him in the heavenly places even while we toil here; and He is with us, working with us, even while He sitteth at the right hand of God.

We may be sure of this, that the love ever increases its manifestations according to our deepening necessities. The darker the night the more lustrous the stars. The deeper, the narrower, the savager the Alpine gorge, usually the fuller and the swifter the stream that runs through it. And the more enemies and fears gather around us, the sweeter will be the accents of our comforter's voice, and the fuller will be the gifts of tenderness and grace with which He draws near to us. Our sorrows, dangers, and necessities, are doors through which His love can come nigh.

So we have had experience of sweet and transient human love; we have had experience of changeful and ineffectual love. Turn away from them all to this immortal deep heart of Christ's, welling over with a love which no change can affect, which no separation can diminish, which no sin can provoke, which becomes greater and tenderer as our necessities increase; and ask Him to fill your hearts with that, that you may know the length and breadth and depth and height of that love which passeth knowledge, and so be filled with all the fullness of God.

THE POSSESSION OF THE SPIRIT OF MIGHT

That he would grant you, according to the riches of his glory, to be strengthened with might by his Spirit in the inner man—Eph. 3:16

It is a miserably inadequate conception of Christianity, and the gifts that it bestows, and the blessings that it intends for men, when it is limited, as it practically is, by a large number—I might almost say the majority—of professing Christians to a simple means of altering their relation to the past and to the broken law of God and of righteousness. His great gift to the world begins in each individual case with the assurance that all the past is canceled, and that He gives that great gift of forgiveness, which can never be too highly estimated unless it is forced out of its true place as the introduction, and made to be the climax and the end of His gifts. I do not know what Christianity means, unless it means that you and I are forgiven for a purpose; that the purpose, if I may so say, is something in advance of the means towards the purpose, the purpose being that we should be filled with all the strength and righteousness and supernatural life granted to us by the Spirit of God.

It is all well that we should enter into the vestibule: there is no other path unto the Throne but through the vestibule; but do not let us not forget that the good news of forgiveness, though we need it day by day, and perpetually repeated, is but the introduction to, and porch of, the Temple, and that beyond it there towers, if I cannot say a loftier, yet I may say a further, gift, even the gift of a Divine life like His, from whom it comes, and of which it is in reality an effluence and a spark. The true characteristic gift of the gospel is the gift of a new power to a sinful, weak world—a power which makes the feeble strong, and the strongest as an angel of God.

We who know how, "if any power we have, it is to ill"; we who understand the weakness, the unaptness, of our spirits to any good and their strength to every vagrant evil that comes upon them to tempt them, should surely recognize as a gospel in very deed that which proclaims to us that the "everlasting God, the Lord, the Creator, of the ends of the earth" [Is. 40:28], who Himself "fainteth not, neither is weary," hath yet a loftier manifestation of His strength-giving power than that which is visible in the heavens above; where, "because he is strong in power, not one faileth" [Is. 40:26]. That of power undiminished, affords a lesser and dimmer manifestation of His strength than the work that is done in the hell of a human heart that has wandered and is brought back, that is stricken with the weakness of the fever of sin, and is drawn again into the strength of obedience and the omnipotence of dependence. It is much to say, "For that He is strong in might, not one of these faileth"; it is more to say, "He giveth power to the faint; and to them that have no might he increaseth strength" [Is. 40:29]. The gospel is the gift of pardon for holiness, and its inmost and most characteristic bestowment is the bestowment of a new power of obedience and service.

December 5

POWER FROM ON HIGH

Ye shall receive power, after that the Holy Ghost is come upon you—Acts 1:8

Power is given to us all through the gift of the Divine Spirit. The very name of that Spirit is the "Spirit of might." Christ spoke to us about being "endued with power from on high" [Luke 24:49]; the last of His promises that dropped from His lips upon earth was the promise that His followers should receive the power of the Spirit coming upon them. Wherever in the early histories we read of a man that was full of the Holy Ghost, we read that he was "full of power." God hath given us the "spirit of power," which is also the spirit "of love and of a sound mind" [2 Tim. 1:7]. So the strength that we must have, if we have strength at all, is the strength of a Divine Spirit, not our own, that dwells in us, and works through us.

And there is nothing in that which need startle or surprise any man who believes in a living God at all, and in the possibility, therefore, of a connection between the Holy Spirit and all the human spirits which are His children. I would maintain, in opposition to many modern conceptions, the actual supernatural character of the gift that is bestowed upon every Christian soul. My reading of the New Testament is, that as distinctly above the order of material nature as is any miracle is the gift that flows into a believing heart. There is a direct passage between God and my spirit: it lies open to His touch; all the paths of its deep things can be trodden by Him. You and I act upon one another from without; He acts upon us within. We wish one another blessings; He gives the blessings. We try to train, to educate, to incline, and dispose by the presentation of motive and the urging of reasons; He can plant in a heart by His own Divine husbandry the seed that shall blossom into immortal life. And so the Christian Church is a great, continual, supernatural community in the midst of the material world; and every believing soul, because it possesses something of the life of Jesus Christ, has been the seat of a miracle as real and true as when He said, "Lazarus, come forth" [John 11:43]. Precisely this teaching does our Lord himself present for our acceptance when He sets side by side, as mutually illustrative, as belonging to the same order of supernatural phenomena, the hour cometh when the dead shall hear the voice of the Son of God, and they that hear shall live, which is the supernatural resurrection of souls dead in sin, "and the hour is coming when all that are in the graves shall hear His voice, and shall come forth" [John 5:28, 29], which is the future resurrection of the body in obedience to His will.

So, Christian friend, do you set clearly before you this: that God's purpose with you is only begun when He has forgiven you, that He forgives you for a design, that it is a means to an end, and that you have not reached the conception of the large things He intends for you unless you have risen to this great thought—He means and wishes that you should be strong with the strength of His own Divine Spirit.

THE DIVINE INDWELLER

He dwelleth with you, and shall be in you—John 14:17

The Divine strength has its seat in, and is intended to influence the whole of, the inner life. "Strengthened with might by His Spirit in the inner man" [Eph. 3:16]. That, I suppose, does not mean the new creation through faith in Jesus Christ—what the Apostle calls "the new man"—but it means simply what another Apostle calls "the hidden man of the heart" [1 Pet. 3:4], and only refers to the distinction which we all draw between the outward, visible, material frame, and the unseen self that animates and informs it. It is this inner self, then, in which the Spirit of God is to dwell, and into which it is to breathe strength. The leaven is hid deep in three measures of meal until the whole be leavened.

And the point to mark is, that the whole inward region which makes up the true man is the field upon which this Divine Spirit is to work. It is not a bit of your inward life that is to be hallowed; it is not any one aspect of it that is to be strengthened—but it is the whole intellect, affections, desires, tastes, powers of attention, combination, memory, will. The whole inner man in all its corners is to be filled, and to come under the influence of this power, until there be no part dark, "as when the bright shining of a candle giveth thee light" [Luke 11:36].

So for this Divine Indweller there is no part of my life that is not patent to His tread. There are no rooms of the house of my spirit into which He is not to go. Let Him come with the master-key in His hand into all the dim chambers of your feeble nature; and as life is light in the eye, and color in the cheek, and deftness in the fingers, and strength in the arm, and pulsation in the heart, so He will come and strengthen your understandings, and make you able for loftier tasks of intellect and of reason, than you can face in your unaided strength; and He will dwell in your affections, and make them vigorous to lay hold upon the holy things that are above their natural inclination, and will make it certain that "their reach shall not be beyond their grasp," as, it so often is in the sadness and disappointments of human loves. And He will come into that feeble, vacillating, wayward will of yours, that is only obstinate in its adherence to the low and the evil, as some foul creature, that one may try to wrench away, digs its claws into corruption and holds on by that; He will lift your will, and make it fix upon the good and abominate the evil, and through the whole being He will pour a great tide of strength which shall cover all the weakness. He will be like some subtle elixir which, taken into the lips, steals through a pallid and wasted frame, and brings back a glow to the cheek and a luster to the eye and a swiftness to the brain, and power to the whole nature. Or as some plant, drooping and flagging beneath the hot rays of the sun, when it has the scent of water given to it, will, in all its parts, stiffen and erect itself, so this Divine Spirit will go searching every corner of the inner man, illuminating and invigorating all.

STRENGTHENED WITH ALL MIGHT

Strengthened with all might, according to his glorious power, unto all patience and longsuffering with joyfulness—Col. 1:11

In no part of Paul's letters does He rise to a higher level than in his prayers, and none of his prayers are more full of fervor than this wonderful series of petitions. They open out one into the other like some majestic suite of apartments in a great palace-temple, each leading into a loftier and more spacious hall, each drawing nearer the presence-chamber, until at last we stand there. Take his prayer in Ephesians. Roughly speaking, that prayer is divided into four petitions, of which each is the cause of the following and the result of the preceding: "That he would grant you, according to the riches of his glory, to be strengthened with might by his Spirit in the inner man" [Eph. 3:16]. That is the first. "That Christ may dwell in your hearts by faith" [Eph. 3:17]. Such is the second; the result of the first and the preparation for the third. "That ye, being rooted and grounded in love, may be able to comprehend with all saints . . . and to know the love of Christ which passeth knowledge" [Eph. 3:17–19]. Such is the next: and all lead up at last to that wonderful desire beyond which nothing is possible—"that ye might be filled with all the fullness of God" [3:19]. Consider that great thought of the Divine strength-giving power which may be bestowed upon every Christian soul. God means and wishes that all Christians should be strong by the possession of the Spirit of might.

It will be a power for suffering. Unless this Divine Spirit were a power for patience and endurance, it were no power suited to us poor men. So dark at times is every life; so full at times of discouragements, of dreariness, of sadness, of loneliness, of bitter memories, and of fading hopes does the human heart become, that if we are to be strong we must have a strength that will manifest itself most chiefly in this, that it teaches us how to bear, how to weep, how to submit.

And it will be a power for effort. We have all of us, in the discharge of duty and the resistance of temptation, to face such tremendous antagonisms that unless we have grace given to us which will enable us to resist, we shall be overcome and swept away. God's grace from the Divine Spirit within us does not absolve us from the fight, but it fits us for the fight. It is not given in order that holiness may be won without a struggle, as some people seem to think, but it is given to us in order that in the struggle for holiness we may never lose "one jot of heart of hope," but may be "able to withstand in the evil day, and having done all to stand" [Eph. 6:13].

It is a power for service. "Tarry ye in Jerusalem until ye be endued with power from on high" [Luke 24:49]. There is no such force for the spreading of Christ's Kingdom and the witness-bearing work of His Church as the possession of this Divine Spirit. Plunged into that fiery baptism, the selfishness and the sloth, which stand in the way of so many of us, are all consumed and annihilated, and we are set free for service because the bonds that bind us are burnt up in the merciful furnace of His fiery power. "Ye shall be strengthened with might by His Spirit in the inner man" [see Eph. 3:16]. A power that will fill and flood all your nature if you will let it, and will make you strong to suffer, strong to combat, strong to serve and to witness for your Lord.

GOD'S BOUNDLESS RICHES

That in the ages to come he might show the exceeding riches of his grace in kindness toward us in Jesus Christ—Eph. 2:7

There is the measure. There is no limit except the uncounted wealth of His own self-manifestation, the flashing light of a revealed Divinity. Whatever there is of splendor in that, whatsoever there is of power there, in these, and in nothing this side of them, lies the limit of the possibilities of a Christian life. Of course, there is a working limit at each moment, and that is our capacity to receive; but beyond our count or measurement. Our hearts may be made more and more capable of God; and in the measure in which they are capable of Him they shall be filled by Him. A limit which is always shifting is no limit at all. A kingdom the boundaries of which are not the same from one year to another, by reason of its own inherent expansive power, may be said to have no fixed limits. And so we appropriate and enclose, as it were, within our own little fence, a tiny portion of the great prairie that rolls boundless to the horizon. But tomorrow we may enclose more, if we will, and more and more; and so ever onwards. For all that is God's is yours, and He has given you His whole Self to use and to possess through your faith in His Son. A thimble can only take up a thimbleful of the ocean, but what if the thimble be endowed with a power of expansion which has no term known to men? May it not, then be that some time or other it shall be able to hold so much of the infinite depth as now seems a dream too audacious to be realized. So it is with us and God. He lets us come into the vaults, as it were, where in piles and masses the ingots of uncoined and uncounted gold are stored and stacked; and He says, "Take as much as you like to carry." There is no limit except the riches of His glory.

When one contrasts the largeness of God's promises and the miserable contradiction which the average Christian life of this generation presents, what can we say? "Hath His mercy left forever? Does His promise fail forevermore?" Ye weak Christian people, born weakling and weak ever since, open your mouths wide! Rise to the height of the expectations and the desires which it is our sin not to cherish; and be sure of this, as we ask so shall we receive. "Ye are not straitened in God." "Ye are straitened in yourselves" [see 2 Cor. 6:12]. And there must be self-suppression if there is to be the triumph of a Divine power in you. You cannot fight with both classes of weapons. The human must die if the Divine is to live. The life of nature, self-dependence on self, must be weakened and subdued if the life of God is to overcome, to fill you. You must be able to say "Not I!" or you will never be able to say "Christ liveth in me" [Gal. 2:20]. The patriarch that overcame halted on his thigh; and all the life of nature was lamed and made powerless that the life of grace might overcome. So crush self by the power and for the sake of the Christ, if you want the Spirit to rule over you.

THE HOLY SPIRIT OF PROMISE

Ye were sealed with that Holy Spirit of promise, which is the earnest of our inheritance until the redemption of the purchased possession, unto the praise of his glory—Eph. 1:13, 14

"The Holy Spirit of promise," given to all who believe, is here declared to dwell in and to seal believers as the "earnest" of their "inheritance"; while, on the other hand, that sealing is declared to last until—or, as seems more probably the rendering of the preposition here, to be done with a view unto—the full redemption of God's purchased "possession." So that the two halves of the thought are intentionally brought together in these words. And about both of them—God's possession of us and our possession of God—it is asserted or implied, that they are partially realized here, and are to be realized more fully in the future.

An "earnest" is a portion of the estate which is paid over to the purchaser on the completion of the purchase, as the token that all is his and that it will all come into his hands in due time. Like that part of a man's wages given to him in advance when he is engaged; like the shilling put into the hand of a recruit; like the half-crown given to the farm-servant at the hiring-fair; like the bit of turf that in some old ceremonials used to be solemnly presented to the sovereign on his investiture—it is a portion of the whole possession, the same in kind, but a very tiny portion, which yet carries with it the acknowledgment of ownership and the assurance of full possession.

So the "Spirit of God is the earnest of the inheritance," a small portion of it granted to us today, and the pledge that all shall be granted in the future. And the same idea of present imperfection is suggested in the corresponding clause, which speaks about God's entire purchase (for there is an emphasis in the Greek word in the original), His possession is also a thing of the future.

We possess God in the measure in which we know Him, love Him, and have communion and sympathy with Him. These things—knowledge, love, communion, sympathy—make a very real and very precious possession of God; and he who has God thus has Him as truly, though not as perfectly, as the angels in heaven that burn before His throne.

But though that is true, there is yet another aspect of the possession of God. The Holy Spirit of promise comes to every man that believes in Jesus Christ, and enters into his heart and becomes his. That is the truest way in which man possesses God. The greatest gift that my faith brings down to me from heaven is the gift of an indwelling Spirit—of an indwelling God. For the Spirit of God *is* God. He that has God in his heart by the dwelling there, in mystic reality, of the Divine Spirit, possesses Him as truly as he possesses love or memory, imagination or hope.

There can be nothing deeper, nothing greater, nothing more real in the manner of possession, than the possession which every one of us may have of an indwelling God for our life and our peace. It passes all human analogy. Love gives us the ownership, most really and most sweetly, of the hearts that we love. But, after all the yearning desires for union, and experience of oneness in sympathy, the awful wall of partition between spirits remains; and life may, and death must, separate—but he that has God's Divine Spirit with him has God for the life of his life and the soul of his soul. And we possess Him when, by faith in Jesus Christ, the Spirit of God dwells in our hearts.

OUR INCOMPLETE POSSESSION OF GOD

Ye have not, because ye ask not. Ye ask, and receive not, because ye ask amiss, that ye may consume it upon your lusts—James 4:2, 3.

We have an Infinite Spirit to dwell with us; how finite and little is our possession of it! The Spirit of God is set forth in Scripture under the symbol of "a rushing, mighty wind" [Acts 2:2]; and you and I say that we are Christ's and that we have Him—how does it come, then, that our sails flap idly on the mast, and we lie calm, and making next to no progress? The Spirit of God is set forth in Scripture under the symbol of "flaming tongues of fire" [see Acts 2:3]; and you and I say that we have it—how is it, then, that this thick-ribbed ice is around our hearts, and our love is all so tepid? The Spirit of God is set forth in Scripture under the symbol of "rivers of water"; and you and I say that we possess it—how is it, then, that so much of our hearts and of our natures is given up to barrenness and dryness and deadness? The present possession of the best of us is but a partial and incomplete possession.

And the same facts of wavering faith and cold affection, of imperfect consecration, which show how little we have of God, show likewise how little God has of us. We say that we are His, and live to please ourselves. We profess to belong to another, and to that other we render fragments—of ourselves, and scarcely even fragments of our time and of our efforts. His! And yet all day long never thinking of him. His! And yet from morning till night never refraining from a thing because we know it is contrary to His will, or spurred to do a thing that is contrary to ours because we know it is His. His! And yet we wallow in selfishness. It is only a little corner of our souls that really belongs to God.

I do not forget that this incompleteness of possession, looked at in both aspects, is to a certain extent inevitable, and must go with us all through life. And so do not let any of us rush precipitately to the conclusion that we are *not* Christians because we find what poor Christians we are. Do not let us say, "If there were any reality in my faith, it would be, not a dotted line, but one continuous and unbroken." Do not let us write bitter things against ourselves because we find that we only have received "the earnest of our inheritance" [Eph. 1:14], and that the inheritance has not yet come. And, on the other hand, do not you make a pillow of laziness of that most certain truth; nor because there must be imperfection always in the Christian career here, apply that as an excuse for the individual instances of imperfection as they crop up. You know, when you are honest with yourself, that each breach of continuity in your faith and obedience might have been prevented; you know that there was no reason that could not have been overcome for any failure of consecration or wavering of faith or act of disobedience and rebellion which has ever marked your course. Granted, imperfection is the law, but also remember that the individual instances of imperfection are to be debited not to *law*, but to *us*, and are not to be lamented over as inevitable, though painful, issues of our condition, but to be confessed as sins. "My fault, O Lord! My fault, and mine only."

THE IMPERFECT PRESENT

For now we see through a glass, darkly; but then face to face: now I know in part; but then shall I know even as also I am known—1 Cor. 13:12

The facts of Christian experience are such as that they inevitably point to the conclusion that there is a life beyond. All that is good and blessed about religion, our faith, the joy that comes from our faith, the sweetness of communion, the aspiration after the increase of fellowship with Him—all these, to the man that enjoys them, are the best proof that they are going to last forever, and that death can have no power over them. "Like thoughts, their very sweetness yieldeth proof that they are born for immortality."

To love, to know, to reach the hands out through the shows of time and sense, and to grasp an unseen reality that lies away beyond, is, to any man that has ever experienced the emotion and done the thing, one of the strongest of all demonstrations that nothing belonging to this dusty low region of the physical can touch that immortal aspiration that knits him to God; but that whatever may befall the husk and shell of him, his faith, his love, his obedience, his consecration, these at least are eternal, and may laugh at death and the grave. And I believe that ever to the men that have not the experience, the fact of religious emotion, the fact of worship, ought to be one of the best demonstrations of a future life.

The very incompleteness of our possession of God and of God's possession of us points onward to, and, as it seems to me, demands a future. The imperfection, as well as the present attainments of our Christian experience, proclaim a coming time. That we are no better than we are, being as good as we are, seems to make it inconceivable that this evidently half-done job is going to be broken off short at the side of the grave.

Here is a certain force at work in a man's nature, the power of God's good Spirit, evidently capable of producing effects of entire transformation. Such being the case, who, looking at the effects, can doubt that sometime and somewhere there will be less disproportion between the two? The engine is evidently not working full power. The characters of Christians at the best are so inconsistent and contradictory that they are evidently only in the making. It is clear that we are looking at unfinished work; and surely the great Master Builder who has laid such a foundation, tried and precious, will not begin to build and not be able to finish! Every Christian life, at its best and noblest shows, as it were, the ground plan of a great structure partly carried out—a bit of walling up here, vacancy there, girders spanning wide spaces, but gaping for a roof, a chaos and a confusion. It may look a thing of shreds and patches, and they that pass by the way begin to mock. But the very fact that it is incomplete prophesies, to wise men, of the day when the headstone shall be brought with shouting, and the flag hoisted on the roof-tree. Fools and children, says the proverb, should not see half-done work—certainly they should not judge it.

Wait a bit. There comes a time when tendencies shall be facts, and when influences shall have produced their appropriate effects, and when all that is partial and broken shall be consummate and entire in the kingdom that is beyond the stars.

Wait! And be sure that the good and the bad, so strangely blended in Christian experience, are alike charged with the prophecy of a glorious and perfect future.

THE FUTURE THE PERFECTING OF THE PRESENT

Who hath also sealed us, and given the earnest of the Spirit in our hearts—
2 Cor. 1:22

The "earnest" points onward to an inheritance the same in kind, but immensely greater in degree. The "redemption of the possession" is a somewhat singular expression; for we are accustomed to regard the great act of redemption as already passed in the sacrifice of Christ upon the Cross. But the expression is employed here, as in several other places, to express not so much the act of purchase, the paying of the price of our salvation, which is done once for all and long ago, as the historical working out of the results of that price paid in the *entire* deliverance of the *whole* nature of a man from *every* form of captivity to *anything* that would prevent his *full* possession by God.

"Through, a glass darkly; but then face to face . . . shall I know even as also I am known" [1 Cor. 13:12] says Paul, suggesting great changes in the degree of our knowledge of, and friendly communion with, God, but also seeming to imply some unknown changes in the manner of our beholding, which may be connected with the new powers of that "body of glory" like our Lord's which will then be ours. It is quite conceivable that the physical universe may have qualities as real as light and heat, and scent and sound, which we could appreciate if we had other senses appropriate, as we have sight and touch, and small and hearing.

And so it is quite conceivable that when clothed upon with our "house which is from heaven" [2 Cor. 5:2], which will have a great many more windows in it than the earthly house of this tabernacle, which is built for stormy weather, there will be sides and aspects of the Divine nature that we do not know anything about today which shall be communicable and communicated to us.

But be that as it may, a deeper knowledge, a fixed love, an unbroken communion, with all distractions and interruptions swept clean away forever, so that we shall dwell forevermore in the House of the Lord—these are the plain elements which make the very Heaven of heavens, and which ought to make the joy of our hope. In the measure in which we know and love Him, in that measure shall we be known and loved by Him. He and we shall be so interwoven as that we shall be inseparable. We shall cleave to God and God shall cleave to us.

Oh, how small and insignificant all other notions of a future life are as compared with that! The accidents of locality and circumstance should ever be kept subordinate in the pictures which imagination may draw of what is beheld through the gates ajar by little pilgrims in the unseen. The representations which seem to aim at making another world as like this one as may be, dwarf its greatness, and tend to obscure the conditions of entering into its rest. "It doth not yet appear what we shall be" is as much a revelation as "when He shall appear we shall be like Him" [1 John 3:2]. As a great painter concentrates finish and light on the face of his sitter, and purposely keeps the rest of the picture slight, there is one face that should fill the dim, dark curtain of the future—the face of Christ—and all else may be thrown together in mere sketchy outline. We know that future chiefly by negations and by symbols, and the one positive fact is that we shall have Him and He will possess us.

December 13

AS WE SOW, WE REAP

They that plow iniquity, and sow wickedness reap the same—Job 4:8
He that soweth iniquity shall reap vanity—Proverbs 22:8

It is a solemn thought that the ultimate perfect possession of and by God is evolved from a germ which must be planted now if it is to flourish there. "The child is father of the man." Every present is the result of all the past; every future will be the result of the past and the present. Everybody admits that about this life, but there are some of us that seem to forget it with regard to another world. We know too little of the effect that is produced upon men by the change of death to dogmatize; but one may be quite sure that the law of continuity will go on into the other world. Or, to put it into simpler English, a man on the other side of the grave will be the same as he was on this side. The line will run straight on; it may be slightly refracted by passing from any atmosphere of one density to another of a different, but it will be very slightly. The main direction will be the same.

What is there in death that can change a man's will? I can fancy death making an idiot wise, because idiocy comes from physical causes. I can fancy death giving people altogether different notions of the folly of sin; but I do not know anything in the physical fact of death, or in the accompanying alterations that it produces upon spiritual consciousness, in so far as they are known to us, that can alter the dominant bias and set of a man's nature. It seems to me more likely that it will intensify that dominant bias, whatever it is; that it will make good men better and bad men worse when the limitations of incomplete organs are gone. At all events, do not run risks with such a very shaky hypothesis as that: but remember that what a man sows he shall reap; that the present is the parent of the future, and that unless we have the earnest of inheritance here, and pass into the other world bearing that earnest in our hands, there seems little reason why we should expect that, when we stand before Him empty-handed, we can claim a portion therein.

I was passing a little town garden a day or two ago, and the man had a young weeping willow that he had put in the plot in front of his door, and he had bent down its branches and put them around the hoop of an old wine-cask to teach them to droop. And after a bit, when they have been set, he will take away the hoop, but the branches will never spring upwards, though it be gone, wherever you transplant the tree. Are you doing that with your souls? If you give them the downward set, they will keep it, though the earth to which you have fastened them be burnt up with fervent heat, and the soul be transplanted into another region.

If you have life, you will grow. If there be any real possession of the inheritance, it will be like the rolling fences that they used to have in certain parts of the country, where a squatter settled himself down upon a bit of a royal forest, and had a hedge that could be moved outwards and shifted on by degrees; and from having begun with a little bit big enough for a cabbage garden, ended with a piece big enough for a farm. And that is what we are always to do, to be always acquiring, "adding field to field" in the great inheritance that is ours.

"WHAT SHALL I RENDER?"

What shall I render unto the Lord for all his benefits toward me?—Ps. 116:12

"What shall I render? . . . Take!" The whole essence of Christianity is in that antithesis, if you think about it. For what does the doctrine that a man is saved by faith mean if it does not mean that the one thing that we all have to do is to accept what God bestows? And the same attitude of reception which we have to assume at the beginning of our Christian life must be maintained all through it. Depend upon it, we shall make far more progress in the Divine life if we learn that each step of it must begin with the acceptance of a gift from God, than if we toil and moil and wear ourselves with vain efforts in our own strength. I do not mean that a Christian man is not to put forth such efforts, but I do mean that the basis of all profitable discipline and self-control and reaching out towards higher attainments, either in knowledge or in practical conformity to Jesus Christ, which he puts forth, must be laid in fuller acceptance of God's gift, on which must follow building on the foundation, by resolute efforts to work God's gift into our characters, and to work it out in our lives.

All around you, Christian friend, there lie infinite possibilities. God does not wait to be asked to give; He *has* given once for all, and continuously as the result of that once-for-all giving, just as preservation is but the prolongation of the act of creation. He has given once for all and continuously all that every man, and all men, need for their being made perfectly like Himself. We hear people praying for "larger bestowments of grace." Let them take the bestowments that they *have*, and they will find them enough for their need. God communicated His whole fullness to the Church forever when He sent His Son, and when His Son sent His spirit. "Open thy mouth wide and I will fill it" [Ps. 81:10]. Take what you have, and you will find that you have all that you need.

What a sin it is that with such abundance lying close to us, we Christian people should live such low and surface lives as we do! The whole fullness of ocean is pouring past us, and our lives are often chapped with thirst. All God's grace is streaming out ever more around us, and we are impoverished and crippled for want of it. A man plunged into the sea of God, and yet empty of God, is like a flask corked and waxed and waterproofed, and sunk into the depths of ocean, with leagues of water on either side, and fathoms below it, and yet dry within.

Remember the blessed transformation in the whole conceptions of our relations to God, our obligations and duties, which this thought affects. Away goes the religion of fear, away goes the religion of reluctant obedience to duties, which we discern but dislike. Away goes the religion of recompense and bartering and bargaining with God. Away goes everything except the religion of a heart turned to love by the reception of God's love. Such a heart is endowed with a kind of shadowy resemblance to the Divine blessedness. Into it, too, though it has nothing, can come the wish to give itself, to give God what He has not unless we give it. And so, with wonderful reciprocity, like the light flashed back from one mirror to another, God—the giving God—gives and loves, and the recipient man receives and loves and gives. "What shall I render? . . . I will take."

THE CUP OF SALVATION

I will take the cup of salvation, and call upon the name of the Lord—Ps. 116:13

Here is a guiding word about plain common duties. How few of us recognize, and receive into our hearts, all the lesser daily blessings which God pours down upon us! How many of us are like Haman, to whom the Persian king's favor, and the real sovereignty over his empire, and everything that gratified ambition could expect, all turned to ashes in his mouth because one poor Jew sat there, and would not get up when he passed. "All this availeth me nothing, as long as Mordecai sits at the gate" [see Esth. 5:13]. We all have our Mordecais, and we say to ourselves, "God has given me this mercy, that blessing, and the other one; but it all turns to bitterness because I cannot get that other thing that I want. It is a little one, but I want it, for without it everything else is nothing." There are some of us who, if there is the faintest suspicion of a cloud away down on the horizon shiver and complain as if there were no sunshine. One sorrow can blot out a thousand joys. One disappointment can more than cancel a whole series of fulfilled expectations. Brother, be sure that you take all the blessings of your daily life that God bestows upon you, and do not be one of God's fractious children, who care for none of His gifts because they are whimpering for the moon, and nothing else will satisfy them. Take what is given, and you will find that it is far more than you expected, and your hands and your heart will be full.

And then there is another plain piece of practical wisdom, "I will take the cup . . . and call upon the name of the Lord." Do not take any cup in your hand that you cannot do that with. You remember the old stories about the demon-prepared banquets spread in the desert to tempt the knight from his quest. When the Name of God was pronounced over them, they vanished, and instead of dainties and gold plate and a luxurious table, there was only a heap of dry sticks and stones on the sand. Name the Name of God over the cup before you put it to your lips; and if you cannot, dash it down. Be sure that it is no cup of salvation unless you do. Unless we do thus associate thankful thoughts of the giving God with all our common blessings, they are no blessings, and will draw us away from Him.

But do not forget that we can render to God something which He does not possess in such a manner as satisfies His heart, unless we give it Him. We can give Him ourselves: and we shall be moved to such self-surrender only when we have taken the full cup of full salvation which Christ has made ours by His giving Himself for, and to, us all. "I beseech you, brethren, by the mercies of God, that ye present your bodies a living sacrifice" [Rom. 12:1].

December 16

TRANSFORMATION THROUGH PRAYER

And as he prayed, the fashion of his countenance was altered, and his raiment was white and glistering—Luke 9:29

And if we have communion with God as deep and real as Jesus Christ had, the fashion of our countenances will be altered too. I do not mean, of course, that any physical change will occur, though I wonder if there are any of us that cannot remember someone who, at some time or other of deep emotion, and of high communion with God, showed a face shining like Stephen's when the heavens were opened; or like Moses when he came down from the mount! I wonder if there are any of us that have not in our hearts the remembrances of, perhaps, very homely features of some poor old man or woman, glorified and transfigured by the love of Christ and faith in God! That miracle is being done all around us every day. And there are people of whom it is true that "A beauty born of" more than "murmuring sound" has passed into their faces, just as there are, on the other hand, men and women who bear written on their foreheads that they belong to the devil, and have the marks of their evil passions, their bad tempers, their lusts, their cunning, stamped on their faces so that nobody can mistake them. We are all physiognomists, and we generally make a pretty correct estimate of a man's character by looking at him.

If we are holding on by God, and if our days are passed in any real sense in communion with Him, whether upon the mountaintop as Christ and the three were, or down in the valley trying to cure demoniacs, as was much more permanently the disciples' place and duty; if we are, in any real sense, in touch with God, we cannot but be made fair, noble, refined, manifestly purified, and having an indwelling and out-saying light in and from us. If there is nothing of the sort in our appearance, it is because God always tells upon a life, and lifts a man above cares, and enables him to put his heel upon his faults, and to master his devilries; and refines him by the presence of elevated and heaven-directed thoughts and aspirations. Does your religion do anything of that sort for you? If it does not, you had better see whether it is real or not.

Of all the things that are given, in God's great mercy, to Christian people, to change their characters and natures for the better, the most powerful is the transforming power of communion with God. It is to that, if you come to look into it, that the New Testament entrusts the almost whole assimilation of men's characters to the image of Christ. Of course, I know that the Divine Spirit comes to sanctify and to cleanse, but here is the law of our being transformed: "But we all, with open face beholding as in a glass the glory of the Lord, are changed into the same image" [2 Cor. 3:18]. Look at Him and you will be like Him. You can tell by the flush that comes over a man's face whether he has it turned full to the sunlight or not. And we ought to be able to tell by the very cut of a man, certainly by the cast of his life and character, whether he knows what it is to go up to the mountaintop, and within the cloud, to walk, in the fire, and catch its radiance and its warmth.

351

THE NEED OF A DEFINITE AIM IN LIFE (PART ONE)

They went forth to go into the land of Canaan, and into the land of Canaan they came—Gen. 12:5

The reference of these words, as we all know, is to Abraham's great act of faith, when he left Haran and his native place to begin the pilgrim life which God had called him to undertake. It is a strange description of a journey to leave out the journey altogether, and only to mark two points—the beginning and the end. The keynotes of the narrative are these two—"went forth"; "came in." The only things worth noticing about any life are wither it was directed and whether it reached its aim. All the toilsomeness of the road, the privations, the weary marches, the hunger and thirst, the perils and foes, are all dropped out of sight. Never mind about these. They "went forth to go"—and they came where they went to go. As one of our modern poets has it, there are

> "Two points in the adventure of the diver,
> One when, a beggar, he prepares to plunge,
> One when, a prince, he rises with his pearl."

"They went forth" for one definite purpose, "to go into the land of Canaan." Now, perhaps, you will remember that the New Testament lays stress upon what might, at first sight, seem a contradiction; and says that Abraham went out, "not knowing whither he went" [Heb. 11:8]. But there is no real contradiction. Both statements are true. In Abraham's case there was a combination of knowledge and ignorance similar to that which we may all have in our lives; for he certainly knew that he was to be led at last to a land which he should afterwards inherit, and he knew, when he crossed the Euphrates and set his face westwards, that Canaan was his immediate "objective point" (as soldiers say), but he did not know, till after his departure from his first home, that Canaan was the promised land. Abraham went forth, as it were, with sealed orders. He was bid to go to a certain place, and, when there, he would get further instructions. He knew that he was to go to Canaan, and beyond that point all was dark, except for the sparkle of the great hope that gleamed on the horizon in front, as a sunlit summit rises above a sea of mist between it and the traveler. Like such a traveler, Abraham could not accurately tell how far off the shining peak was, nor where, in the intervening gorges full of mist, the path lay; but he plunged into the darkness with a good heart, because he had caught a glimpse of his journey's end. So with us. We may have clearly before us the ultimate aim and goal of our lives, and also the step which we have to take now, in pressing towards it; while between these two there stretches a valley full of mist, the breadth of which may be measured by years or by hours, for all that we know, and the rough places and green pastures of which are equally hidden from us. We have to make sure that the mountain peak which we think we see, with the sunlight playing on its sides, is not delusive cloud, but solid reality, and we have to be very certain that God has bid us step out on the yard of ground in front of us which we can see; and, having secured these certainties, we have to cast ourselves into the obscurity before us, and to carry in our hearts the bright vision of the end, to encourage us in the difficulties of the road.

THE NEED OF A DEFINITE AIM IN LIFE (PART TWO)

I have chosen the way of truth: thy judgments have I laid before me—Ps. 119:30

Many will remember how strongly one of the great teachers of the past generation laid hold of one of these two thoughts (referred to in the previous day's note)—and, only of one of them—when he insisted, with reiteration that would have been wearisome if it had not been so earnest, on doing the duty that lies nearest us. It is a shame that he did not, with equal decisiveness, insist on the reality of the Christian vision of the ultimate goal, which glorifies the smallest proximate duties! But we should combine both in our view, that the sight of the land that is very far off may both hearten us for, and direct us to, the next step in our march. Abraham "went out, not knowing whither he went" [Heb. 11:8]; but ye he knew whither, in the first instance, to shape his course, for he "went forth to go into the land of Canaan."

One condition of a blessed life—certainly a condition of a strenuous, fruitful, and noble one—is to make very clear to ourselves, and even to reiterate to ourselves, what is the ultimate aim to which we are shaping our conscious efforts. I believe that nine-tenths of all the failures in this world come from men not interrogating themselves and answering honestly and thoroughly this question, "What am I living for?" Of course, all the nearer aims which our physical necessities, our tastes, and our appetites, prescribe to us are clear enough to everybody; but back of them—suppose I have made my fortune, won my wife, filled my home with blessings, made my position as a student, an artist, a man of "commerce"; behind all these lies—What then? *What then?* These are not ends; they are means. What is the *end* that I am living for—back of all these and above them all? Oh, if the average, unreflecting man, who lives from hand to mouth, recognizing only the aims for life which the necessities of living impose upon him, would but wake up to ask himself, for one reflective half-hour, "What is it all about? What does it all lead to? What am I going to do after I have attained these nearer aims?" There would not be so many wasted lives; there would not be so many bitter old men who look back upon a life in which failure has been at least as conspicuous as success. Let us be sure that we know where we are going, and let our aim be the highest, noblest, ultimate aim, befitting creatures with hearts, minds, consciences, and wills like ours. What that aim should be is not doubtful. The only worthy aim is God. Canaan is usually regarded as an emblem of heaven, and that is correct. But the land of our inheritance is not wholly across the river, for "the Lord is the portion of mine inheritance." [Ps. 16:5]. God *is* Heaven. To dwell with Him and in Him, to have all the current of our being setting towards Him, to remember Him in the struggle and strenuous effort of life, and to look to Him in hours of solitude and sadness, are the conditions of all blessedness, and of all strength and peace.

DETACHMENT FROM OLD ASSOCIATIONS

By faith Abraham, when he was called, to go out unto a place which he should after receive for an inheritance obeyed; and he went out, not knowing whither he went—Heb. 11:8

Every great purpose requires restriction in other directions. A man cannot learn to play the fiddle unless he will consent to shear off a good many hours of leisure, and give them to it. There is nothing worth doing to be done except upon condition of resolutely stopping eyes and ears to attractions that lie around us. Jesus Christ demands no more than the artist pays for success in his art, no more than the man of business pays for making his wealth, no more than the student pays for attaining the mastery of his science; and that is, that everything else shall be subordinated, and, if necessary, shall be thrown aside, in order to secure the one aim. And when He said, "No man can follow me that does not take up his cross and deny himself" [see Luke 9:23], he was just putting into language the experience that Abraham and his company had to go through when, if ever they were to go into the land of Canaan, they had to go out of the land of Haran. Always subordinated, and often cast aside, must everything else be if Christian men are to make God what He ought to be—their aim and end. The compass in an iron ship gets deflected by the iron around it, and so the resolute pointing of our spirits toward God gets drawn aside and warped by the many things that lie around us. Therefore rigid self-control and the continual effort to regard all external things mainly as means to an end, and possibly as hindrances thereto, are absolutely essential for success in the Christian life.

There is no patent way of getting to God. There is no easier path to be trodden today than of old. There are no rails laid to travel without effort to heaven by. We have still to journey in the old pilgrim fashion which Abraham set, and thereby became "the father of the faithful." "They went forth"—and unless we are prepared to leave behind us native country and companionship, such as Abraham left behind him in Haran, and to dwell, if needful, in a wilderness and a solitude, we shall never see "the land that is very far off" [Is. 33:17]. It is near us if we will forsake self and the things seen and temporal, but it moves away and recedes from us when we turn our hearts to these.

A mournfully large number of professing Christians have lost the very notion of progress, and content themselves with saying, "Oh! We shall always be imperfect; as long as we are here in this world, we cannot make it any different." No, you cannot make it different in that respect; but if you are not growing at all, ask yourself if you are living at all. Do not be content, as so many are, to be like invaders, who have pitched their tents, and after years of occupation have been unable to advance beyond the strip of shore which they seized at first, while all the interior lies unconquered and in arms against them.

THE CHRISTIAN AIM ULTIMATELY REALIZED

And he led them forth by the right way, that they might go to a city of habitation—Psalm 108:7

The man that has one definite purpose in view is the strong man. Such distinction of aim gives what most of our lives so sadly lack—continuity right through them. There is only one aim so great and so far that we never can reach it, and never outgrow it. And is not that a blessing? Look back on your lives. Have they not been like the course of a ship with a headwind, tacking first in one direction and then in another? Have they not been like the navigation of the ancients, who could not push out to sea for fear of losing their landmarks; and so had first to make for one headland and then for another, and to leave them one by one behind them as they sailed on their devious course? We too often live fragmentary lives. But if we have far before us, beyond the furthest reach of thought, apprehension, or attainment, the one great aim to be with God, to be in God, to be like God, to be flooded with God, why, then, we can never need to substitute another purpose for that, or say, "It has served its turn, and we can leave it behind." So the whole life may be of a piece, strong, solid, continuously progressive and increasing; and everything that we do may be brought into harmony with and subjection to this aim. There is only one purpose that lasts a lifetime there is only one that can be followed, amid all the variety of occupations which so often break up our lives into fragments. "This one thing I do" [Phil. 3:13], is the secret of all blessedness.

No man honestly wants God and does not get Him. No man has less of goodness and Christlikeness than he truly desires and earnestly seeks. We all experience many failures, for disappointments, for hopes unfulfilled, and even for those which, when accomplished, turn out not to be worth fulfilling. Thank God for all the times in which He has made the harvest from our servings a very poor one, so that we have sown much and brought home little! It is His way of teaching us to turn away from the paths in which effort has no assurance of success, into the paths in which it cannot fail. "I have never said to any of the seed of Israel, Seek ye My face in vain." We may not reach other lands which to us seem to be lands of promise; or when we get there we may find that the land is "evil and naughty." But this land we shall reach if we desire it, and if, desiring it, we go forth from the vain world. Canaan is the symbol of the rest that remains for the people of God. No pilgrim with his face set Zionward ever perished in the wilderness or lost his road. "They go from strength to strength; every one of them in Zion appeareth before God" [Ps. 84:7]. And when they get there, nothing will be thought by them about the sandy deserts, the salt wastes, and the waterless wildernesses; nothing about the weariness and the solitude and the dangers and the toils. This, and this alone, will be worth recording as the summing up of the lives of the happy pilgrims who have accomplished all at which they aimed, that they are at rest forever in the mother-country which they sought.

A HOPE BORN IN THE DARKNESS

That we through patience and comfort of the scriptures, might have hope—
Rom. 15:4

Who can tell how many struggling souls have taken heart again, as they pondered over the sweet stories of sorrow subdued which stud the pages of Scripture like stars in its firmament? The tears shed long ago which God has put "in His bottle," and recorded in "His book," have truly been turned into pearls. That long gallery of portraits of sufferers, who have all trodden the same rough road, and been sustained by the same hand, and reached the same home, speaks cheer to all who follow them. Hearts wrung by cruel partings from those dearer to them than their own souls turn to the pages which tell how Abraham, with calm sorrow, laid his Sarah in the cave of Machpelah; or how, when Jacob's eyes were dim that he could not see, his memory still turned to the hour of agony when Rachel died by him, and he sees clear in its light her lonely grave, where so much of himself was laid; or to the more sacred pages which record the struggle of grief and faith in the hearts of the sisters of Bethany. All who are anyways afflicted in mind, body, or estate find in the Psalms men speaking their deepest experiences before them; and the grand majesty of sorrow that marks "the patience of Job" [James 5:11], and the flood of sunshine that bathes him, revealing the "rod of the Lord," have strengthened countless sufferers to bear and to hold fast and to hope. We are all enough of children to be more affected by living examples than by dissertations, however true; and so Scripture is mainly history, revealing God by the record of His acts, and disclosing the secret of human life by telling us the experiences of living men. But Scripture has another method of ministering encouragement to our often fainting and faithless hearts. It cuts down through all the complications of human affairs, and lays bare the innermost motive power. It not only shows us in its narratives the working of sorrow and the power of faith, but it distinctly lays down the source and the purpose, the whence and the whither, of all suffering. No man need shrink or faint before the most torturing pains, or most disastrous strokes of evil, who holds firmly the plain teaching of Scripture on these two points: they all come *from* my Father, and they all come *for* my good. It is a short and simple creed, easily apprehended. It pretends to no profound wisdom. It is homely philosophy, which common intellects can grasp, which children can understand, and hearts half-paralyzed by sorrow can take in. So much the better. Grief and pain are so common that their cure had need to be easily obtained. Ignorant people have to writhe in agony as well as wise ones; and till grief is the portion only of the cultivated classes, its healing must come from something more universal than philosophy, or else the nettle would be more plentiful than the dock, and many a poor heart would be stung to death. The Christian view of sorrow, while it leaves much unexplained, focuses a steady light on these two points: its origin and its end. The slings and arrows which strike are no more flung blindly by an "outrageous fortune," but each bears an inscription, like the fabled bolts, which tells what hand drew the bow, and they come with His love.

A HOPE BORN OF THE DAY

To whom God would make known what is the riches of the glory of this mystery among the Gentiles, which is Christ in you, the hope of glory—Col. 1:27

There is a river in Switzerland fed by two uniting streams bearing the same name, one of them called the "white," one of them the "gray," or dark. One comes down from the glaciers, and bears the half-melted snow in its white ripple; the other flows through a lovely valley, and is discolored by its earth. They unite in one common current. So in the two verses (Rom. 15:4, 13) we have two streams, a white and a black, and they both blend together and flow out into a common hope. In the former of them we have the dark stream—"through patience and comfort," which implies affliction and effort. The issue and outcome of all difficulty, trial, sorrow, ought to be hope. And in the other verse we have the other valley, down which the light stream comes—"the God of hope fill you with all joy and peace in believing, that ye may abound in hope." So both halves of the possible human experience are meant to end in the same blessed result; and whether you go around on the one side of the sphere of human life, or whether you take the other hemisphere, you come to the same point, if you have traveled with God's hand in yours, and with Him for your Guide.

I have traced the genealogy of the hope which is the child of the night. But we have also a hope that is born of the day, the child of sunshine and gladness, and that is set before us in the second of the two verses I have quoted. The darkness and the light are both alike to our hope, in so far as each may become the occasion for its exercise. It is not only to be the sweet juice pressed from our hearts by the winepress of calamities, but that which flows of itself from hearts ripened and mellowed under the sunshine of God-given blessedness.

We have seen that the bridge by which sorrow led to hope was perseverance and courage; in this second analysis of the origin of hope, joy and peace are the bridge by which faith passes over into it. Observe the difference: There is no direct connection between affliction and hope, but there is between joy and hope. We have no right to say, "Because I suffer I shall possess good in the future"; but we have a right to say, "Because I rejoice—of course with a joy in God—I shall never cease to rejoice in Him." Such joy is the prophet of its own immortality and completion. And, on the other hand, the joy and peace which are naturally the direct progenitors of Christian hope are the children of faith. So that we have here two generations, as it were, of hope's ancestors. Faith produces joy and peace, and these again produce hope.

Faith leads to joy and peace. Paul has found—and if we only put it to the proof, we shall also find—that the simple exercise of simple faith fills the soul with "*all* joy and peace." Gladness in all its variety, and in full measure, calm repose in every kind, and abundant in its still depth, will pour into my heart as water does into a vessel on condition of my taking away the barrier and opening my heart through faith. Trust, and thou shalt be calm. In the measure of thy trust shall be the measure of thy joy and peace.

THE BELOVED SON

This is my beloved Son, in whom I am well pleased—Matt. 3:17

All Christ's work for us, and its sweetness and preciousness to us, all His power as the Revealer of God and of man, all His power as Redeemer, Savior, Sympathizer, Helper, Friend, Judge, Recompense, Life, all depends on and stands or falls with this conception of His birth into the world as the coming, by His voluntary act, of the Eternal Word into the brotherhood of our humanity. "Forasmuch as the children were partakers of flesh and blood, he also himself likewise," and yet how differently, actively, "took part of the same" [Heb. 2:14].

And then from this flows the other great thought which our Lord announces, that His birth is the assumption of a true and yet unique manhood. He is "Son of man," body, soul, and spirit, one of us; "bone of our bone, flesh of our flesh" [see Gen. 2:23], knowing the aspirations of the spirit and the limitations of the body; proved to be the Son of David, and the Brother of us all according to the flesh, in that He hungered and thirsted and wearied and wept, and suffered and died; proved to be a man in spirit and in heart like us all, in that He sorrowed and rejoiced, was grieved and was angry, willed and purposed, thought and loved.

And not only is perfect and a true manhood revealed to us in the name by which He comes so near to us all, but a manhood which, in all its reality, was yet singular and unique. Others are "sons of men"; this is "*the* Son." In Him, as it were, is contained all which is proper to humanity, and is scattered elsewhere through the race. He is the one pearl of great price [Matt. 13:46], the entire and perfect chrysolite. To Him all other men are but as fragments. He alone is the full true Man, according to the Divine ideal; the *second* Man, *the* Man Christ Jesus. In Him all the strengths, beauties, holinesses, proper to, or possible to, humanity are gathered, and abide. Others, saints, sages, preachers, teachers, by the side of Him are like a tiny cup of water by the side of the everflowing fountain. You might take millions of blocks to be fashioned into the fairest forms of manly strength and womanly beauty, out of this great marble cliff, in which everything that is lovely and of good report, all that is virtuous and deserves praise, is found in stainless perfection.

In every religion is some tradition that "the gods are come down in the likeness of men" [Acts 14:11]. Is this but one more dream like those others, expressing unfulfilled longings and vain desires? Nay, this is the reality of which those are but confessions of the need. They are man's wistful and half-despairing hopes. This is God's answer, meeting and surpassing all their expectations, giving a real, perfect, and eternal incarnation, instead of apparent partial and temporary assumptions of shadowy manhood.

THE INCARNATION IN ORDER TO A LIFE OF SERVICE

The Son of man came not to be ministered unto, but to minister, and to give his life a ransom for many—Matt. 20:28

As a king might enter poor men's huts, and learn their condition, and live their lives, and share their squalor, and weep their tears, and staunch their wounds, so Christ wills to be born that He may help and serve us. He comes "not to be ministered unto, but to minister." The infinite condescension of the incarnation, looked at as I have suggested it must be looked at, is the fit vestibule to a life likewise marked by infinite condescension and lowliness. He comes to serve. Think of the outward circumstances of the life; of how He stole into the world, as it were, in lowly guise, and chose the condition of poverty. Think of how, all through His life, you find unwearied diligence, readiness to help everybody, whatsoever their weakness, their need, to turn away from no vileness, to be disgusted by no profanity, to despair of no abject of alienated heart. He ever recognizes the claims of others upon Him, and never thinks of His claims upon them except for their good. He requires nothing, never for a moment shows that He thought of Himself, but forever devotes His loving heart and hand, His wise words, His miracle-working power, to the blessing of men.

Such a life stands absolutely alone. There is not a flaw in the marble, not a black vein running through it that spoils the statue, not a speck. No man can put his finger upon any action recorded of Jesus Christ, and say, "He did that for His own advantage, He did that from a motive that centered upon self."

Do not let us forget that in this we have Christ's revelation of God. The Highest of all is highest, in order that He may stoop to the lowliest, and being Lord of all serve the needs and supply the emptiness of every creature that lives.

That revelation of the Master's relation to us is not antiquated by His present exaltation. He is still your Servant and mine, ready to help and to succor. And, more wonderful than all, He has given it us, as the highest conception that we can form of the heavenly world, that He Himself will come forth and gird Himself, and serve them who have been His servants here.

That life of service was also a true revelation of the law of His kingdom and of the true greatness and blessedness of men. He proposes His own utter self-suppression and devotion to our advantage, as the pattern to which all professing Christians are to conform. In Him we learn the dignity of service; in Him we learn the obligations of superiors. This example is meant to shame us out of our self-seeking, vulgar ambition, and misuse of advantages which raise us above our fellows. It says to us all, "Do not stand on your rights; forget your claims; consecrate your capacities to your brethren's service, and learn that position means obligation, and that the only true order of rank in Christ's kingdom is determined, not by what we are, but by our use of what we are to help all who will accept our help." Does the world believe that the servant of all is the chiefest of all? Does it believe that the chiefest of all should be servant of all? Does the church believe it? Do we? Do we act as if we did, either in regard to our judgment of others or to the regulation of our own lives?

December 25

CHRIST'S VICARIOUS AND REDEEMING DEATH

I lay down my life for the sheep. . . . I have power to lay it down, and I have power to take it again—John 10:15, 18.

We can imitate Christ in His service, but not in His sacrifice; we can tread in His footsteps to the gate of Gethsemane, but He has to wrestle in His agony alone; alone He has to stand before His judges, and to die alone. He *gives* His life. As at its beginning He willed to be born, so at the end He wills to die. He is the Lord of Life and the Lord of Death; and never did He witness the completeness of His authority over that awful form, which yet is His servant, more marvelously and entirely than when He seemed to submit to its blow.

Like the King of Israel who bade his armor-bearer fall upon him and slay him [see 1 Sam. 31:4], so Christ commanded and Death obeyed. If you will read with an eye to this thought the stories of the Crucifixion, you will see that all the evangelists, as of set purpose, choose expressions which are at least consistent with, and I think were selected on purpose to express, the thought of the voluntariness of our Lord's death. He "yielded up the ghost," [Matt. 27:50], "He gave up the spirit," with a mighty cry which indicated unexhausted strength, "Father! Into thy hands I commend my Spirit" [Luke 23:46].

The same witness is born, as I believe, by the remarkable language employed in the account of the Transfiguration, when these three, each of whom stood in a peculiar relation to death, Moses, Elijah, and Christ, conversed in solemn words, "concerning the *departure* which He should *accomplish* at Jerusalem" [see Luke 9:31]—by Himself willing to go, and therefore going. You will not understand either birth or death unless you interpret them both according to His own profound saying: "I came forth from the Father, and am come into the world." Again, "I leave the world and go unto the Father" [John 16:28].

And, still further, we have here set forth our Lord's voluntary death as a ransom. A ransom is a price paid for the deliverance of a slave from captivity. And Christ distinctly, beyond all quibbling on the part of honest interpretation, as it seems to me, sets forth His death here as the crown of His service and the climax of His work, because in it there is the power by which the bonds of sin and condemnation are broken, and liberty is proclaimed to the captive, and the opening of the prison to them that are bound. He dies, not as the hero dies who closes his heroism by a brave death. He dies, not as the martyr dies who seals his witness with his blood. He dies, not as the saint dies, leaving behind him sweet and pathetic memories that draw us onward upon a course like his own. Other men's deaths are but the closing of their activity; Christ's death is the climax of His. It is not enough that He should serve in our stead; He must die our death if we are to be set free. It is not enough that He should witness of God by the wisdom of His Word, the purity of His life, the graciousness of His deeds, the tenderness of His compassion, the pathos of His tears. A nobler revelation of the love of God triumphing over man's sin; of the consistency of that life with perfect righteousness—a revelation, too, of the darkness and the foulness of man's evil which nothing else could have given, is given to us when, and only when, we recognize the voluntary death of Jesus Christ as the ransom and propitiation for the sins of the world.

WATCHFULNESS

Blessed are those servants whom the lord when he cometh shall find watching—
Luke 12:37

The first idea in watchfulness is keeping awake, and the second is looking out for something that is coming. Both these conceptions are intertwined in both our Lord's use of the metaphor of the watching servant and in the echoes of it which we find abundantly in the Apostolic letters. The first thing is to keep ourselves awake all through the sleepy night, when everything tempts to slumber. Even the *wise* virgins, with trimmed lamps and girt loins, do in some degree succumb to the drowsy influences around them, and, like the foolish ones, slumber, though the slumbers of the two classes be unlike. Christian people live in the midst of an order of things which tempts them to close the eyes of their hearts and minds to all the real and unseen glories above and around them and that might be within them, and to live for the comparatively contemptible and trivial things of this present. Just as when a man sleeps he loses his consciousness of the solid external realities, and passes into a fantastic world of his own imaginations, which have no correspondence in external facts, and will vanish like the baseless fabric of a vision if but a poor cock shall crow, so the men who are conscious only of this present life and of the things that are seen, though they pride themselves on being wide awake, are, in the deepest of their being, fast asleep, and are dealing with illusions which shall pass and leave nothing behind, as really as are men who lie upon dreaming couches and fancy themselves hard at work. Keep awake; that is the first thing, which, being translated into plain English, points just to this, that, unless we make a dead lift of continuous effort to keep a firm grasp of God and Christ, and of all the unseen magnificences that are included in these two words, as surely as we live we shall lose our hold upon them, and fall into the drugged and diseased sleep in which so many men around us are plunged. It sometimes seems to one as if the sky above us were raining down narcotics upon us, so profoundly are the bulk of men unconscious of realities and fooled by the illusions of a dream.

Many of us have to acknowledge that the fervor of early days has died down into coldness. The river that leapt from its source rejoicing, and bickered among the hills in such swift and musical descent, creeps sluggish and almost stagnant among the flats of later life, or has been lost and swallowed up altogether in the thirsty and encroaching sands of a barren worldliness. Do not let your Christian life be like that snow that is on the ground—when it first lights upon the earth, radiant and white, but day by day more covered with a veil of sooty blackness until it becomes dark and foul. Even early failures, recognized and repented of, may make a man better fitted for the tasks which once he fled from. Just as they tell us that a broken bone renewed is stronger at the point of fracture than it ever was before, so the very sin that we commit, when once we know it for a sin, and have brought it to Christ for forgiveness, may minister to our future efficiency and strength.

The past is no specimen of what the future may be. The page that is yet to be written need have none of the blots of the page that we have turned over shining through it. The sin which we have learned to know for a sin and to hate teaches us humility, dependence—shows us where the weak places are; sin which is forgiven knits us to Christ with deeper and more fervid love, and results in a larger consecration.

REMEMBER AND BE THANKFUL

And thou shalt remember all the way which the Lord thy God hath led thee—
Deut. 8:2

There are few of us who have much time for retrospect, and there is a very deep sense in which it is wise to "forget the things that are behind," for the remembrance of them may burden us with a miserable entail of failure, may weaken us by vain regrets, may unfit us for energetic action in the living and available present. But oblivion is foolish if it is continual, and a remembered past has treasures in it which we can little afford to lose. It is hard to recognize our Father God in the bustle and hurry of our daily life, and the meaning of each event can only be seen when it is seen in its relation to the rest of a life. Just as a landscape, which we may look at without the smallest perception of its beauty, becomes another thing when the genius of a painter puts it on canvas, and its symmetry and proportion become more manifest, and an ethereal clearness broods over it, and its colors are seen to be deeper than our eyes had discerned, so the common events of life, trivial and insignificant while they are passing, become, when painted on the canvas of memory, nobler and greater, and we understand them more completely than we can do while they are passing.

We need to be at the goal in order to judge of the road. The parts are only explicable when we see the whole. The full interpretation of today is reserved for eternity. But, by combining and massing and presenting the consequences of the apparently insignificant and isolated events of the past, memory helps us to a clearer perception of God and a better understanding of our own lives. On the mountain summit a man can look down all along the valley by which he has wearily plodded, and understand the meaning of the divergences in the road, and the rough places do not look quite so rough when their proportion to the whole is a little more clearly in his view.

Only, if we are wisely to exercise remembrance, and to discover God in the lives which, while they are passing, had not perception of Him, we must take into account what the meaning of all life is—that is, to make men of us after the pattern of His will.

> "Not enjoyment, and not sorrow,
> Is our destined end or way."

But the growth of Christlike and God-pleasing character is the Divine purpose, and should be the human aim of all lives. Our tasks, our joys, our sorrows, our gains, our losses—these are all but the scaffolding, and the scaffolding is only there in order that course upon course may rise the temple—palace of a spirit, devoted to, shaped and inhabited by, our Father, God.

It is possible to remember vanished joys, and to confer upon them by remembrance a kind of gentle immortality; and, thus remembered, they are ennobled, for all the gross material body of them, as it were, is gotten rid of, and only the fine spirit is left. The roses bloom, and over bloom, and drop, but a poignant perfume is distilled from the fallen petals. The departed are greatened by distance; when they are gone, we recognize the angels that we entertained unawares [see Heb. 13:2]; and that recognition is no illusion, but it is the disclosure of the real character, to which they were sometimes untrue and we were often blind.

REMEMBER AND REPENT

Remember, therefore, from whence thou art fallen, and repent and do the first works—Rev. 2:5

We look back upon a past, of which God gave us the loom, and we had to put in the threads. The loom is all bright and pure. The threads that have crossed it from our shuttles are many of them very dark, and all of them stained in some part. So let us take the year that has gone, and spread them out by the agency of this servant of the court, Memory, before the supreme judge, Conscience.

Let us remember, that we may be warned and directed. We shall understand the true moral character of our actions a great deal better when we look back upon them calmly, and when all the rush of temptation and the seducing whispers of our own weak wills are silenced. There is nothing more terrible, in one aspect, there is nothing more salutary and blessed in another, than the difference between the front view and the back of any temptation to which we yield—all radiant and beautiful on the other side, and when we get past it and look back at it, all hideous. Like some of those painted canvases upon the theater stage: seen from the pit, with the delusive brilliancy of the stage thrown upon them, they look like beautiful works of art; seen at the back, dirty and cobwebbed canvas, all splashes and spots and ugliness. Let us be thankful if memory can show us the reverse side of the temptations that on the near side were so seductive.

It is when you see a sketch of your life that you understand the significance of the single deeds in them. We are so apt to isolate our actions that we are startled, and it is a wholesome shock when we see how, without knowing it, we have dropped into a habit. When each temptation comes, as the moments are passing, we say, "Oh, just this once! Just this once!" And the acts that we thought isolated we find out to our horror—our wholesome horror—have become a chain that binds and holds us. Look back over the year, and drag its events to the bar of Conscience, and I shall be surprised if you do not find out that you have fallen into wrong habits that you never dreamed had dominion over you. So I say, "Remember and repent."

I do not want to exaggerate, I do not want to urge upon you one-sided views of your character or conduct. I give all credit to many excellences, many acts of sacrifice, many acts of service, and yet I say that the main reason why any of us have a good opinion of ourselves is because we have knowledge of ourselves; and that the safest attitude for all of us, in looking back over what we have made of life, is, hands on mouths, and mouths in dust, and the cry coming form them, "Unclean! Unclean!"

A little mud in a stream may not be perceptible when you take a wineglassful of it and look at it, but if you take a riverful or a lakeful you will soon see the taint.

The best use the memory can serve for us is that the remembrance should drive us closer to Jesus Christ, and make us cling more closely to Him. That past can be canceled, these multitudinous sins can be forgiven. Memory should be one of the strongest strands in the cord that binds our helplessness to the all-forgiving and all-cleansing Christ.

FUTURE ANTICIPATION

Looking for and hasting unto the coming of the day of God—2 Pet. 3:12

Keep yourself awake first, and then let the waking, wide-opened eye, be looking forward. It is the very *differentia*, so to speak, the characteristic mark and distinction of the Christian notion of life, that it shifts the center of gravity from the present into the future, and makes that which is to come of far more importance than that which is, or which has been. No man is living up to the height of his Christian responsibilities or privileges unless there stands out before him, as the very goal and aim of his whole life, what can never be realized until he has passed within the veil, and is at rest in the "secret place of the Most High" [Ps. 96:1]. To live for the future is, in one aspect, the very definition of a Christian.

It is not for us, as it is for men in the world, to fix our hopes for the future on abstract laws of the progress of humanity, or the evolution of the species, or the gradual betterment of the world, and the like—all these may be true; I say nothing about them. But what we have to fill our future with is that the same Jesus "shall so come in like manner as ye have seen him go" [Acts 1:11]. No man can rightly understand the whole contents of the blessed proclamation, "Christ has come," unless he ends the sentence with "and Christ will come." Blessed is "that servant whom the lord, when he cometh, shall find watching" [Luke 12:37].

Of course, I need not remind you that much for which that second coming of the Lord is precious, and an object of hope to the world and the Church, is realized by the individual in the article of death. Whether Christ comes to the world or I go to Christ, the important thing is that there result union and communion, the reign of righteousness and peace, the felicities of the heavenly state.

And so, dear brother, just because of the uncertainty that drapes the future, and which we are often tempted to make a reason for dismissing the anticipation of it from our minds, we ought the more earnestly to give heed that we keep that end ever before us, and whether it is reached by His coming to us, or our going to Him, anticipate, by the power of realizing faith grasping the firm words of Revelation, the unimaginable, and—until it is experienced—the incommunicable blessedness revealed in these great, simple words, "So shall we ever be with the Lord" [1 Thess. 4:17].

OUR UNREVEALED FUTURE

For I reckon that the sufferings of this present time are not worthy to be compared with the glory which shall be revealed in us—Rom. 8:18

The fact of sonship makes us quite sure of the future. I am not concerned to appraise the relative value of the various arguments and proofs, or, it may be, presumptions, which may recommend the doctrine of a future life to men, but it seems to me that the strongest reasons for believing in another world are these two: first, that Jesus Christ was raised from the dead and has gone up there; and, second, that a man here can pray and trust and love God, and feel that he is His child. We are the *children* of God now, and if we are children now, we shall be grown up some time. Childhood leads to maturity. The infant becomes a man.

That is to say, he that here, in an infantile way, is stammering with his poor unskilled lips the name "Abba! Father!" will one day come to speak it fully. He that dimly trusts, he that partially loves, he that can lift up his heart in some more or less unworthy prayer and aspiration after God, in all these emotions and exercises, has the great proof in himself that such emotions, such relationship, can never be put an end to. The roots have gone down through the temporal, and have laid hold of the eternal. Anything seems to me to be more credible than that a man who can look up and say, "My Father!" shall be crushed by what befalls the mere outside of him; anything seems to me to be more believable than to suppose that the nature which is capable of these elevating emotions and aspirations of confidence and hope, which can know God and yearn after Him, and can love Him, is going to be wiped out like a microscopic insect by the finger of Death. The material has nothing to do with these feelings, and if I know myself, in however feeble and imperfect a degree, to be the son of God, I carry in the conviction the very pledge and seal of immortality. "That is a thought whose very sweetness yieldeth proof that it was born for immortality." "We are the sons of God" [1 John 3:2], therefore we shall always be so, in all worlds, and whatsoever may become of this poor wrappage in which my soul dwells.

The consciousness of belonging to another order of things, because I am God's child, will make me sure that when I have left this earth, the tie that binds me to my Father will not be broken, but that I shall go home, where I shall be fully and forever all that I so imperfectly began to be here, where all gaps in my character shall be filled up, and the half-completed circle of my heavenly perfectness shall grow like the crescent moon into full-orbed beauty.

THE FUTURE UNKNOWN

Ye know not what shall be on the morrow—James 4:14

You can only know facts when the facts are communicated. You may speculate and argue and guess as much as you like, but that does not thin the darkness one bit. The unborn child has nor more faculty or opportunity for knowing what the life upon earth is like than man here, in the world, has for knowing that life beyond. The chrysalis's dreams about what it would be when it was a butterfly would be as reliable as a man's imagination of what a future life will be. So let us feel two things:—Let us be thankful that we do not know, for the ignorance is a sign of the greatness; and then, let us be sure that just the very mixture of knowledge and ignorance which we have about another world is precisely the food which is most fitted to nourish imagination and hope. If we had more knowledge, supposing it could be given, of the conditions of that future life, it would lose some of its power to attract.

Ignorance is not always repellent—blank ignorance is; but ignorance shot with knowledge like a tissue which, when you hold it one way seems all black, and when you tilt it another, seems golden, stimulates men's desires, hopes, and imagination. So let us thankfully acquiesce in the limited knowledge. "Fools can ask questions which wise men cannot answer, and will not ask."

There are questions which, sometimes, when we are thinking about our own future, and sometimes when we see dear ones go away into the mist, become to us almost torture. It is easy to put them; it is not so easy to say, "Thank God, we cannot answer them yet!" If we could it would only be because the experience of earth was adequate to measure the experience of heaven; and that would be to drop the future down to the low levels of this present. Let us be thankful, then, that so long as we can only speak in language derived from the experiences of earth, we have yet to learn the vocabulary of heaven. Let us be thankful that our best help to know what we shall be is to reverse much of what we are, and that the loftiest and most positive declarations concerning the future lie in negatives like these: "I saw no temple therein" [Rev. 21:22]. "There shall be no night there" [Rev. 21:25; 22:5]. "There shall be no curse there." "There shall be no more sighing nor weeping, for the former things are passed away" [see Rev. 21:4].

The white mountains keep their secret well; not until we have passed through the black rocks that make the throat of the pass on the summit, shall we see the broad and shining plains beyond the hills. Let us be thankful for, and own the attractions of, the knowledge that is wrapped in ignorance, and thankfully say, "Now are we the sons of God, and it doth not yet appear what we shall be" [1 John 3:2].

Subject Index

Scripture Index